THE RUSSIAN ORTHODOX CHURCH
UNDERGROUND

The Russian Orthodox Church Underground, 1917-1970

WILLIAM C. FLETCHER

LONDON
OXFORD UNIVERSITY PRESS
NEW YORK TORONTO
1971

Oxford University Press, Ely House, London W.1

GLASGOW NEW YORK TORONTO MELBOURNE WELLINGTON
CAPE TOWN SALISBURY IBADAN NAIROBI DAR ES SALAAM LUSAKA ADDIS ABABA
BOMBAY CALCUTTA MADRAS KARACHI LAHORE DACCA
KUALA LUMPUR SINGAPORE HONG KONG TOKYO

ISBN 0 19 213952 5

PRINTED IN GREAT BRITAIN
BY EBENEZER BAYLIS & SON LIMITED
THE TRINITY PRESS, WORCESTER, AND LONDON

Contents

**To
Diane**

Preface

All serious scholarship is descended from a long line of progenitors, and is able to make some contribution to knowledge only by exploring, initially at least, paths charted by previous analysis. The attempt at scholarship which follows, perhaps more than many others, is indebted to preceding works, and it is my pleasant obligation to acknowledge this inheritance with all possible gratitude.

Soviet scholarship must come first in the lists of pioneers in the study of illegal forms of Orthodoxy in the U.S.S.R. The results of a field study of religious sects which were published in 1961 under the title *Sovremennoe sektantstvo* ('Contemporary sectarianism'), and in particular the contributions by Academicians L. N. Mitrokhin and Z. A. Nikol'skaia to that volume, opened up an entire vista of study, making possible a detailed, coherent examination of a phenomenon which had been lacking from the purview of serious scholarship, Soviet and Western alike, since the works of F. C. Conybeare, V. D. Bonch-Bruevich, and their contemporaries in the twenties. Mitrokhin and Nikol'skaia, by their careful and dispassionate presentation of concrete data, provided a basis on which other scholars could build, regardless of whether or not they might agree with the ideological guidelines and conclusions of this initial exploration into a serious analysis of underground Orthodoxy.

My own interest in the subject was aroused by Dr. N. A. Teodorovich who, with her remarkable alertness, insight, and painstaking research, of which all who labour in this field of scholarship are benefactors, published an article on underground Orthodoxy in the *Bulletin of the Institute for the Study of the U.S.S.R.* in 1965. If my approach and conclusions depart from hers this in no way should detract from my indebtedness to her work, for she was alert to the subject and had laboured in it before others in the West had given serious attention to it.

A similar, and even more substantial, share of credit is due to those others in the West, particularly among the Russian emigration, who for numerous reasons have long been devoting care and attention to discovering and preserving documents, reports, and information concerning underground Orthodoxy. An especially large debt of gratitude is owing to those individuals, nameless and many of them already forgotten, who were responsible for the compilation and preservation of *Delo Mitropolita Sergiia* ('The Metropolitan Sergii affair'), a collection of documents in typescript originating in the U.S.S.R. early in the thirties, without which the crucial events of the time would remain more obscured by the mists of time than they are now.

No less valuable was the 1965 dissertation of Archimandrite Ioann (Snychev), written on the basis of similar archival materials, which was generously made available to me through the good offices of the Moscow Patriarchate. If I have had the temerity to make my own interpretations from these materials which may not conform in every respect with those of the author, I can only plead the perversity of independent scholarship, reiterating my gratitude for the knowledge to which I was so kindly given access and emphasizing that any mistaken conclusions are mine alone.

Every scholar owes a debt to the authors and publishers of works which he has used, and no amount of meticulous attribution can fully express the gratitude rightfully due to them. In particular, the authors, researchers, and administrators associated with the Holy Trinity Monastery in Jordanville, New York, deserve every encomium, both for their painstaking efforts at gathering and preserving data on the underground Orthodox and for their readiness in making published treatments available, meeting and exceeding every request with dispatch and efficiency.

On a more personal level, I am greatly indebted to the doyen of study of religion in the U.S.S.R., Dr. Paul B. Anderson. In this work as in nearly every other, those valid insights which I have discovered are often directly, and nearly always indirectly, attributable to his greater knowledge and understanding, from which I have benefited and continue to benefit. In particular, Dr. Anderson very generously made available to me immensely helpful materials from his extensive personal collection of Soviet publications, which greatly expanded the range of data to which I had access. As so often is the case, I am greatly in his debt.

Richard H. Marshall, Jr., of the University of Toronto, spent many hours of unrewarded labour on my behalf in the course of this study. In large measure, this work would not have extended to its present scope, and probably would not have been carried through to completion, without his kind and unmerited concern and help, and in many particulars it was his insight which provided the key to a rational explication of an otherwise obscure and confusing point. I am in his debt. Bohdan R. Bociurkiw, of Carleton University, was very kind in extending my own inadequate knowledge from his inexhaustible store of understanding, especially with regard to the Ukraine in general and concerning individuals in particular. Thomas A. Bird, of Queens College, New York and Andrew Q. Blane, of Hunter College, both gave me extensive help, the latter with his meticulous, time-consuming, and generous comments at an early stage in the study, and the former by his consistent encouragement and valuable insights on numerous occasions.

My special thanks are due to my former colleague, Mlle Silvia Stöcker. While this study was in the incubation and parturition process, she endured my cogitations and intellectual struggles far beyond the call of duty, contributing many insights and eliciting many more, always with great grace and charm responding to my endless questions and queries which I am sure, in retrospect, must have been very tedious indeed at times. I shall remain grateful. Miss Sarah Hearn was more than once burdened with the noisome task of transcribing, typing, and re-typing, and her cheerful and diligent labours deserve my complete thanks.

All of these, and many others, have made an immense contribution to this study, doubtless more than sufficient to account for any good things contained therein. But not, of course, sufficient to account for the inaccuracies, mistakes, and perverse conclusions. These are my own, and I emphasize that none of my sources, none of my colleagues and helpers, and none of my mentors can be held accountable for them. On the contrary, it is only due to their generous and incalculable contribution that this study may hope to have any value at all.

Finally, my wife merits a special degree of my gratitude, for the demands of research and scholarship, a direct source of pleasure and excitement for the student himself, are a source of indirect burdens and annoyances to his wife. As she has done in the past (and, dismally, will doubtless be called upon to do in the future), my wife has borne these burdens, and has done so willingly, cheerfully, and without complaint, taking an interest in the subject and feigning one when her husband became tiresome and a bore on it. Her contribution to the resulting work has been great, meriting my devoted and enduring thanks.

Lawrence, Kansas   W.C.F.
10 March 1971

I

Introduction

Underground Russian Orthodoxy has been a constant factor in the religious situation in Russia throughout the Soviet period. Operating in deepest secrecy and subject to severe pressure, the underground movements have never been well illuminated nor well understood by students of the country's religions, either within the U.S.S.R. or abroad. This book will attempt to trace the history of these movements over the past half century.

This study will attempt as far as possible to remain within fairly strict definitions of the subject matter. The subject to be traced and analysed will be confined to the underground Russian Orthodox movements and organizations. Technically speaking, 'underground Orthodox' will imply not only a direct relationship to Russian Orthodoxy, but also (1) activities which are illicit from the point of view of the laws of the State or the policies of the regime, and (2) the lack of current, recognized ecclesiastical relationship with the legalized Russian Orthodox organization, the Moscow Patriarchate. Naturally, the phenomena to be studied are not textbook paradigms but living movements, and hence these restrictive definitions will tend to become blurred as syncretism with other religious movements takes place, as ambiguities in State policy make it difficult to determine the practical legal status at a given moment, and as the relationships of the movements to the Moscow Patriarchate fluctuate between the congenial and the hostile.

Common to all of the movements to be included in this study is the immense influence of the religious policies of the Soviet regime in their formation and development. State pressure has been the overwhelming, if not the sole, factor which has accounted for the existence of the underground Orthodox movements. And indeed, in these movements a mirror image of the history of religious policy in the U.S.S.R. can be discerned.

Marxism-Leninism maintains a deep commitment to the eradication of religion in society, and this atheistic pre-supposition has remained constant in the ideology of the ruling forces in Soviet society since 1917. The regime has not, however, remained consistent in the application of this ideological commitment, but instead in its religious policy it has at times willingly, at times unwillingly, embraced measures of expedience dictated by the times and circumstances. Thus, during the first ten years of communist rule in Russia the regime's religious policy reflected little of that energetic atheism which characterized certain later periods. The Russian Orthodox Church was immediately disestablished, and attempts were made to reduce its power in society by various machinations ranging from arrest of key leaders to the attempt to create competitive movements to weaken the Church from within. In 1929, the Soviet regime undertook a vigorous anti-religious campaign with exceedingly stern measures designed to eliminate organized religion from society in the briefest possible time. This campaign continued more or less unabated for the next dozen years. With the crisis of World War II, however, the regime was in critical need of such support as the Church could give to it, and as a consequence, an informal concordat was struck in 1943. In return for the Church's co-operation in political matters, a limited degree of religious opportunity, sufficient to ensure the viability of organized religion, was granted within the U.S.S.R. But in the late fifties the State began to withdraw from this bargaining situation, and the decade since 1960 has been characterized by a vigorous, well conceived and energetically applied anti-religious campaign. In this most recent campaign, the churches, which had almost succumbed to the pre-war campaign, have again suffered crippling losses, and religious life in the country has become subject to an intense degree of pressure affecting all religious people, clerical and lay, of every religious faith and denomination.

That the churches have survived fifty years of this sort of pressure seems somewhat of an anomaly, particularly in view of the immense power possessed by the State and in view of its total success in eradicating any other form of social institution not ultimately founded on communism. According to Nathaniel Davis,

One cannot get around the fact that a Communist government has sufficient power to crush religious opposition whenever it is prepared to pay the price. Therefore the price of suppression is a key element in the churches' defense. Basically, the task of the churches is to ensure that the Communists find the price of suppression greater than the discomfort of toleration.[1]

It is precisely the subject of this study, underground Orthodoxy, which provides the ultimate argument inhibiting the State in its attempt to eradicate religion. At any given time, the State could by fiat effect the closure of the churches and religious institutions which remain in the country. That it has not done so is explicable, in the last analysis, by the actual and potential threat presented by underground movements which arise when pressures against open observance of religion become too great. Communist leaders from Lenin to the present generation have specifically cautioned against too precipitate application of measures against functioning churches, for the closing of a church prematurely will inevitably result in the burgeoning of illegal religious organizations.

Religious organizations which are allowed to function openly, publicly, and legally are at least subject to a measure of supervision. Once believers have been denied this minimum toleration, however, their worship is subject to no possible day-to-day control, but can only be disrupted by the most diligent application of investigatory and police power. Indeed, the many fluctuations of the regime's religious policy might suggest considerable controversy within the ranks of ruling authorities, between those ideological purists who would advocate immediate liquidation of organized religion, regardless of consequences, and those of a more pragmatic bent (doubtless including the secret police) who prefer a situation which can be controlled to one which would be subject to no control whatsoever. Thus the phenomenon of underground religious organizations constitutes the primary factor which so far, at least, has inhibited the State from simply eliminating the churches from Soviet society.

Ultimately, this is the major importance of the subject of this study. The underground religious organizations are in the last analysis the single, overwhelming influence restraining the State's

---

[1] Nathaniel Davis, *Religion and Communist Government in the Soviet Union and Eastern Europe* (unpublished Ph.D. dissertation, Fletcher School of Law and Diplomacy, 1960), p. 180.

anti-religious designs. Regardless of how large or how small these organizations may be, and irrespective of how influential or inconsequential their actions may seem, the very existence of these movements and the huge potential which they represent, should no alternative means of religious practice be available, are the single overwhelming factor in ensuring to organized religion that degree of toleration by a hostile State which has allowed the continued survival of the Church in the U.S.S.R.

It should be noted from the beginning that this historical study will by no means endeavour to present an exhaustive analysis of this crucial phenomenon in the U.S.S.R. Such an attempt would require volumes and could scarcely be made to fit into the procrustean bed of a single, manageable study. Hence this work will subject itself to certain limitations, endeavouring to provide a comprehensible analysis of an important part—but by no means of the totality—of this phenomenon.

First, the subject of study will be limited in time, concentrating on the Soviet period (1917 to the present).

Second, as has been noted, this study will attempt to remain within a strict definition of terms. In particular, the term 'underground' will be treated as a technical term. This study will endeavour to avoid that broader use of the term which has become so popular that indeed, in many respects, 'underground' is now a meaningless, if not a contra-productive, designation. Some researchers have used the term to include anyone who at one time or another indulges in any illegal religious practice, and thereby conclude that vast numbers of believers are in the 'religious underground'.[2] Others, arguing with some justification that anyone who is religious at all, in the technical sense, denies the communist ideology, include all religious people in the 'religious underground'.[3] Whether or not such definitions may be justifiable, this study will not treat the term 'underground' so broadly, but will remain within the more limited definition described above.

The most serious of the limitations which this study will impose upon itself will be in restricting its coverage to the *Orthodox* underground. There are vast numbers of other underground organiza-

[2] Joseph Johnston, *God's Secret Armies within the Soviet Union* (New York: Putnam, 1954), p. 18.

[3] Cf. Richard Wurmbrand, *Underground Saints* (Old Tappan, New Jersey: Fleming H. Revell, 1968), pp. 7–44.

tions and movements which will not be treated in this study. For example, in the 1960s the Russian Baptist organization has been deeply divided by a highly developed, well-founded, and ably led opposition movement, which very quickly has been driven into the underground by State measures against it. Exceedingly dramatic events have surrounded this movement, such as the plea of the thirty-two 'Siberian Christians' for asylum at the U.S. embassy in Moscow in 1963, or the 'sit-in' of Baptist protesters inside the Kremlin in 1966.[4] Furthermore, in earlier periods in their history, such as before the war, the Baptists have been almost entirely an underground organization. Numerous other Christian and semi-Christian organizations have persisted without benefit of any legal recognition and hence in complete secrecy, such as Pentecostals, Jehovah's Witnesses, and indigenous movements such as Dukhobors, Molokans, and the vast array of *Khlysty* sects. In addition, underground religious organizations have sprung up from time to time in the past and exist today among Jews, Muslims, and Buddhists in the U.S.S.R.

Hence underground religion in the U.S.S.R. is a highly complex and immensely variegated phenomenon. The topic is vast. This study, subject as it is to limitations of space and time, must, perforce, content itself with making a contribution to the subject, rather than entertain any pretentions of treating so complex a matter comprehensively in a single volume. Instead this study will focus its attention on one of the most significant elements in that underground, the Russian Orthodox underground.

The schisms of the twentieth century were by no means a new or unique phenomenon in the history of the Russian Orthodox Church. Indeed, from its inception the Russian Church has undergone numerous periods of discontent and schism. The most influential of these schisms was the Old Believer movement, which reached immense proportions and which has survived three hundred years as a fully independent branch of Orthodoxy in Russia, with no relationship (other than the historical) with the modern Russian Orthodox Church.

The Old Believers schism arose over the issue of certain liturgical reforms introduced by Patriarch Nikon in the middle of the seventeenth century. The immediate issues of this schism—crossing oneself with three fingers instead of two, spelling Jesus *Iisus*

[4] Michael Bourdeaux, *Religious Ferment in Russia* (London: Macmillan, 1968).

instead of *Isus*, five *prosphorai* instead of seven, etc.—seem piquant from the vantage point of historical retrospect, but they contained within them the symbolic representation of deep and important issues within the Russian Church of the time. These issues ranged from justifiable fears of Greek or Latin influence on theology, to ecclesiastical dissatisfaction with the dictatorial pretensions of the Patriarch and his bishops, and to a vast array of sociological discontent related to the monarchy's then current drive to complete the process of replacing the popular democracy of the village with a centralized and, as future events were to prove, despotic rule over the country's life.

The Old Believers very quickly separated into two movements, the *Popovtsy* ('with priests') and the *Bezpopovtsy* ('without priests') depending, as their names suggest, on whether or not the members could reconcile themselves to the use of priests without Old Believer ordination (no bishop had joined in the schism, and hence the Old Believers could not consecrate their own priests). The *Popovtsy* managed to utilize priests who converted to them after ordination in the Russian Orthodox Church, and ultimately acquired an ordained bishop through the good offices of the Austrians. The *Bezpopovtsy* were forced to innovate, and eventually engendered a wide range of sects further and further removed from traditional Orthodox practice. Entire communities of both groups were established in various remote places in the country, and, in addition, in the eighteenth century the *Beguny* ('runners') arose among the *Bezpopovtsy*, claiming no fixed domicile but spending their lives wandering secretly throughout the Russian countryside.

From the very beginning of their history, the Old Believers have been subject to intense pressure. Especially during the first half-century, the movement was fiercely persecuted. On apprehension, they were subject to torture followed by burning at the stake, and as a result, on numerous occasions entire communities committed self-immolation when capture seemed imminent. Even at the best of times, they experienced severe, and sometimes crippling, discrimination, and it was only in the early twentieth century that they enjoyed anything like toleration from the State. With the advent of the communists to power in Russia, however, the Old Believers very soon found themselves under State pressure once again.

The Old Believers were of immense importance in the history of pre-revolutionary Russian society. Devout, committed, and frugal, they offered an exceedingly attractive alternative to the Russian Orthodox Church, which during the last centuries of tsarist rule had been increasingly stagnant and corrupt. Economic prosperity virtually flowed to these hard-working and diligent people, and especially by the close of the tsarist period, they had made great contributions to the rapid industrialization which was then beginning in Russia, and many of the Old Believers were men of immense wealth and economic influence in the country. On the eve of the communist revolution there were as many as twenty to twenty-five million Old Believers in the country.[5]

The influence of the Old Believers, which bid fair to transform Russian society, was abruptly terminated by the advent of the communists, and the movement has declined precipitately since then. At present there are an estimated 1,000,000 Old Believers in the country.[6] Prior to the anti-religious campaign of the sixties they could claim as many as 900 churches,[7] and at present they may be found in numerous areas of the U.S.S.R.[8] Where no Old Believer churches are operative, members of the movement will travel great distances to functioning churches for important rites and celebrations.[9] The majority of the Old Believer congregations still active are located in the western regions which were acquired by the U.S.S.R. during World War II.[10]

It is not surprising that the Old Believer movement, long accustomed to surviving intense State pressure, should at many points have exercised an influence on the members of the modern Russian Orthodox underground movements. Detailed analysis of the experiences of the Old Believers under the reign of the communists

[5] F. Fedorenko, *Sekty, ikh vera i dela* ('The sects, their faith and works') (Moscow: Publishing House for Political Literature, 1965), p. 102.
[6] Ibid.
[7] S. D. Bailey, 'Religious Boom in Russia,' *Christian Century*, 12 March 1958, p. 305.
[8] E.g., V. F. Milovidov, 'Staroobriadchestvo i sotsial'nyi progress' ('The Old Believers and social progress'), in Academy of Sciences of the U.S.S.R. (hereafter cited as AN SSSR), *Voprosy nauchnogo ateizma* ('Problems of scientific atheism') (Moscow: 'Mysl',' semi-annually since 1965), II, 220; A. Podmazov, 'O sovremennom staroobriadchestve v Latvii' ('The contemporary Old Believers in Latvia'), *Kommunist Sovetskoi Latvii*, No. 1 (January 1967), pp. 69–74.
[9] V. N. Vasilov, 'Etnograficheskoe issledovanie religioznykh verovanii sel'skogo naseleniia' ('Ethnographic research on the religious faiths of the rural population'), in A. I. Klibanov, ed., *Konkretnye issledovaniia sovremennykh religioznykh verovanii (metodika, organizatsiia, rezul'taty)* ('Concrete research on contemporary religious faiths (methodology, organization, results)') (Moscow: 'Mysl',' 1967), p. 153.
[10] Milovidov, op. cit., p. 208.

8   THE RUSSIAN ORTHODOX CHURCH UNDERGROUND

would be beyond the scope of this study, but the movement nevertheless exerts a noticeable influence in the background. Religious movements tend to coalesce under pressure, and there is much syncretism and crossing of denominational boundaries as various movements, suffering from the same disabilities and pressures, tend to learn from each other's experiences. Thus the Old Believers, no less than the other clandestine religious movements, had an influence on the underground Orthodox, and it should continually be borne in mind that those groups with which this study will be concerned were not operating in a vacuum, but formed a part of a larger process far beneath the surface of Soviet society.

One insuperable difficulty which is encountered by any study such as this is inadequacy of data. Clandestine by nature and by necessity, these groups devote great energy precisely to avoiding any public knowledge of their activities. Hence even at the best of times the student of these movements will find many lacunae and inadequacies in the information. In addition, at various periods in the past fifty years, the Soviet regime has followed a policy of withholding even such information as it has been able to discover, and at no time has the regime encouraged or permitted a complete public disclosure of the data it has gathered concerning these groups. Hence this study can in no wise pretend to comprehensive knowledge, but must remain content with reconstructing as accurate a picture as possible from the scattered and incomplete data available.

Naturally, the temptation of speculation where evidence is lacking looms large in any study of such a subject as this. Scholarship dealing with the Soviet Union entails a chronic susceptibility to the argument from silence, and particularly with regard to underground religious activities this dubious procedure leads the observer far astray. In 1959, Harrison Salisbury wrote that 'the Church indulges in no undercover activities'.[11] Similarly, Dimitry Konstantinov, who subsequently found much to say about underground Orthodoxy, in 1956 was compelled to discount the likelihood of any significant underground activity.[12]

[11] Harrison E. Salisbury, *To Moscow—And Beyond* (New York: Harper, 1959), p. 249.

[12] Dmitrii Konstantinov, *Pravoslavnaia molodezh' v bor'be za tserkov' v SSSR* ('Orthodox youth in the struggle for the Church in the USSR') (Munich: Institute for the Study of the U.S.S.R., 1956), pp. 50–1; cf. his *Gonimaia tserkov'* ('The persecuted Church') (New York: All-Slavic Press, 1967), *passim*.

Even Nathaniel Davis, a careful and competent scholar, wrote in 1960, 'The plethora of official and unofficial information about underground church activity during that particular period [the late thirties] strengthens the probability that activities on such a scale are not presently being carried on, or else there would be more information.'[13] Even though a decade later new evidence had demonstrated that these views were greatly mistaken, based as they were on the argument from silence, they are not subject to over-much criticism in that regard, for scholarship does impose the eminently justifiable requirement of remaining within the available evidence. In addition, certain apologists of Soviet religious policy made their own contribution to the obfuscation of this problem by claiming definitely that there was no such phenomenon extant in the U.S.S.R.[14]

To some degree, the mistaken assumption that underground Orthodoxy was non-existent could have been avoided by exhaustive attention to the Soviet press. In nearly every period there have been references to religious activities which eventually have proved to be connected with clandestine organizations. In the absence of other evidence, however, it is extraordinarily difficult to evaluate these few scattered references, and certainly it is not

---

[13] Davis, op. cit., p. 271.

[14] Georgii Grabbe, *Pravda o russkoi tserkvi na rodine i za rubezhom* ('The truth about the Russian Church in the motherland and abroad') (Jordanville, New York: Holy Trinity Monastery, 1961), p. 182. One of the victims of this argument from silence was the pseudonymous work by 'Father George,' *God's Underground* (New York: Appleton-Century-Crofts, 1949). Purporting to be an eyewitness appraisal by a secret Roman Catholic priest who claimed to have had much contact with underground Orthodox organizations, it was reviewed with extreme scepticism by Matthew Spinka in *Westminster Bookman*, Vol. IX, No. 1 (September–October 1949), and was called an outright fabrication by Paul W. Facey, S.J., 'The Case of the Missing Underground,' *America*, 16 July 1949. Even N. S. Timasheff agreed with Facey's hypothesis that it was constructed on the basis of his own *Religion in Soviet Russia, 1917–1942* (New York: Sheed and Ward, 1942); see his article, 'Religion in Russia, 1941–1950,' in Waldemar Gurian, ed., *The Soviet Union, Background, Ideology, Reality* (Notre Dame, Indiana: University of Notre Dame Press, 1951), pp. 173–4. Despite the fact that excerpts of 'Father George's' work had been printed in *Colliers* (29 May 1948), these criticisms were sufficient to nullify the book's influence on subsequent scholarship. However, in one of the ironies of history, recent Soviet scholarship has presented materials dealing with the immediate post-war period which corroborate this work in so many details that it would now appear that the learned critics were somewhat hasty in their judgements, and however much the book may have been edited, it seems to have been based on actual experience. (If indeed it was a fabrication, then it was constructed with an almost clairvoyant knowledge of details which would not be available for another dozen years.)

possible on their basis alone to construct anything like a full picture. Furthermore, stories in the Soviet press display no particular immunity from the common journalistic tendency to sensationalize, and when this predilection is combined with pronounced hostility towards religion on ideological grounds, great care must be exercised in the employment of such evidence. In particular, when Soviet journalism must serve as almost the sole source of data concerning truly radical experiments in underground Orthodoxy (cf. Chapter IX), satisfactory estimates of the real size or importance of the movement in question become quite impossible. Past experience has demonstrated that even obviously sensational reports in the Soviet press can seldom be ignored with impunity by the scholar; due notice must be taken of the phenomena reported, but a certain caution and, perhaps, scepticism must obtain until corroborating evidence is forthcoming.

Until comparatively recently, the only evidence in favour of the existence of underground religious groups was to be found in the literature of the *émigré* religious community in the West. A number of Russian *émigré* writers, particularly in the jurisdiction of the Russian Orthodox Synod Abroad, devoted no little energy to attempting to establish that an underground Orthodox Church is extant in the U.S.S.R. Their argument, however, was almost totally ignored outside their own, relatively small circle.

There was good reason for treating this case by *émigré* authors with caution. The bulk of their documentation consisted of reminiscences solicited from those who had fled the U.S.S.R., and were quite unverifiable. Many of them were contributed anonymously. Furthermore, these testimonies were largely vitiated by the compilers' almost completely uncritical acceptance of their validity, deriving in large measure from the prejudice in favour of such a phenomenon on the part of these *émigré* authors. Hence most serious scholars tended to use such material sparingly, if at all.

However, during the past ten years, these materials have been verified by new evidence, to a sufficient degree to allow some sort of differentiation to be made between the probably accurate and the possibly spurious within the body of evidence painstakingly gathered by Russian *émigrés* over the past half century. For example, the publication of Aleksandr Solzhenitsyn's *One Day in the Life of Ivan Denisovich* provided independent verification for the great body of prison literature written by escapees from the prison system who had reached the West, and demonstrated that their reports, always suspected of being somewhat exaggerated, were quite realistic. Materials specifically dealing with the history of underground Orthodox organizations have been presented in recent years by the Academy of Sciences of the U.S.S.R. which similarly corroborate much of the material hitherto available only from *émigré* sources. Therefore this body of Russian *émigré* literature becomes of some importance for the student of the phenomenon, for certain details therein available can be found nowhere else.

To be sure, the student must exercise considerable caution when using these materials, attempting to filter out as much as possible the glosses deriving from the prejudices of the authors. In particular, care must be taken with regard to assessment of the degree to which political hostility was the guiding motivation of the underground Orthodox movements, for these Russian *émigré* authors, many of them outspokenly anti-communist, have a tendency to see in all such movements a vehement protest against the political system. Despite the deficiencies, however, this body of material remains of importance, and can no more be ignored on grounds of possible distortion by anti-communist sentiments than can the materials of Soviet scholars be ignored on opposite grounds.

Of special importance for this study is the anonymous work entitled *Delo Mitropolita Sergiia* ('The Metropolitan Sergii Affair'). This is an unpublished collection of a large number of reactions of bishops within the U.S.S.R. to the change of political policy of the Russian Orthodox Church in 1927. These materials, which are known to have originated within the U.S.S.R. and which were there collected during the two years following that change in policy, present a unique insight into the events which formed an important chapter in the history of underground Russian Orthodoxy, and serve to corroborate or perhaps refute evidence gathered from other sources.

Of similar importance is the complementary study of Archimandrite Ioann (Snychev) in his dissertation at the Moscow Theological Academy in 1965, entitled *Tserkovnye raskoly v russkoi tserkvi* ('Church schisms in the Russian Church'). This work, which was generously made available for the present study through the good offices of the Moscow Patriarchate, deals with the same period covered by the collection described above, and is based on an archive collected in Russia similar to but far more extensive than its counterpart in the Western archives. Many of the materials quoted or cited by Archimandrite Ioann are also available in the latter, and hence the two works provide an indispensable means of mutual verification and validation of their contents, as well as illuminating events which hitherto have been exceedingly obscure for the Western scholar.

The most important materials for this study are to be found in the considerable body of research which has been published in the past decade by Soviet authors. Indeed, ten years ago this study could not have been written, for the materials provided by the Soviet Academy of Sciences and affiliated research institutions have been of incalculable importance in illumining what heretofore had been a little known (and in many respects completely unknown) aspect of Soviet religious life. While it remains true that the materials made available by Soviet research represent only a small portion of the data compiled by them during the past ten years, even this partial glimpse into the fruits of recent Soviet scholarship is of critical importance to any study such as this.

Of particular importance are the numerous field studies which have been conducted at selected locations throughout the country since 1959. A new development in Soviet research methodology, these sociological field studies of the actual circumstances and particular histories of local religious life have resulted in an immense flow of data.

A number of different approaches have been used by Soviet researchers in the sociological field studies. Both questionnaire procedures and interviews in depth have been used, although it should be noted that because of the fear and secrecy of underground Orthodoxy, these methods have not been particularly fruitful with regard to this specific sector of the local religious population.[15] Documentary research is also conducted, both in

[15] A. I. Klibanov, 'Nauchno-organizatsionnyi i metodicheskii opyt konkretnykh issledovanii religioznosti' ('Scientific organizational and methodological experience of concrete research on religiousness'), in Klibanov, *Konkretnye issledovaniia*, op. cit., p. 15; Z. A. Iankova, 'O nekotorykh metodakh konkretno-sotsial'nogo izucheniia religii' ('Certain methods of concrete social study of religion'), in ibid., pp. 113, 117.

the archives of the local press and in materials produced by the
religious groups. With regard to the latter,

among research materials are compositions of a theological character,
documents of religious polemics, religious *belles lettres*, poems, songs,
and tracts. As a rule, these are handwritten and typed compositions,
less frequently compositions printed on duplicating apparatuses, and
even more rarely printed by typographic means.[16]

Of particular importance is the access which these state-sponsored
studies have had to the court records in the localities under
study. These materials, hitherto absolutely secret and unobtainable, have included a great wealth of data concerning the
individual leaders of various underground Orthodox groups, as
well as confessions extracted from them during the court processes.[17]

    This body of materials is not without weaknesses, for sociological
research remains an infant discipline in Soviet scholarship.
Perhaps the most debilitating weakness in the research conducted
to date has been the high degree of ideological prejudice among the
researchers. This research is firmly committed to the tenets of
Marxism-Leninism in advance, and hence will tend to emphasize
certain aspects congenial to that ideology, while ignoring other
data which might be of even greater interest to the non-Marxist
student. One curious result of this pre-judgement on the part of
the researchers is that with rare exceptions, these underground
Orthodox groups are considered to be motivated primarily by
political factors. Other motivations, if they are noted at all,
receive much lesser emphasis than the alleged or real political
hostility of these groups. It is exceedingly ironic that in this
regard, both the communist and the anti-communist students of
underground religious movements are in absolute agreement in
considering these groups primarily as political phenomena.
Ideological prejudices of the Soviet scholars also result in frequent
controversies concerning the social and economic origins of
various underground Orthodox movements forty years ago,

16 Klibanov, 'Nauchno-organizatsionnyi i metodicheskii opyt,' op. cit., p. 22.
17 Iu. V. Gagarin, 'Otkhod ot sektantstva v Komi ASSR' ('Departure from sectarianism in the Komi ASSR'), in N. P. Krasnikov, ed., *Po etapam razvitiia ateizma v
SSSR* ('Stages of the development of atheism in the U.S.S.R.') (Leningrad: 'Nauka,'
1967), p. 169, n. 1; Klibanov, 'Nauchno-organizatsionnyi i metodicheskii opyt,' op.
cit., pp. 7, 24.

which, however interesting they may be to the communist theoretician, seem all but irrelevant to a pragmatic understanding of the contemporary movement.

Much of the inherent weakness of such Soviet research is due to methodological inexperience. Soviet scholarship has by no means achieved complete success in purging itself of neo-medieval Soviet scholasticism, and hence much of the writings even of the present-day Soviet scholars consists of rather sterile repetition of authorities of the past, without any particular attempt to gain fresh insight into the phenomena those stalwarts described. Furthermore, Soviet scholars occasionally seem content to draw far-reaching conclusions from an inadequate fund of data, in some cases apparently relying on a single interview.[18] Finally, Soviet scholarship often is insufficiently critical of the data which it collects. Testimony of former members of a religious group is used without consideration of whether the subject's memories may have been coloured or distorted by his experiences since his conversion to atheism. In utilizing confessions deriving from court processes against leaders of underground Orthodox organizations, there is very little evidence that the contemporary Soviet researchers have made any allowance whatsoever for the distortions which may have entered into these confessions as a result of coercion. Nor is sufficient allowance made in these field studies for the degree to which fear on the part of the participants of the clandestine movements may distort their answers; recent Soviet scholars seem aware of this phenomenon, but to date have not tempered their results gained in such field surveys sufficiently to compensate for this factor.[19]

The most serious limitation in contemporary Soviet scholarship concerning the underground religions is to be found in the motivation of the research. These studies in the past decade have not been undertaken primarily from a thirst for knowledge, nor from a desire to understand reality objectively and for its own sake, but first and foremost have been designed to equip anti-religious workers for more successful efforts in attempting to overcome religion's influence in society. The primary purpose of

[18] E.g., Milovidov, op. cit., p. 219.

[19] Cf. A. I. Klibanov, 'Sovremennoe sektantstvo v Tambovskoi oblasti' ('Contemporary sectarianism in Tambov oblast'), in AN SSSR, *Voprosy istorii religii i ateizma* ('Problems of the history of religion and atheism') (Moscow: AN SSSR, annually, 1950–64), VIII, 63.

these studies is to provide more effective weapons for the arsenal of atheist propaganda. To be sure, the practitioners of these arts have become sufficiently sophisticated to understand that knowledge is essential to achieving maximum success, and therefore there is a wealth of accurate information in these studies. Nevertheless, the studies are not designed primarily to render objective, detached knowledge, and therefore the student who is not engaged in this struggle in the Soviet countryside and whose purposes are not to serve this or that ideology but simply to describe and understand, will often search in vain for data which, however interesting they might be, are not applicable to the anti-religious needs motivating these studies of Soviet scholarship.

Obviously, then, this study will suffer from certain limitations inherent in the available data. Nearly all of the factual material which this study might utilize falls short of true objectivity, but is instead coloured—and sometimes transmogrified—by the ideological designs of the one side or the other. Furthermore, even should this study achieve perfect success in filtering out the ideological pre-suppositions in the data (scarcely a realistic hope), it would still suffer from the lacunae which are inherent in any materials dealing with a movement which itself seeks to remain hidden. For all these limitations, and despite the undoubted inaccuracies which will find their way into the study at this point or that, the fact remains that the underground Orthodox organizations play an important role in the determination of Soviet religious policy, and indeed to some degree in the religious life of the country as a whole. It can therefore be hoped that even the incomplete picture which will emerge in the course of this study will be sufficiently reliable as to promise a contribution to understanding the contemporary phenomena of religion in the U.S.S.R.

II

The Gathering Clouds

The abdication of the Tsar and the fall of the monarchy in February 1917 evoked an astonishingly passive response from the Russian Orthodox Church. Although certain leaders of the Church had pronounced grave warnings against the various forms of radicalism which were rampant during the turbulent months preceding the revolution, when the actual event occurred the Church all but remained silent. No particularly noteworthy attempts were made to rally to the side of the throne during the desperate hours preceding the abdication, and once the revolution was a *fait accompli* the Church made no attempts to reverse the event or to undertake work toward a restoration. It seemed almost as though the Church were indifferent to the fate of the monarchy.

This might seem somewhat strange in view of the intimate relationship between the institutional Orthodox Church and the autocracy. Particularly since the reforms of Peter the Great, the Church had been intimately identified with the monarchical regime and, indeed, so dependent was it on the latter that in many important respects it was scarcely distinguishable from other departments of the state bureaucracy. The organs of church government on every level above that of the parish were dependent on State subsidies for their financial existence. Decision-making was located in the Holy Synod, appointed by the Tsar and under the direct and almost absolute control of the Over-Procurator, a layman responsible only to the Tsar. Such intimacy with the monarchical structure of the Government augured ill for the Church's ability to survive the fall of tsarism.

That the Church was indissolubly wedded to the pre-revolutionary form of governmental structure had seemed all the more apparent after the abortive revolution of 1905. The Church almost immediately rallied round the Tsar and expended great energies in frustrating the reforms which he had conceded to those who were challenging the Government. In the parliamentary Duma following 1905, the Church regularly lent its weight to the most conservative elements in their consistently successful attempts to frustrate the designs of more radical representatives. Many of the leaders of the Church gained a great deal of fame (or, as the future course of events would demonstrate, notoriety) for their participation in the Union of Russian People (commonly called the Black Hundred), an exceedingly reactionary body dedicated to the preservation of the *status quo*.

Not even the years of mismanagement of the ignorant peasant Rasputin had succeeded in shaking the Church hierarchy's apparent dedication to the monarchical structure. Many of the ruling hierarchs owed their position directly to the whims of this peasant, whose self-proclaimed mystical powers had won him the devotion of the empress and the Tsar. During the brief period between Rasputin's murder and the February Revolution the Church did little or nothing to rebuild the chaos left by his rule, and indeed seemed all but incapable of acting in the absence of direct governmental initiatives.

This heritage of acceptance and support of the monarchy, however, proved to be very ephemeral indeed. The fall of the monarchy in 1917 was met by an attitude of indifference—perhaps of numbness—on the part of the institutional Church, and the Church appeared to be sublimely non-political in its approach, willing to accept whatever form of political organization seemed at the moment to be in command.

It was quickly demonstrated, however, that this non-political, indifferent approach to the governmental structure was more apparent than real. If the Russian Orthodox Church initially refrained from attempting to play any particular role in the political life of the nation, this acquiesence to the political realities of the moment endured only for so long as the direct interests of the Church were not in jeopardy. The Church made it plain that it expected its interests and privileges to be continued despite the change of Government. In a resolution adopted on 13 July 1917 by the commission charged with preparing for a Council (Sobor) of the Church it was stipulated that the Church should continue to enjoy such privileges as autonomy in internal affairs, State recognition of the marriage and divorce rules of the Church, church holidays and records, and the church school system together with compulsory Orthodox religious instruction in all schools; the Government must also continue to render to the Church the financial subsidies to which it was accustomed.

It was apparent, however, that the Provisional Government was little inclined to grant these privileges to the Church in every particular. By the time the Sobor convened on 16 August, the fear that the new Government would not leave the privileged position of Orthodoxy undiminished, together with the increasing chaos in the country as social disintegration spread at an alarming rate, had produced a notable reaction within the Church. The earlier political indifference of the Church was fast being replaced by a much more militant attitude toward politics, predominantly of a conservative bent. The Sobor very nearly entered directly into the political life of the nation during the brief rebellion of General Kornilov. Active political support of his abortive *coup d'état* was openly—and largely approvingly—discussed by the Sobor, and it would seem that it was only the lethargy of the Sobor machinery, together with the astonishingly rapid collapse of the Kornilov *putsch*, that saved the Church the considerable embarrassment that would have ensued upon attempting outright political intervention in a lost cause.

One reason for this relatively rapid increase in political interest within the Church Government was the threat to its cherished privileges. On 20 July the parochial schools had been placed under State control, and the Provisional Government was showing less and less inclination to support religious education in the secular schools with any degree of vigour. In addition, there was apprehension that the Government was not going to be especially indulgent in the matter of State subsidies for support of the Church. As a result, the Sobor gave serious consideration to entering directly into the election campaigns for the Constituent Assembly later in the year.

Thus the February Revolution and ensuing events demonstrated that the Church, however apolitical it might appear to be, was by no means willing to remain politically neutral where its own interests were concerned. While these events demonstrated that it had no particular commitment to any single form of political organization of the country's life, the Church was more than willing to consider active engagement in political questions in order to defend its own position within the society. While in actual practice the distinction may seem to be minor, inasmuch as in its desire to retain its position the Church seemed no less hostile to innovation in political affairs than would have been the case had it been openly committed to a conservative form of political government, the distinction is of great importance in evaluating the reaction of the Church to the storm of events which descended upon the country with the Bolshevik revolution of October 1917.

The Church's initial reaction to the Bolshevik *coup d'état* was mute, reminiscent of its response to the February Revolution that same year. Again, in the first days following the communist accession to power the Church gave the impression of being thoroughly non-political and indifferent to the forms of power in the governmental structure. However, the new Bolshevik Government was much less hesitant with regard to the privileges of the Church, and a series of three decrees in December and January declared that all land (including church property) was nationalized, registration of birth, marriage, and death was secularized, and financial support for clergymen was ended. On 23 January 1918, the Decree of Separation of Church from State and of School from Church was published, which the Church rightly interpreted as an unqualified withdrawal of every privilege from the Orthodox Church. The Church reacted to these infringements on its privileges with immediate and outright hostility, and for the following year at least engaged in a militant, political struggle against the new regime.

It is important to note that this political hostility of the Church to the communist regime was not expressed in terms of any sort of ideological hostility to the goals of the radical socialist Bolsheviks. Subsequent Soviet historians have made it axiomatic that this initial hostility was due to an ideological commitment to some more traditional political order on ideological grounds. However, such a political predilection on the part of individual churchmen should be balanced against a no less outspoken minority of the Church which was positively in favour of the ideals of socialism. The Church itself, speaking officially or corporately, at no time indulged in an ideological struggle against the new Government.

The hostility of the Church during the first year of communist rule in Russia was instead evoked by twin motivations. As has been suggested, the Church was quick to resist any encroachment upon its privileges. Perhaps more important than this, however, was the parallel theme in its hostile pronouncements against the new Government, an objection not so much to the form which the new political rulers were instituting in the governmental structure, nor to their stated goals, but to the means by which they were achieving power. It was quite obvious that the *coup d'état* of October had by no means represented the wishes of the people at large, but was instead a forcible overthrow of a more or less representative government by a highly organized, armed minority. The initial months and indeed years of Soviet rule in Russia were accompanied by excesses against traditional norms of orderly, legal process, or indeed any sort of truly democratic fulfilment of the wishes of the population. Many transgressions against traditional morality were committed by the authorities, and in particular they seemed totally unconcerned with those virtues and ethical norms traditionally espoused by Christianity.

Thus the Church reacted strongly against brutality and un-ethical procedures while at the same time giving expression to hostility evoked by loss of privileges. Both of these themes were evident in the first message of Patriarch Tikhon excommunicating the communists four days before the promulgation of the Decree of Separation.

It is a hard time that the Holy Church of Christ is now going through in the Russian land. Both the open and secret enemies of the truth of Christ persecute this truth and aim at destroying the work of Christ, and, instead of Christian love, sow everywhere the seeds of evil, of hatred, and of fratricidal struggle. The Commandments of Christ— to love one's neighbour—are forgotten and trampled underfoot. Every day, there comes to us news of horrible and cruel massacres, the victims of which are innocent men and even people lying on a bed of pain, guilty only of having accomplished in all honesty their duty towards their country, of having used their strength in the service of the good of the people. And all this is accomplished in our time, not only at night under the cover of darkness, but even in full daylight, with an audacity unknown to this day, and with a cruelty that knows no mercy, without any judgement, and with the trampling underfoot of all right and all law, and all this takes place almost in all the towns and villages of our country, in the capitals just as in distant border regions.[1]

The second motivation for the Church's political hostility—fear of loss of its prerogatives—was also apparent in the same proclamation:

We call to all of you, the faithful sons of the Church, rise to defend your Holy Mother, which is being outraged and oppressed today! The enemies of the Church have seized power over the Church and its good property through the force of fire. . . .

And you brothers, bishops and pastors, without relaxing for an instant your religious activities, call your flock to defend with an ardent zeal the rights of the Orthodox Church which are at present being trampled underfoot. Create immediately spiritual unions, invite the faithful to enter, not from necessity, but with good will, into the ranks of spiritual fighters who against the forces from outside will pit the strength of their sacred zeal; and we are absolutely confident that the enemies of the Church will be humiliated and scattered, dispersed by the force of the Cross of Christ, for the promise of the divine bearer of the Cross is immutable. 'I shall establish my church and the gates of hell shall not prevail against it.'[2]

At no point in this initial proclamation (nor, indeed, in subsequent official acts of the Church) did the Church express its political hostility to the new regime in theoretical or ideological terms. The hostility was consistently in terms either of resistance to loss of privilege or of indignation at the tramelling of Christian morality in the Government's conduct, and at no time was the expressed political hostility of the Church incompatible with the possibility of political neutrality should these two areas be ameliorated.

However, it would be gratuitous to claim that the proclamations of the Church during the initial period were not political actions. Even though the initial decree of Patriarch Tikhon was expressed in religious rather than political terms, its effect could only be political, for if pronouncement of anathema promised little effect among the Bolsheviks themselves, who were formally and openly committed to atheism, it could have a great effect in

[1] Translation from Nikita Struve, *Christians in Contemporary Russia* (London: Harvill Press, 1963), p. 343.
[2] Ibid., pp. 344–5.

increasing their difficulties in securing the loyalty of the Russian populace, among whom the Orthodox Church was still a force with substantial influence. Furthermore, during the first year the Patriarch issued communion bread to the imprisoned Tsar and held requiems following his execution, and denounced in fiery terms the peace treaty of Brest-Litovsk with Germany. Even though such actions as these had substantial religious motivation (pastoral in the case of the Tsar and jurisdictional in the case of the treaty of Brest-Litovsk, which separated large numbers of Orthodox in previously Russian lands from direct communion with the central authorities of the Church), they also represented direct interference of the Church in the political arena and were interpreted with some justification by the Bolsheviks and subsequent Soviet historians as acts of anti-Soviet political opposition.

After the autumn of 1918 Patriarch Tikhon changed his political approach from open hostility to political neutrality. In his letter to the Council of People's Commissars on the first anniversary of the *coup d'état* the Patriarch reiterated his hostility in the terms of his first proclamation.

The attacks on freedom in matters of faith are particularly painful and cruel. Not a day passes without the organs of your press publishing the most monstrous slander and heinous blasphemy against the Church of Christ and its servants. You mock the servants of the altar, you force bishops to dig trenches (e.g., Bishop Ermogen of Tobolsk), and you send priests to do low, manual labour. You have laid your hands on the patrimony of the Church which has been amassed by generations of the faithful, and you have not hesitated to act in a manner contrary to their final wish. You have closed a whole series of monasteries and chapels without any pretext or reason. You have forbidden access to the Moscow Kremlin—that sacred patrimony of all the faithful. You are destroying the traditional framework of the ecclesiastical community—the parish. You are closing down brotherhoods and other charitable and educational organizations maintained by the Church. You break up diocesan assemblies. You interfere in the internal administration of the Orthodox Church. By excluding all sacred images and forbidding the teaching of the catechism in schools, you deprive children of the spiritual food which is indispensable for their education as Orthodox.[3]

Not only did the Patriarch reiterate his hostility against the

---

[3] Ibid., pp. 348–9.

infringement of what the Church considered its rights, he also reiterated the ethical motivation:

Now then to you, who use power for persecuting your neighbours and for wiping out the innocent, we extend our word of admonition: celebrate the anniversary of your taking power by releasing the imprisoned, by ceasing bloodshed, violence, havoc, restriction of the faith; turn not to destruction, but to organizing order and legality, give to the people their wished-for and deserved respite from fratricidal strife. Otherwise all righteous blood shed by you will cry out against you, and with the sword will perish you who have taken up the sword. (Matt. 26:52)[4]

However, along with such expressions of hostility, in the same message the Patriarch also laid the basis for his subsequent efforts to disengage from the political struggle and take a non-political position in the Church: 'It is not our work to judge the earthly power; all power permitted by God would draw upon itself our blessing, if it verily showed itself to be "God's servant", for the good of those under it.'[5]

Subsequent events were to prove that once having entered into outright political struggle against the Soviet regime, the Church would find it all but impossible to disengage. The State accepted the Church's challenge in political contest and for the next quarter of a century refused to lay down its arms, despite the obvious sincerity of Patriarch Tikhon and his followers who had renounced political opposition to the regime. The communists seized upon the image of political hostility which the Church had created for itself in the first year.

More importantly for this study, in this initial year of hostility Patriarch Tikhon created for himself an image of anti-Soviet hostility which would become a tradition among the more politically militant of the illegal, underground Orthodox groups. His subsequent attempts to come to an understanding with the Soviet Government were largely ignored among the 'Tikhonites' who, in choosing him as their patron, tended to see only his initial, outright resistance to the encroachments of the Soviet Government upon religion. Thus Patriarch Tikhon, because

---

[4] Translation from John Shelton Curtiss, *The Russian Church and the Soviet State, 1917–1950* (Boston: Little, Brown, 1953), p. 65.
[5] Ibid.

of his policies in his first year of rule over the Church, became the archetypal image of valiant resistance for the politically oriented segments of subsequent illegal Orthodox organizations.

In addition, during his initial year Patriarch Tikhon also made a beginning of instructing the religious populace in forming their own organizational machinery for carrying out their religious convictions despite the desires of the State. According to John S. Curtiss,

> The Patriarch also issued detailed instructions to the local churchmen concerning opposition to the decree of separation of church from state. The clergy were told to unite the believers and to encourage them to defend the church, chiefly by forming organizations of laymen to protect the holy things; these leagues were to be organized by parishes.[6]

Furthermore, these organizations were designed to be united in a single, nationwide structure through an All-Russian Council of parish organizations.[7]

It would not be completely correct to consider such organizational attempts as the initiation of an underground form of Russian Orthodoxy. In view of the highly tenuous control of the Soviet authorities over society, such organizations could exist openly and without resorting to clandestine procedures. Furthermore, they were organized on the express and open instructions of the duly constituted church authorities. Nevertheless, they did represent organizational endeavours which were technically outside the scope of legally permissible activities, and so soon as the Soviet authorities should gain sufficient stability to enforce the law sternly, they could be expected to attract the wrath of the State. Perhaps most importantly, in this very early period the local parishes did receive some experience in formation of new organizational capabilities in response to the times, rather than being restricted, as formerly, to working within already existing organizational structures created from above. During the coming years, any experience gained in such spontaneous, local creation of organizations for carrying out religious activities would be immensely valuable.

The Russian countryside was soon aflame in civil war as the

⁶ Ibid., p. 56.   ⁷ Ibid., p. 60.

Bolsheviks found themselves in desperate struggle against domestic and foreign opposition armies. While Patriarch Tikhon and the central authorities of the Russian Orthodox Church were careful to avoid becoming embroiled in the Civil War, the same is not true of the local and regional leaders of the Church. Particularly in disputed areas, a great number of religious organizations sprang up in support of the White armies and participated in an exceedingly fierce struggle against the Soviet regime. Such religious organizations, however, do not appear to have survived the collapse of the White forces and exerted no considerable direct, organizational influence on the life of the Russian Church after the close of the Civil War.

One event during the Civil War, however, was to have considerable effect in subsequent years. Because of the exceeding great confusion then obtaining in the country, with large areas either under White control or in dispute as the fortunes of war waxed and waned for one side or the other, Patriarch Tikhon and the Holy Synod authorized diocesan leaders to act independently by a decision of November 1920.

In case the eparchy is without all communication with the Supreme Church Administration, or the Supreme Church Administration, headed by the Most Holy Patriarch, for any reason discontinues its activity, the eparchical bishop immediately gets into communication with the bishops of the neighbouring eparchies on the subject of organizing a supreme level of Church authority. In case this is impossible, the eparchical bishop assumes all authority.[8]

This decision was to have vast significance in subsequent developments within Russian Orthodoxy, for it provided a canonically valid basis for independent action on the part of local bishops. In cases of need or disputed validity of subsequent Church leadership, local bishops, on the basis of this order of Patriarch Tikhon, could take upon themselves the prerogatives of organizing religious life within their dioceses to suit their own evaluation of the most effective approaches.

During this period the State embarked upon a serious campaign to reduce the influence of monastic institutions within the country.

[8] Translation from Nadezhda Teodorovich, 'The Belorussian Autocephalous Orthodox Church,' in Boris Iwanow, ed., *Religion in the USSR* (Munich: Institute for the Study of the U.S.S.R., 1960), p. 70 n. 1.

Begin

In a relatively short time a great number of monasteries were arbitrarily closed down. By 1920, of the 1,025 monasteries in 1914, 673 had been dissolved.[9] Vast numbers of monks and nuns, who found themselves precipitately cast out of the cenobitic life to which they had pledged themselves, were forced to depart into the surrounding world to make their way as best they could. Some, of course, found it possible to give up the external observance of monastic life and enter into the working force. Large numbers, however, were forced to innovate and seek ways of continuing their vocation. 'The black (monastic) clergy were scattered over the face of the Russian land like cockroaches swept out from under the stove by the hand of a tidy housewife.'[10]

This early religious diaspora would become traditional among certain segments of the Orthodox population in subsequent decades. No longer able to live legally according to their religious convictions, these monks and nuns were forced to adopt those innovations which would soon become the hallmark of the various forms of illegal religious life. Some of the monasteries hastily utilized the expedient of forming themselves into 'working collectives' or artels, consonant with the Soviet theory of optimum agricultural organization.[11] This practice of forming co-operative communities, overt or covert, would also play a role in the subsequent development of underground Orthodoxy. Others of the dispossessed monastics appeared to be thoroughly alienated from society, and chiliasm made its appearance among them as they wandered about the population preaching against the coming of the anti-Christ and the rapidly approaching end of the world.[12] This apocalyptic theme would play a large role in the subsequent life of illegal Orthodoxy in Russia.

The waning of the Civil War brought no respite to the Russian Orthodox Church, for it soon found itself confronted with a well-conceived and eminently successful manœuvre on the part of the State. Partly because of peculiarities of the weather and partly because of the havoc which had been wreaked during the Civil War, the Russian countryside was in the grips of a catastrophic famine in 1921. The State found it possible to utilize the crisis of

[9] Curtiss, op. cit., pp. 82–5.
[10] Ibid., p. 84, quoting *Vestnik Sviashchennogo Sinoda Pravoslavnoi Tserkvi* (Moscow), No. 1 (1926), p. 18.
[11] Curtiss, op. cit., p. 85.
[12] Ibid., p. 168.

the famine against the Church. In order to aid the starving the State declared the confiscation of church valuables. Patriarch Tikhon, while willing to co-operate to the best of his ability in regard to unconsecrated valuables, felt himself constrained to resist the expropriation of valuables which had been specifically consecrated to religious usage. Nevertheless, the State persevered in its designs and declared the confiscation of all church valuables except vessels actually necessary to the conduct of religious worship. Patriarch Tikhon attempted to resist, but the resources of the Church were insufficient to deter the State from confiscating the valuables. A large number of riots occurred as the faithful attempted to carry out the Patriarch's orders against expropriation of consecrated valuables, and a number of court trials of church leaders resulted. The net result was a significant defeat for the Church, for Soviet propaganda was able to make a persuasive case that the Church was indifferent to human suffering, preferring to hoard its (allegedly) vast wealth for the sake of ancient rules of doubtful validity.

As a result, Patriarch Tikhon was placed under house arrest in June 1922, and, operating as his locum tenens, Metropolitan Agafangel issued an epistle which reiterated Patriarch Tikhon's decree of 1920 granting each bishop the right to independence if free intercourse with the patriarchal administration was unavailable.

Beloved in God reverend bishops,
Bereaved temporarily of supreme administration, govern your dioceses now in independence according to the Holy Scriptures, the Holy Canons; in future, until the restoration of the Supreme Church Administration, decide definitively the questions which before you referred to the Holy Synod; and in doubtful cases apply to our humility.
Honest Priests and all servants in Christ of the Altar and the Church,
You are closely connected with the life of the people. Their progress in the spirit of the Orthodox Doctrines must be dear to you. Increase your holy zeal. When the believers will see in you the blessed burning of the Spirit they will not turn away from their holy altars.[13]

[13] Translation from Boleslaw Szczesniak, *The Russian Revolution and Religion* (Notre Dame, Indiana: University of Notre Dame Press, 1959), p. 81. The Russian text is available in Sergei Viktorovich Troitskii, *Razmezhivanie ili raskol* ('Separation or schism') (Paris: Y.M.C.A. Press, 1932), p. 75.

Begin [handwritten in margin]

Like the earlier decree of the Patriarch, this epistle of the patriarchal locum tenens Agafangel provided a basis which could in future be claimed in canonical justification of independent diocesan action when the central administration of the Church was in doubt.

Perhaps as important to the subsequent illegal forms of Orthodoxy were the numerous trials growing out of resistance of Church authorities to the State's confiscation of valuables during the famine. A number of such trials were held in 1922, and they 'seemed to have eliminated, either permanently or temporarily, many of the hierarchs most hostile to the Soviet regime.'[14] Only a small proportion of those found guilty in court were executed; the remainder were given various terms of prison or exile, and thus were not permanently removed from the life of Russian Orthodoxy. While in prison, they could form nascent clandestine organizations and conduct worship services in the absence of duly constituted facilities. On their release they could apply these mechanisms in society. In addition, their prison experience might well intensify their initial hostility to the regime.

Thus in this early period the prerequisites for the formation of underground religious organizations were already extant. According to I. Stratonov,

In 1920–22 many were attracted by this idea. From the middle of 1922 the whole unsuitableness of this idea was made manifest quite obviously, since there was no better condition for the appearance of pseudo-priests and hierarchs of doubtful ordination, to say nothing of the fact that for the mass of the believers a transfer to a catacomb position was generally impossible. Even the opposition itself could not become catacomb, but it became underground, composing proclamations against that very church government which, with such labour overcoming all possible difficulties, bore the heavy cross of church government.[15]

Despite the manifest dangers of canonical irregularities there were schismatic movements which appeared during this early period. Many of these were short-lived and exerted no considerable influence on the subsequent course of Orthodox life in

[14] Curtiss, op. cit., p. 128.

[15] I. Stratonov, *Russkaia tserkovnaia smuta (1921–1931 gg)* ('The Russian Church confusion (1921–1931)') (Berlin: Parabola, 1932), p. 172.

Russia. Some of these illegal organizations, however, did survive and had an impact on the general course of Orthodox underground organizations.

According to a Russian Orthodox scholar writing a half-century later, many obscure schisms appeared in the Russian Church almost immediately after the Sobor of 1917.

A number of lay participants in the Sobor, whom the October Revolution deprived of their wealth or positions of privilege (in their number were several ministers of the Tsarist or Provisional Government and members of the monarchical faction of the State Dumas) quickly emigrated beyond the borders of the country, or went into the deep underground within its confines. We testify that among those who concealed themselves in these days there were almost none who bore spiritual rank.[16]

If there were few priests or prelates among these early dissenters, the same cannot be said of those remnants of the Civil War organizations which did not emigrate with the collapse of the White forces, as will become apparent below.

There were early, minor schisms which refused to recognize the Patriarch at all.[17] Among these was the 'Independent Orthodox Soviet Church' organized by the deposed Archbishop Vladimir of Penza. This early schism was exceedingly ephemeral and short-lived, and did not receive the support of the believers inasmuch as it was totally in favour of the Soviet regime.[18] As such it had little in common with the subsequent schismatic movements with which this study is concerned.

Of more enduring influence was the sect of the Ioannity. This sect arose in the 1880s among followers of the Orthodox mystic, John of Kronstadt.[19] This movement very rapidly developed into a sect sufficiently far removed from traditional Orthodox doctrine and practice as to constitute almost another Christian denomination. The followers of John of Kronstadt were able to form a religious organization after the revolution of 1905, and from 1906

---

[16] I. Shabatin, 'Russkaia pravoslavnaia tserkov' v 1917–1967 gg' ('The Russian Orthodox Church, 1917–1967'), *Zhurnal Moskovskoi Patriarkhii* (hereafter cited as *ZMP*), No. 10 (October 1967), p. 35.

[17] Donald A. Lowrie, *The Light of Russia* (Prague: Y.M.C.A. Press, 1923), pp. 214–15.

[18] Curtiss, op. cit., pp. 101–2.

[19] Fedorenko, op. cit., pp. 206–7.

to 1912 were able to publish their own journal. In 1908 the sect was led by the merchant, V. F. Pustoshkin, who took the name of Feodosii the Elder. According to Soviet sources the sect went underground after the October revolution.

The Ioannity were a highly mystical movement. Members of the sect held that John of Kronstadt was Christ incarnate and made a practice of referring to the leaders as members of the Holy Family, archangels, etc. Thus the sect in its developed form was very far from traditional Orthodoxy.

Nevertheless, because of its historical Orthodox origins the sect was able to attract certain of those who either were unable or felt themselves unable to worship with the patriarchal Church. The advent of the Soviets in Russia thus elevated this sect from being a rather minor aberration on the fringes of Orthodoxy to an option for the dispossessed Orthodox, which was of some influence in ensuing years. Particularly important was the fact that this sect produced written documents which circulated widely among dissident Orthodox in subsequent years. According to Soviet scholars, these documents, produced after 1917, were filled with and motivated by direct hostility to the Soviet authorities.

The Imiaslavtsy ('glorifiers of the Holy Name') were another mystical schismatic movement in the Orthodox tradition. Formed in the second decade of the twentieth century, this sect arose on Mt. Athos as a result of an uncommonly subtle dispute over the proper worship of God. Holding that it is *hubris* for sinful man to presume that he can approach the awesome holiness of God, the Imiaslavtsy held that man cannot glorify God directly, but can only glorify His Holy Name. In 1915 the Russian Orthodox Church decided against this refinement, and as a result its adherents were declared excommunicate and schismatic.

Following the Soviet attack on the monasteries, adherents of this group dispersed, with many of them fleeing to the Northern Caucasus. They continued to proselytize among the Orthodox, claiming that the Church had fallen from grace and that the Soviet regime was the servant of the anti-Christ. The movement's leaders in 1923–4 advocated complete isolation from society under the slogan of 'preservation of the Orthodox faith in the wilderness by the powers of the true believers', and underground cells and illegal monasteries were formed. In the Kuban, one of the leaders organized eight hermitages of thirteen members each, and united these into a monastic commune for agricultural work.[20]

Similarly, the sect of Innokent'evtsy attained a degree of prominence during this period.[21] Founded by the monk Levisor Innokentii in 1908, this was an apocalyptically oriented sect. Innokentii proclaimed himself the Third Person of the Trinity, and after the Bolshevik revolution participated directly in armed conflict against the Red Army. In one incident the Innokent'evtsy had collected weapons at one of their monasteries and succeeded in liquidating the entire force of two hundred soldiers which the Red Army sent to capture the monastery. Innokentii himself was murdered in 1919 by one of the members of the sect, allegedly for immoral conduct. A struggle for leadership in the sect ensued and the sect disintegrated into a number of allied groups, some of which preserved their existence during subsequent decades.[22]

The Fedorovtsy were another of the sects founded in the years prior to the revolution which continued to exist in the U.S.S.R. Their name was derived from that of their founder, Fedor Rybalkin. This was a highly ascetic movement, which, like its counterparts, placed considerable emphasis on apocalypticism.[23]

Despite the appearance of early schisms and the ability of existing schismatic movements to capitalize on the discontent with the Soviet regime, in this early period the times were as yet premature for the rise of a truly significant underground movement within Orthodoxy. Far more important than these schisms in preparing the way for such a phenomenon was the Living Church Adventure. Under the benign gaze of State authorities, a group of liberal and radical clerics conspired to seize control of the Church, and for a brief period, at least, achieved astonishing success. The group was led by Bishop Antonin and the priests Vvedenskii, Kalinovskii, and Krasnitskii. In response to persuasion by this group, Patriarch Tikhon, under house arrest at the time, agreed to transfer his powers as Patriarch to the Metropolitan of Iaroslavl, Agafangel, who would administer the Church in his place until a successor could be chosen. In May 1922, Tikhon

[20] Ibid., pp. 209–10.

[21] Ibid., pp. 207–9.

[22] A. Babii and V. Gazhos, 'Tak lozhnaia mudrost' bledneet' ('Thus false wisdom fades'), *Nauka i Religiia*, No. 9 (September 1969), pp. 27–30.

[23] Fedorenko, op. cit., p. 210.

agreed to turn over the archives to this group of clerics so that they might transfer them to Metropolitan Agafangel and so that in the brief interval before his arrival they might take care of routine matters such as correspondence, etc.

Metropolitan Agafangel never did arrive in Moscow. Shortly thereafter he was arrested and exiled to the far north. In the vacuum of power which resulted (Patriarch Tikhon was still under arrest) the group of radical priests took advantage of the situation and in July 1922 formed an administration which they entitled the Living Church. At a congress held in July and a Sobor convened by the Living Church in April and May of 1923, a series of reforms were pushed through, chief among which were the translation of the liturgy into the vernacular, the acceptance of the new (Gregorian) style for the Church calendar, and the stipulation that married clergy may be elevated to the episcopate and that widowed priests may remarry (both clearly in contradiction to Canon Law).

From the beginning, the Living Church movement was plagued by fissiparous tendencies and very quickly split into a congeries of more or less closely allied groups whose adherents came to be designated the renovationists. The Living Church movement was composed almost exclusively of the white, or parish, clergy and never did succeed in attracting the great mass of believers. When the State reversed itself by releasing Patriarch Tikhon (who had been stripped of his office and demoted to a simple layman by the Living Church Sobor of 1923), the movement quickly began the deterioration which led to its final demise during World War II.

Nevertheless, the initial success of the Living Church was very impressive indeed. The Living Church Metropolitan N. F. Platonov stated that at its peak some 15,000 parishes were allied with the renovators.[24] According to incomplete data from 1925, they held 12,593 churches in 108 of the dioceses.[25] A recent Soviet scholar places the figure still higher: 'By the time of the Sobor of 1923 the renovators had more than half of all the parishes; by 1925 the balance had changed in favour of the Tikhonites; in the thirties only one-third of all the parishes

[24] V. E. Titov, *Pravoslavie* ('Orthodoxy') (Moscow: Publishing House for Political Literature, 1967), p. 116.
[25] Curtiss, op. cit., p. 190.

remained with the renovators.'[26] According to a Western estimate, the renovators still retained some 35 per cent of the total
number of Orthodox parishes by the end of the decade.[27]

The initial success of the Living Church group was phenomenal,
and in some respects difficult to account for. To be sure, the
movement enjoyed the vigorous support of the Government.
While the regime's support of the Living Church movement was
by no means unanimous—the Communist Party retained its
hostility to all religion—the Living Church did win numerous
important concessions from the Government. These concessions
included permission to maintain a central administration, permission to publish, and permission to organize a theological
academy. All of these had been denied to the patriarchal Church.
In addition, the State indicated that it was not unwilling to use
the requirement of registration of local parishes against the
opponents of the Living Church.[28] Even more important, the
Living Church movement enjoyed a great deal of practical help
from the regime. Particularly in disputed parishes, the regime did
not show itself especially hesitant to arrest those members of the
clergy who resisted the Living Church. A goodly number of the
parishes won by the Living Church, and perhaps a greater number
of the cathedrals (the renovators captured nearly all of the
cathedrals), were won by default as the State conveniently
removed clerics who objected to the Living Church.

Important as it was, however, the connivance of the secular
authorities scarcely provides sufficient explanation for the extent of
the Living Church's initial success. Other factors must be sought
to explicate the truly formidable ability of the Living Church
group to gain control over the churches in the initial period.

Perhaps one of the more important reasons for this success was
the great confusion which was rampant within the Russian
Orthodox Church during this period. The Patriarch was in
prison and there were reports that he had abdicated.[29] Indeed,

[26] M. M. Sheinman, 'Obnovlencheskoe techenie v russkoi pravoslavnoi tserkvi
posle oktiabria' ('The renovation movement in the Russian Orthodox Church after
October'), in AN SSSR, *Voprosy nauchnogo ateizma*, op. cit., II, 58.

[27] Matthew Spinka, *Christianity Confronts Communism* (New York: Harper, 1936),
p. 78, citing W. H. Chamberlin, 'The Struggle for the Russian Soul,' *Atlantic Monthly*,
September 1929, p. 397.

[28] *Izvestiia*, 27 April 1923.

[29] Wassilij Alexeev, *Russian Orthodox Bishops in the Soviet Union, 1941–1953* (mimeographed, in Russian; New York: Research Program on the U.S.S.R., 1954), p. 73.

there were even rumours that he had been killed in prison.[30] To add to the confusion, the Living Church was inaccurately claiming that Tikhon had transferred all authority to them.[31] So great was the confusion that the Living Church group did succeed in winning the temporary allegiance of a number of hierarchs who were far from sympathetic with the aims and methods of the movement, including the future Patriarch, Metropolitan Sergii.[32]

Perhaps most important of all was the intrinsic appeal of the Living Church reformers to the white clergy—an appeal which had sociological roots.[33] For the preceding two hundred years at least the white clergy had been an oppressed caste within the Russian Empire. Prior to the reforms of 1860, the clergy by law had been socially immobile, unable to aspire to any profession other than the ministry. Children of clergymen had only the options of following in their father's footsteps or being conscripted as peasants into the army. Even after the reforms of 1860, the white clergy had been largely ignored in the decision-making of the Church. While the tsarist State had provided subsidies for the functioning of the diocesan machinery of the Church, the parish priests had to remain content with the donations of an often hostile peasantry, and in many cases had no hope of escaping from a very low standard of living. In addition, in their ecclesiastical functions the parish clergy were at the mercy of the vast and cumbersome network of rules and regulations of the Church bureaucracy as administered by the bishops.

The Sobor of 1917, which had restructured the Church, had done little to remove the dissatisfactions of the white clergy. The chief effect of the reforms of 1917 was to restore to the episcopacy

---

[30] Mikhail Pol'skii, *Novye mucheniki rossiiskie* ('Modern Russian martyrs') (Jordanville, New York: Holy Trinity Monastery, two volumes, 1949 and 1957), I, 105-6.

[31] Gleb Rar (pseudonym of A. Vetrov), *Plennenaia tserkov'* ('The captive Church') (Frankfurt: Posev, 1954), pp. 14-15.

[32] Ibid.; cf. Sviashchennik Mikhail (pseudonym of Mikhail Pol'skii), *Polozhenie tserkvi i Sovetskoi Rossii. Ocherk bezhavshego iz Rossii sviashchennika* ('The position of the Church in Soviet Russia. An essay by a priest who fled Russia') (Jerusalem: Goldberg's Press, 1931), p. 105.

[33] For sociological backgrounds of the Living Church Adventure, I am indebted to the Rev. Dr. Georges Florovsky, in an unpublished address entitled, 'A Pattern from the Past: Zeal for Reform and the Living Church,' delivered on 11 September 1967, at the conference, 'Trends in the Changing Society: Religious and Intellectual Ferment in the U.S.S.R.,' organized by the Centre de Recherches et d'Etude des Institutions Religieuses, in Geneva, Switzerland.

a degree of authority which had been denied it under the Petrine regulations of the Empire. Many of the white clergy, however, continued to feel themselves largely ignored in the structure of the Church and were profoundly dissatisfied with the limitations on the role which they could take in Church life.

The Living Church movement was by and large a reflection of this dissatisfaction on the part of the lower clergy. With very little theological or theoretical basis, and with a patchwork programme constructed more on emotions than on any stable system of goals, the advocates of renovation were able to strike a sympathetic chord in a large number of the white clergy, who in their general dissatisfaction with their conditions could join enthusiastically in the rather ill-defined programme of the renovators.

It was precisely this emotional expression of dissatisfaction, however, which contained in it the seeds of collapse, as well as the grounds for the initial success of the Living Church movement. No coherent programme was worked out by the Living Church leadership, and a great deal of the potential energy of the movement was dissipated in the rash of subsequent schisms within its ranks. More important, this dissatisfaction of the white clergy was not felt especially strongly by the laity, and parish priests who joined the movement were unable to bring their congregations with them. As a result, the movement was exceedingly ephemeral, and though it embraced a large proportion of the lower clergy, it never did have that base of popular support necessary to its survival.[34]

The renovators ran into considerable resistance in the parishes. Supporters of Patriarch Tikhon travelled about the parishes organizing the parish councils against renovating priests.[35] In June 1922, Metropolitan Agafangel issued a message from his place of exile in the far north which was secretly circulated among the faithful and called them to remain true to the Patriarch.[36] The supporters of the Patriarch expended funds, issued printed propaganda, and sent special instructors around to the parishes warning them against the renovators.[37] According to *Izvestiia*, in

[34] Shabatin, op. cit., p. 38.
[35] N. F. Platonov, 'Pravoslavnaia tserkov' v 1917–1935 gg' ('The Orthodox Church, 1917–1935'), in AN SSSR, *Ezhegodnik muzeia istorii religii i ateizma* ('Annual of the Museum of the History of Religion and Atheism') (Moscow: AN SSSR, annually since 1957), V, 254–5.
[36] Curtiss, op. cit., p. 134.
[37] Platonov, op. cit., p. 255.

August 1922, 'Not withstanding the extreme vigilance of the G.P.U., a series of secret meetings of the faithful were held in Vladimir, Kursk, Riazan, Perm, and other cities, and everywhere it was resolved to disavow the Supreme Church Administration and support Patriarch Tikhon.'[38] Mikhail Pol'skii cites as an example one individual who was appointed by his bishop to be a missionary against the renovation and travelled about the area organizing patriarchally oriented churches in areas where the renovators had captured all of the churches,[39] and as another example cites a priest of patriarchal orientation who, during the Easter fast of 1924, was in one of the only two non-renovation churches in one city:

It is not surprising that during the Great Fast all the believers that did not accept the renovation confessed only at [these churches]. Father Mikhail confessed some 200–300 per day, the confessions lasting not more than two to three minutes, for all understood that one must not delay him, but merely to appear in his church signified faithfulness to Orthodoxy.[40]

Such agitation in favour of the patriarchal orientation could be very effective indeed, especially in areas where 'many of the laity did not even know that they had renovationist priests'.[41]

There were a number of reactions to the Living Church movement among the laity which resulted from and in part explain the hostility to the renovators. According to a historian of the Moscow Patriarchate,

Very, very many believing laymen spurned the renovation because of the incomprehensible, unquenchable, boundlessly clear hatred of its leaders towards monasticism. They considered the latter as 'an unnatural institution,' monasteries as 'hotbeds of obscurantism and sloth,' and the monastic clergy as endowed with all the fancied vices.[42]

Veneration for monastics is deeply rooted in the Orthodox tradition. In addition, this attack on monasticism was easy to recognize as a direct attack on the monastic bishops. The position of the bishop is solidly entrenched in the Orthodox tradition and the

---

[38] Paul Miliukov, *Outlines of Russian Culture*; Part I: 'Religion and the Church' (Philadelphia, Pennsylvania: University of Pennsylvania Press, 1942), p. 178.
[39] Pol'skii, op. cit., II, 149–50.
[40] Ibid., p. 145.
[41] Ibid., p. 155.
[42] Shabatin, op. cit., p. 38.

affection and respect of Orthodox people for the bishop is an important factor in Orthodoxy.

Almost immediately, apocalyptic interpretations of the Living Church Adventure appeared. According to Curtiss,

Rumours circulated about the appearance of anti-Christ; gossip in Petrograd had it that Vvendenskii was using an automobile with 'the number of the Beast' upon it—the mystic number '666'—as his car had a licence plate numbered '999,' or '666' inverted.[43]

According to data drawn from one area in 1923, the Orthodox population considered the Living Church 'a new faith', and the population refused to enter the renovationist churches from fear of receiving 'the seal of anti-Christ'.[44]

Probably the dominant motivation in the hostility to the Living Churchmen was their willingness to support and collaborate with the Soviet Government. Despite their often sincere avowals of desire to reform the Church, the political interpretation of their action very quickly arose. According to W. Alexeev, 'The overwhelming majority saw in the renovators only adventurers and Soviet agents.'[45] Interestingly enough, Soviet scholars are in agreement with this view, claiming that the major reason for hostility to the Living Church was its collaboration with the Soviet State, and that the patriarchal parish councils served as centres for uniting reactionary forces against the regime.[46] The most visible immediate result of the Living Church Adventure was indeed a polarization within the Church; because of the challenge of the renovators, parishes were forced to take a stand on the political issue of acceptance or rejection of the Soviet Government and its policies.

This political coloration continued to prevail in the Church even after the release of Patriarch Tikhon, which marked the beginning of the decline and ultimate dissolution of the Living Church movement. Those who had interpreted the Living Church Adventure politically continued to see in Patriarch Tikhon the symbol of resistance to the Soviet regime, interpreting his widely

[43] Curtiss, op. cit., p. 144.
[44] A. I. Klibanov, 'Sovremennoe sektantstvo v Lipetskoi Oblasti' ('Contemporary sectarianism in Lipetsk Oblast'), in AN SSSR, *Voprosy istorii religii i ateizma*, op. cit., pp. 159–60.
[45] Alexeev, op. cit., p. 79.
[46] Sheinman, op. cit., pp. 48–9.

publicized confession as a tactical manœuvre by the Patriarch, a statement extracted by the regime under duress as the price of his release. So great was the impact of the release of the Patriarch that many of the adherents of the Living Church quit the struggle and repented of their schismatic actions.[47]

The very existence of a Patriarch proved a rallying point for the great mass of the believers. Despite the fact that the restrictions applied against him by the regime even after his release were sufficient functionally to immobilize him, making it impossible for him actually to administer the Church,[48] the patriarchal Church continued to regain ground previously lost to the Living Churchmen during the remaining two years of Tikhon's life.

The crisis of the Living Church Adventure for the first time created a widespread capability for *ad hoc* and clandestine means of resistance among Orthodox people. It would be somewhat misleading to denote these nascent groupings and activities by the term underground, for if in the majority of cases they were obliged to avoid the observation of State authorities during the period of the Living Church Adventure, these activities were conducted in direct affiliation with the legally operating patriarchate. Although widespread underground movements did not originate during this period, a great number of believers gained some initial experience —with the blessing of the duly constituted Church authorities— in the techniques and procedures of clandestine religious organization and life.

According to the Living Church hierarch, Platonov, laymen formed special 'councils of twenty', undertaking semi-clandestine measures against Living Church priests in their parishes. They formed networks of cells within the parishes, and often enjoyed the help of itinerant monks from liquidated monasteries.[49] According to the Soviet academician, L. N. Mitrokhin, Patriarch Tikhon himself encouraged and initiated just such activities. Mitrokhin quotes a priest:

Tikhon called me to active church work and struggle with communist teaching and the Soviet government, as a government which had

[47] Ibid., p. 57.

[48] For example, the Commissariat of Justice on 8 December 1923, ruled that prayers for 'citizen Belavin' might be considered evidence of a disloyal attitude of a congregation, and might result in the 'reconsideration' of the contract allowing the church to remain functioning. See Curtiss, op. cit., p. 150.

[49] Platonov, op. cit., pp. 256–9.

renounced religion. According to his words, having accepted the position of a priest, I was obliged to educate the people in the spirit of non-acceptance of the Soviet government, to fortify them against participation in Soviet measures. He recommended that I found circles and groups among the people, and that I entice into them first of all people who do not accept the Soviet government and who are zealously attached to religion. He told me that I should have in my parish not less than twelve such activists, according to the number of the apostles. The Patriarch gave special attention to the education of youth in a religious, anti-communist spirit, he recommended that I entice them into circles, and that I organize with them activities of studying prayers and religious songs.[50]

Pol'skii cites a similar case of a daughter whose father had joined the renovationists; she asked him for his blessing and then departed and joined the Tikhonite movement.[51] Secretly ordained priests circulated among the laity during the Living Church Adventure.[52] Pilgrimages were made to holy places in lieu of church services,[53] and apocalypticism was rampant.[54] All of these experiences would become significant in the future should further necessity arise, and, indeed, Mitrokhin finds evidence for a direct connection between these opponents of the Living Church and later underground Orthodox organizations:

In the beginning of the twenties a schism developed among the clergy and believers in Kozlov, whose transmission line was the prescription of the Tambov diocesan council on the propagation of a change in church government, the renovation of the church service, and the transfer of all church festivals to the New Style ... At this time the special epistle of Tikhon appeared, in which he condemned all innovations in the church. In connection with this call a Kozlov 'clerical committee' was formed in 1923, into which entered the priests N. Sosnovskii, V. Sokolov, and the protodeacon P. Sergievskii. . . .

The most active was N. Sosnovskii, who, while he was in charge of the Nikitovskii Church, began to form groups of religious fanatics

[50] L. N. Mitrokhin, 'Reaktsionnaia deiatel'nost' "istinno-pravoslavnoi tserkvi" na Tambovshchine' ('The reactionary activity of the "True Orthodox Church" in the Tambov area'), in AN SSSR, *Sovremennoe sektantstvo* ('Contemporary sectarianism'), Volume IX of the series AN SSSR, *Voprosy istoriia religii i ateizma*, op. cit., pp. 147–8.
[51] Pol'skii, op. cit., II, 249.
[52] Ibid., p. 253.
[53] Klibanov, 'Sovremennoe sektantstvo v Lipetskoi oblasti,' op. cit., p. 160.
[54] Platonov, op. cit., p. 263.

4

who were inimically disposed to the Soviet government. Among the people close to him we find Archimandrite Kol'tsov (monastic name 'Illarii'), who was one of the authorities of the [later] True Orthodox Church. (A secret funeral was held locally by the remaining members of the True Orthodox Church on his death.) In 1923, Illarii enticed into his organization P. P. Filatov, who later was one of the most eminent leaders of the Michurin and Tambov True Orthodox Church.

We have not been able to establish the numbers and composition of Sosnovskii's groups, known by the name 'Nikitovskii schism,' but, all things considered, it was comparatively numerous and had links with other organizations of like nature. Thus, Sosnovskii was linked with the prominent old-church Metropolitan Iosif of Leningrad, and, especially importantly, with Bishop Bui of Voronezh. The link with Bui, who was located then in Elets, existed through 'Illarii,' who regularly received instructions for the organization of anti-Soviet groups from the Voronezh bishop.[55]

Mitrokhin goes on to relate other, analagous cases in which members of the opposition to the Living Church became active participants in later underground organizations.

Even if the Living Church Adventure did not result in an immediate and widespread underground movement in the Orthodox Church, there were underground sects which became visible within Orthodoxy during this period. Chief among them were the Fedorovtsy. In one area, according to a Soviet scholar,

In 1923 a new religious sect was established by a certain Fedor Doroshenko with the knowledge of the Bishop of Voronezh, Vladimir. . . . The leaders of the sect were former participants in the kulak uprisings: the commander of the 'Novokalitvenskii Insurrectionary Regiment,' Dmitrii Parkhomenko, his brother Petr, 'Inspector of the Cavalry Insurrectionary Regiment,' and others. The sect received the name 'Fedorovtsy' from the name of the monk Fedor Rybalkin, who in the past had served in the Kolchak regiment, 'Jesus Christ'.[56]

A rather aberrational form of underground Orthodoxy was the sect of Apokalipsisty. This was founded by a former Roman Catholic priest, N. F. Guminskii, who, because of his claim that he was the representative of the Prophet Elijah, had been unfrocked by Pius XI.

[55] Mitrokhin, op. cit., pp. 150–1.
[56] I. A. Aleksandrovich, et al., 'Sektantstvo v voronezhskoi oblasti i rabota po ego preodoleniiu' ('Sectarianism in Voronezh oblast and work for overcoming it'), in AN SSSR, Ezhegodnik muzeia istorii religii i ateizma, op. cit., V, 61.

In 1923–1924, utilizing the schism in the Russian Orthodox Church, Guminskii began to gather about himself fanatically inclined church-men, laying the basis for the religion of the sect of the Apokalipsisty. He called his closest assistants apostles. These apostles travelled around through the Ukraine, preaching the religion of Guminskii, ascribing to him the praise of a saint and miracle worker.[57]

This rather syncretistic sect attracted adherents not only from the Orthodox population but from other sectarians as well. In their religious structure they were quite similar to Orthodoxy, with three ranks of clergy (bishops, presbyters, deacons), utilization of icons (including portraits of the founder), use of the sign of the cross, confession, etc. Unlike the Orthodox, the believers remained seated during worship, and baptism was performed only on adults.[58] The sect was oriented eschatologically, as its name indicates.

In the far north an exceedingly alienated sect calling themselves the 'True Orthodox Christians in Hiding' appeared during this period.[59] This group, whose members cut themselves off com-pletely from society and hid deep in the forest, contained many similarities to the analagous variant of the Old Believer movement, and will be discussed in a subsequent chapter.

Thus the exigencies of the first decade of communist rule in Russia had created conditions which gave rise to a large number of the prerequisites for the formation of an underground Orthodox movement within the country. Clandestine Orthodox and semi-Orthodox movements had been formed and were already in existence and operational. The early excesses of the regime against the monasteries, as well as the Living Church Adventure, had already created a tradition of a wandering clergy, able to service Orthodox groups existing outside the framework of the institu-tional Church. The Living Church Adventure had given a large number of Orthodox believers experience in the techniques of clandestine religious life and had created—especially in areas where the renovators controlled all the churches—groups of Orthodox believers already dependent on their own resources for the expression of religious commitments. Most important, in the

---

[57] Fedorenko, op. cit., pp. 216–17.

[58] S. D. Skazkina, ed., *Nastol'naia kniga ateista* ('Reference book for the atheist') (Moscow: Publishing House for Political Literature, 1968), p. 136.

[59] Gagarin, op. cit., p. 169.

person of Patriarch Tikhon the future underground Orthodox movement had acquired a patron saint. For those of political orientation, his initial year of resistance against the State provided a basis for subsequent political hostility to the communist regime. Neither his confession, which such believers considered extracted from him by coercion, nor the 'testament' written the day before he died in 1925, which they considered altogether spurious, were sufficient to tarnish the image of Patriarch Tikhon in the minds of those who were politically hostile to the Soviet regime.

What was missing was leadership, for the believers who had resorted to clandestine measures in resisting the encroachments of the Living Church remained loyal to their duly constituted bishops. These bishops, inasmuch as they remained in affiliation with the legally accepted Patriarch, could not at this time be considered adherents of an underground, illegal form of Orthodoxy. If an underground movement were to develop, leadership would be required, and the events of 1927 would provide that leadership.

III

The Storm

Patriarch Tikhon died on 7 April 1925, and for the next two years the central organization of the Russian Orthodox Church experienced increasing difficulty. The State obviously was no longer prepared to remain content with the apolitical position of Tikhon and began arresting his successors one by one. By mid-1927 it seemed as though the State were determined on liquidating the central government of the Church entirely, and, indeed, was not far from having done so. This process was only reversed when the patriarchate, in the person of Metropolitan Sergii (Stragorodsky), abandoned the apolitical position in favour of a carefully defined position of political loyalty to the Soviet State. It was the controversy which ensued from this decision which marked the real beginning of underground Orthodoxy in the U.S.S.R.

Metropolitan Petr of Krutitskii became locum tenens of the patriarchate upon the death of Patriarch Tikhon. Before his death the Patriarch had named Metropolitans Kirill, Agafangel, and Petr as his successors until such time as a Sobor could be convened to elect a new patriarch. Both Kirill and Agafangel were in exile, however, and there seemed to be no opposition to the appointment of Petr as the locum tenens.

The subsequent course of events gave to Petr, whether he wanted it or not, a large role in the life of that element in the Church which was politically ill-disposed to the Soviet regime. In view of the scant data concerning him it is difficult to determine precisely what his own political attitudes were. According to Russian *émigré* writers, Petr was quite unwilling to countenance any compromise whatsoever with the atheist regime. I. M. Andreev states that the Soviet State had even put pressure on Tikhon to declare himself in political support of the regime:

The Holy Patriarch did not give such a declaration, fully satisfactory
to the Soviet authority. Metropolitan Petr also refused it, for which
he went into exile, where he died (in 1936). Metropolitan Sergii in
1926 published a declaration which was acceptable to the Orthodox
population, but not satisfactory to the Soviet Government, for which
he was arrested. Archbishop Serafim of Uglich also refused to publish
a declaration. There are witnesses that both Metropolitan Kirill and
Metropolitan Iosif had proposals to write the declaration required by
the Soviet authority, but also refused.[1]

It is difficult, however, to reconcile such a postulated attitude of
political hostility with what few facts are available concerning the
position of Metropolitan Petr.[2] For example, at one point Petr
actually transferred his authority for a short time to the collegiate
group of the Grigorievtsy (see below, pp. 46-9) precisely because he
was led to understand that they had received governmental
approval.[3]

After the arrest of Metropolitan Petr on 23 December 1925, the
problem of his attitude towards the State became especially acute,
inasmuch as various pretenders to authority in the Russian Orthodox Church claimed his putative sanction. It would appear that
since he had personally designated Metropolitan Sergii as the
guardian of the locum tenens in case he should be unable to
exercise his duties, the issue would be settled. Nevertheless, after
Metropolitan Sergii had taken a position of political loyalty to the
Soviet State, those hostile to such a position questioned whether in
so doing Metropolitan Sergii was indeed properly carrying out
his responsibilities as the representative of Metropolitan Petr.
According to one report, a member of a scientific expedition to
Siberia claimed to have met with Metropolitan Petr and quoted
Petr as having said, 'I trusted Metropolitan Sergii and I see I
made a mistake.'[4] According to Pol'skii,

Copies were received of letters from the locum tenens of the patriarchal
throne himself, Metropolitan Petr of Krutitskii, in which this hierarch,

---

[1] Ivan Mikhailovich Andreev, *Kratkii obzor istorii russkoi tserkvi ot revoliutsii do nashikh
dnei* ('A brief survey of the history of the Russian Church from the revolution to the
present') (Jordanville, New York: Holy Trinity Monastery, 1952), p. 50.

[2] Stratonov, op. cit., p. 170.

[3] Ibid., p. 152.

[4] *Delo Mitropolita Sergiia* ('The Metropolitan Sergii Affair') (unpublished typescript,
np, np, nd [1930?]), Document No. 30, p. 56.

clearly and simply disclosing the illegality of the action of Metropolitan Sergii, in several letters with Christian love prayed Metropolitan Sergii to turn aside from the path he had taken. The writer of these lines himself heard and read these letters with indisputable proof of their authenticity.[5]

Another document, however, claims that Bishop Vasilii, the vicar of the Riazan diocese, had stated authoritatively that Petr felt that 'it was quite timely that this appeal has appeared, as the product of the necessity of the contemporary moment of the historical situation of our native Orthodox Church'.[6]

In short, it would not appear possible on the basis of available data to determine Metropolitan Petr's position with regard to the patriarchate's search for legalization. This entire question, however important it may have been in establishing the legitimacy of the succession within the patriarchal Church and within the *émigré* jurisdictions abroad, in actual fact proved to be largely irrelevant to the underground Church groupings who claimed Metropolitan Petr as their immediate superior. Because he was in exile at the time that the patriarchate, in the person of Metropolitan Sergii, revised its attitude towards the Government, his name was eminently suitable for use as a point of legitimacy for the alienated groups. In the course of time, however, such allegations of legitimacy, whether spurious or valid, became of diminishing importance to the underground movement.

The death of Patriarch Tikhon seemed a golden opportunity to the renovators, and they made great efforts to increase their influence in the Russian Church.[7] A Sobor was convened in 1925 and the adherents of the Living Church groups made considerable efforts to offer concessions in order to induce the patriarchal Church to attend. Metropolitan Petr was adamant in refusing to join the schismatics in this venture, and as a result, the Sobor of 1925 was unable to arrest the continuing decline of the Living Church. The increased activity of the renovators, however, did

---

[5] Pol'skii, op. cit., II, 156.

[6] *Delo Mitropolita Sergiia*, op. cit., No. 59, p. 154.

[7] Archimandrite Ioann (Snychev), *Tserkovnye raskoly v russkoi tserkvi 20-kh i 30-kh godov XX stoletiia—grigorianskii, iaroslavskii, iosiflianskii, viktorianskii i drugie. Ikh osobennost' i istoriia* ('Church schisms in the Russian Church of the 20s and 30s of the twentieth century—the Grigorian, Iaroslav, Josephite, Viktorian, and others. Their peculiarity and history') (unpublished Master's dissertation, Moscow Theological Academy, 1965), pp. 8–11.

make a contribution to the already considerable confusion reigning in many of the parishes.

A more immediate challenge was raised by Archbishop Grigorii of Ekaterinoslav.[8] Metropolitan Petr was attacked in the Soviet press on 15 November 1925,[9] and Grigorii persuaded him to call a synod of bishops to give the strongest possible refutation of the charges.[10] Before he could issue a proclamation to this effect, however, he was arrested.[11] Under the leadership of Grigorii, a synod of bishops met on 22 December and agreed to form a Temporary Higher Church Council (T.H.C.C.) to provide for the administration of the Church.[12] Pol'skii, apparently basing his argument on the fact that Petr was arrested the following day, interprets this affair as a new Living Church Adventure, in which the G.P.U. sought to fragment the Church even further.[13] In the interpretation of the Russian Orthodox scholar, Archimandrite Ioann, however, the motivation for Grigorii's attempt to seize power was probably egotism interlaced with a measure of personal incompatibility with Metropolitan Petr.[14] The Government did not seem displeased with the attempt, nevertheless, and not only granted permission for the initial gathering, but, when the T.H.C.C. had been formed, granted it legal recognition.[15]

The advantages which accrued from legal recognition were sufficiently impressive to induce Petr to countermand his previous appointment of Metropolitan Sergii as his deputy and, in some-

[8] Sheinman, op. cit., p. 60.

[9] *Izvestiia*, 15 November 1925.

[10] *Izvestiia*, 7 January 1926.

[11] Ioann (Snychev), op. cit., pp. 22–3. Ioann introduces considerable confusion into his treatment of these events. Referring to the arrest with periphrastic euphemisms, he says, 'However, Metropolitan Petr was unable to fulfil his promise. . . . On 10 December, i.e., three days after the publication of the act [designating successors], Metropolitan Petr was removed from power.' Although inadequacies of data preclude absolute certainty, it would not appear that Petr was arrested until 23 December; the discrepancy would be accounted for by the 13 day difference between the New (Gregorian) Style of calendar and the Old (Julian) Style still used by the Church. Hence Petr's arrest occurred the day after Grigorii had convened the founding meeting for his group. Ioann, however, operating on what appears to be the false premise that Sergii had already succeeded to power and sufficient time had elapsed for Grigorii to be informed of this event, proceeds to argue that Grigorii's meeting broke the canonical requirement of subordination to his superior (Sergii).

[12] See the proclamation issued by the synod of bishops, quoted in ibid., pp. 31–3.

[13] Mikhail, op. cit., p. 23.

[14] Ioann (Snychev), op. cit., pp. 20–1.

[15] Ibid., pp. 32, 50.

what ambiguous terms, to transfer his power to a collegiate group.[16] This action was also accepted by the Government.[17] However, Sergii, after some hesitation, finally elected to ignore this action and placed Grigorii and his bishops under a ban, an action which Petr supported in a decree of 9 June 1926, in which he annulled his previous support of the collegiate approach.[18] Thus Sergii was able to survive the challenge of Grigorii, a challenge which was immensely complicated by the simultaneous attempt of Metropolitan Agafangel to assume leadership in the Church in the spring of 1926.[19]

At its peak, the Grigorian movement was able to claim some twenty-six bishops,[20] and hence posed a serious challenge to Metropolitan Sergii. Understandably, subsequent Russian Orthodox scholarship has found the challenge uncanonical; the Church's official journal summed up the matter thus:

Inasmuch as Metropolitan Petr had officially transferred his rights as head of the Supreme Church Government to Metropolitan Sergii, the activities of this group of bishops contradicted Apostolic Rule 34, according to which no bishop may exceed his authority and act independently of the first bishop, i.e., in this case it was impermissible to act independently of the guardian of the patriarchal locum tenens, who at that time was Metropolitan Sergii of Nizhegorod.

---

[16] Ibid., pp. 55–6. The ambiguity was introduced by Petr's authorizing a collegial group to be formed by Grigorii and two other prelates, neither of whom was involved in the already formed T.H.C.C. Grigorii applied this decision to his T.H.C.C., but it remains questionable whether such application was consonant with Petr's intent in making the transfer of power. Furthermore, there was some confusion as to the conditions which Petr attached to this transfer. In his proclamation of 1 February 1926 (as quoted by Ioann, ibid.) he stated, 'With deep sorrow we have been informed by papers in hand that divisions, or to express it more strongly, a new schism, have begun in the Orthodox Church, that His Eminence Metropolitan Sergii is not living in Moscow. ... If on our part for the calming of the believers and the grace of the Church a special arrangement changing those of 5 [sic] December 1925, is needed. ...' However, in his proclamation of 1 January 1927, he states, 'But even then, when I composed the resolution of 1 February, the Lord, evidently, did not forsake me: in that resolution I wrote in the conditional form: IF IT IS TRUE that Metropolitan Sergii is deprived of the possibility of governing ...' (ibid., p. 76). Hence it would appear that Ioann's quotation of one of these passages is in error, or (more probably) Petr's memory was faulty. In any case, Sergii, in refusing to yield to the order of 1 February, was correctly following Petr's intent, at least retrospectively.

[17] Ibid., pp. 54–5.

[18] Ibid., pp. 65, 70.

[19] *Izvestiia*, 13 June 1926.

[20] Ioann (Snychev), op. cit., p. 111; cf. I. Glukhov, 'Patriarkh Sergii i ego deiatel'nost' ' ('Patriarch Sergii and his activity'), *Z.M.P.*, No. 3 (March 1967), p. 64.

The very principle of collegiality, in the sense given it by the T.H.C.C., does not conform to the decision on the character of the government of the Russian Church which was made by the Local Sobor of 1917, which placed a Patriarch at the head of the bishops. Furthermore, the T.H.C.C., even though formed of bishops, did not enjoy the confidence of the entire episcopate and could not be the expression of the will of the whole Russian Church. Metropolitan Sergii addressed the members of the T.H.C.C. with an epistle pointing out to them their uncanonical actions, and finally laid a ban on them which was also supported by Metropolitan Petr.[21]

More important for this study than the question of canonicity is the question of the political position of the Grigorian movement. The very fact that the collegiate group had succeeded in winning the acceptance of the Government would seem to imply that the regime, at the very least, found the movement's attitudes congenial. This indication of the regime's interest in the movement is further supported by Ioann, who, without indicating his source, relates that the eminent and revered Archbishop Ilarion (Troitskii) was briefly released from the Solovky prison camp in 1927 and was provided with special transportation to Moscow so that Grigorii could try (unsuccessfully, as it turned out) to secure his support.[22] To some degree, however, such support by the regime seems incongruous, for the stated political attitude of the Grigorian group was by no means comparable to the uncritical acceptance which the Living Church had offered to the State.

We consider it our duty to attest to our complete obedience to the laws of the Government of the U.S.S.R. which is in power and our trust in its good will, in the purity of its measures in service of the good of the people. Reciprocally, we ask for trust in our loyalty and readiness to serve the good of that same people to the extent of our power, intelligence, and ability.[23]

As will become evident below, this is a rather carefully delimited statement, which contrasts markedly even with the subsequent position taken by Sergii himself, and hence, despite indices of governmental support, it would seem correct (particularly in view

---

[21] N. I., 'Zashchita magisterskoi dissertatsii v moskovskoi dukhovnoi akademii' ('Defence of a Master's dissertation in the Moscow Theological Academy'), *Z.M.P.*, No. 8 (August 1966), pp. 8–9.

[22] Ioann (Snychev), op. cit., pp. 96–7.

[23] Proclamation of 22 December 1925, quoted in ibid., p. 33.

of the Grigorian group's strict preservation of dogmatic, canonical, and liturgical orthodoxy) to classify this as a 'schism of the right'.[24]

The apparent incongruity of State support for a movement which was, by and large, moderate in its politics is perhaps best resolved by considering the regime's actions in this affair as a part of its then current policy of encouraging confusion within the Church. The State had not yet embraced its subsequent commitment to direct confrontation with the Church, and in this period appeared to be content with fostering divisions from within (of which the Living Church Adventure was the most overt example) in the hope of weakening the institutional structure.

Even though at no time did it attain the proportions of the Living Church schism, the Grigorian schism was a serious challenge to the patriarchal party. A considerable number of parishes saw fit to affiliate with this group, and it preserved its existence for almost twenty years. As late as 1938 the Grigorian collegiate group was estimated to have approximately 5 per cent of the Orthodox churches in Russia,[25] and the schism was not finally liquidated until 1943.[26]

Shortly before his arrest, on 6 December 1925 Metropolitan Petr had taken the precaution of designating successors.

In case of impossibility for any circumstances of my carrying out the duties of Patriarchal Locum Tenens, I temporarily turn over the fulfilment of such duties to His Eminence Sergii, Metropolitan of Nizhegorod. If it is not possible for this Metropolitan to accomplish this, then it will be the Exarch of the Ukraine, His Eminence Metropolitan Mikhail, and if he is deprived of the possibility, then His Eminence Iosif, Archbishop of Rostov. . . .[27]

Almost immediately upon succeeding Petr, Metropolitan Sergii had to survive the challenge of the Grigorian collegiate group, and then in April 1926, Metropolitan Agafangel, who was senior to Metropolitan Petr in the list of successors designated by Patriarch Tikhon, returned from exile. Ultimately, however, he was persuaded to withdraw his claims.[28]

Early in 1926 Metropolitan Sergii was arrested and brought to

[24] Ibid., *passim*.
[25] Curtiss, op. cit., p. 286, citing *Antireligioznik*, No. 4 (1938), p. 34.
[26] Ioann (Snychev), op. cit., p. 118.
[27] Glukhov, op. cit., p. 64.
[28] Cf. Ioann (Snychev), op. cit., pp. 128–58.

Moscow for discussions with regime officials, then returned to his diocese. In June he circulated a letter to the bishops in which he proposed a platform for the Church's attitude towards the State. Essentially a repetition of Patriarch Tikhon's non-political position, this letter made no attempt to minimize the difference in point of view between Church and State.

But let us be sincere to the end. We cannot pass over in silence the contradictions which exist between our Orthodox [people] and the communists who govern our Union. The latter struggle against God and his rule in the hearts of the people, while we see the significance and aim of our entire existence in the confession of faith in God as well as in the widest dissemination and affirmation of that faith in the peoples' hearts. They accept exclusively the materialistic conception of history, while we believe in divine Providence, in miracles, etc.

Far from promising reconciliation of that which is irreconcilable and from pretending to adapt our faith to communism, we will remain from the religious point of view what we are, i.e., members of the traditional church.[29]

This position received powerful support during the summer of 1926 in a letter which was written by a group of eminent bishops imprisoned on Solovky Island in the far north and widely circulated among the Orthodox believers. In this letter, which despite their experience of the regime's hostility towards religion the imprisoned bishops considered a workable platform for Church-State relations, frank admission was made of the occasions on which the Church had trespassed against non-interference in politics, and a list of the regime's transgressions against the rule of separation of Church and State was included.

Even though these two definitions of a proper church attitude towards the Government proved ineffectual (the regime was unwilling to accept any such position of neutrality on the part of the Church), the letters received wide support among the Orthodox faithful and their circularization among the people left a profound imprint. Subsequently, according to a bishop who had left the legalized Church and entered the underground movement, this circularizing of proposals to determine the consensus of the faithful constituted a Sobor, and the theory was advanced that if it is impossible for representatives of the Church to meet in one

[29] Translation from Matthew Spinka, *The Church in Soviet Russia* (New York: Oxford University Press, 1956), p. 158.

place, this sort of consensus by correspondence was a valid means of making decisions in the Church.[30] That Metropolitan Sergii's subsequent decisions were not preceded by such a survey of attitudes within the Church was held to invalidate them.

Such a continuation of Patriarch Tikhon's apolitical position, however, obviously was not sufficient to ameliorate the State's hostility towards the Orthodox Church. Metropolitan Sergii was twice more arrested, and in June 1927, he issued a proclamation which radically altered the political stand of the Orthodox Church and determined the official Church's course for the ensuing decades. Despite the fact that the proclamation claimed to be fulfilling the desires of the late Patriarch, its substance was abandonment of the non-political position in favour of the Church's positive support of the regime in political matters.

We must show, not in words, but in deeds, that not only people indifferent to Orthodoxy, or those who reject it, can be faithful citizens of the Soviet Union, loyal to the Soviet government, but also the most fervent adherents of Orthodoxy, to whom it is as dear with all its canonical and liturgical treasures as truth and life. We wish to be Orthodox and at the same time to claim the Soviet Union as our civil motherland, the joys and successes of which are our joys and successes, the misfortunes of which are our misfortunes. Every blow directed against the Union, be it war, boycott, or simply murder from behind a corner, like that in Warsaw, we acknowledge as a blow directed against us. Remaining Orthodox we remember our duty to be citizens of the Union 'not from fear, but from conscience,' as the Apostle has taught us (Rom. 13:5). And we hope that with God's help, by your general cooperation and support, we shall resolve this matter.[31]

This was a profound and important change in the position of the Russian Orthodox Church, one which evoked a storm of protest, for the faithful were by no means unanimous that such outspoken and uncritical acceptance of an atheistic regime was justifiable or necessary.[32] There were a number of factors, however, which

---

[30] *Delo Mitropolita Sergii*, op. cit., No. 122, p. 170.

[31] *Izvestiia*, 18 August 1927; translation from William C. Fletcher, *A Study in Survival: The Church in Russia, 1927–1943* (New York: Macmillan, 1965), pp. 29–30. *Note:* throughout the present study, the 'orthographic atheism' of Soviet journalism, whereby Soviet authors refuse to capitalize divine or sacred appellations, will be dispensed with. Translated passages from Soviet sources will capitalize 'God', etc., according to accepted English (or rather, non-Soviet) usage.

[32] Glukhov, op. cit., p. 66.

necessitated some such change of course in the policies of the Church.

Of overwhelming importance was the chaos then prevalent in the higher Church government. The organizational structure of the Church was on the brink of dissolution. Ten of the eleven designated successors of Patriarch Tikhon were in prison or in exile. Unless something were done to reverse this situation the traditional governmental structure of the Church could not survive. According to Metropolitan Sergii, 'Only impractical dreamers can think that such an immense community as our Orthodox Church with all its organizations may peacefully exist in this country by hiding itself from the Government.'[33] The previous Church policy of non-interference between Church and State had in practice evoked the active hostility of the State against the Church, hostility which could prove fatal to the Church as an institution. In its place Metropolitan Sergii apparently hoped that by offering active political support the Church could in return receive sufficient concessions from the Government to allow its continued survival. The effectiveness of this approach received token validation almost immediately, as the Government allowed Sergii on the basis of this statement to organize a Holy Synod and to publish a journal. Ultimately (after a delay of some sixteen years), Sergii's approach proved to be quite effective. For the two decades following the beginning of World War II Church and State acted in a tense and limited, but nevertheless effective, harmony, with the Church receiving sufficient privileges to allow its functioning in return for its political co-operation with the State. Had Metropolitan Sergii not found some such means of tempering the adamant hostility of the State it is highly doubtful whether the Church could have continued to exist much beyond 1927 as an institution within Soviet society.

A second factor necessitating some form of action on the Church's part was the challenge of the Living Church. While in 1927 the competition offered by the Living Church no longer seemed so overwhelming as it had four years previously, nevertheless the Living Church did enjoy the ability to exist as a structured institution within society. With the institutional framework of the patriarchal Church approaching disintegration, the very existence of a competitive body which was able to organize religious activities

[33] Ibid., p. 30.

without the disadvantage of an implied transgression of State law was a formidable challenge indeed. By reversing the political position of the patriarchal Church in a manner analogous to, but in many respects different from, that approach which the Living Church had effectively used to secure legal recognition, the patriarchal group might be able to neutralize the single, chief advantage possessed by the competitive groups of the Living Church.[34] Unless some sort of normality could be achieved in relations between his Church and the State, Sergii evidently felt that the depredations of the Living Church competition might decimate his Church.[35]

A similar threat which was facing the Church should the central authority collapse was the danger that the Church, having to go *en masse* into an underground or illegal position, would rapidly disintegrate. Without the stabilizing effect of functional central authority the Orthodox parishes might very quickly degenerate into sectarian congregations further and further removed from canonical validity.[36] As will become apparent in the course of this study, Metropolitan Sergii's change of position in 1927 did not entirely solve this problem of centrifugal tendencies within the Church, and those portions of the Church which went underground for one reason or another did indeed display a marked tendency towards sectarian aberrations with the passage of time.

W. Alexeev, despite his own evident hostility towards the patriarchate's policy of political collaboration with the communist regime, gives what appears to be a valid summary of the motivational aspects of this change in course.

Of course, Metropolitan Sergii knew all about these currents and moods, and, of course, they had an influence on him. Constant conversations with all sorts of people about the declaration and the emphasis of its requirements witnessed to the uneasy conscience of the Metropolitan. We can suppose that his confidence that it was possible to outwit the Bolsheviks gradually dissipated in the locum tenens. Before the beginning of World War II the position of the patriarchate was desperate. Even if the Metropolitan exaggerated in his interview published in *Izvestiia* from 16 to 19 February 1930, that he then had 163 bishops, then all the more, considering that in

[34] Shabatin, op. cit., p. 41.
[35] Glukhov, op. cit., p. 64.
[36] Ibid.

1939 less than 10 of them remained, the difference turns out to be great.[37]

The change of policy itself was a carefully delimited programme. Like the Living Church, Sergii was offering to the Government the unreserved support of the Church in political matters (albeit perhaps in less outspoken terms). Unlike the Living Church, however, Sergii was careful to limit his support to political matters only; in no other area of Church life was he willing to yield. The traditions and canons of the Church remained sacrosanct, and it was only in political affairs that Sergii was willing to adapt his policy.

The passage of his declaration which caused the greatest hostility among its recipients was the recognition of 'the Soviet Union as our civil motherland, the joys and success of which are our joys and successes, the misfortunes of which are our misfortunes'. A subtle distinction exists in the Russian phrasing of this statement, for the word 'motherland' is feminine in gender, while 'Soviet Union' is masculine. The possessive pronoun in 'the joys and successes *of which*' is feminine, and therefore the exact meaning of the phrase is that it is the joys and successes of the motherland, not of the Soviet Union, with which the Church identifies. This left the Church room to disagree with the regime as to what precisely constitutes a 'joy and success' for the motherland (e.g., the growth of atheism in society might be considered a joy by the Soviet Union, but by the Church a misfortune to the motherland).[38]

It would appear that this distinction was somewhat too subtle for a portion of the proclamation's intended audience. *Émigré* churchmen, for example, mistakenly attacked the proclamation on the basis of the possessive pronoun's being masculine.[39] Similarly, according to an open letter composed by churchmen imprisoned on Solovki Island on 14 September 1927,

We cannot accept and approve the proclamation in its entirety, for the following considerations:

[37] Alexeev, op. cit., p. 83.
[38] Sergei Viktorovich Troitskii, *O nepravde Karlovatskogo raskola; razbor knigi Prot. M. Pol'skogo 'Kanonicheskoe polozhenie vysshei tserkovnoi vlasti v SSSR i zagranitsei'* ('On the falsity of the Karlovtsi schism; an analysis of the book by Protopriest M. Pol'skii, "The canonical position of the supreme Church government in the U.S.S.R. and abroad"') (Paris: Editions de l'Exarchat Patriarcal Russe en Europe Occidentale, 1960), pp. 47–8.
[39] Ibid.; cf. Alexeev, op. cit., p. 77; Arfved Gustavson, *The Catacomb Church* (Jordanville, New York: Holy Trinity Monastery, 1960), p. 64.

In paragraph 5 the concept of subordination of the Church to the civil order is expressed in such a categorical and unreserved form that it easily could be understood in the sense of a complete interlacing of Church and State. The Church cannot undertake before the State (whatever the form of government may have been in the past) the obligation to consider 'all joys and successes *of the state* her own joys and successes and every misfortune, her own misfortune'.[40]

A Moscow document of August 1927 paraphrases this statement as follows: 'The joys and successes *of the Soviet Union* are our joys and successes.'[41] Perhaps such a distinction was entirely too subtle after all, for even a subsequent scholar of the Moscow Patriarchate makes the same mistake concerning the 'declaration, the substance of which implied that the children of the Russian Orthodox Church are loyal citizens of their motherland, the Soviet Union, whose [masculine] joys and successes are their joys and successes, and misfortunes, their misfortunes'.[42]

Even where this distinction was duly noted, however, the proclamation was not unassailable so far as a portion of the clergy were concerned. In a statement composed by clergy on 14 March 1928, the following observation is made:

The Christian cannot consider all the joys and successes of the motherland his own successes and joys and every misfortune his own misfortune.

The civil motherland has its own earthly joys and griefs far removed from God and sometimes even contrary to Him. If the Christian takes all these joys and all these griefs as his own he takes on the world's flavour and becomes 'a friend of the world', he finds himself in the impossible position of serving Christ, God and the world at the same time and becomes an enemy of God. For the word of God says that friendship with the world is enmity against God (James 4:4).[43]

[40] *Delo Mitropolita Sergiia*, op. cit., No. 25, p. 163. Italics mine.

[41] Ibid., No. 38, p. 86. Italics mine.

[42] N. I., op. cit., p. 9. It would perhaps be unjust to place too much opprobrium on this unfortunate scholar, for he was misled by the uncommon subtlety of Ioann (Snychev), whose dissertation he was reviewing. In his reserved and exceedingly brief treatment of this delicate matter, Ioann paraphrases this passage by using the word 'fatherland' (*Otechestvo*), which is neuter in gender. Inasmuch as in the possessive pronominal form there is no morphological distinction between masculine and neuter, this innovation avoids the distinction entirely in the subordinate clause, 'its [neuter] (the Fatherland's) joys and successes or misfortunes completely become, as it were, the joys and misfortunes of the Russian Church itself.' Op. cit., p. 188.

[43] *Delo Mitropolita Sergiia*, op. cit., No. 54, pp. 144–5.

Despite attempts by subsequent commentators to minimize the opposition to this declaration,[44] there was a great deal of hostility in the stormy reaction which ensued. A large number of documents circulated throughout the country, some in support of the proclamation, but the majority objecting to it.[45] Among the supporters of the policy, a great number recognized the difficulty of the times and accepted the change of course. The overwhelming necessity for the continued preaching of the Word of God in Russia was more than sufficient to compensate for whatever distasteful measures must be undertaken in the field of politics.[46] Furthermore, there was recognition that such a change of political policy did not necessarily introduce changes into other areas of the life of the Church. According to a document in support of Sergii in the autumn of 1927, the proclamation

changes only the relationship of the Church to the Soviet Government but the faith and the Orthodox Christian life remain immovable. Consequently, the words of the declaration, 'the joys and successes of which are our joys and successes and the misfortunes our misfortunes,' do not relate to our faith and to the Orthodox Christian life but relate only to the economic sphere and our state life, and therefore to point to the declaration as something dangerous for the church does not follow at all.[47]

M. Kurdiumov, in support of the policy, claims that the proclamation caused trouble only abroad; in Russia everybody understood it and considered it 'a great moral feat' on Sergii's part.[48] A large proportion of the believers did accept the declaration of loyalty, bitterly perhaps, but as an unavoidable necessity for the preservation of open churches in Russia.[49] Indeed, the émigré theologian, Nikolai Berdiaev, persuasively argued that Tikhon and Sergii had submitted themselves to a deeper martyrdom by renouncing personal integrity and the right to physical martyrdom instead of speaking a lie or a half-truth, because of their greater concern for the needs of the Church; the Church cannot avoid politics entirely

[44] Troitskii, *O nepravde . . .*, op. cit., p. 46.
[45] For documentary treatment of the controversy surrounding the Declaration of 1927, see *Delo Mitropolita Sergiia*, op. cit., *passim*, and Andreev, op. cit., pp. 53–76.
[46] Rar, op. cit., pp. 26–7.
[47] *Delo Mitropolita Sergiia*, op. cit., No. 97, p. 35.
[48] Mikhail Grigor'evich Kurdiumov, *Komu nuzhna tserkovnaia smuta?* ('Who needs the Church confusion?') (np: np, nd [1928?]), pp. 9–10.
[49] Rar, op. cit, p. 31.

in its duty to bring the Christian faith to every society, regardless of that society's form or structure.[50] Finally, supporters of the proclamation pointed out with some sorrow that it was not, after all, the Church but the State which had necessitated this change in policy, for had the State been willing to abide by its proclaimed policy of separation of Church and State there would have been no need whatsoever to raise the question at all.[51]

The opposition to the change in policy, however, was much more vociferous than its support. Letters, statements, and analyses were circulated from hand to hand.[52] A number of arguments were raised against the new policy.

One of the chief objections was that by proclaiming loyalty to the Soviet Government, Sergii was in fact capitulating to the programme of the renovators, accepting the political position of this radical minority on behalf of the Church at large. Even according to a Soviet scholar, 'After the Patriarchal Church changed its relationship towards the Soviet State, undertaking a position of loyalty, in the eyes of the believers any substantial difference whatsoever between the Orthodox Church and the renovators disappeared.'[53] However, even among those adamantly hostile to this political policy, it had to be recognized that it was not correct to equate Sergii with the renovators, for he had broken none of the canons of the Church.[54] This compounded the difficulties of those who were unwilling to accept the position, for not only did those who refused to follow Metropolitan Sergii now become, by implication, suspect of counter-revolution (as had those who rejected the Living Church movement earlier), they also became guilty of breaking their canonical obligation to their superior. There was no escape: either they became illegal and excommunicate or they became apostate by entering into a pact with the godless.[55]

Not everybody, however, remained satisfied that Sergii's action was unimpeachable from a canonical point of view. Considering the magnitude of this decision, and in view of the fact that it was made not by the Patriarch or even the locum tenens, but the mere guardian, the question was raised as to whether Sergii had not

[50] *Delo Mitropolita Sergiia*, op. cit., No. 118, pp. 143–7.
[51] Ibid., No. 37, pp. 77–8.
[52] Pol'skii, op. cit., II, 126.
[53] Titov, op. cit., p. 116.
[54] Mikhail, op. cit., p. 94.
[55] Ibid., pp. 48–9.

exceeded his canonical authority in making this decision. Sergii had been careful in the text of the proclamation to foresee such objections and to state clearly that this decision was provisional only and for final ratification would be subject to the decision of the next Sobor.

We shall now only express our firm conviction that the future Sobor, having solved many of the most troublesome problems of the inner life of the Church, will at the same time give its final approval with one mind and voice to the task undertaken by us in establishing regular relations between our Church and the Soviet regime.[56]

The difficulty, of course, was that no Sobor would be held for the next sixteen years (and curiously enough, neither of the subsequent Sobors bothered to discuss the issue of the political policy which had been initiated by Sergii in 1927). In a letter of May 1928, Sergii dealt with this problem also. Referring to his detractors, he stated,

They write that we cannot accept legalization before all that is necessary for a fully independent existence of the Church has been granted. In particular, the Synod should be composed of those who are now in prison. Of course all these desires are near to all of us; but one must not be so naive as to await their realization in practice, and that by way of ultimatums. One cannot expect that the Government, which to the present time has considered us counter-revolutionary, will suddenly become generous: release all to freedom and then grant that we decide on whatever we like to propose to the State.

It is clear that such an ultimatum would result in the unending degeneration of our illegal position.[57]

Resistance to Sergii's proclamation was not confined to the realm of ideas alone, but resulted in a great number of concrete acts of resistance. According to Alexeev,

Both Professor Andreev and Protopriest Mikhail Pol'skii write about the storm evoked by the declaration among the laity and among the clergy. The author of the present work, having been in Moscow at the time of the publication of the declaration, can testify to the truth of the picture drawn by Professor Andreev and Father Mikhail Pol'skii.[58]

---

[56] *Izvestiia*, 18 August 1927; translation from Fletcher, op. cit., p. 31.
[57] *Delo Mitropolita Sergiia*, op. cit., No. 117, p. 142.
[58] Alexeev, op. cit., pp. 75–6.

Letters received by the Russian emigration told of massive popular hatred for the new policy,[59] and there was considerable evidence that Sergii was widely scorned as a mere tool of the Bolsheviks.[60] There were demonstrations against him in the Moscow churches.[61] His new course 'evoked the appearance in Moscow of a great number of anonymous leaflets and tracts directed against him and his church work, and also several hierarchs who individually spoke out against him with accusations and censure'.[62] Those of conservative persuasion found the compromise quite unacceptable.[63]

Although certain observers, particularly in the West, have suggested that the majority refused to follow Sergii,[64] it is difficult to determine precisely how large the number of those profoundly dissatisfied with the decision was. Certainly it was immense. According to Archimandrite Ioann,

... one must accept as true that the majority of the church congregation had not yet advanced to that degree of regard for the new governmental structure to which Metropolitan Sergii and his Temporary Patriarchal Synod had arrived. This served as the reason for the Orthodox who were divided in their views both on the proclamation itself and on the church policy of Metropolitan Sergii.[65]

Without disclosing his source of data, Ioann relates that 5,000 copies of the proclamation were printed and distributed to the parishes, but many of the recipients were so overwhelmed by its contents that they simply returned it to the sender; 'almost 90 per cent of the Orthodox parishes reacted to the proclamation [in this manner]'.[66]

---

[59] Georgii Petrovich Fedotov, 'K voprosu o polozhenii russkoi Tserkvi' ('On the question of the position of the Russian Church'), *Vestnik Russkago Studencheskago Khristianskago Dvizheniia*, No. 11 (November 1930), p. 12.

[60] Mikhail K. Gorchakov, *Itogi politiki mitropolitov Sergiia i Evlogiia* ('The sum of the policy of Metropolitans Sergii and Evlogii') (Paris: 'Doroi zlo!', 1930), pp. 5–7.

[61] Fedotov, op. cit., p. 12.

[62] *Delo Mitropolita Sergiia*, op. cit., No. 115, p. 134.

[63] V. E. Ladorenko, 'K voprosu ob izmenenii politicheskoi orientatsii russkoi pravoslavnoi tserkvi (1917–1945)' ('On the problem of the change of political orientation of the Russian Orthodox Church (1917–1945)'), in AN SSSR, *Voprosy istorii religii i ateizma*, op. cit., XII, 116–17.

[64] Nadezhda Teodorovich, 'The Political Role of the Moscow Patriarchate,' *Bulletin of the Institute for the Study of the U.S.S.R.*, No. 7 (July 1960), p. 46.

[65] Ioann (Snychev), op. cit., p. 189.

[66] Ibid., pp. 189, 196. This widespread refusal to disseminate the proclamation (cf. ibid., p. 363) may, in part, explain *Izvestiia*'s unusual decision to publish it in full subsequently.

Particularly before the groups in opposition to the policy had had time to form such organizational structures as were within their capacity, and especially in areas where there were no churches which provided an alternative to either the Living Church or the new policy of Sergii, believers who disagreed with the policy were bereft of facilities for worship. As a result, services began to be held in private homes and apartments.[67] This was an expedient which in coming years would be widely utilized for various reasons.

Very quickly, however, organized opposition began to appear, as a number of dioceses refused to submit to the new political policy and severed relations entirely with Metropolitan Sergii.[68] Opposition reached very bitter levels indeed. For example, Ilarion, vicarial bishop of Smolensk,

was a most irreconcilable enemy of the declaration of Metropolitan Sergii of 1927; he denied the sacraments when performed by Sergiites, and for a second time baptized infants and married those already married in a 'Soviet' Church.[69]

A number of dioceses refused to continue to recognize Sergii as their superior, and he had to devote considerable efforts to correspondence and explanations with the bishops of such dioceses.[70]

Nor was the opposition passive only. Those in opposition to Sergii pursued their cause with great vigour.

The leaders of the groupings and the oppositionists, spreading orally and in writing various slanders against the higher church government, persuaded believers to break prayer relations with Metropolitan Sergii and his Synod as alleged sinners against the purity of Orthodoxy and the freedom of the Church. Calling them traitors to Orthodoxy and murderers of church freedom, they persuaded the people that the temples of Sergii's orientation were without grace, and, not considering themselves guilty of spreading confusion in the Church, openly required 'the traitors of the Church to resign their positions and transfer the government administration into other hands, or tearfully repent of doing evil and lead the ship of the Church in the old channel.'[71]

---

[67] Pol'skii, op. cit., II, 155.
[68] Andreev, op. cit., p. 52.
[69] Pol'skii, op. cit., II, 124.
[70] Several examples of this correspondence are included in *Delo Mitropolita Sergiia*, op. cit., 'Supplement' (unpaginated).
[71] Glukhov, op. cit., p. 66.

In a number of places parishioners physically attacked bishops and priests of patriarchal orientation.[72]

The immediate result was a great deal of confusion throughout the Russian Orthodox Church. In the parishes, already disoriented by the conflicting claims of renovationists, followers of Metropolitan Grigorii, etc.,

the simple, believing people went from one church to another, not knowing which of them was with grace and which without grace. Some, seeking peace for themselves, departed into the sects. Others, seduced by schism and arguments, left the faith altogether and became people outside the Church.[73]

To the extent that he was able, Metropolitan Sergii attempted to meet the many challenges ensuing from his proclamation of 1927 with the counsel of Gamaliel, 'If this matter is of man it will perish.'[74] 'He often said that their actions, built upon sandy ground, were not durable and sooner or later would perish with them, just as the branch cut off from the vine perishes (John 15:1–7).'[75]

Such a passive response, however, was not sufficient, particularly in view of the great confusion reigning in the Russian Church. In his letter of 31 December 1927, Metropolitan Sergii wrote:

There are dioceses and even parishes which, wandering gropingly among the uninformed, live a separate life and often do not know whom to follow in order to preserve Orthodoxy. What a propitious field for the dissemination of all sorts of fables, intentional deceits and all sorts of pernicious errors! What a broad field for all sorts of self-appointed![76]

Sergii made a point in this epistle of emphasizing the canonical rule that a subordinate may sever relations with his duly appointed superior only if the superior has publicly espoused an obvious heresy which has already been judged by a council; in all other cases he is canonically obliged to remain in communion with his superior pending the resolution of disputed issues by a Sobor.[77] In answer to this claim, Metropolitan Iosif wrote:

Those who defend Sergii say that the canons allow separation from a

---

[72] Shabatin, op. cit., p. 42.

[73] Glukhov, op. cit., p. 66. He appears to be quoting, without acknowledgement and in slightly altered form, Ioann (Snychev), op. cit., p. 270.

[74] Shabatin, op. cit., p. 42.

[75] Glukhov, op. cit., p. 67.

[76] *Delo Mitropolita Sergiia*, op. cit., No. 44, p. 120. Also quoted in Ioann (Snychev), op. cit., p. 186, and Glukhov, op. cit., p. 65.

[77] *Delo Mitropolita Sergiia*, op. cit., No. 44, p. 122.

bishop only for heresy judged by a Sobor; it can be replied that the actions of Metropolitan Sergii have led to just that state if one has in view such clear destruction of the freedom and dignity of the one Holy, Conciliar, and Apostolic Church.

But beyond this there is much that the canons cannot foresee, and can one dispute the fact that it is worse and more dangerous than any heresy when a knife is plunged into the very heart of the Church—her freedom and dignity? Which is worse—heresy or murder?[78]

The ultimate weapon to which Sergii had recourse was the ban and excommunication. In defence of this step Sergii wrote to Metropolitan Kirill in July 1929,

You are deeply grieved that we call them departed ones and schismatics. But they call our Church, led by me, 'the kingdom of anti-Christ,' our temples 'the den of satan,' us his servants, the Holy Eucharist 'demon food,' they spit on our Holy things, and the like.[79]

Obviously, feelings were running at a high pitch in consequence of the decision of 1927. Accusations were flung unsparingly by both sides and the opposition not infrequently resorted to apocalyptic imagery to explain what had happened to the Russian Church.[80] The biblical books of *Daniel* and *Revelation* were enlisted in support of the argument of Sergii's opposition that his action represented the final, eschatological apostasy.[81]

A number of organized schismatic movements resulted from dissatisfaction with Sergii's proclamation. These movements, unlike their predecessors, enjoyed significant backing from an important part of the episcopacy and the church leadership, and not only exerted an influence in the countryside during the years which followed, but also provided the leadership for subsequent underground Orthodox organizations. The impact of these early schisms was immense, influencing and in many respects determining the attitudes and approaches of all subsequent underground Orthodox groups.

The most influential of these schismatic movements was the Josephite schism, centred in Leningrad. The leader of the schism, Metropolitan Iosif (Petrovykh), was an important figure in the

[78] Ibid., No. 85, p. 14.

[79] Ibid., 'Supplement'.

[80] Mikhail Grigor'evich Kurdiumov, *Tserkov' i novaia Rossiia* ('The Church and modern Russia') (Paris: Y.M.C.A. Press, 1933), pp. 15–16; cf. Ioann (Snychev), op. cit., p. 294.

[81] *Delo Mitropolita Sergiia*, op. cit., No. 116, p. 140.

Church. While Archbishop of Rostov (Iaroslav oblast) he had been designated by Metropolitan Petr as an alternate to Sergii. In 1926 Sergii had appointed him Metropolitan of Leningrad; however, Iosif was able to visit Leningrad only once, and then the State denied him the necessary residence permit to allow him to move to the city.[82] Apparently the grounds for the denial were false allegations of connections with the Ioannity,[83] although why the State should consider such connections grounds for denial of residence permit remains unclear. Iosif returned to Rostov and continued to be the diocesan leader *in absentia*.

On 19 October 1927, Sergii and his Synod ordered Iosif to be transferred to Odessa.[84] Iosif refused to accept this latest transfer and continued to claim Leningrad as his see.[85] This created an exceedingly tense situation in the Leningrad diocese, and the dissatisfaction of the believers was further exacerbated by an order of 21 October prohibiting mention of exiled diocesan leaders in the prayers of the liturgy.[86] Independently of Iosif, the clergy of Leningrad made preparations to sever relationships with Sergii, and very quickly they had completed their organizational work and were ready to function as an independent diocese.[87] On 26 December 1927, the vicarial bishops Sergii and Dimitrii, with Iosif's support, issued a declaration of independence from Metropolitan Sergii.[88] This move had been preceded by vigorous correspondence between Leningrad and Metropolitan Sergii in Moscow, as well as by attempts to avoid an irrevocable schism by means of sending delegations from Leningrad to Moscow to seek a way of reconciliation.[89] The laity went so far as to appeal to Bishop Nikolai (Iarushevich) to intercede with Sergii on Iosif's behalf.[90]

[82] Ioann (Snychev), op. cit., pp. 222–3.

[83] Ibid. According to Ioann, Iosif was innocent of the charges. Like nearly all others, he of course bore great respect for John of Kronstadt. Cf. the report of Pol'skii, op. cit., II, 296, that it was a mark of Kirill's great eminence in the Church that John specifically asked that he conduct his funeral service.

[84] *Delo Mitropolita Sergiia*, op. cit., No. 47, p. 129.

[85] Spinka, *The Church in Soviet Russia*, op. cit., pp. 74–5; *Delo Mitropolita Sergiia*, op. cit., No. 48, p. 130.

[86] Ioann (Snychev), op. cit., pp. 232–3; *Delo Mitropolita Sergii*, op. cit., No. 45, p. 123.

[87] Platonov, op. cit., p. 253.

[88] Text in Ioann (Snychev), op. cit., pp. 264–5; also in *Delo Mitropolita Sergiia*, op. cit., No. 64, p. 167, dated 27–29 December.

[89] Ioann (Snychev), op. cit., pp. 245–55; cf. Pol'skii, op. cit., II, 136–7.

[90] *Delo Mitropolita Sergiia*, op. cit., No. 46, pp. 125–8.

The members of the new movement had especially strong convictions regarding the political compromise of Metropolitan Sergii. According to one of the sympathizers of the new movement, Archbishop Varlaam,

The unwilling complicity of Orthodoxy with the socialist republic has become aggravated through the acceptance of the godless government by Metropolitan Sergii. The Church may not carry on external struggle, but the Church should devote itself to spiritual struggle with such a government.[91]

The Josephite movement gained the adherence of a number of churches in Leningrad,[92] and it quickly spread to other areas in the country.[93]

Quite evidently, the fundamental motivation for the schismatic movement was political, the conviction that any sort of support for the godless political regime was incompatible with Christian conscience.[94]

The true causes of the schism were the dissatisfaction of a part of the episcopacy with the decree on the separation of Church from State. Some of them did not succeed in understanding the deep motivations of Patriarch Tikhon, who by his counsel determined the concrete relationship of his followers to the state Government of our motherland.[95]

The opinion of the schismatics was that in view of the proclamation of separation of Church and State 'the Church should no longer take an active interest in the fate of the State'[96] and therefore, because Metropolitan Sergii had transgressed against this ideal in offering the positive support of the Church to the State, the schismatics felt in duty bound to sever their affiliation with him. Thus it would appear that the primary motivation of the schism was political.

Sergii's change of political policy, however, was not the immediate issue at stake in the schism, but rather it was the unacceptable

[91] Platonov, op. cit., p. 264.
[92] Pol'skii, op. cit., II, 138.
[93] Shabatin, op. cit., p. 42.
[94] Ibid., p. 41.
[95] N. I., op. cit., p. 9.
[96] Anton Ciliga, *The Russian Enigma* (London: Labour Book Service, 1940), pp. 161–2.

transfer of Iosif. The believers in Leningrad had unwillingly accepted Sergii's proclamation, waiting to see what fruits it would bring; with the attempt to transfer Iosif, this policy had borne fruit.[97] By this action, according to the dissidents, Sergii demonstrated that in its seemingly unconditional acceptance of the State the Church had lost the freedom to order its internal affairs according to the needs and desires of the believers. Furthermore, the order that exiled or imprisoned diocesan leaders may no longer be mentioned in the liturgy, while it made obvious sense as a corollary of the Church's position of loyalty (none of such leaders was convicted on religious charges, and hence the Church could hardly continue publicly to support convicted criminals), could also be interpreted as subjugation to the State in the matter of diocesan leadership. Without a diocesan bishop who could be recognized in the liturgy, the diocese could be considered vacant, and hence the State, merely by arresting a hierarch it disliked, could induce the Church leadership to transfer to that diocese another bishop more amenable to the State's desires.[98] Sergii himself may have admitted as much in his written answer to one of the questions posed by a delegation from Leningrad:

The transfer of bishops is a temporary phenomenon, related in its origin to a significant degree to the circumstance that the relationship of our church organization to the civil government remains unclear to the present time. I agree that transfer is often a blow, not for the Church, but for the personal feelings of the bishop himself and the flock. But keeping in mind the extraordinary situation and the efforts of many to tear the body of the Church asunder by one means or another, both the bishop and the flock should sacrifice their personal feelings in the name of the good of the Church at large.[99]

It was this immediate issue of the attempted transfer of Iosif which provided the catalyst for the formation of the schism.[100]

The chief argument of Metropolitan Iosif and his followers in

---

[97] Ioann (Snychev), op. cit., pp. 241–2.

[98] This rationale would perhaps explain the claim of the schismatics that Sergii was guilty of up to 40 such transfers (ibid., p. 254), a figure which Ioann finds hard to believe (p. 290); the dissidents may have been referring to dioceses whose bishops were in exile, operating on the assumption that Sergii's ban on mentioning them in the liturgy amounted to transferring them away from the dioceses which they were still, in theory, ruling *in absentia*.

[99] Ibid., pp. 251–2.

[100] N. I., op. cit., p. 9.

refusing to accept the transfer was the canonical impermissibility of a bishop's being removed from his diocese against his will; furthermore, Metropolitan Sergii, as the mere guardian of the locum tenens (rather than Patriarch) lacked the authority to order such a transfer. To this the supporters of Sergii quite cogently argued that if he lacked authority to transfer Iosif away from Leningrad, then it should follow that he also lacked the authority to transfer him from Rostov to Leningrad in the first place.[101] In actual fact, there was a degree of casuistry on both sides in this debate over the canonical implications of the transfer, for the chief complaint was not so much the canonicity of such appointments and transfers as the fact that they were arbitrary and very often seemed inspired by the State.[102] Furthermore, those who were opposed to such practices saw in such transfers a very present danger for the life of the local church.

In our difficult time, when heresies and schisms abound, to receive into a diocese a bishop whose purity of Orthodoxy is not known to the believing people in exchange for one whose Orthodoxy is pure, cannot serve the good of the Church. And the new bishop, who does not know the conditions of life in which the Orthodox Church of the given locality lives, who does not know which of her clergy is truly Orthodox and which is a renegade, can make many mistakes, as has happened in many places, where renegades are rewarded and Orthodox priests suffer persecutions.[103]

In actual fact, none of these arguments appears to touch on the real issue in the transfer of Metropolitan Iosif. Had Sergii not ordered his transfer to some other diocese he would have risked bringing the Church to an outright confrontation with the State, for, as has been noted, the secular authorities forbade Iosif to remain in Leningrad.

In the initial organization of the Josephite schism, Leningrad remained the focus despite Iosif's enforced absence. There the schismatics enjoyed the services of a number of very capable leaders, including former professors of the Petersburg Theological Academy.[104] Iosif continued to exercise leadership through correspondence, such as the following statement addressed to the Leningrad flock:

[101] *Delo Mitropolita Sergiia*, op. cit., No. 97, p. 38.
[102] Ibid., No. 96, p. 30.
[103] Ibid., No. 119, p. 149.
[104] Shabatin, op. cit., p. 42.

Calling God's blessing on them, I ask and pray that the pastors and all believers be faithful to our leadership and archpastoral care, peacefully and quietly continuing the business of prayer, of the salvation of the soul, and of divine services, humbly submitting to the civil authority, which has not yet found it possible to allow [me to return].[105]

In addition, Metropolitan Iosif, in view of his exalted rank in the Church hierarchy, undertook to extend his sanction to other bishops who were separating from Metropolitan Sergii. Again this was carried on by correspondence:

Dear *Vladyko*. Having learned from———about the decision you have taken, I find after acquaintance with all the materials that there was no other alternative. I approve your step, I unite myself to you, but, of course, I am deprived of the possibility of helping you more substantivally. Structure your church affairs correctly, so that we each may rule independently, turning all glances and hopes toward the uniquely legal locum tenens, Metropolitan Petr, and the future Local Sobor of all present bishops, not a chance selection and their own individual followers. This legal Sobor should be held even now by all rulers and the Synod, and if they are powerless to do this they should themselves honourably come out from behind the scenes, and say openly that we are prepared for every martyrdom, that we will never subject the truth of Christ to sacrifice and mockery by the obscurantism of godlessness. The Lord help you. Let not faith in the veracity of the promises of the Lord disappear among us to the end of the age.

Metropolitan Iosif.[106]

Iosif had powerful support in this attempt to encourage diocesan life out of communion with Sergii. He was in close relationship with the important and powerful Metropolitan Agafangel,[107] and, according to one document at least, shared with Metropolitan Agafangel the explicit jurisdictional sanction of Metropolitan Petr himself.[108]

The Josephite movement very quickly expanded, with several bishops travelling as widely as possible to win adherents, with numerous letters and correspondence, and by means of missionaries (primarily monks and priests) travelling throughout the

---

[105] *Delo Mitropolita Sergiia*, op. cit., No. 87, p. 15.
[106] Pol'skii, op. cit., II, 5.
[107] Glukhov, op. cit., p. 64; Andreev, op. cit., p. 52.
[108] *Delo Mitropolita Sergiia*, op. cit., No. 86, p. 14.

diocese and beyond.[109] Many of the participants in the movement had already won distinction as leaders in the earlier struggle against the Living Church.[110] The special emissaries of the movement apparently enjoyed a considerable degree of success, combining their message concerning the jurisdictional dispute with the convenient imagery of apocalyptic warnings concerning the end of the world, the Second Coming of Christ, etc.[111]

In order to 'electrify' the people, a special approach to them was necessary. The Josephite leadership dressed in the clothes of ascetics and utilized, in the first place, 'mystical' survivals in the name of the celebration of mysticism—an inner relationship with God, stimulating people to resistance of the measures of the government.[112]

One innovation which would leave a deep imprint on subsequent underground Orthodox endeavours was the dissemination of anonymous tracts claiming to have originated from visions of the Mother of God, etc.[113] Many of the Josephites, according to Platonov, placed great hope in the expectation of Western intervention and, in preparation for such an event, liberally interlaced their messages with elements of Catholicism, the idealist philosopher Solov'ev, etc.[114] Undue emphasis should not be given to such expectations of Western intervention, however, for curiously enough the attempts of the Karlovtsy Synod of the *émigré* Russian Church to bring the Josephites under their jurisdiction were without success.[115]

Despite the extensive geographic distribution of the movement's adherents,[116] the Josephites were an exceedingly loosely organized, de-centralized movement united by a common affiliation with Metropolitan Iosif and little else.

They had their own particular goals and plans, which quite excluded the question of any sort of organized, central administration. Factually speaking, the Josephites did not attempt to found a schism or a special society outside the unity of the Church. Their primary goal was limited to preserving the freedom of the Church by their departure from

[109] Platonov, op. cit., p. 265.
[110] Ioann (Snychev), op. cit., p. 241.
[111] Platonov, op. cit., p. 266.
[112] Ibid., p. 265.
[113] Ioann (Snychev), op. cit., pp. 297–8.
[114] Platonov, op. cit., p. 266; cf. Ioann (Snychev), op. cit., p. 307.
[115] Ibid., p. 348.
[116] Ibid., pp. 299–305.

Metropolitan Sergii and of guarding themselves and the flock from the allegedly pernicious activity of the first hierarch. Furthermore, as Metropolitan Iosif clearly stated, they did not consider that it was they who had gone into schism, but Metropolitan Sergii and all the hierarchs who were in agreement with him. Consequently, they had contrived to understand that they were and would remain in the bosom of the Orthodox Church. The question, then, of the organization of an administration, which belonged by right to each bishop, they considered thus: Metropolitan Iosif is the head of the Leningrad eparchy. To him, as the eparchial hierarch, the vicarial bishops, pastors and all the laity are subordinated. The regional Church governs itself independently in autonomous rights.[117]

The same theory seemed to obtain for other dioceses which affiliated with the Josephite movement, and rather than an organized, unified movement, the Josephites represented a loose association of independent local and regional groups affiliated in name only.

According to Orthodox scholarship, the schismatic movement reached its peak by the middle of 1928 and declined thereafter.[118] However, this estimate may not be precisely correct, for it would not appear that the G.P.U. made a concerted attempt to disrupt the movement until the winter of 1929, when most of its leaders were arrested.[119] Many of the movement's most ardent supporters went underground, abandoning normal society altogether and embracing a wandering form of life thereafter.[120] Police pressure against the Josephites—and other groups disagreeing with Sergii— was endemic after 1929,[121] and the Josephite schism, which had begun as a fairly visible and well-founded movement, was quickly reduced to the tenuous existence shared by all such underground groups during the following decade.

Soviet scholarship has, by chance as it were, provided fairly detailed information on one of the branches of the Josephites which provides considerable insight into the nature of the movement. The Buevtsy organization arose in the Tambov area in response to the events of 1927, led by Bishop Aleksii (Bui) of Voronezh, and

[117] Ibid., pp. 309–10.
[118] Ibid., p. 345.
[119] Pol'skii, op. cit., II, 138. According to Ioann (Snychev), op. cit., p. 350, the arrests began in April 1929; by the end of the year the movement had been effectively decapitated, with its leaders and most active adherents removed from the scene.
[120] Ibid., p. 351.
[121] Ciliga, op. cit., p. 162.

was affiliated with the larger Josephite movement. Apparently it was less a new schismatic organization within Orthodoxy than a reorganization and expansion of earlier movements which had been extant in that area. As has been noted, Soviet scholarship finds direct connections both in terms of organization and in terms of personnel with a movement headed by the monk Illarii which arose during the Living Church crisis.[122]

Bishop Aleksii was unwilling to accept the decision of Sergii in 1927. On 22 January 1928 he wrote:

Standing on guard for Orthodoxy and closely following the phenomena of church life not only in the dioceses entrusted to our humility, but in general in the patriarchate, we to our great sorrow have discovered in the recent actions of the guardian of the patriarchal locum tenens Sergii, Metropolitan of Nizhegorod, who has returned to his duties, an aspiration to deviate to the side of the renovators, exceeding the rights and powers given to him, and breaking the holy canons (decision of the principal questions of independence, transfer and dismissal of bishops without judgement and trial, and the like; see Kirill, Law I, Apostolic Rule 34).

By his actions contrary to the spirit of Orthodoxy, Metropolitan Sergii had torn himself from unity with the Holy, Conciliar and Apostolic Church and lost the right of presiding over the Russian Church. . . .

I take as my higher spiritual leader His Eminence Iosif, who was named by the patriarchal locum tenens, His Eminence Petr, Metropolitan of Krutitskii, the third candidate for guardian of the patriarchal locum tenens on 6 December, 1925.[123]

Thus the movement which was begun by Bishop Aleksii and which became known by his (secular) name, the Buevtsy, formed a part of that congeries of similar movements more or less united under the wing of the Josephite schism. Inasmuch as the Buevtsy movement maintained its identity, however, and exerted an historical influence of its own, it may also be considered separately.

The Buevtsy movement appeared to be primarily a local movement centred in Voronezh and with its influence concentrated in the surrounding area. According to Soviet research, however, it did have direct links in many other regions as well.[124] Organiza-

[122] Mitrokhin, op. cit., pp. 150–1.
[123] Pol'skii, op. cit., II, 68–9.
[124] Mitrokhin, op. cit., p. 151.

tionally, the movement appears to have been relatively sophisticated and well founded.

The Buevtsy formed a central organization. Its leadership was largely
composed of anti-Soviet clergy, monastic elements, kulaks and merchants. Among 74 leaders of the organization there were: bishops—1;
priests, deacons, and psalmists—13; monks and nuns—44; vagabond
churchmen—4; former members of the police—2; kulaks and merchants—2; home craftsmen—1; servants—1. The organization spread
among the kulak elements who were dissatisfied with the policy of
collectivization, but it also tried to conduct agitation among the
worker-peasant masses. But it had no success at all among them.[125]

The size of the movement is difficult to determine, but apparently
it was relatively substantial, well able to attract adherents.

With the help of God and on your action, more than 20 congregations
have united, which also constitutes a cell for future unification of such
congregations within the bounds of possibility.

But having in view God's work and for God's glory, and also in view
of our weakness, in order that no one reproach us for oblique or other
forms of love of pre-eminence, I turn over your congregations to the
guidance and leadership of Bishop Aleksii, administrator of the
Voronezh diocese.[126]

Soviet researchers thirty years later had discovered traces of some
forty congregations with a general membership of over 700
belonging to the Buevtsy movement in 1930.[127] In view of the
peculiar circumstances necessitated by clandestine Church life,
however, it is difficult to imagine that Soviet historical research
was able to identify more than a fraction of the adherents of a
movement such as this, and these figures may indeed be without
much value in estimating the size, strength, and influence of the
movement.

Bui himself was arrested on 21 February 1929,[128] but it would
not appear that the arrest of the movement's titular head seriously
impeded the progress of the Buevtsy. For the next three years at
least, they continued their activity with great vigour, and for the
following decade their influence continued to be felt, as will be
described in the following chapter.

[125] Ibid., p. 152.
[126] *Delo Mitropolita Sergiia*, op. cit., No. 93, p. 24.
[127] Mitrokhin, op. cit., p. 151.
[128] Pol'skii, op. cit., II, 16.

Another influential schism arising out of protest against the proclamation of 1927 was the 'Iaroslav Church Oblast' led by Metropolitan Agafangel. Agafangel, it will be recalled, had been Patriarch Tikhon's first choice as locum tenens, and prior to Sergii's change of course in 1927 had briefly challenged his leadership before deferring to him in the interests of the harmony of the Church. In February 1928 he and his vicars met to form an independent unit renouncing affiliation with Metropolitan Sergii.[129] Metropolitan Iosif participated in this meeting.[130] Subsequently, the schism led by Agafangel declined the offer of the Josephites to join in their movement,[131] and the 'Iaroslav Church Oblast' apparently remained within the confines of the single area of Agafangel's jurisdiction.[132] Nevertheless, it did number among its adherents some twenty bishops,[133] and hence was a formidable competitor to Sergii. Despite its refusal to join the Josephite movement, close relations between the two movements were maintained.

In the initial announcement of the formation of the new jurisdiction, great care was taken to play down any political dissatisfaction with the Government.[134]

We welcome this [1927] requirement and testify that we have always been, are, and will be loyal and obedient to the civil government; always have been, are, and will be honourable and conscientious citizens of our mother country; but this, we consider, has nothing in common with the policy called for by you and does not invite and require the children of the Church to voluntary renunciation of those rights of freely organizing the inner religious life of the society of the Church which that policy itself grants to the civil government (allowing congregations of believers to elect their own clerical leaders).[135]

The statement goes on to say that the reason for the decision to break relations was Sergii's arbitrary policy of appointing and transferring clergy to the advantage of his own favourites.

Thus it would seem that the 'Iaroslav Church Oblast' formed by

[129] Glukhov, op. cit., p. 64; Ioann (Snychev), op. cit., pp. 164–7.
[130] Ibid.
[131] Ibid., pp. 174, 281.
[132] Ibid., p. 169.
[133] Sheinman, op. cit., p. 60.
[134] Delo Mitropolita Sergiia, op. cit., No. 99, pp. 40–1.
[135] Ibid., No. 66, p. 170; Ioann (Snychev), op. cit., p. 165.

Metropolitan Agafangel was similar to the Josephite schism and, indeed, it might be more accurate to consider both organizations component parts of the same movement. The primary difference would be that the 'Iaroslav Church Oblast', even though led by (from one point of view) the most senior prelate in the Church, had an influence which was primarily local and by no means could compare with that of the Josephite schism, despite the fact that Iosif was junior to Agafangel in the Church hierarchy.

A great number of other schismatic organizations sprang up following the proclamation of 1927. Many of these were local organizations, independently organized but with a more or less close affiliation to the Josephite schism. Many of them were rather ephemeral, and with the regime's increasing harshness of the next few years, quickly disappeared, either permanently or only to reappear again under the same or a different name. Unfortunately, the poverty of concrete data from these years makes it extraordinarily difficult to identify and differentiate among these movements.

One of the more evanescent of these movements was the Viktorianskii schism.[136] Taking its name from Viktor, vicarial bishop of the Viatsk eparchy, this schism was closely connected with the Josephites in Leningrad. Viktor, who had protested against the proclamation of 1927 and then severed relations with Sergii when the latter ordered him to be transferred, was arrested in April 1928, and in prison was led to repent. The movement, however, seems to have survived his defection by a few years.

The Varlaamovtsy appear in Platonov's list of these schismatic movements, but little information is available concerning them.[137] It remains uncertain whether this was a distinct movement or whether it was subsumed in the Buevtsy or Josephite movements.

Two other movements were rather more substantial, and much more subtle in their tactics than the groupings described above. Rather than renounce Sergii and his leadership in the Church, they remained in canonical relations with him, but did everything in their power to frustrate his policy and nullify his influence on their parishes.[138] The more substantial of these was the Danilovskii

---

[136] Ibid., pp. 362–83; Glukhov, op. cit., p. 66.

[137] Platonov, op. cit., p. 265.

[138] Such covert opposition was also employed by sympathizers of the Josephites. Cf. Ioann (Snychev), op. cit., p. 347.

movement, which embraced, in addition to a large number of monks, priests, and laymen, at least seven bishops from various dioceses.[139] The Mechevtsy included at least five bishops, and were very active.[140] In Moscow,

> there appeared semi-oppositionists or 'Mechevtsy'—followers of Father Sergii Mechev, who had not formally broken with Metropolitan Sergii, but in fact had sabotaged the decisions and orders of the so-called 'Patriarchal Synod'.
>
> In substance, a huge majority of the Moscow churches belonged to the secret adherents of Father Sergii Mechev. Among them, contrary to the decree, the proclamations of the Soviet government were not followed.[141]

Finally, some mention should be made of Metropolitan Kirill, the first of Patriarch Tikhon's three designated successors. In voluminous correspondence with Sergii he bitterly contested the latter's actions.[142] However, the resistance of this towering figure in the Church hierarchy was probably without considerable influence in the development of the underground Orthodox movements, for he apparently adhered to his promise not to interfere in the life of the Church. Elements in the Russian emigration name him as the leader of the underground Church along with Petr until their deaths in 1936,[143] but no evidence is adduced in support of this assertion, and for practical purposes, at least, it is almost certainly spurious.[144]

Two other branches of the underground Orthodox movement have been identified with the period immediately following 1927 by Soviet researchers. The True Orthodox Church has at times been traced back to the declaration of 1927[145] and has been listed

---

[139] Ibid., p. 384; P. Kurochkin, 'Evoliutsiia sovremennogo russkogo pravoslaviia' ('The evolution of contemporary Russian Orthodoxy'), *Nauka i Religiia*, No. 4 (April 1969), p. 50.

[140] Ioann (Snychev), op. cit., p. 384.

[141] Pol'skii, op. cit., II, 23.

[142] Ioann (Snychev), op. cit., pp. 385–402.

[143] Andreev, *Kratkii obzor*, op. cit., p. 71.

[144] There would seem to be some confusion regarding Kirill's death. Andreev (ibid.) states that he died in exile in 1936. Pol'skii, op. cit., II, 296, notes later evidence that he was returned to Moscow and shot in 1937. Ioann (Snychev), op. cit., p. 401, however, without citing his source of data, states that Kirill finally made his peace with Sergii 'not long before his death from a snake-bite in August 1941'.

[145] R. F. Filippova, 'K istorii otdeleniia shkoly ot tserkvi' ('The history of the separation of school from Church'), in Krasnikov, *Po etapam razvitiia*, op. cit., p. 92.

among the various underground organizations which were already extant and active during 1928 and the years following.[146] However, in such Soviet historical writing it remains unclear whether the True Orthodox Church actually existed as such during this period, or whether Soviet scholarship makes use of the term as a generic designation to summarize the local and regional organizations which subsequently did form the True Orthodox Church.[147] In view of this methodological possibility it would seem wise to postpone a discussion of the True Orthodox Church until a subsequent chapter.

Similarly, at least one scholar locates the cognate movement, the True Orthodox Christians, in this period. 'This reactionary sect was founded at the end of the twenties by those who did not agree with the last testament of Patriarch Tikhon with his call to cessation from struggle against the Soviet Government.'[148] More reliable Soviet scholarship, however, indicates that the True Orthodox Christians were the heirs of the traditions established by other groups during these and subsequent years.[149] It would appear obvious that the term is being used generically in this case, for according to one authoritative Soviet scholar, this 'new movement in Orthodoxy' arose in the mid-forties.[150] Therefore discussion of the True Orthodox Christians will also be postponed until a subsequent chapter.

Summarizing, it would appear that the events of 1927 resulted in a number of distinct types of underground Orthodox activity. First would be the large body of more or less highly organized groups within the Josephite movement. These can be subdivided into those groups feeling so strongly about the events of 1927 that they permitted no contact whatsoever with churches of patriarchal jurisdiction, and those who were less vehement, allowing their followers to follow their own consciences concerning the degree of contact with the Sergiite churches. Second are a number of groups which lacked organization and hence were less well equipped to

[146] A. Nikol'skaia, 'K kharakteristike techeniia tak nazyvaemykh istinno-pravoslavnykh khristian' ('The characteristics of the movement of the so-called True Orthodox Christians'), in AN SSSR, *Sovremennoe sektantstvo*, op. cit., p. 166.

[147] Mitrokhin, op. cit., p. 148. Fedorenko specifically states that the Josephites established the True Orthodox Church in 1928; op. cit., p. 211.

[148] A. Vasin, 'Nachalo polozheno' ('A beginning has been made'), *Nauka i Religiia*, No. 7 (July 1968), p. 17.

[149] Klibanov, op. cit., p. 167.

[150] Nikol'skaia, op. cit., p. 166.

function. Third were individual churches which were open and functioning, but which because of the general confusion of the times were unknown either to the Government or to the Church authorities. Finally, there were the individual schismatics who, either because of strong convictions concerning the change in policy of 1927 or for other reasons (often with no relation whatsoever to politics, such as inability to pay the tax), led a vagabond life, wandering about the countryside and conducting and participating in religious functions on an *ad hoc* basis.[151]

This last phenomenon was to assume important proportions in 1928 and the years that followed. According to an Orthodox historian,

Small lots of fanatics (a few laymen gathered around every unrepentant schismatic bishop) went into an illegal position and according to their ability tried surreptitiously to do harm to the self-denying labour for church peace of the helmsman of the patriarchal Russian Church.[152]

Considering the jurisdictional and social confusion of the times, it was difficult indeed for the simple laity to choose selectively in religious matters, and as a result there was a great deal of jurisdictional fluidity throughout the country.[153]

The position of those who felt constrained to sever relations with Sergii but who had no convenient alternative organization was especially acute, forcing them into complete isolation.[154] According to a letter written in January 1928, 'Last autumn more than two thousand monks went into the world, having lost their native cloisters in which they had spent their entire lives.'[155] Even the higher clergy were on occasion forced to this expedient. According to the letter of a bishop who had severed relations with the Sergiite Church and was devoting himself to an eremitic, lonely life,

By all appearances it is evident that I will not again be brought out of the wilderness; yea, and I myself hasten thither, to be hidden there while the wrath of God passes by. I grieve only that among the archpastors of the Russian Church there are not a few followers of the

[151] Alexeev, op. cit., p. 82. Cf. the description in Ioann (Snychev), op. cit., p. 403, of Bishop Amphilokhii, a follower of Metropolitan Kirill, who, in despair, fled to the *taiga* and became a hermit from 1929 until his death in 1946.
[152] Shabatin, op. cit., p. 42.
[153] Ibid.
[154] *Delo Mitropolita Sergiia*, op. cit., No. 42, p. 114.
[155] Ibid., No. 73, p. 182.

Sergiite theology, which is offensive in practice. Forgive me and pray for me, and repent before it is too late. Later on you will not be able to break free—you yourself know why.[156]

Such unfortunates, deprived as they were of the ministrations of an organized Church, were reduced not only to supporting themselves physically by whatever means possible; even spiritually they had to have recourse to expedients of individual worship without the consolation of corporate support.[157]

There was a great danger, of course, that such independent worship would degenerate into distorted practices further and further removed from traditional Orthodoxy. One of the Josephite bishops in Leningrad in January 1928, in reply to a letter from a fellow bishop who had expressed a desire to 'leave the world', argued in this manner: 'You want to go into obscure wandering in order to pray without trespass against conscience in every temple without distinction.' He advised against this, for such an approach would eventually imply acceptance of every religion. Furthermore, it would imply that such bishops are schismatic, whereas according to the Josephites, those who disagree with Sergii are not schismatics but, to the contrary, are the only true representatives of the Russian Orthodox Church.[158] According to another dissenting bishop,

The Old Believers schism took on a sick, abnormal, anti-church appearance, inasmuch as it accounted the Russian State of the seventeenth and eighteenth centuries as a lawless, apocalyptic state (Rev. 13), and the Orthodox Church as the Church of anti-Christ. It is not surprising that the monstrous ideology of the Old Believer schismatics took extremely monstrous forms in sects and the most extreme fragmentation (*Beguny*, *Stranniki*, and other sects in the schism).

The departure of the Orthodox Church into God's wilderness, however, is a phenomenon of entirely different order.[159]

Nevertheless, in developing his argument in the same letter, this bishop resorts to the same sort of extreme apocalypticism as that of the Old Believers which he condemns.[160]

[156] Ibid., No. 114, p. 133.
[157] Ibid., No. 95, p. 29.
[158] Ibid., No. 91, p. 18.
[159] Ibid., No. 122, p. 166.
[160] Ibid., pp. 169–70.

Eschatological themes were a most attractive temptation for such alienated believers. Indeed, according to the same bishop,

I am sure that if in a series of theological lectures you thought to explain the church dogmatic doctrine of anti-Christ and other allied questions in a strictly Orthodox spirit, you would scarcely complete the cycle of lectures and remain in one place—whether you wished to or not, you would complete your sermons in the wilderness.[161]

Russia was on the brink of a very difficult phase of her modern history. The conditions which would fall upon the Russian people in the next few years would greatly amplify all the themes of religious dissent which had appeared in response to the change in Church policy in 1927. These dissatisfactions found their initial expression in the series of important schismatic movements in the months following Sergii's announcement of the change of policy.

It is difficult to determine the extent to which these schismatic movements prevailed in the Russian Church in terms of number of followers. It is not impossible that at the time these were relatively minor schisms numerically. Very quickly, however, the course of events would magnify the impact of such schismatic movements out of all proportion to their beginnings, which could possibly have been relatively small. The decade which followed forced great numbers into these movements or analogous expedients, willingly or not.

Perhaps most important, the schisms of 1927 were the most severe the Church has suffered during the Soviet period in terms of the stature of leadership which went into schism. The episcopate had remained faithful to the patriarchal jurisdiction during the Living Church Adventure, with very few exceptions. In 1927, however, influential, important, and highly respected bishops went into schism, renouncing affiliation to the Moscow Patriarchate. This wealth of leadership in the clandestine Orthodox movement would be of immense significance during the next decade.

[161] Ibid., p. 168.

IV

Years of the Red Dragon

From 1928 until World War II Soviet society went through a convulsive period. Throughout the country there was turmoil and confusion as nearly all aspects of life—politics, economics, social institutions, etc.—were overturned by the regime's vigorous attempts to transform Russian society as quickly as possible. The effects of these years of confusion were felt especially keenly in the religious life of the society.

In 1928, any previous religious tolerance was suspended,[1] as the U.S.S.R. embarked on a frantic campaign of rapid industrialization and enforced collectivization of agriculture. Throughout the country traditional institutions and practices of peasant life were overturned and the rural population was enrolled into collective enterprises, whether they desired such changes or not. Resistance to collectivization was widespread and exceedingly fierce. Revolts and uprisings took place in many areas, and indeed for four years it appeared that portions of the country— especially the Ukraine—were on the brink of civil war. Millions were dispossessed of their property, moved to new and unfamiliar surroundings in population transfers decreed and enforced by the Government, arrested *en masse* into the burgeoning penal and forced labour system, allowed to starve, or executed.

The Church felt the effects of the collectivization campaign especially keenly, for concurrently with the collectivization of the countryside a vigorous anti-religious campaign was waged by the regime. During the initial years of collectivization, 1928–32, the Church suffered under the onslaught of the State's intense hostility, which was unremitting except for the briefest of breathing spaces in 1930. During these years, church leaders were arrested on a mass scale, and churches were closed either in connection with the

[1] Cf. *Pravda*, 9 May and 7 June 1928.

transformation of the village into the collective farm system or outright through use of force. Churches which were not closed down found themselves confronted with legislation introduced in 1929 subjecting them to a sweeping range of restrictions on their permissible activity and encroachments on their freedom within the Church. Individual believers were subjected to a broad range of sanctions rendering the observance and practice of religious convictions exceedingly difficult, if not impossible. In the space of a very few months the post-revolutionary situation of the Church— difficult though many of the believers may have felt it to be—was replaced by a vast, well conceived and highly organized programme of vigorous restrictions against religion in the Soviet Union.

The initial onslaught against religion (and indeed against other areas of society) came to an end in 1932, and for the next four years the religious population enjoyed a period of somewhat decreased tension. To be sure, the anti-religious campaign was by no means abandoned, but was pursued with considerable vigour throughout these middle years of the thirties. Nevertheless, in comparison with the ferocious onslaught of 1928–32, the years which followed seemed less filled with crisis for the religious segment of the population. Despite the fact that pressure continued, churches continued to be closed, and large-scale arrest of believers remained an ever present threat, the churches were able on a very small scale to recoup some of their initial losses, and the most miniscule hints of the beginnings of a renewed vitality for religion in the U.S.S.R. began to appear.

The rise of the Great Purges marked an end to this hiatus, however, and as the Terror reached its peak in 1936–8, the churches along with other sectors of society, particularly including the Communist Party, came under vigorous attack. The anti-religious campaign was resumed with all ferocity and the great majority of the surviving religious leaders were subjected to propaganda attacks, arrest, incarceration, and execution as saboteurs, fifth columnists, spies, and traitors. By the end of the Great Purges the Church was prostrate, and although the anti-religious campaign was continued, albeit with somewhat diminished vigour, until the advent of World War II, it seemed as though the regime's long struggle with religion was all but won.

The effects on the institutional Russian Orthodox Church were staggering. In the space of a decade, the Church had been almost completely destroyed as an institution. Of the 163 bishops claimed by Metropolitan Sergii in 1930, only four survived the decade in office. The 30,000 churches which he had claimed in 1930 had been reduced to 4,225 by official figures, while independent estimates suggested that even that figure was inflated and only a very small number of churches continued to function legally within the country. The administrative machinery of the Russian Orthodox Church had been liquidated almost entirely; the diocesan network continued to exist in little more than name only, as communications within the central organization were all but impossible. Parish life within the dioceses was reduced to the most extreme of expedients, and, except for the traditional theory of diocesan organization within Orthodoxy, were in effect reduced to single, independent parishes functioning as best they could in the extraordinarily difficult times. The anti-religious campaign had achieved almost complete success against the institutional Orthodox Church.

The campaign's successes were not quite so evident, however, with regard to the population's continued adherence to religion. If the churches had been largely eliminated, the religious convictions of the population had displayed a surprising tenacity. The census of 1937 originally included a question of religious adherence, and even though the census was finally aborted (allegedly due to improper procedures in the compilation of data) subsequent estimates apparently based on the census indicated that well over half the population of the Soviet Union declared themselves religious believers. Thus the anti-religious policies of the State resulted in a situation in which a majority of the population continued to adhere to religion despite the fact that to all intents and purposes the institutional Church had disappeared from society. This situation naturally provided exceeding fertile soil for the appearance of clandestine, underground religious practices among the people.

The religious population was by no means completely acquiescent to this threat to the continuation of religious life. Illegal, clandestine religious practices abounded during this period, and there was much evidence of underground activity on the part of the believing population.[2] According to Metropolitan Sergii

[2] E.g., *Komsomol'skaia Pravda*, 11 April 1937; cf. the collection of evidence in Pol'skii, op. cit., II, xvi–xxiii.

(Voskresenskii), who defected to the Germans in 1941, in the U.S.S.R. during the thirties,

There was in general a very active secret religious life—secret priests and monks, catacomb churches and liturgies, baptism, confession, the Eucharist, weddings, secret theological courses, secret stores of utensils for divine service, icons, service books, secret relations between congregations, dioceses, and the patriarchal administration. In order to destroy a catacomb patriarchate as well, it would have been necessary to execute all bishops also, including the secret ones who doubtless would have been ordained in case of need. And if one imagines the impossible, that complete destruction of the entire church organization was successful, faith would remain nonetheless, and atheism would not have won a step.[3]

The situation of the clergy in such conditions was especially acute, as many of them were torn between abhorrence of the compromises made inescapable by the tenor of the times, and the desire to serve the religious needs of the population. Mikhail Pol'skii reports a conversation he had early in this period with a bishop who remained in communion with Metropolitan Sergii and the patriarchal administration:

I showed him the necessity of separating himself from Metropolitan Sergii and, of course, again going to prison. He said to me that doing that would not correct the situation. That would change nothing in the created order. To deny one's post was not possible: he pitied the people, the people were still there for him, and these people knew not which way to go; only the Sergiite churches remained under the sign of Orthodoxy.[4]

Especially in the middle thirties, after the first storm of the anti-religious campaign had passed, the believers did their best to reverse the tide, particularly with regard to churches which had been closed arbitrarily. In one case, a priest offered his services to the newly formed *kolkhoz* (collective farm): if they would open a church in which he could preach, he would use his considerable influence among the believing peasantry to persuade them to join the *kolkhoz*.[5] The believers used whatever measures were available —possibly even including work slowdowns—to persuade the

[3] Grabbe, op. cit., p. 88.

[4] Mikhail, op. cit., p. 65.

[5] M. Mitin, 'O nashikh zadachakh na antireligioznom fronte' ('Our tasks on the anti-religious front'), *Pod Znamenem Marksizma*, No. 2–3 (March 1936), p. 91.

authorities to allow them to worship.[6] There were many reports of agitation to open churches.[7] Such agitation was particularly vigorous after the publication of the 'Stalin Constitution' of 1936, which diminished somewhat the range of sanctions applied against the clergy.[8] Obviously, though, whatever success such attempts achieved was inadequate, for, as has been noted, the State continued its vigorous and active opposition to the churches. Other expedients had to be devised in order to make religious observances possible.

Perhaps the most obvious of such expedients was to travel to the nearest open church after the local church had been closed.[9] According to an anti-religious author in 1933, 'We know many cases where the *kolkhozniks*, having closed their church, travelled to neighbouring churches, where they pray among themselves at home, where they have taken the icons from the walls, keeping them in their own trunks.'[10] The traditional parish structure of the local Orthodox churches was thus modified as the actual geographic area of many churches was multiplied many times.[11] Local parish churches came to serve as regional and even inter-Oblast churches.[12] Late in the decade, an anti-religious author wrote, 'Until 1939, believers flowed here from the neighbouring Chkalovskii Oblast, from Tataria. Here the churchmen built their nest, collecting donations for repair of the church.'[13] Obviously, this measure could only provide limited accommodation for the needs of the population, depending upon the distances which had to be travelled, the primitive transportation facilities available, and, ultimately, the limits imposed by the total number of believers who can be effectively served by a single church. Furthermore, in Soviet conditions, where all travel is controlled

---

[6] Georges Bissonette, *Moscow Was My Parish* (New York: McGraw-Hill, 1956), p. 256.

[7] I. Aleksandrov, 'Dat' otpor agitatsii tserkovnikov' ('Repulse the agitation of the churchmen'), *Vlast' Sovetov*, No. 19 (October 1937), p. 23.

[8] N. Amosov, 'Oktiabr'skaia revoliutsiia i tserkov'' ('The October revolution and the Church'), *Antireligioznik*, No. 10 (October 1937), p. 54; F. Oleshchuk, 'O zadachakh antireligioznoi propagandy' ('Tasks of anti-religious propaganda'), *Pod Znamenem Marksizma*, No. 4 (April 1937), p. 104.

[9] Timasheff, *Religion in Soviet Russia, 1917–1942*, op. cit., pp. 77–9.

[10] Quoted in Pol'skii, *op. cit.*, II, xvi.

[11] Cf. *Sotsialisticheskoe Zemledelie*, 29 June 1937.

[12] P. Kogan, 'Uchitelia-anti-religiozniki v chuvashskom sele' ('Anti-religious teachers in a Chuvash village'), *Antireligioznik*, No. 8 (August 1939), p. 58.

[13] Ibid.

by passport, this expedient depended upon the goodwill of the governmental officials, which during this period, at least, was not especially pronounced.

Closing of churches was not everywhere as effective as the most ardent adherents of the anti-religious campaign might have wished. Many of the churches listed as legally closed continued business as usual, with services twice a week; many others were active, but nowhere legally registered.[14] 'In Nizhnii Tagil the local City Soviet does not know at all how many active churches exist in the region.'[15] In part, the success of the campaign to close churches depended upon the attitudes of local authorities, for where they were lax in applying the anti-religious measures, churchmen could continue to work openly.[16] In other cases, a church would be successfully closed for a period; later on a priest would appear, and the Church would again resume its former activity.[17] Thus the regime's authorities could by no means feel completely confident about their success in closing churches.[18] In some cases even after the elimination of the priest the laity continued to keep the Church functioning.

It is interesting that while there is no church in this Village Soviet, there is a chapel. The individual, Tarasov, and two *kolkhoz* women constitute the church council; there is no priest, but they perform services, a choir of *kolkhozniks* and school children sings. The chapel is well equipped.[19]

The formation of 'house churches' became a widespread practice. Where other means of worship were not available, dispossessed parishioners would organize religious services in their homes or apartments.[20] Such 'churches in the home' conducted complete liturgies (when clergy were available), truncated liturgies led by

---

[14] *Komsomol'skaia Pravda*, 15 November 1936.

[15] Ibid.

[16] *Trud*, 27 August 1937.

[17] N. Krupskaia, 'Antireligioznuiu propagandu—na bolee vysokuiu stupen'' ('Anti-religious propaganda—on a higher level'), *Revoliutsiia i Natsial'nosti*, No. 3 (March 1937), pp. 27–8.

[18] *Komsomol'skaia Pravda*, 15 November 1936.

[19] Emel'ian Iaroslavskii, 'Zadachi antireligioznoi propagandy' ('The tasks of anti-religious propaganda'), *Antireligioznik*, No. 5 (May 1941), p. 5; the same passage is presented verbatim in his posthumous collection *O religii* ('On religion') (Moscow: State Publishing House for Political Literature, 1957), p. 333, dated 6 April 1941.

[20] Curtiss, *op. cit.*, p. 288, citing *Antireligioznik*, No. 2 (1940), p. 24.

members of the minor clergy, lay services, or even simple prayer
meetings of individuals or small groups of laymen.[21] Mikhail
Pol'skii after his release from Solovky claims that he personally
conducted such services in the homes, and knew several other
priests who did likewise.[22] This practice was considerably facilitated
by the incompetence or carelessness of local officials in closing the
parish church in question, for on numerous occasions the believers
were able to salvage the various church materials such as icons,
crosses, candlesticks, and even the vessels of divine service
(chalices, patens, etc.) and the antimension (consecrated altar
cloth), preserving them from destruction or loss by storing them in
private premises.[23] Such materials greatly facilitated the institution of house services. According to an atheist scholar,

After the closure of the church, the icons and other church property
were dismantled by the inhabitants of the villages in the vicinity, and
therefore to the present time in several houses one can meet with
materials of church furnishings, and sometimes even entire iconostases.[24]

These materials greatly enhanced the attempts of the laity to conduct
a semblance of worship in the absence of priests.[25] This informal
practice of Orthodoxy continued throughout the decade.[26]

Fully operational secret churches were also established during
this period.[27] If the local clergy survived the closure of their
church it was not unlikely that the Church would continue to
function, but at locations which were not known to the State
authorities.[28] 'Lately there have been reports of quiet meetings
(without singing) held in the dead of night and of secret Orthodox

[21] Z. A. Iankova, 'Sovremennoe pravoslavie i antiobshchestvennaia sushchnost' ego
ideologii' ('Contemporary Orthodoxy and the anti-social essence of its ideology'), in
AN SSSR, *Voprosy istorii religii i ateizma*, op. cit., XI, 70.

[22] Pol'skii, op. cit., II, xv.

[23] Konstantinov, *Gonimaia tserkov'*, op. cit., pp. 47–8.

[24] G. A. Nosova, 'Opyt etnograficheskogo izucheniia bytovogo pravoslaviia'
('Experience of ethnographic study of the way of life of Orthodoxy'), in AN SSSR,
Voprosy nauchnogo ateizma, op. cit., III, 153.

[25] Timasheff, op. cit., p. 85, citing *Antireligioznik*, No. 2 (1930).

[26] Harvey F. Fireside, *The Russian Orthodox Church under German Occupation in World
War II* (unpublished Ph.D. dissertation, New School for Social Research, 1968), p. 227,
quoting International Military Tribunal, Documents: Staff Evidence Analyses, No.
2950, 1 August 1941.

[27] Timasheff, op. cit., pp. 79–80.

[28] Semashko, 'Odna iz zadach izbiratel'noi kampanii' ('One of the tasks of the
election campaign'), *Vlast' Sovetov*, No. 10 (May 1938), p. 21.

services in the forests.'[29] According to a report from Smolensk collected by Pol'skii:

The priest Konstantin Oletskii and his son were arrested in 1935 upon the discovery of a church which was under ground, beneath the old tower 'Veselukha' in the rampart wall constructed in the time of Boris Godunov in the Ratovka suburb of Smolensk. By chance, children playing near the tower heard singing and called the attention of a passing militiaman to it. The place was surrounded and they tracked a woman who was entering into the tower with wine for the service. In connection with this discovery many clergy and laymen were arrested, inasmuch as a list of the parish of this secret church was found. Local newspapers gave much attention to this event.[30]

A similar secret church managed to function for three years following the beginning of the collectivization period.[31] According to Constantine Krypton,

In 1933, for example, I was married in an illegal church. The priest asked only for my future wife's name and my own. We were required to take an oath that, in the event of divorce, we should request permission for such a step from the nearest duly-constituted bishop of the Orthodox Church.[32]

Such secret churches represented the phenomenon of underground methods being employed by churches which had by no means renounced affiliation with the patriarchate. In fact, during this period it would seem that the patriarchal Orthodox Church itself was an organization which was both legal and illegal, with many of its duly constituted parishes having to resort to illegal methods to continue their operations.

It was not always possible, however, to utilize such expedients as those described above. By far the most widespread phenomenon of this difficult period in the religious life of the Soviet Union was individual 'internal emigration'. Deeply religious people would simply attempt to conceal their convictions from outside observation and to get along as best they could without overt satisfaction

[29] Vladimir Filimonovich Martsinkovskii, *With Christ in Soviet Russia* (Prague: Kniktiskarna V. Horak, 1933), p. 327.

[30] Pol'skii, op. cit., II, 212–13.

[31] Ibid., p. 271.

[32] Constantine Krypton, 'Secret Religious Organizations in the U.S.S.R.,' *Russian Review*, XIV (April 1955), p. 127, n. 16.

of their religious needs. Many of the minor clergy (and, as will become evident below, the other branches of the ordained clergy) concealed their religious convictions and merely kept themselves in readiness for any eventual relaxation of conditions which would allow the resumption of their religious services.[33] Others abandoned the organized churches entirely and created their own substitutes. One such incident was reported in the Soviet press in 1964:

The little village of Sergeevka is located far away from a town and from the railroad. With its log cabins and fences made of planks, it virtually nestles in the *taiga* and hides under huge cedars and firs. Kirill Longinovich Maerov liked Sergeevka, and late in the twenties he moved here, escaping collectivization. 'I do not want to work together with the anti-Christs,' said he.

Long hours would he kneel in front of the icons, bow to the cold boards of the floor, and pray to God for His grace. Seven children followed their father's example. Continually, he impressed upon the children that people are merely guests on earth and, in order to get into Paradise, one must not offend God.

Sasha had difficulties in his studies. For one year he did not attend school at all, and two winters he spent in the fifth grade. For this his church was responsible. Nobody in the school knew that in the evenings Sasha had to burn the incense for the church, put the candles in place, and take care of the articles of the church service.[34]

Despite the cumbersome administrative and institutional machinery which had become traditional over the centuries, Russian Orthodoxy was peculiarly well endowed for this sort of individual practice of the faith. To a large extent Russian Orthodoxy has depended more on the devotion and activity of the laity than on the clergy. 'Parents and, still more, grandparents continued to teach their children and grandchildren religion, as they have done throughout all the centuries of Russian history.'[35] Baptism, in particular, which in case of necessity can be administered by laymen, continued to be performed secretly on such a large scale that when children were baptized in the Church the formula was often made conditional in recognition of the validity of a baptismal ceremony which may

---

[33] Konstantinov, *Gonimaia tserkov'*, op. cit., pp. 54–5.

[34] *Komsomol'skaia Pravda*, 10 April 1964.

[35] Nicholas Zernov, *The Russians and Their Church* (London: S.P.C.K., 1945), p. 166.

7

already have been performed secretly.[36] Secret believers existed throughout society on all levels.[37]

Many in Russia, both young and old, small and great, pray 'under the covers'. They pray to God even though secretly, because ashamed or afraid openly to confess their faith. There lives yet in that land the spirit of secret confession exhibited by Nicodemus.[38]

Of especial applicability to such believers was the Orthodox tradition of continual prayer in the heart.[39]

Among the Russian people there is a widespread practice of reciting the 'Jesus prayer'. This short prayer, 'Lord Jesus Christ have mercy upon me a sinner,' is usually repeated mentally only. It is repeated a great many times with the purpose of intense concentration on the idea of God and of the preclusion of all other thoughts. In this way is attained the spiritual sobriety which, according to the Orthodox view, is the foundation of spiritual life.[40]

Thus believers in the U.S.S.R. during this period were forced to adopt a wide range of temporary and provisional expedients. It would be strange indeed if more highly organized underground forms of religion had not sprung up and flourished in such conditions.

Despite the mass arrests and subsequent enrolment of clergymen into the forced labour system, large numbers of clergy of all ranks survived the precipitate dissolution of the institutional Church. Deprived of the possibility to continue their accustomed religious life and ministry, these clergymen were obliged to discover means of coping with the situation, and in so doing provided a large reservoir of leadership potential on which underground organizations could draw.

In the ranks of the episcopacy, prelates of all grades were reduced to unusual methods. In some instances, this would merely be due to the difficulties of maintaining communications in such

---

[36] Zinaida Schakovskoy, *The Privilege Was Mine* (New York: Putnam's, 1959), p. 268.

[37] Alex Inkeles and Raymond A. Bauer, *The Soviet Citizen* (Cambridge, Massachusetts: Harvard University Press, 1959), p. 217.

[38] Martsinkovskii, op. cit., p. 302.

[39] Spinka, *The Church in Soviet Russia*, op. cit., p. 135; cf. Kallistos Timothy Ware, '"Pray Without Ceasing": The Ideal of Continual Prayer in Eastern Monasticism,' *Eastern Churches Review*, II, 3 (Spring 1969), pp. 263–61.

[40] Vasily V. Zenkovsky, 'The Spirit of Russian Orthodoxy,' *Russian Review*, No. 1 (January 1963), pp. 50–1.

confused times; without proper central liaison institutional Orthodoxy was forced to develop administrative expedients on the diocesan, and even sub-diocesan, level.[41] Because of the imminent possibility of arrest, local bishops often appointed successors secretly.[42] There were reports of bishops and even archbishops disguising their vocation to avoid detection, some of them even occupying important positions in the economy of the country.[43] 'When the head of the largest state hospital in Tashkent died he was buried, to the great astonishment of the communists, in the robes of an Orthodox archbishop, for such he was in Central Asia.'[44] Clerics on occasion found the medical profession a convenient refuge;[45] Archbishop Luka, who subsequently attained great prominence in the Church, served in the dual role of prelate and one of the most capable surgeons in the country.[46] The local believers were intensely devoted to their clergy and their bishops, and as a result such concealment was a practical option for clerics threatened by the hostility of the regime.[47]

The monastic profession proved to be particularly tenacious in refusing to yield to measures designed to force monks to renounce the life to which they had pledged themselves. Upon the dissolution of their monastery, many had recourse to jobs in industry, maintaining their vows inwardly while taking a place in the economy of the community.[48] With the partial relaxation of conditions during World War II, a great number of such secret monks declared themselves and resumed their former, monastic form of life.[49] In one city a group of secret monks once a year would

[41] The difficulties of maintaining communications are reflected in the opening lines of a letter of Sergii to one of his bishops on 21 May, 1940: 'Dear *Vladiko*: Since I now have your address, I am making use of the possibility to reply to your Easter greetings. . . .' Orthodox Eastern Church, Russian, *Patriarch Sergii i ego dukhovnoe nasledstvo* ('Patriarch Sergii and his spiritual legacy') (Moscow: The Patriarchate, 1947), p. 226.

[42] Pol'skii, op. cit., II, 13–14.

[43] Mikhail Grigor'evich Kurdiumov, *Rim i Pravoslavnaia Tserkov'* ('Rome and the Orthodox Church') (Paris: Les Editeurs réunis, 1939), p. 39.

[44] Timasheff, op. cit., p. 81.

[45] *Trud*, 20 December 1937.

[46] Alexeev, op. cit., pp. 124–5.

[47] Mikhail, op. cit., p. 5.

[48] Paul B. Anderson, *People, Church, and State in Modern Russia* (New York: Macmillan, 1944), p. 16.

[49] E. Behr-Sigel, *Prière et Sainteté dans l'Eglise Russe* (Paris: Les Editions du Cerf, 1950), p. 179.

reportedly open a closed Church for services a few miles outside the city. In 1933 the secret police surrounded the Church during the service and arrested all of them; ten were shot two months later.[50]

Monks who had been deprived of their monasteries were quick to seize upon a provision of Soviet policy peculiarly adaptable to their purposes. Communist agricultural policy had always emphasized collective rather than individual organization of rural life. Monastics, by conviction and tradition ideally suited to such work, quickly organized themselves into communes under the provisions of Soviet law.[51] The Commissariat of Justice attempted to counter such practices by making it mandatory that any applicant to join such a collective must be accepted. This proved to be ineffective, however, for understandably enough, very few non-monastics sought membership in a collective organization consisting exclusively of monks.[52] Finally, the State was obliged to take stern action against all such organizations. These measures were probably contra-productive, for on dissolution such communities were fragmented into smaller groups even more hostile to the Soviet regime.[53] Many of the monks, without bothering to form a collective agricultural unit, quite naturally congregated into small eremitic groups.[54] Nor were the authorities particularly successful in disrupting this form of secret monastic organization, for reports continued to appear concerning them, both among observers in the West[55] and in the Soviet press.[56] In 1937 one of the best state farms in the Caucasus proved to be composed of priests and monks led by a bishop.[57]

The formation of secret monastic communities was not confined to the countryside. Cenobitic communities sprang up throughout the country.[58]

An interesting by-product of overcrowding in big cities emerged through the compulsory redistribution of living space which forced several

[50] Pol'skii, op. cit., II, 182–3.

[51] A. A. Valentinov, *The Assault of Heaven* (Berlin: Max Mattisson, 1924), pp. 91–3.

[52] Timasheff, op. cit., p. 25.

[53] Nadezhda Teodorovich, 'The Catacomb Church in the U.S.S.R.,' *Bulletin of the Institute for the Study of the U.S.S.R.*, No. 4 (April 1965), p. 10.

[54] Pol'skii, op. cit., II, xvi, quoting *Bezbozhik*, 1931.

[55] Kurdiumov, *Tserkov' i novaia Rossiia*, op. cit., pp. 16–17; Timasheff, op. cit., pp. 79–80; Pol'skii, op. cit., II, 248.

[56] *Trud*, 20 December 1937; *Sotsialisticheskoe Zemledelie*, 11 January 1938.

[57] Pol'skii, op. cit., II, xix.

[58] Anderson, op. cit., p. 16.

families to live together in one apartment and to use the same kitchen. Naturally Christian families chose to move to apartments where the other occupants believed as they did; thus little communities were formed where prayers were customary and the Orthodox way of life was followed as far as it could be.[59]

Early in this period there was a secret convent in a Leningrad apartment where services were held, sometimes with neighbours in attendance. The services were all conducted in whispers, even the singing. The organization apparently had several branches in the city.[60] Complaints of similar phenomena appeared in the Soviet press later in the decade.[61] In 1937 an illegal monastery was discovered in Smolensk.[62] In Nizhni Novgorod a government official was discovered to be the prior of a secret monastery,[63] and one of the accusations levelled against Metropolitan Feofan during the Great Purges was that he had himself organized an underground monastery.[64]

During the years of collectivization and the decade following, the practice of a wandering life continued to be popular among dispossessed monks. Many such vagrants were uncovered during the campaign of the years of the Great Purges.[65] Throughout the period such vagabond monks and nuns were a relatively common feature of Russian life.[66] Indeed, some of these illegal monastics even attempted to influence society, urging citizens to boycott elections.[67]

Like their monastic cousins, priests also were forced to devise measures to avoid detection and continue their religious vocation after the closure of their churches. Many priests could be persuaded to renounce their exclusive devotion to their profession by the difficulty of making a living in a society consciously organized against them.[68] With the initiation of the collectivization campaign clergymen were deprived of economic rights and made subject to

[59] Timasheff, op. cit., p. 63.
[60] Krypton, op. cit., pp. 125–6.
[61] *Komsomol'skaia Pravda*, 15 September 1937.
[62] *Izvestiia*, 23 November 1937.
[63] Timasheff, op. cit., p. 81.
[64] *Trud*, 20 December 1937.
[65] *Sotsialisticheskoe Zemledelie*, 11 January 1938.
[66] *Trud*, 15 April 1937.
[67] *Izvestiia*, 23 November 1937.
[68] Alexandre Marc, 'The Outstretched (?) Hand . . . in the U.S.S.R.,' in François Mauriac, *Communism and Christians* (Westminster, Maryland: The Newman Press, 1949), p. 188.

severe taxation.[69] This reduced many of them to outright penury.[70] Whether it was due to such economic sanctions, the closure of the churches, or other reasons, Emel'ian Iaroslavskii, the titular head of the anti-religious campaign, in March 1931, could point with pride to the fact that 'of late years we have had a mass renunciation of their trade by priests (literally thousands of them)'.[71]

Large numbers of priests responded to the changing society by undertaking unobtrusive social activity, supplementing their incomes by work in secular occupations.[72] Many quite naturally gravitated towards the schoolteaching profession.[73] Many worked in the factories, singing in factory choirs, etc.[74] Other became farm workers, members of road gangs, and the like.[75] Such priests, even though they had temporarily interrupted their sacerdotal vocation by secular work, were available to perform priestly functions when opportunities should arise.[76] For example, in Odessa each Easter at the single open Church, which had no priest, a priest who had been living as a worker would come forward, conduct the service, and be arrested.[77] Other priests disappeared completely within society. Dimitry Konstantinov relates the story of a priest who managed to escape from a marching convoy of some 150 clergymen on their way to the prison camps, hid in the forest, and finally made his way to Moscow by train, where the believers helped him to assume a disguise with false documents, etc. He remained in hiding until the more relaxed conditions of World War II made it possible for him to resume the priesthood.[78] In addition to such priests as these, many laymen in nearly every profession agreed to receive secret ordination to the priesthood.[79]

[69] Spinka, *Christianity Confronts Communism*, op. cit., pp. 102–4.

[70] Donald Attwater, *The Christian Churches of the East* (London: Chapman, 1961), II, 66.

[71] Emel'ian Iaroslavskii, 'Zadachi antireligioznoi propagandy v period sotsialisticheskogo nastupleniia' ('Tasks of anti-religious propaganda in the period of the advance of socialism'), *Pod Znamenem Marksizma*, No. 3 (March 1931), p. 48.

[72] Attwater, op. cit., II, 66–7.

[73] *Pravda*, 23 December 1928.

[74] Fireside, op. cit., p. 312.

[75] Ibid., p. 250.

[76] Ibid., pp. 326–7.

[77] P. J. Huxley-Blythe, 'Modern Christian Martyrs,' *American Mercury*, No. 88 (February 1959), p. 25.

[78] Konstantinov, *Gonimaia tserkov'*, op. cit., pp. 52–4.

[79] Adolph Keller, *Religion and Revolution* (New York: Revell, 1934), p. 183.

A common phenomenon during this period was the wandering priest, roaming the Russian countryside at will without any stable parish.[80] Such priests were to be found throughout the country.[81] In some cases they had been led to this expedient by the Government's refusal to allow them to resume parish work on their return from prison or exile.[82] Generally these priests were paid in kind by the population for performing religious ceremonies, and thus managed to make their living.[83]

The need for their services was immense. In one case a wandering priest baptized eighteen children at once, ranging in age from one to fifteen years.[84] Given the precipitate decrease in the number of functioning churches, the need was endemic throughout the country for the various Christian ceremonies which could be conducted by such wandering priests.[85] According to Iaroslavskii,

It is stupid to think that if a priest is deprived of his parish he ceases to be a priest. We know of hundreds of cases where after the closing of churches their priests change into 'itinerant priests' and with their simple inventory of divine items, wander about the villages and workers' settlements, conducting religious rites, reading prayers, the Bible, the psalter. Such an 'itinerant priest' is sometimes more dangerous than one who serves openly.[86]

Concurrently with the phenomenon of the wandering priests who could bring the consolations of the Church to the people, the practice grew up of having ceremonies conducted by correspondence.[87] Rites could be conducted *in absentia*[88] or by proxy.[89] Weddings could be conducted by sending the wedding ring to a priest for his blessing, and, similarly, funerals could be performed by the priest blessing a bit of earth sent to him from the grave.[90]

---

[80] Anderson, op. cit., p. 178; Mitropolit Evlogii, *Put' moei zhizni* ('The path of my life') (Paris: Y.M.C.A. Press, 1947), p. 652; Nicholas Nyaradi, *My Ringside Seat in Moscow* (New York: Thomas Y. Crowell, 1952), p. 171.

[81] Teodorovich, 'The Catacomb Church in the U.S.S.R.,' op. cit., p. 4.

[82] Pol'skii, op. cit., II, xvi.

[83] Fireside, op. cit., p. 312, quoting Harvard Refugee Interview Project, 'Hans Koch,' Protocol of 1 June 1951, pp. 8–9.

[84] *Komsomol'skaia Pravda*, 1 March 1938.

[85] Attwater, op. cit., II, 67.

[86] *Trud*, 15 April 1937.

[87] *Antireligioznik*, No. 8 (August 1937), p. 54.

[88] Anderson, op. cit., p. 17.

[89] Timasheff, op. cit., pp. 77–9.

[90] Pol'skii, op. cit., II, xvi, quoting *Bezbozhnik*, No. 7 (1936).

Wandering priests very quickly learned to conduct their lives with the greatest secrecy, using numerous clandestine methods to avoid detection.[91] As an example, during the second part of the decade,

Father Varsonofii, in order to fulfil the major goal—strengthening the believers—took off his priestly clothes and assumed the guise of an old man in the usual long Russian shirt girdled with a belt. In such a guise he was able for some time to visit a whole series of his faithful children unnoticed, both in his former parishes and in other places: Kuban, Donbas, Belorussia, several cities of the Ukraine, and finally Odessa. The major goal of the visits was to conduct secret divine liturgies, confessions, and the Eucharist. Only his faithful, who knew each other or could offer similar verification, gathered at these services.

The writer of these lines was a witness to one of these trips of Father V., made somewhat earlier than these years. There at the edge of the city in a house located in a remote place and protected by a high fence (but activities were also held in the centre of the city itself) Father V. confessed for two days and in the evenings, as much as he had strength, the people who arrived, who passed on from one to another the word concerning his location. There was not even time for him to eat.[92]

Interestingly enough, some of these priests when captured were apparently confined in mental hospitals, thereby avoiding the inconvenience of formal imprisonment.[93]

The services rendered by such vagabonds were not exclusively limited to meeting the religious needs of the population. In some cases wandering priests helped out in the kitchen, took care of children, or even engaged in small-scale distribution of goods to the poor.[94] In addition to priests, the desperate need for religious literature induced some to become wanderers serving as colporteurs, distributing what little was available to meet this need.[95] Similarly, religious minstrels occasionally appeared, making their living by singing religious songs in the villages.[96]

A number of other surreptitious means of fulfilling religious needs began to appear during this period. In particular, the

[91] Pol'skii, op. cit., II, 190–1.
[92] Ibid., p. 161; cf. p. 226.
[93] Teodorovich, 'The Catacomb Church in the U.S.S.R.,' op. cit., p. 5.
[94] *Bezbozhnik*, 21 April 1939.
[95] *Trud*, 27 August 1937.
[96] Timasheff, op. cit., p. 69.

problem of education was acute, for the State during the twenties and thirties allowed the Church no facilities for the education of its adherents. In 1929, religious education for children was limited to groups of no more than three persons. The Church's immediate response was a secret letter suggesting the formation of a network of three-member groups to carry out the religious education of children.[97] For a time this expedient enjoyed considerable success.[98] Among adults, numerous informal (and illegal) study groups of four or five people began to meet in order to study the Bible, theology, and the like.[99] Old works of theology which had been preserved from the pre-revolutionary period were passed from hand to hand.[100]

The problem of the education of clergy was especially important, although not so acute as it might seem at first glance. The Russian Orthodox tradition was well suited to the informal preparation of priests.

With few exceptions, the parish clergy is married, and the successor to the priest is his son. If the clergy has an exclusively liturgical function, there is no need for the young man to spend many years in a seminary preparing himself to become a priest. All he needs to do is help his father at the altar until he knows the rites of the different sacraments.[101]

Metropolitan Sergii alluded to this phenomenon of informally prepared priests in 1941,[102] and indirect evidence of informal theological education was given in the by-laws of the post-war theological academies, which allowed admission to people already well grounded in theology but lacking seminary training.[103]

Even in the early twenties there was a clandestine theological seminary in the U.S.S.R.[104] During the thirties a secret theological

[97] M. Kuznetsov, 'Antireligioznoe vospitanie v shkolakh balashovskogo okruga' ('Anti-religious education in the schools of the Balashov region'), *Antireligioznik*, No. 5 (May 1930), p. 84.

[98] Camille Maximilian Cianfarra, *The Vatican and the Kremlin* (New York: Dutton, 1950), pp. 55-6.

[99] Konstantinov, *Pravoslavnaia molodezh' v bor'be za tserkov' v SSSR*, op. cit., pp. 20-1.

[100] Schakovskoy, op. cit., p. 268.

[101] Bissonette, op. cit., p. 255.

[102] Wallace Carroll, *We're in This with Russia* (Boston: Houghton Mifflin, 1942), pp. 149-50.

[103] *Z.M.P.*, No. 6 (June 1953), pp. 67-70.

[104] Francis McCullagh, *The Bolshevik Persecution of Christianity* (New York: Dutton, 1924), p. 72.

school was operating in Moscow, organized by Archbishop Varfolomei (Remov).[105] As a consequence, he was arrested and shot in 1936,[106] and the theological school was finally closed in 1938.[107]

There was considerable traffic during these years in illegally produced literature,[108] and numerous secret printing presses were operational.[109] In 1934 an anti-religious author complained of the existence of secret typewriters, printing presses, and even the production of counterfeit money among religious believers.[110]

Thus a broad range of underground activities was commonplace during the years following the decision to collectivize. In view of the extreme tension of the times and the great energies devoted by the regime to the anti-religious campaign, very few believers in Russia could avoid indulging in some form of illegal and clandestine activity at one time or another. It is hardly surprising, therefore, that underground religious organizations flourished during these years.

There were many considerations compelling people to join the underground movements during this period. Particularly among the leadership, the compelling reason was political or at least had political overtones. As has been noted, a significant and influential portion of the leadership of the Russian Orthodox Church disagreed with the propriety of offering political support to the regime in the hope of receiving concessions. Allied to this motivation, and perhaps behind it in many cases, was the desire to preserve the integrity and freedom of the Church rather than allowing the designs of the State to creep into internal church matters, as, for example, seemed to be the case in the controversies over the transfer of Metropolitan Iosif and other bishops.

Particularly with the initiation of the collectivization campaign and the rise of the regime's vigorous anti-religious effort, which during the late twenties and early thirties was at times very un-

---

[105] Pol'skii, op. cit., II, 125.

[106] Struve, op. cit., French edition, p. 355.

[107] Timasheff, op. cit., pp. 80–1.

[108] 'Vreditel'skaia deiatel'nost' tserkovnikov i sektantov' ('Wrecking activity of churchmen and sectarians'), *Antireligioznik*, No. 5 (May 1930), pp. 97–9.

[109] William C. White, 'The Triple-Barred Cross,' *Scribner's Magazine*, LXXXVIII, 1 (July 1930), p. 76.

[110] L. Lagovskii, 'Itogi bezbozhnoi piatiletka' ('A summary of the godless five year plan'), *Vestnik Russkago Studencheskago Khristianskago Dvizheniia*, No. 1 (January 1934), p. 28.

restrained indeed, the political ambivalence or hostility towards the regime of these leaders, who had in a sense rightly foreseen the coming course of events, could be expected to find an ever growing response in the Church at large. It would be most unnatural if the regime's excesses in the anti-religious campaign did not result in a reciprocal hostility on the part of the campaign's victims. Lenin himself had warned that anti-religious excess results in the alienation of the religious population. As the storm of collectivization descended upon the country, many local and Party officials succumbed to boundless enthusiasm in their anti-religious activities. The only result could be the deepening of political hostility on the part of believers. People who heretofore had viewed the various changes in the governmental structure with a degree of equanimity, who had been relatively uninterested in politics, suddenly would tend to respond with sharp hostility to the regime which had ordered the encroachments on their religious freedom. The net result was a radical increase in the believing population's hostility to the political regime.

In some cases the clergy themselves contributed to the deepening alienation of a portion of the Orthodox population. Parish priests who were not particularly well in tune with the prevailing sentiments in their parish (a phenomenon which was not uncommon in the Russian tradition), or who miscalculated the depth of the convictions of certain of their parishioners, might contribute to the growing hostility of the latter by a too enthusiastic acceptance of the actions of the regime. In the Urals, for example,

in Cheliabinsk, in one of the churches in line with the icons they hung portraits of comrades Lenin and Kalinin, causing a disturbance among the illiterate and half-blind old women, who did not know to which of the 'saints' to kneel and mumble prayers.[111]

Practices such as this would be anathema to certain of the sincerely convinced believers, not on political grounds, but on grounds of sacrilege. The result, however, would be to direct the initial shock of the believers—shock arising from purely religious considerations—against the political leadership of the State, thereby transforming religious discontent into political hostility.

Some priests, perhaps interpreting Sergii's offer of political

[111] P. Zarin, 'Politicheskii maskarad tserkovnikov i sektantov' ('The political masquerade of churchmen and sectarians'), *Antireligioznik*, No. 10 (October 1931), p. 15.

support a bit too literally, actively supported the *kolkhoz* move-ment.[112] In some cases, priests went so far as to refuse the sacraments of confession, absolution, and the Eucharist to peasants who had not joined the *kolkhoz*.[113] Naturally, such enthusiasm could only alienate those believers who were unwilling to join in the collectivization movement, either because of general hostility towards it or for any of the very real grounds presented by its several implications—loss of personal property, collective owner-ship, subordination to State appointed *kolkhoz* directors, increased expropriation of crops by the State, drastic reduction in standard of living, or even anti-religious overtones implicit in the *kolkhoz* movement.

Further exacerbating the already tense situation in the Church, Sergii had ordered his churches to cease the practice of holding religious memorials for those who had been arrested. This was a logical consequence of his policy of political loyalty to the regime, for the Government arrested such unfortunates, not on overtly religious grounds, but on the claim that they were counter-revolutionary. Therefore, if the churches continued to remember these people in their prayers, this itself would imply counter-revo-lutionary aspirations within the churches.[114] This was explicitly borne out in the interviews Sergii gave to domestic and foreign journalists in February 1930:

Metropolitan Sergii stated that all believers who have suffered in the U.S.S.R. from the Bolsheviks suffered not for their religious but for their political convictions. This was the interpretation of the Soviet Government itself for all the arrests, martyrdoms, exiles, and murders of many pastors and laymen of the Church. Metropolitan Sergii con-sidered it necessary and useful to the Church to accept this interpreta-tion in front of the foreign journalists who had been thirsting, of course, to hear, this time from the mouth of Metropolitan Sergii, a protest against the persecution of belief. The interview of Metropolitan Sergii for many bore the bitter sense of his (and all his hierarchs') renunciation of their own martyrs.[115]

In view of the deep tradition of reverence for martyrdom and for local religious superiors, such a trespass against the honoured

[112] Ibid., pp. 13–14.
[113] Curtiss, op. cit., p. 262.
[114] Mikhail, op. cit., p. 51.
[115] Bishop Ioann (Shakovskoi), *Russkaia tserkov' v SSSR* ('The Russian Church in the U.S.S.R.') (New York: Rausen Brothers, 1956), pp. 13–15.

memory of those popular heroes of the faith who had been victimized by the regime's policy would be an unbearable shock to Orthodox believers who for one reason or another had been deeply affected by the arrest, incarceration, or death of a particularly revered or beloved member of the Church. Not all the Orthodox believers were sufficiently sophisticated to realize that even a concession such as this, distasteful and indeed bitter though it may have been to accept, surely could by no means detract from whatever glory may have been achieved by such martyrs.[116] The net result would be an increasing alienation within the Orthodox parishes, making a further contribution to the motivation to abandon the open churches entirely for some other form of religious observance.

To the catalogue of pressures impelling believers towards the religious underground should be added the contra-productiveness of the regime's own measures against the Church. An important segment even of the atheist apparatus had warned that use of over-zealous measures, such as forbidding children to speak or think about God, would only result in the use of conspiratorial methods.[117] Thus the excesses of anti-religious zeal in some cases could be expected merely to confirm any existing sentiments that in view of the distastefulness of the times, the believer might just as well abandon all pretence of conforming to the rules of a society specifically organized to deny his religious needs and enter the underground without further ado.

All of these motivations, and many others of course, contributed to the rising popularity of underground forms of Orthodoxy during this period. Nevertheless, it is doubtful that the underground movement would have achieved anything like the pre-war proportions had it not been for the single overwhelming inducement to join the conspiratorial movements: the closure of churches.[118] The success of the regime's campaign against the institutional Church left millions of believers without any permissible outlet for their religious needs and desires. It would be absurd to presume that all such dispossessed believers would immediately cease to worship together, and that the tradition of a millennium could be terminated by the simple mechanism of padlocking a church door. Therefore,

---

[116] Ibid.

[117] *Za Kommunisticheskoe Prosveshchenie*, 10 August 1937.

[118] Konstantinov, *Gonimaia tserkov'*, op. cit., p. 21.

vast numbers of believers were all but desperate for some form of religious life, and the result was a vast burgeoning of the underground movement. No longer was this a live option only for those who were sufficiently agitated by political considerations to object vehemently to Sergii's change in policy in 1927.[119] Vast numbers now began to join the underground movements for many other reasons, chief among which was the lack of any alternative form of religious observance.[120]

A general historical pattern of the development of the underground movement can be discerned for this period, even though the evidence is far from complete. While there were deviations from this pattern among individual underground organizations and from one part of the vast country to another, in view of the fact that the chief determinant of the development of the underground movement was the policy of the regime, the underground Orthodox (and, indeed, non-Orthodox) organizations shared a general pattern in the course of events from 1928 until World War II.

The collectivization campaign was a time of special growth and proliferation of these organizations.[121] Such groups became 'especially visible when the country moved to the establishment of the policy of industrialization and collectivization'.[122] The first two years, 1928–30, were marked by an especially vigorous proliferation, development, and expansion of the underground movements, for during this period the regime threw caution to the winds in its collectivization campaign and the confusion throughout the countryside was so rampant as greatly to facilitate the underground movement. Throughout the decade, however, new groups continued to appear.[123]

Beginning about 1930, the regime began to devote special attention to this problem, and exceedingly fierce methods were employed to attack these potentially dangerous, *sub rosa* organizations. Police powers were widely utilized and succeeded rather well in disrupting the illegal organizations; 'in the beginning of the thirties many organizations ended their existence'.[124] To be sure,

[119] Konstantinov, *Pravoslavnaia molodezh' v bor'be za tserkov' v SSSR*, op. cit., p. 34.
[120] Ibid.
[121] Cf. Iuliia Nikolaevna Danzas, *The Russian Church* (New York: Sheed and Ward, 1936), p. 158.
[122] Sheinman, op. cit., p. 61.
[123] Ibid.
[124] Glukhov, op. cit., p. 67.

subsequent Soviet scholarship has ascribed the increasing difficulties of the underground movements to other causes:

The general tendency—decrease in the numerical strength of sectarian congregations—made its way through a whole series of temporary vacillations, ebbs and flows. Beginning with 1930–1932, when the first five-year plan was successfully completed and agriculture was restructured on socialist beginnings, the rapid decline of numerical strength of sectarian congregations became marked.[125]

Thus it was the successful transformation of the social environment which is held responsible for the decline of the underground movements in the early thirties.[126] In view of the rapidly burgeoning powers of the secret police during this period, however, one may perhaps be forgiven for raising alternative hypotheses to account for the decline. Interestingly enough, a Russian Orthodox historian suggests that after 1930 the patriarchal Church began to grow. In view of the decimation suffered by the Church during the thirties, however, with its institutional organization all but inoperative at the end of the decade, such a statement, at first glance, appears to be very unlikely indeed. Nevertheless, the reason given by this Orthodox historian—the return of schismatics—would seem credible in view of the success of the measures applied against the underground organizations.[127] The dramatic increase in the severity of social control exercised by the regime during this period would render illegal organizations a much less attractive option where legally permissible services were available in an open Church.

It would appear that during the slight relaxation in the anti-religious campaign from 1932 to 1936, underground organizations were able to function somewhat more easily in the Russian countryside, and indeed there may have been a slight increase in their success during these years. By 1936 religious life in the country was enjoying a quiet but nevertheless noticeable revival.[128]

Whatever ground had been regained was quickly lost during the tension of the Great Purges, for in the fierce anti-religious

[125] Federenko, op. cit., p. 102.
[126] Sheinman, op. cit., p. 63.
[127] Ibid, p. 43.
[128] O. Putintsev, 'O svobode sovesti v SSSR' ('Freedom of conscience in the U.S.S.R.'), *Pod Znamenem Marksizma*, No. 2 (February 1937), p. 79. *Pravda*, 15 April 1937; *Izvestiia*, 1 May 1936; Timasheff, op. cit., pp. 67–9; *New York Times*, 3 May 1937.

campaign of 1937 and 1938 great emphasis was placed upon alleged (and doubtless in some cases real) underground machinations of religious people. Underground organizations which had managed to preserve leadership structure through the first wave of attack of the early thirties, or which had been able to reorganize themselves since, again were decimated and their traces were lost entirely.[129]

It appears, however, that the success of the attack against illegal Orthodoxy in 1937–8 was no less ephemeral than that achieved in the earlier attack. No sooner had the storm passed than the underground organizations again began to operate within the countryside in the more relaxed conditions which prevailed between 1938 and the beginning of World War II.

Thus the general historical pattern of underground Orthodoxy during these years was a sharp increase from 1928–30, a vigorous and largely successful repression early in the thirties, moderate increase until the Great Purges again reduced their activities, and finally another resumption of activity towards the beginning of World War II.

The 'Tikhonites' were by far the dominant movement in underground Orthodoxy during this period. The name was a generic term applied both by the atheists and by the members of the movement themselves to a large number of more or less related organizational movements which claimed as their *raison d'être* the continuation of the heritage of the late Patriarch. According to a Soviet scholar,

The Declaration of Sergii was a positive act. Its appearance did not signify that the entire Orthodox Church, all its hierarchs, accepted a position of loyalty to the Soviet social order. There still remained groups who were for the continuation of the first, Tikhonite course of enmity to the Soviet order. This became especially evident when the country moved to the establishment of the policy of industrialization and collectivization. . . .

Among the old churchmen, new groups continued to appear, especially during the years of collectivization.[130]

It is impossible to determine the numerical strength of this movement, of course. Despite his vested interest in the existence of

[129] Ioann (Shakovskoi), *Russkaia tserkov' v SSSR*, op. cit., p. 4, n. 2.
[130] Sheinman, op. cit., p. 61.

such a movement, Pol'skii was rather pessimistic as to its size, admitting that those who went into schism were only a scattered few.[131]

The Orthodox Church is in Russia, it remains. It is not with Metropolitan Sergii, as also he is not with it. The Tikhonite, patriarchal Church in Russia, just as it existed before, before Metropolitan Sergii, so also it now exists in an illegal position. It is not great as to its numbers. . . . Who is the leader of this Church of Christ? How many are they, and where? Few. You could count them on your fingers. They are in concentration camps, prisons, exile, and who knows where.[132]

It would appear that this assessment is somewhat pessimistic, however, for the underground movement reached significant proportions during the pre-war years. Particularly during the collectivization campaign, when the kulaks (wealthy peasants, or, as events were to demonstrate, almost anyone who opposed collectivization) were to be eliminated as a class, 'the Tikhonites discovered their natural ally in the angry kulak and were not slow to equip kulak hostility to collectivization with the slogans of church monarchical counter-revolution'.[133] The many general references to the underground movement in the anti-religious propaganda of the period,[134] or more specifically to the Tikhonites,[135] testify to the considerable importance of the movement, at least so far as the State was concerned. For example,

In this region a group of sectarians, so-called 'Tikhonites', built themselves a strong nest. Among these 'Christ-like brothers' there were not a few hardened enemies of the people. . . .

From time to time on the farm there appeared old men of suspicious appearance, sectarian preachers. They are practised in cultivating gullible and unsophisticated people. Cleverly and subtly they sidle up to young people and children in search of donations.[136]

It should be noted that in this period it was the practice of underground groups to take as the name of their organization the name of a particular founder or hero. This practice not only led to the

---

[131] Mikhail, op. cit., p. 53.
[132] Ibid., p. 111.
[133] Klibanov, 'Sovremennoe sektantstvo v Tambovskoi oblasti,' op. cit., p. 93.
[134] Cf. Hélène Iswolsky, Soul of Russia (London: Sheed and Ward, 1944), p. 154.
[135] Pravda, 2 March 1937.
[136] Komsomol'skaia Pravda, 23 December 1938.

practical deification of such stalwarts in subsequent years,[137] but also considerably increased the complexity of determining the component parts, extent, size, and influence of the Tikhonite movement.

The dominant organization within the Tikhonite genus was the Josephite movement. Again this is a generic designation, to some degree embracing a large number of local or regional sub-organizations generally claiming jurisdictional validity on the basis of Metropolitan Iosif's leadership. In common with nearly all of the other underground Orthodox groups, the Josephites enjoyed considerable success during the tumultuous years of collectivization. With the mobilization of the regime's forces against underground religious organizations, however, the movement came under considerable pressure, and by 1930–1, 'the Josephite Church leadership, considering the situation in the locales, were forced to retrench—to yield a large part of their churches to the Sergiites, concentrating their attention on individual cultivation of believers in the spirit they desired'.[138] The application of police power apparently enjoyed considerable success in breaking up the organization.[139]

The movement was not totally disrupted, however. In 1932, two of the 425 churches in the Bashkir Republic were known to belong to the Josephite movement.[140] As will become evident below, various branches of the Josephite movement continued vigorous activity throughout the decade.

The Josephite movement claimed to be loyal to the patriarchal locum tenens, Metropolitan Petr. While it would seem that questions regarding the person of Metropolitan Petr exercised émigré Orthodox a great deal more than those within the country, nevertheless his position did have a bearing on the movement. Unfortunately, the confusion reigning during the thirties has surrounded Metropolitan Petr in a mist which is almost impenetrable to the historian, and little or no reliable information is

[137] A. S. Onishchenko, 'Tendentsii izmeneniia sovremennogo religioznogo soznaniia ('Tendencies of change of contemporary religious understanding'), AN SSSR, *Vopros Nauchnogo Ateizma*, op. cit., II, 98.

[138] Platonov, op. cit., p. 268.

[139] I. Andreev, *O polozhenii pravoslavnoi tserkvi i sovetskom soiuze. Katabombnaia tserkov v SSSR* ('The position of the Orthodox Church in the Soviet Union. The catacomb church in the U.S.S.R.') (Jordanville, New York: Holy Trinity Monastery, 1951) p. 8.

[140] Pol'skii, op. cit., II, xiv, citing *Antireligioznik*.

available concerning him. Pol'skii alleges that he was offered his freedom during the thirties but refused because the offer was made contingent on unacceptable prerequisites. However, he submits no documentation to support this assertion, and at least as he presents it, it appears to be intrinsically improbable.[141] He also alleges (somewhat less improbably) that Petr may have been released for a short period in 1935 for a conversation with Metropolitan Sergii.[142]

Metropolitan Petr died late in 1936.[143] According to the emigration the succession then descended upon Metropolitan Kirill.[144] Thereafter the emigration apparently selected Iosif himself as the successor to the patriarchate, more or less, one suspects, by default.[145]

There is one report that Metropolitan Iosif had direct contact with Petr while Iosif was in exile.

A direct witness tells of his stay in exile. In August, 1936, the comparatively young Archimandrite Arsenii lived in Alma Ata. It was from him that I first learned, says she, that a secret, catacomb church exists, led by Metropolitan Iosif of Petersburg and organized by him with the blessing of Metropolitan Petr Krutitskii, with whom he, living in exile in Chemkent, 100 *versts* from Alma Ata, had secret relations the whole time.

Incidentally, the Church was apparently in an earth dug-out entered through Arsenii's apartment. He and Metropolitan Iosif conducted services in it whenever Iosif could get there from Chemkent.[146]

Despite the intense interest of the *émigré* churchmen in determining a line of succession, it would appear that the question of the attitudes of Metropolitan Petr and his actual relations with Iosif— and even, perhaps, questions concerning the person of Iosif himself—were academic within Russia, particularly after Iosif was shot late in 1938.[147] With the increasing competence of the Soviet

---

[141] Ibid., I, 142–3; cf. Fletcher, *A Study in Survival*, op. cit., pp. 73–4.

[142] Pol'skii, op. cit., II, 287–8.

[143] Sergii's elevation to the office of locum tenens on 27 December 1936, implies Petr's death by that date, although it was not officially announced until some months later, and in the emigration there was a body of opinion that he did not die until January 1937. Cf. Pol'skii, op. cit., I, 143, II, 287–8.

[144] Ibid., II, 296.

[145] Andreev, *O polozhenii pravoslavnoi tserkvi v sovetskom soiuze*, op. cit., pp. 8–9.

[146] Pol'skii, op. cit., II, 1.

[147] Andreev, *O polozhenii pravoslavnoi tserkvi v sovetskom soiuze*, op. cit., pp. 8–9.

secret police there was no chance whatsoever of maintaining any kind of regular or normal contact with the nominal leader of the Josephite movement. His function, indeed, was not at all that of leader for the great majority of the movement's adherents, but rather that of founder and inspirer of the movement. His role thus was almost entirely figurative, and in view of the impossibility of communications his particular actions or attitudes at a given time could have little bearing on his image within the movement.

The Josephite movement continued throughout the decade, despite the pressure and the decimation of its leadership. (Dimitrii, the bishop of Gdovsk, allegedly Iosif's locum tenens, was killed in 1938, for example.[148]) Nevertheless, the Josephite churches continued to function. In Moscow itself, there was apparently a functioning Josephite Church in 1938.

At the apartment of N.N., whose last name was well known to them, 30–40 people would gather. A priest whose name was also known to them would serve. In order to enter it was necessary to go through a water pipe with a password. It was curious that in the same house a *chekist* [member of the secret police] lived. The secret churchmen had links with higher spiritual leaders and elders, whose place of residence was kept a strict secret. They lived somewhere in the countryside and, in addition, constantly changed place.[149]

Similar groups were known to exist in Leningrad, and throughout the country the Josephite schism was able to utilize to some degree the practice of the conduct of religious ceremonies by correspondence.[150]

The lack of reliable data concerning the details of the Josephite movement and its branches is somewhat less acute with regard to one of the branches, the Buevtsy. This is probably not so much due to the intrinsic importance of this group as compared with other branches of the movement, but is more the result of the vagaries of subsequent Soviet historiography in selecting the geographic region in which the Buevtsy had been dominant for a case study of the general problem of sectarian organizations.

As has been noted, the Buevtsy movement was a sub-unit of the Josephite schism enjoying the explicit sanction of Metropolitan

---

148 Pol'skii, op. cit., II, 5.
149 Ibid., p. xv.
150 Ibid.

Iosif.[151] Although its organizational centre was in Voronezh, it enjoyed great success in the regions surrounding Tambov, 100 miles to the north-east, and, indeed, was active over a wide area of the Caucasus and the Ukraine.[152] As has been noted above, the Buevtsy movement had a highly centralized organization. Its actual formation appeared to be by way of a process of unifying independently existing, local underground organizations. For example,

It is important to note that a special Kozlov union which was led by the merchant's daughter, P. P. Filatova, joined the Buevtsy.

According to the words of the believers with whom we conversed, P. Filatova quite explicitly spoke of her theological and political predecessors: 'Metropolitan Petr and Archbishop Aleksii (Bui—L.M.) did not recognize the Soviet government, and we, the true Orthodox Christians, as disciples of Metropolitan Petr and Bishop Aleksii also are opponents of the Soviet government.' In those years, of the nine groups under her leadership, one was municipal (in Kozlov). Several other anti-Soviet groups also joined the Buevtsy, in particular the group of Archimandrite A. P. Filippenko, who had served with Bui in the Vladimir Cathedral in Voronezh.[153]

Apparently there was a fierce attack against the movement, which resulted in the conviction of its leaders and the dissolution of its organizational structure in 1930 or 1931.[154] Prior to this attack, the Buevtsy in the Tambov area (at least that portion of them which Soviet investigators were able to discover) 'consisted of about 40 groups with general membership above 700'.[155] After this initial attack the movement was reorganized by a subordinate and, again according to Soviet investigators, had a following of some 200 people in 1932.[156] The Soviet academician Mitrokhin states that 'at the end of 1932 the organization of the Buevtsy ended its existence and its most active workers were convicted of anti-Soviet activity',[157] but goes on to state that its adherents, despite the alleged destruction of the movement's organization, conducted anti-Soviet agitation during the election campaign in 1939.[158]

[151] Mitrokhin, op. cit., p. 148.
[152] Curtiss, op. cit., p. 260.
[153] Mitrokhin, op. cit., pp. 151–2.
[154] Ibid., p. 151. It is unclear whether or not this is the same trial as that described by Curtiss, op. cit., p. 260.
[155] Mitrokhin, op. cit., p. 151.
[156] Ibid.
[157] Ibid., p. 154.
[158] Ibid.

Thus it would seem that even though two successful investigatory and penal processes were initiated against the Buevtsy organization (in 1930 and 1932), the movement continued its activity throughout the decade.

During the collectivization campaign, the Buevtsy, like cognate movements throughout the country, conducted vigorous agitation against the *kolkhozes*.[159] Priests belonging to the movement apparently refused to give absolution of sins to those who would not break with the *kolkhozes*, and attempted to convince people that entrance into the *kolkhozes* was 'a breach of the counsel of the Lord'.

They spread absurd, slanderous rumours, such as that in the *kolkhozes* all would sleep under one blanket, that old people would be reworked into fertilizer, while young people would be shaved so that their hair could be sent abroad as wool in exchange for tractors.[160]

Nor was such agitation without success. According to one informant's recollection of that period,

Our farm was in the *kolkhoz* 'Zarech'e' and before the harvest we left, and besides us several other farmers left. We left because all the time the monk Evgenii Beliaev (an active worker of the Buevtsy—L.M.) was saying to us, 'If anyone does not get out of the *kolkhoz* before the harvest he will remain a slave for ever, because soon the Soviet Government will not exist but a bourgeois government will exist, and it will take for itself all the land of the *kolkhoz*, but the private farmers will live in freedom and the land which they use will remain to them.' We, the ignorant people, considered the monk Beliaev a knowledgeable person, one worthy of God, and the nuns also believed him and left the *kolkhoz*.[161]

Nor was such agitation confined to persuasion alone. Throughout the country numerous riots and uprisings occurred in the popular attempts to resist the forcible collectivization of agriculture. In the Tambov area, the Buevtsy were directly involved in one such uprising. In 1932,

Suddenly a crowd appeared from nowhere. The cry was heard: 'Orthodox, thrash the anti-Christ. It will not be a sin for us, the Lord will help us deliver ourselves from Satan.'[162]

[159] Platonov, op. cit., p. 265.
[160] Mitrokhin, op. cit., pp. 152–3.
[161] Ibid., p. 153.
[162] Ibid., p. 154.

In the conduct of their work the Buevtsy used active laymen to supplement the ranks of the clergy.

Taking of monastic vows was practised in secret, and strong attempts were made to seek out or fabricate various kinds of 'holy men', 'sages', and 'prophets'. Periodically instructed, they went about the villages and conducted agitation among the peasants, convincing them that entrance into the *kolkhozes* was a 'breach of the counsel of the Lord'. Some of them passed themselves off as people who had purportedly entered a *kolkhoz* unwittingly but had been ruined, and were now forced to live off of 'good people' and were vagabonds.[163]

Because the number of churches which the Buevtsy could utilize was far from adequate, a cult of informal shrines sprang up, thus giving the movement the advantage of locales which could attract people from numerous villages without the disadvantages of a fixed location, such as a normal church, which would be more susceptible to police pressure.

As an example we cite the development of the 'Holy Apple Tree' in the village of Podgornyi. 'Sages' and 'holy men' spread this sort of rumour: 'You will die in the *kolkhoz*. Go, ride to the holy apple tree.' The apple tree was described as 'able to work miracles'. The number of pilgrims at times reached several hundred people. They gathered together in secret, preferably at night. At the apple tree itself divine services were held, the *akafists* were read, anti-Soviet speeches were delivered, and the leaders administered confession.[164]

In addition to the Bible, the Buevtsy placed great emphasis on a work entitled, 'The Visions of John of Kronstadt', an apocalyptic composition thought to have originated during the Living Church Adventure.[165] In addition, the Buevtsy also appear to have made use of the notoriously anti-Semitic 'Protocols of the Elders of Zion'.[166]

Eschatology played a considerable role in the doctrine of the Buevtsy. Subsequent Soviet scholarship suggests that this eschatological motif was intertwined with definite aspirations towards engineering a restoration of the monarchy.[167] Apocalyptic imagery

[163] Ibid., pp. 152–3.
[164] Ibid., p. 154.
[165] Ibid., p. 153.
[166] Ibid.
[167] Klibanov, 'Sovremennoe sektantstvo v Tambovskoi Oblasti,' op. cit., pp. 92–3.

was utilized in agitation against collectivization,[168] as well as against ration cards and passports, which were called 'seals of anti-Christ'.[169]

Certain Soviet observers have also discovered a similar movement, the True Orthodox Church, during this pre-war period. Unfortunately, it remains uncertain whether this represents the uncritical application of the name of a subsequent underground Orthodox organization to those movements from which it was derived, or whether this early in the history of underground Orthodoxy this appellation had already come into vogue. The designation 'true Orthodox' is cited as one of the branches of the Josephite movement in the composition of Metropolitan Platonov written in the late thirties.[170] Inasmuch as this article, whose author died during World War II, was published posthumously in 1960 and 1961 in abridged form, it remains uncertain whether he actually used the designation or whether it was inserted by the editors.[171]

South-east of Moscow, 'the most reactionarily inclined part of the clergy of the Riazan area broke with the Church and founded in the north-east regions of the area small, illegal groups of partisans of the so-called True Orthodox Church, connected with similar groups in other central areas'.[172] This movement organized secret home monasteries and utilized written materials similar to those used by the Buevtsy. Apparently monarchical aspirations were very strong in the movement.[173] The True Orthodox Church, according to Soviet scholarship, was active in spreading the Tikhonite influence in Orthodox parishes in other areas as well.[174]

Even less convincing is the attempt to find members of the True Orthodox Christians movement during this period. The few references offered by Soviet scholarship seem almost certainly to be a generic misnomer applied to a period prior to the rise of the True Orthodox Christians in the underground movement as a whole. According to the study of the Riazan area referred to above,

[168] Mitrokhin, op. cit., pp. 152–3.
[169] Platonov, op. cit., p. 265.
[170] Ibid.
[171] Ibid., p. 206, editor's n. 1.
[172] Iankova, 'Sovremennoe pravoslavie,' op. cit., p. 69.
[173] Ibid.
[174] Klibanov, 'Sovremennoe sektantstvo v Lipetskoi oblasti,' op. cit., p. 160.

during the thirties the True Orthodox Christians were also active. They let only trusted fellow believers enter their homes and in order to protect themselves from the influence of the surrounding world placed chalk signs of the cross all over their homes in every conceivable place and kept the building tightly shuttered with the doors locked. 'The basic means of subsistence of the True Orthodox Christians consisted of seasonal labour for personal hire as sawyers, carpenters, stove makers, and also the production of hand-made icons and neck crosses, in which many of them engaged in speculation.'[175]

Similarly, one branch of this movement, the True Orthodox Christians in Hiding are extant in the Komi republic in the far north, and Soviet scholarship has traced its existence under this name back as early as the twenties.[176] A more widespread variant, the True Orthodox Christians Wanderers have also on occasion been postulated for the period of collectivization.[177] Both of these movements, which will be discussed in a subsequent chapter, have numerous points of similarity with Old Believer organizations, and hence the assertion that they may have existed during the pre-war period seems slightly less improbable than the attempt to find the True Orthodox Christians movement as a whole during these years.

Another underground Orthodox organization which was active in the Komi Republic, but apparently without connection to the movement described above, called themselves the *Burs'ylys'*, or 'singers of the good'. Founded in the nineteenth century, their goal was to translate Orthodoxy into the Komi language. They were much involved in the anti-collectivization resistance, and on one occasion, forty families slaughtered their cattle and moved into the deep forest. Leaders were brought to trial in the early thirties, but the movement was able to revive during and immediately after World War II.[178]

A large number of small, local organizations sprang up from time to time during these years, and can be roughly categorized in the Josephite schism. In 1931 a monarchist conspiracy was discovered in Ivanovo led by Bishop Avgustin and seven priests.[179] Numerous

[175] Iankova, 'Sovremennoe pravoslavie,' op. cit., p. 71.
[176] Gagarin, op. cit., p. 183.
[177] V. F. Milovidov, op. cit., p. 218.
[178] Gagarin, op. cit., pp. 170–3.
[179] Curtiss, op. cit., p. 260.

conspiracies of this sort were discovered in the anti-religious campaign during the Great Purges.

In Borovichskii region, Leningrad area, an illegal monastery was liquidated in 1937. The monks of this monastery went about the *kolkhozes*, gathered espionage data, and spread counter-revolutionary rumours. The leaders of the monastic spy gang were the local archbishop, a former Kolchak general, a former prince, and a former tsarist police officer.[180]

According to Pol'skii, Bishop Ioasaf of Chistopol' was in 1936–7 head of a secret Tikhonite group of fourteen people, including an archpriest and three nuns.[181] In another instance he describes a secret village led by a Bishop M. which had links with other underground groups all over the U.S.S.R. The village was so secret that even some of the surrounding underground groups did not know of its existence. Wooden crosses, toys, and the like were made and couriers were sent out to trade them for needed supplies. The secret police finally discovered the village and executed some of its inhabitants, imprisoning the rest.[182] Similarly, Pol'skii describes the return of a priest to Kharkov from prison, who organized church services in various apartments in the city in order to avoid the risks inherent on attending the legally open churches.[183] A priest such as this could act as

a sort of centre of a known circle of churchmen; he was visited by the clergy of monasteries which had been burned down, and priests, monks, nuns, and laymen of every age and every calling. All came: some to receive consolation in sorrow, some on church business, some for personal spiritual instruction.[184]

The various underground organizations embraced by the Josephite schism were by no means the only form of illegal religious activity available to the Russian populace during these years. The turmoil of collectivization and the subsequent years of confusion resulted in a swift rise in the influence of those illegal Orthodox and semi-Orthodox organizations which were already in existence, and a proliferation of similar groupings arising spontaneously in response to the times.

[180] *Krasnaia Zvezda*, 9 January 1938.
[181] Pol'skii, op. cit., II, 125.
[182] Ibid., pp. xix–xxi.
[183] Ibid., pp. 160–1.
[184] Ibid., p. 157.

The Imiaslavtsy again became prominent during the collectivization campaign, and joined in the agitation against the
kolkhozes: 'Think, Orthodox, where you are going: . . . it doesn't
matter, the end of the world is soon. . . .'[185] The believer, according
to the Imiaslavtsy, should 'whether he eats, whether he drinks,
whether he sits, whether he walks on the way, or whatever else
he does, continually call out, "Lord Jesus Christ, Son of God,
have mercy on me".'[186] One Soviet scholar reports that 'in
1928–29 [this] underground was liquidated and its leadership was
sentenced to forced labour'.[187] Many of its leaders were executed
in 1930.[188] Inasmuch as the movement was able to resume operations in 1944[189] and in 1947,[190] it seems unlikely that the liquidation was complete and that the movement ceased to exist entirely
during the thirties.

The Ioannity were also active during this period. In 1938,
organizations of Ioannity were uncovered in widely separated
areas of the country.[191] They constructed complex organizations
with couriers, go-betweens, missionaries, and colporteurs distributing their literature. They operated

under the cover of so-called co-operative and agricultural industrial
artels, had conspiratorial apartments and secret addresses, hiding
places and forged documents. The leaders often changed their place of
residence and entered into fictitious marriages. People who were singled
out for recruitment were assiduously studied for a long time.[192]

In their worship practices, the Ioannity refused to visit Orthodox
churches but conducted the Orthodox rites in home churches,
complete with the various paraphernalia of Orthodox worship
(icons, icon lamps, crosses, etc.). They 'deified the person of the
founder of the sect, they preached the nearness of the end of
the world, and they advocated renunciation of marriage'.[193]

[185] Klibanov, 'Sovremennoe sektantstvo v Tambovskoi oblasti,' op. cit., p. 94.
[186] Nikol'skaia, op. cit., pp. 165–6.
[187] Fedorenko, op. cit., p. 210.
[188] Boris Kandidov, *Tserkov' i shpionazh* ('The church and espionage') (Moscow: State Anti-religious Publishing House, 1938), p. 69.
[189] Fedorenko, op. cit., p. 210.
[190] *Z.M.P.*, No. 1 (January 1948), p. 76.
[191] Struve, op. cit., p. 230.
[192] Fedorenko, op. cit., p. 207.
[193] Ibid. It should be noted that any aberrations which may have been practised by the Ioannity are scarcely attributable to John of Kronstadt himself, whose Orthodoxy was unimpeachable.

Apparently the Ioannity were able to survive the decade handily.[194]

Similarly, the Apokalypsisty were also exceedingly active during the thirties. In 1934 they were able to establish groups in Vladivostok, Kirgizia, and the Voronezh area, and in 1941 underground Apokalypsisty were discovered in three different oblasts.[195]

A large number of other sects responded vigorously to the collectivization trauma. Among the more influential of these were the Fedorovtsy, whose activities intensified in direct response to the policy of enforced collectivization.[196] The doctrine of the sect had no substantial differences from normative Orthodox doctrine.[197] In the Voronezh area the sect had a developed network of branch organizations.

In 1928 there were ten to fifteen thousand sectarians of various sorts on the territory of the Voronezh area. The most numerous was the sect of the Evangelical Christians, consisting of 4,010 members united in 178 congregations. Besides the Evangelical Christians, in the area there were the following sects: Old Believers—1,172 people, Baptists—1,118, The New Union of Spiritual Israel—972, Mennonites—422, Sabbatarians—443, New Israelites—408, Molokans—247, Seventh Day Adventists—161, Ioannity—132, 'Followers of the Sacred Scripture'—48, Khlysty—44, Skoptsy—28, the sect of Zion—24, Tolstoyites—3, Fedorovtsy—several hundred.[198]

These figures might imply that the Fedorovtsy were very influential indeed, for the aggregate total of sectarians in the list is 9,232, and if the higher estimate of the total number of sectarians is at all accurate, the Fedorovtsy, by simple process of elimination, might seem astonishingly dominant.

The Fedorovtsy would adorn the walls of their huts with such slogans as 'Christ is risen', 'Blessed is the man that walketh not in

[194] Ibid.

[195] Ibid., p. 217.

[196] Klibanov, 'Sovremennoe sektantstvo v Tambovskoi oblasti,' op. cit., p. 93.

[197] M. B. Mitin, 'O nauchno-ateisticheskoi propaganda v svete postanovleniia TsK KPSS, "O zadachakh partiinoi propagandy v sovremennykh usloviiakh" ' ('Scientific atheistic propaganda in the light of the decision of the CC CPSU, "The tasks of Party propaganda in contemporary conditions" '), in AN SSSR, Uspekhi sovremennoi nauki i religiia ('Contemporary science's successes and religion') (Moscow: AN SSSR, 1961), p. 29.

[198] Aleksandrovich, op. cit., p. 62.

the counsel [soviet] of the ungodly', and 'Let God arise and scatter his enemies and let all that hate him flee from his face'.[199] Apocalypticism was a dominant theme among them; 'they considered themselves the angelic retinue of Christ in the approaching hour of his Second Coming'.[200] Not infrequently, this apocalyptic emphasis had direct tsarist overtones, and, indeed, one of their most popular hymns was not immune to a monarchistic interpretation:

> *Nadezhda i sila*
> *Na kniazia Mikhaila,*
> *Poslannika bozh'ego k nam.*
> *Pust' on okazhetsia strakhom velikim*
> *Vsem bezbozhnikam—*
> *Nashim vragam.*

(Hope and power/ To Prince Michael,/ Sent to us by God./ Let him show terrible judgement/ To all the godless—/ Our enemies.)[201]

The Fedorovtsy held that with the advent of collectivization, the world had entered the Last Times, and the end of the world was near.

The Fedorovtsy preached that 'the kingdom of anti-Christ has begun, the enemy of the human race is on the throne, and the time of the Second Coming and Terrible Judgement draws near'.

They preached that together with Christ will be the captain of the 'white army', the Archangel Michael, understanding by the latter the Grand Duke Michael. Evidently in order to help the coming Christ not to confuse the righteous with the sinners, the Fedorovtsy sewed a cross on their garments. The cottages of the Fedorovtsy were turned into home churches. Inhabitants visiting them, according to a witness, 'are struck with an innumerable quantity of icons hung everywhere. In several cottages, icons almost covered three walls.'[202]

In view of the imminence of the Second Coming of Christ, they

---

[199] Klibanov, 'Sovremennoe sektantstvo v Tambovskoi oblasti,' op. cit., p. 94. Interestingly enough, this last ('Let God arise,' etc.), which is known as the 'Prayer to the Cross of Honour' and was the most popular of all prayers among the Fedorovtsy (Nikol'skaia, op. cit., p. 165), was used to close the first message of the Sobor of 1917 after the Bolsheviks had taken Moscow. See Curtiss, op. cit., p. 41.

[200] Nikol'skaia, op. cit., p. 184.

[201] Aleksandrovich, op. cit., p. 61.

[202] Klibanov, 'Sovremennoe sektantstvo v Tambovskoi oblasti,' op. cit., p. 93.

advocated strict asceticism, without any contact whatsoever with the surrounding world of collective farmers.[203]

Not surprisingly, the Fedorovtsy came under fierce attack by the regime. One of the leaders was accused of having received 62,000 roubles from the U.S.A.,[204] and, apparently, was induced to confess this crime.[205] A mass trial was held in Voronezh in 1930, and yet the sect reappeared again in 1938 in the Donbas, and has survived to the present.[206]

The Cherdashniki were a new sect which arose in direct response to the collectivization campaign. They appeared to have been a rather syncretistic combination of Orthodox and *Khlyst* practices.[207]

In their rites the Cherdashniki placed 'a naked "Christ" on a table (shroud) half covered with a sheet (winding-sheet) and kissed him. Finally they reproduced the Resurrection and Ascension. They lifted the naked Khakilev (the leader of the Cherdashniki—A.K.) and climbed to the attic (*cherdak*) through an opening in the ceiling, and the followers cried in ecstasy, "Take us with you too," seizing him by the legs. The "appearance to the people" was reproduced in reverse order. From "heaven", i.e. from the attic, they lowered Khakilev on two towels to the table. At this time those present cried out "Lo, he approaches, he comes...." All of this is carried out with singing, reading, and instructions.'[208]

The Cherdashniki called themselves apostles, and their local surroundings Palestine. The *kolkhozes* were to be replaced by 'evangelical' arrangements, and 'dressed in long black clothes they went from village to village and agitated against the *kolkhozes*, for the triumph of the "kingdom of God on earth".'[209]

A great number of other underground religious sects flourished during the thirties. One study identified sixty-three discrete religious sects during this period.[210] Drifting further and further away from Orthodoxy, many of these underground groups seemed

---

[203] Fedorenko, op. cit., p. 210.

[204] Aleksandrovich, op. cit., p. 62.

[205] M. Sherwood, *The Soviet War on Religion* (New York: Workers' Library Publishers, 1930), p. 15.

[206] Struve, op. cit., p. 244.

[207] Fedorenko, op. cit., p. 210.

[208] Klibanov, 'Sovremennoe sektantstvo v Tambovskoi oblasti,' op. cit., p. 94.

[209] Nikol'skaia, op. cit., p. 165.

[210] V. F. Zybkovets, *Ot boga li nravstvennost'* ('Is morality from God') (Moscow: State Publishing House for Political Literature, 1961), p. 33.

more similar to the traditional 'priestless' organizations of the Old Believers.[211] Other groups developed their own aberrations. According to one accusation of dubious merit, a certain Bishop F. converted to Roman Catholicism and began helping the Jesuits in central Russia.[212] In another case a mystic enjoyed considerable influence over a Komsomol youth, leading him to wear a crown of barbed wire.[213]

A large number of sects were commonly designated *Krasnodrakonovtsy* or Sects of the Red Dragon. Such underground organizations were united by a common apocalyptic emphasis in their outlook. Considering the communist regime the Red Dragon, in allusion to the twelfth Chapter of *Revelation*, one of these sects, the Korneevtsy,

would not cut their hair in order to be like Christ; they lived locked up and would not send their children to school ('it doesn't matter, the end of the world is soon'). In the sect marriage was also postponed to that day when each man would have seven women. The sectarians believed that such a time would come after the Red Dragon came out of the rock. They did not participate in social life, for the entire secular world, according to their words, was marked with the seal of the Red Dragon— the five pointed star.

Entry into the sect was accomplished by savage rites. Aside from the fact that the recommendation of trusted people was obligatory for entry into the sect, and it was necessary to pay a considerable sum of money to Father Kornei, the one joining the sect had to pass under 'Dido's trousers'. Kornei dressed in white trousers and stood on two benches, and the apprentice would pass between his legs trying not to touch the old man's trousers. If he succeeded, it meant that the apprentice 'was worthy of God'; if not, it meant that he was dishonourable and unworthy of admission to the sect.[214]

The Shashkovtsi were another local example of the Sects of the Red Dragon. 'The Shashkovtsi predicted the imminent end of the world, the Terrible Judgement when fire from heaven would burn the "Red Dragon" and all non-believers and everything on earth in general.'[215] The Shashkovtsi specifically identified

[211] Timasheff, op. cit., pp. 85–6.

[212] *Izvestiia*, 23 November 1937.

[213] *Komsomol'skaia Pravda*, 22 June 1931.

[214] Fedorenko, op. cit., p. 206.

[215] A. Terskoi, *U sektantov* ('Among the sectarians') (Moscow: Publishing House for Political Literature, 1965), p. 28.

the Soviet Government as the Red Dragon.[216] Unfortunately, in the case of this local Red Dragon sect, classification becomes difficult, for the founder, Shashkov, was originally a *Khlyst*.

There were great numbers of these groups, usually exceedingly small in size and circumscribed in their influence.[217] The great majority of the sects of the Red Dragon were spontaneous in origin and ascribed to practices far removed from traditional Orthodox Christianity. Many of them, sharing as they did common features with indigenous Russian traditions such as the *Khlysty* or with Protestant Christian groups such as the Pentecostals, fall outside the scope of this study. Nevertheless, it should be noted that these Sects of the Red Dragon not only shared many features (apocalypticism, alienation from society, etc.) with the more traditionally Orthodox underground groups; they also may be presumed during this period to have drawn a large proportion of their adherents from the Orthodox tradition. Thus the Sects of the Red Dragon, however bizarre, represented a live option for individuals of Orthodox faith who were gravitating towards the underground, and these sects exercised a considerable influence on the less extreme versions of underground religion.

We repeat, the stronghold of religious fervour in the U.S.S.R. is not within the Orthodox Church but in the 'mystical' sects. The deepest manifestation of the people's religion is expressed in them, and they are waging a fight to the death against the materialism of Soviet actuality.[218]

Towards the fringes of the underground Orthodox movement, the distinction between the various discrete groupings began to become obfuscated. This does not seem unusual in view of the conditions of secrecy and danger in which these movements flourished.[219] There was a general tendency to forget religious differences in the common struggle,[220] and much interchange of ideas and influence took place between such groups as the Fedorovtsy, Imiaslavtsy, Cherdashniki, and the like, and the dominant Tikhonite movement.[221] Not unexpectedly, this tendency of common effort extended to the various branches of

---

[216] Ibid., p. 38.
[217] Timasheff, op. cit., p. 87.
[218] Danzas, op. cit., p. 163.
[219] Pauline B. Taylor, 'Sectarians in Soviet Courts,' *Russian Review*, XXIV, 3 (July 1965), p. 279.
[220] Lagovskii, op. cit., p. 30.
[221] Klibanov, 'Sovremennoe sektantstvo v Tambovskoi oblasti,' op. cit., pp. 94–5.

the Old Believers on the local level.[222] Nor indeed did such common action remain within the general Orthodox family, for in times of crisis Baptists were observed joining with Orthodox in a common front against attack by the regime.[223] Indeed, on occasion Orthodox priests showed a willingness to forget religious differences to the extent of joining with unbelievers in common goals.[224] Thus there was a widespread tendency to overcome the traditional exclusiveness of the sectarian mentality, and as a result exact classification of the various divisions within the underground religious movements becomes all but impossible.

There were a number of elements common to all branches of underground religious organizations during this period, and, indeed, many of these attitudes were quite prevalent in the legally existing churches as well. The entire countryside was hostile to the enforced collectivization movement, and religious people shared in resisting it.[225] Despite the attempts to limit their impact on society, clergy of all denominations attempted to reach into the villages to conduct individual persuasion among the believers.[226] Nor were such active religious workers without support in the local population. In one village a note was affixed to the door of the local party organizer warning, 'If you don't quit talking against religion we'll break your legs'.[227] In part such hostility as this was elicited by the regime itself, which often succumbed to the temptation of convicting the priest as a plausible moral instigator of such action, whether or not he was actually guilty.[228] Religious opposition to measures of the regime continued even after the worst of the collectivization campaign was over. Revised farming methods, the continuous work week, 'socialist competition,' schools, theatres, newspapers, and the like became targets of religious opposition.[229] For example, there

[222] *Komsomol'skaia Pravda*, 15 November 1936.
[223] *Pravda*, 13 April 1928.
[224] L. Dunaevskii, 'II Vsesoiuznaia konferentsiia nauchno-issledovatel'skikh uchrezhdenii po antireligioznoi rabote' ('The II National conference of scientific research institutions on anti-religious work'), *Vestnik Kommunisticheskoi Akademii*, No. 4 (1934), p. 100.
[225] 'Vreditel'skaia deiatel'nost' tserkovnikov i sektantov,' op. cit., pp. 97–8.
[226] *Antireligioznik*, No. 10 (October 1937), p. 56.
[227] P. Fedoseev, 'Marksizm-leninizm o bor'be s religiei' ('Marxism-Leninism on the struggle with religion'), *Pod Znamenem Marksizma*, No. 3 (March 1937), p. 153; cf. Krasnikov, op. cit., p. 194.
[228] W. H. Chamberlin, *Russia's Iron Age* (Boston: Little, Brown, 1934), p. 321.
[229] Sherwood, op. cit., pp. 23–4.

9

were numerous charges that churchmen were spreading rumours that influenza epidemics were caused by the increased strain of 'socialist competition' among the workers.[230]

All of these may be taken as indications of a general—and acute—phenomenon prevalent among religious people throughout the period: alienation from society, or at least from that society which the regime was bent on imposing by whatever means necessary. Conditions for all religious believers were exceedingly tense, and such alienation was a common and indeed almost inescapable result. If this was true of those who were attempting to remain within the legalized religious organizations, it was magnified many times among those who had either abandoned the few remaining legalized churches, or who had had their churches closed against their will. All of the underground movements were deeply infected with alienation against society or against the dominant forces in society.

A second common feature throughout the country was the result of the State's rigorous proscription of the publication and circulation of religious literature. Particularly among the underground groups, the body of religious literature available to them was relatively scant. Hence a very small number of devotional, doctrinal, or mystical treatises (such as 'The Visions of John of Kronstadt') were utilized by various independent, local and regional organizations, thereby accounting for a large measure of similarity between otherwise isolated underground sectarian groups. Furthermore, the restriction of literature applicable to their interests to these few early works guaranteed that to a measure, at least, subsequent underground organizations would share the political hostility towards the central regime which these earlier compositions had contained.

In addition, a peculiar sort of informal substitute for the lack of literature was utilized, not only in all branches of the religious underground but in the legalized parishes as well. These were a form of 'chain letter' which would receive wide (and, of course, always anonymous) circulation among believers.[231] Commonly called 'letters from God' or 'letters from heaven', these messages, purporting to be of supernatural origin, regularly contained threats against the collectivization movement during the early

[230] Fedoseev, op. cit., p. 153: *Komsomol'skaia Pravda*, 15 November 1936.
[231] Amosov, op. cit., p. 51.

years.[232] Iaroslavskii gave examples of this genre of literature in 1931:

I am thy Lord God, and I say unto thee: the moment has come when the devil will lead the people astray into his nets, into the *kolkhozes*. He who is not seduced by the *kolkhoz* will be saved, but in the days to come I shall wipe out all the *kolkhozes*, and I shall also wipe out those who do not wear a cross on their breasts.

Dear *kolkhoz* comrades: I send you a letter from the heavenly kingdom, in which I ask you to withdraw from the *kolkhoz* and to take upon yourselves the shock work of ruining the *kolkhoz*. He who does not assume this task will go directly to hell, while he who assumes it will be received by me among the Holy Saints and will attain the heavenly kingdom.[233]

In addition to such politically oriented exhortations, 'letters from heaven' would often contain simple ethical or devotional instructions, and in the complete absence of other forms of devotional literature could be so utilized by the recipient. 'Letters from heaven' remained a common phenomenon throughout the period.[234]

The most pronounced attribute which was common to all branches of the underground movement was the large role played by apocalypticism.[235] A habitual concomitant of social alienation, apocalypticism 'increased in the U.S.S.R. in the period 1929–32'.[236] In particular, the collectivization drive was interpreted in apocalyptic imagery.[237]

In the Soviet Union counter-revolutionary elements among churchmen and especially in the sectarian organizations made extensive use of the tale of the coming of anti-Christ and the drawing near of 'the end of the world', to frighten the workers and to distract them from active participation in the building of socialism. A great number of absurd counter-revolutionary tales about 'anti-Christ' and 'the end of the world' were disseminated by the kulaks in the period of intensive collectivization in order to restrain the peasants from entering *kolkhozes*.[238]

[232] M. M. Sheinman, *Religion and the Church in U.S.S.R.* (Moscow: Cooperative Publishing Society of Foreign Workers, 1933), pp. 31–2.

[233] Iaroslavskii, 'Zadachi antireligioznoi propagandy v period sotsial'nogo nastupleniia,' op. cit., pp. 47–8.

[234] E.g., Oleshchuk, op. cit., p. 104.

[235] *Pravda*, 15 April 1937; Danzas, op. cit., pp. 158–9.

[236] *Komsomol'skaia Pravda*, 24 September 1937.

[237] Sheinman, *Religion and the Church in U.S.S.R.*, op. cit., p. 33.

[238] 'Antikhrist' (Anti-Christ), *Antireligioznik*, No. 5 (May 1941), p. 44.

This apocalyptic orientation continued throughout the decade, and particularly as the clouds of World War II appeared on the horizon, apocalypticism became intense. 'A world war has blazed up, and churchmen and preachers carry on conversations that this is the last war and next will come "the end of the world".'[239]

Thus the years prior to World War II were marked by a relatively intense degree of underground Orthodox activity, deeply alienated from society and increasingly prone to eschatological (and, indeed, chiliastic) interpretations of their surroundings. Primarily a response to measures taken against religion by the regime, underground religious activity very quickly became an inseparable part of pre-war life in the Russian countryside and exerted an influence which survived the most vigorous attempts of the Government to put an end to such potentially dangerous activity. Regardless of how quiescent or militant such groups might be, they represented a segment of society which was profoundly and outspokenly hostile to the ruling forces in society. This hostility precluded any hope of securing the co-operation or of utilizing the capabilities of this element in the population, and the only means the regime could devise to reduce their hostile influence within society was to apply the most Draconian of measures—arrest, imprisonment, confinement with forced labour, and execution. Even these measures were far from successful, however, for the ingenuity of the adepts of underground religious life managed to frustrate every attempt to put an end to their activity. The State was able to uncover and close down specific cells and groups of the underground Orthodox movements only with the greatest difficulty, and very often the success achieved against one unit of an underground organization would be counterbalanced by the continuing activities of other units which managed to escape detection.

Underground Orthodox movements survived the decade and continued to exercise an influence in the turbulent conditions of the pre-war Soviet Union. Just as important was the potential which these experienced veterans of underground Orthodoxy possessed for influencing the subsequent clandestine Orthodox organizations which were to spring up in the U.S.S.R.

---

[239] F. M. Putintsev, in a speech of January 1941, in *Antireligioznik*, No. 3 (March 1941), p. 49.

V

The Prison System

Underground Orthodox movements in the U.S.S.R. have always operated quite outside the law, and as a result the threat of the prison system has always loomed large in their activities. At various times a large number of the adherents, and possibly a majority of the leaders of these organizations have spent a period in prison or exile, and as a result the experiences of such believers in the Soviet penal system have formed an influential part of the background of all underground Orthodox organizations throughout the Soviet period.

In general, the Soviet prison system may be divided into three separate aspects: the actual prisons existing in every city and town, and used primarily as places of detention during investigation and as places of confinement for a very small portion of those convicted of crimes; the labour camps in which the vast majority of the convicts served; and the various forms of exile imposed directly or upon completion of the prescribed term at the labour camps. The prison system has played a far larger role in Soviet society than in many other countries, both because of the regime's reliance on arrest and detention (threatened or carried out) in enforcing its will upon society, and because of the sheer size which the prison population attained in various periods.

At its peak, an estimated eight to twelve million people or perhaps more were serving in the prison system of the U.S.S.R. Forced labour camps with immense populations were established in numerous locations of the country, most of them very remote and with rigorous climatic conditions inhibiting voluntary population of the area. An immense administrative machinery under the direct jurisdiction of the secret police was required to operate this vast system. Its population was supplied by mass arrests, and the majority of its inhabitants were convicted on political grounds.

Non-political criminals formed only a small percentage of the prison population.

Initially, the prison system was developed primarily in order to remove potentially dangerous elements from society. Serving as places of confinement, the prison camps performed the function of temporarily or permanently eliminating potentially or actually harmful elements from the population. Very quickly, however, the regime came to realize that work performed by such prisoners could be of considerable value and was much preferable to allowing the incarcerated to remain in idleness. With the burgeoning of the prison population during the collectivization and industrialization campaign, the State had at its disposal a large working force which could be made to produce, and the labour camps very quickly assumed a position of importance in the Soviet economy. At its peak, an estimated one-sixth of the State budget was allocated to the prison system, and the State received an immensely profitable return from the labour extracted from its prisoners. A large proportion of domestic fishing, mining, and forestry was accomplished by the forced labour system, and numerous vast projects of transformation of nature (dams, canals, etc.) were made possible by the immense prison system. If the cost in lives was staggering, the benefits derived by the State from this forced labour were exceedingly rich, when compared with the relatively small amount of non-human capital which had to be invested to achieve these results. In any case, the regime apparently felt that the human cost was insignificant, in view of the fact that many of the convicts might otherwise have been executed outright.

Thus the prison system served the dual function of eliminating a large mass of politically undesirable people from the population and at the same time giving the State a means to achieve results with minimum investment, particularly in projects which required large expenditures of manual labour. In view of the relatively small amounts of capital available to the State for investment, and particularly inasmuch as the programme of enforced industrialization necessitated the allocation of all available capital to heavy industry to the complete neglect of other sectors of the economy, such a means of achieving maximum, immediate results with minimum investment was very attractive indeed to the regime.

A third function of the prison system was widely publicized in the Soviet press. The prisons allegedly were designed, not to exact punishment according to some theory of retributive justice, but to re-educate those who had been convicted. According to Soviet propaganda, the utilization of forced labour in the prison system would re-educate recalcitrant individuals into that love of work on which communism bases its theoretical system. In view of the realities of the prison system, this alleged function may safely be ignored.

The history of the Soviet prison system went through several stages. Prior to the late twenties conditions in the prison camps, while rigorous enough, were by no means completely unbearable. Particularly with regard to religion, a large role was played during these years by the prison complex of the Solovky Islands in the far north. Here a large number of clerics and laymen were sent after their arrest, and at least when contrasted with conditions facing similar unfortunates during later periods, living conditions were tolerable. Considerable opportunity was available for religious worship, group discussions among fellow believers, etc.

With the discovery that the labour camps were economically important in the late twenties, this period of relative relaxation came to an end. Religious convicts, together with all others, were subjected to exceedingly difficult conditions and mere survival became their chief consideration. The system of forced labour camps expanded vigorously with the programme of enforced collectivization, and, in particular, the decision to 'eliminate the kulaks as a class' made a large contribution to its population. Throughout the thirties an exceedingly large prison population was maintained.

World War II brought a brief hiatus in the operations of the prison system. Labour camps in areas subject to possible occupation by the Germans were transferred to safer areas, or in some cases their inhabitants were executed *en masse* to prevent their defection to the Germans. A considerable number of convicts were released in advance of the completion of their sentences in order to provide for the man-power needs of the Red Army. As will become evident below, a small number of others were also released for other reasons.

The prison system resumed full-scale operation with the waning of World War II. Prisoners-of-war were arbitrarily enlisted in its ranks, and large numbers of Soviet citizens who had been exposed to the dangerous influences of contact with non-Soviet societies were summarily transferred to the forced labour population. In addition, a considerable portion of the populations of newly acquired areas were remanded to the prisons before and after the war, together with a number of minority nationalities considered by the regime to be unreliable or to have acted treasonably during the war. From World War II until the death of Stalin, the forced labour system operated with all the vigour to which it had become accustomed during the pre-war decade.

The death of Stalin, and particularly the reduction of the secret police which followed the execution of Beria in 1953, resulted in a vast reduction in the forced labour system. The majority of the convicts were emancipated in the mid-fifties, and of the remainder only a small percentage were kept confined in the few remaining labour camps, while the rest were released to rigidly supervised exile, generally in the area adjacent to the camp in which they had served. This form of exile, while still subjecting its inhabitants to rigorous conditions of life, was immensely preferable to actual confinement in the labour camps.

It would appear that by the middle sixties, the forced labour system had begun to enjoy a revival. The increasing severity of the regime against any form of dissent provided a flow of candidates for the camps, and as a result the forced labour system began to awaken from its dormancy of the preceding decade. While the prison system has by no means yet assumed anything like the proportions it enjoyed during the Stalin period, nevertheless the latter part of the sixties showed a marked increase in the regime's reliance on this form of punishment, as contrasted with the decade following Stalin's death.

Conditions in the labour camps were extreme. Inmates were required to fulfil staggering work assignments. Tasks were generally designed to approach the maximum manual achievement of which the human body is physically capable. Work quotas were sufficiently large to demand intense exertion during nearly every waking hour.

In addition, the food level was held to the barest minimum. Generally consisting of bread and exceedingly thin soup or gruel, the daily rations normally were set so low as to make survival doubtful. Malnutrition was almost universal, and starvation was a very real possibility. Vitamin deficiencies were common, causing bleeding gums, loss of teeth, etc., and were an unavoidable fate awaiting the great majority of those prisoners who managed to survive long terms in the labour camps.

Generally the daily ration of food was made contingent upon fulfilment of the prescribed work norm. Those who for any reason fell short of fulfilling their work norm were given a correspondingly reduced daily food ration. Thus began a vicious circle, in which weakness caused by the diminished diet reduced the ability to work, causing further reductions in the food ration, in a descending spiral which could only end in death. Conversely, those who were strong enough could aspire to an increased food ration by attempting to exceed the already staggering daily work norm. The disadvantage to this approach, however, was that such immense exertions nearly always resulted in death from heart failure within two to five years. In addition, because many of the labour camps were located in areas of extreme climatic conditions, the death rate due to exposure was also exceedingly high. Those populations transferred from warm areas of the south to the arctic climate of the far north very quickly succumbed. All of these factors combined to give an average life expectancy of three to five years at some of the worst camps. Only the hardiest could look forward with any degree of hope to surviving the ten or twenty-five year sentences which were common at various periods.

The degree of supervision varied considerably from one camp to another. Some camps were under an exceedingly strict regime, while others were run in a somewhat more relaxed manner. Even the inmates at the best of the camps, however, were subject to the rigorous discipline of work, food, and weather. Escape was a vain hope; once reaching the camps, very, very few managed to make good their escape. Generally the camps were in areas so remote that even if the escapee could avoid detection by the guards, he had almost no hope of surviving the vast distances to be travelled to the nearest point of civilization. In less remote areas, the secret police organized the indigenous population very effectively against any escapees, offering attractive inducements for their capture.

If for no reason other than its immense size, the prison system is of direct relevance to an understanding of illegal religion in the

U.S.S.R. This is particularly so in view of the fact that any sort of affiliation with underground Orthodox practices was punishable upon discovery by incarceration in the labour camps. The very existence of this form of penal servitude thus would hover in the background for every member of the underground movement, and for a very large proportion of them the labour camps were their ultimate destination.

In a way, the camps served as a sort of 'theological seminary' for the leadership of underground Orthodoxy. A large proportion of its active leaders, at one time or another, passed through the forced labour system. In many respects, this experience coloured their outlook and determined the forms of worship which they imparted to their followers when they resumed their activity.

With regard to religion, the labour camps served as a great equalizer. The distinction between a legalized priest and an underground priest disappeared entirely in the camps. Once one had been arrested and sentenced to forced labour, it made no practical difference whatsoever whether he considered himself affiliated to an illegal Orthodox organization or to one of the legal groups. Thus members of illegal organizations were thrown into intimate contact with former members of the legalized Church, and the earlier controversies and disagreements were overshadowed by the general struggle to survive. In particular, the question over the Church's political attitude towards the regime became largely irrelevant in practice, for it would be very difficult indeed for victims of the regime to continue to place great emphasis on the advantages of loyalty.

Living conditions in the labour camps necessitated the use of clandestine techniques if any expression of religious life were to be achieved at all. Thus the mechanics of underground religious practices—services held in secret, methods which could be used to avoid detection, production of items necessary for divine services from materials at hand, independent organization of religious life in the absence of a functioning Church hierarchy, etc.—were learned by every active believer in the prison population. Experience in the camps could be applied directly to the organization of underground religious life upon release from confinement.

Individualism was forced upon every religious believer in the forced labour system. Only rarely were groups able to worship together. Despite the Orthodox tradition of collective worship, the conditions in the camps forced all believers to rely upon themselves if their faith were to be expressed at all. The necessity to stand alone in the faith and the realization with the passage of time that one can do so was of immense value to those who had passed through the prison experience, for in their subsequent life they could act with greater resilience to meet the difficulties imposed by the State's attack against organized, collective religion.

Finally, the experience of prison conditions resulted in a considerable broadening of outlook for many of the religious inmates. There simply was not sufficient time or energy available to indulge in religious disputes, and in the face of the extreme struggle for mere survival, religious differences generally remained in the background. All branches of Orthodoxy were thrown together in intimate and inescapable association, and Orthodox found themselves closely allied with Protestants of all kinds, members of indigenous Christian and semi-Christian sects, and even Jews and Muslims in the common effort to retain some measure of faith in the face of the extreme challenge of camp life.

Thus an examination of Orthodoxy in the prison camps is imperative for a proper understanding of underground Orthodoxy in the U.S.S.R. Unfortunately, no comprehensive, systematic studies of the phenomenon are available. A large number of memoirs and reports of former inmates are available, but even this relatively extensive literature is insufficient for the derivation of a balanced assessment of religion in the entire prison system, either in terms of its various historical periods, or in terms of its geographic extent. At best one can gain an impression of Orthodoxy in the prison system through the random observations of such believers which may be found in the prison literature. It does not seem feasible, however, to attempt to classify these observations either in terms of time or geography, and hence one can only hope at best to derive an impressionistic understanding of Orthodoxy in the prison camps.

There is no way of estimating with any degree of accuracy the proportion of the prison population at any given time who were serving sentences as a result of their religious activities. According to N. Teodorovich, 'Returnees from such camps report that of every thousand prisoners, at least twenty are priests, and of these at least one-half are Russian Orthodox.'[1] Clergymen of all denominations—not only Orthodox priests, but Roman Catholic priests or Protestant pastors, and Jewish rabbis, were a common feature of the labour camps.[2] According to Victor Tchernavin:

During my stay in the Shpalernaya prison, there were always in each cell from ten to fifteen persons held in connection with cases involving questions of religion. And there were some of them in isolation cells, so that their number must have been about ten per cent of all the prison inmates.[3]

Andreev asserts that 'according to official data of the Scientific Research Criminological Cabinet in 1928, in the Soviet concentration camps, the number of those condemned for Church affairs reached twenty per cent of all prisoners of the concentration camps'.[4] However, unless Andreev is here exercising more critical judgement than usual, it might be well to treat this figure somewhat cautiously. Surely it is a low figure if one refers to that proportion of the prison population who would consider themselves religious believers, for the prisoners represented a fairly broad cross-section of society, and therefore fifty per cent or more would probably fall into this category. On the other hand, if the figure refers to those convicted specifically for religious offences, then it would seem an uncommonly high estimate not only for the early collectivization period, when the kulaks were being eliminated as a class, but also for other periods. The secret police were exceedingly democratic in their practices of indiscriminate arrest, and it would not seem that the problem of religion occupied as much as one-fifth of their attention at any given period.

Even less persuasive is the statement of Bishop Antonii of Los

[1] Nadezhda Teodorovich, 'The Russian Orthodox,' in Institute for the Study of the U.S.S.R., *Genocide in the U.S.S.R.* (New York: Scarecrow Press, 1958), p. 209. It would not appear that such reports should be used for facile generalizations. If 8–12,000,000 inmates be taken as the estimated peak population of the prison system, these proportions would yield a clerical population of 160–240,000, of whom 80–120,000 would be Russian Orthodox priests. In view of the fact that in 1914 the Church had only 50,150 deans and priests in the whole Russian Empire (Curtiss, op. cit., p. 10), the proportion of priests to the entire prison population accepted by Teodorovich seems intrinsically improbable.

[2] F. Beck and W. Godin, *Russian Purge and the Extraction of Confession* (London: Hurst and Blackett, 1951), p. 128.

[3] V. Tchernavin, *I Speak for the Silent* (New York: Hale, Cushman, and Flint, 1935), p. 145.

[4] Andreev, *O polozhenii pravoslavnoi tserkvi v sovetskom soiuze*, op. cit., p. 8.

Angeles. Referring to recent *émigrés* who had spent ten years in the post-war prison camps, he states:

These witnesses report that not far from Vorkuta a special concentration camp was built for 'unmasked churchmen', i.e. members of the secret church who do not recognize the Moscow Patriarchate. The significance of the revelation of the existence of this camp is indicated by the fact that usually the Soviet Government does not construct a concentration camp for less than 50,000 prisoners. And if so many are 'revealed churchmen', how many should remain 'unrevealed'?[5]

Konstantinov repeats this story, claiming that a special camp for clergy was transferred from the Solovky Islands (apparently used during the twenties as a special receiving point for those arrested on religious grounds) to the steppes near the Aral Sea. He states that this camp survived the reduction of the prison camp system during the mid-fifties with some 30,000 clergy incarcerated in it.[6] According to George Grabbe, a special camp for monastics existed.[7] Almost certainly these reports are without foundation; nevertheless, the fact remains that clergy were no strangers to the prison system.

Russian Orthodox bishops were by no means exempt from sentence in camps. This was especially true of the twenties, when prison conditions were sufficiently relaxed as to allow a degree of differentiation among the prisoners. In subsequent periods, the extreme conditions in the camps tended to blur distinctions of rank among prisoners, and bishops generally were absorbed into the great sea of grey along with all other prisoners and were seldom more visible than lower clergy or even simple believers.

On the Solovky Islands, however, bishops were commonly to be found among the estimated 400 clergymen incarcerated there in the middle twenties. According to Dallin and Nikolaevsky,

Prominent among them were Bishop Illarion (Troitski) who was closely associated with the late Patriarch Tikhon, Bishop Manuil (Lemeshevski) who managed the Leningrad bishopric after the execution of Metropolitan Benjamin; Bishop Peter of Tambov, who died in 1924 in the

[5] Bishop Antonii, *O polozhenii tserkvi v sovetskoi rossii i o dukhovnoi zhizni russkago naroda* ('The situation of the Church in Soviet Russia and the spiritual life of the Russian people') (Jordanville, New York: Holy Trinity Monastery, 1960), p. 49.
[6] Dimitry Konstantinov, 'The Results of Soviet Persecution of the Orthodox Church,' *Bulletin of the Institute for the Study of the U.S.S.R.*, No. 5 (May 1965), pp. 45–6.
[7] Grabbe, op. cit., p. 184.

penal section on Sekirny mountain; the vicar of Saratov (Sokolov);
Bishop Serafim of Kolpino; the Father Superior of the Kazan
monastery, Pitirim (Krylov).[8]

Among them, Bishop Illarion was especially revered. His fellow
prisoners called him locum tenens of the patriarchal throne,
according to an apocryphal story which circulated among the
prisoners that he had been secretly appointed to this position by
Patriarch Tikhon.[9]

These imprisoned bishops maintained an active religious life,
continuing even while in prison to do whatever possible for the
good of the Orthodox Church. Andreev relates,

Their Graces Viktor, Illarion, Nektarii and Maksim not only often
served in secret, catacomb services in the forests of the island, they even
conducted secret ordination of several new bishops. They did this in
strictest secrecy even from their very closest associates so that in case
of arrest and examination they could not betray the truth of the secret
bishops to the G.P.U. Only on the eve of my departure from Solovky
did I learn from my close friend, one celibate priest, that he no longer
was a priest, but a secret bishop.[10]

Such secret ordinations in the prison camps continued after the
beginning of the collectivization campaign, and apparently were
carried out in other camps throughout the country as well.[11]
This concern for the continued viability of the institutional Orthodox Church seemed to remain constant among the imprisoned
bishops, even though the Orthodox prisoners were by no means
unanimous in their evaluation of whether, indeed, there was any
hope for the future of the Church.

His Grace Maksim was a pessimist and prepared for the worst trials of
the last times, not believing in the possibility of a rebirth of Russia. But
His Grace Viktor was an optimist and believed in the possibility of a
brief but bright period as the last gift from heaven for the weary Russian
people.[12]

[8] David J. Dallin and Boris I. Nicolaevsky, Forced Labor in Soviet Russia (New Haven,
Connecticut: Yale University Press, 1947), p. 175.
[9] Boris Shiriaev, Neugasimaia lampada ('The inextinguishable icon-lamp') (New
York: Chekhov Press, 1954), p. 318.
[10] Pol'skii, op. cit., II, 30.
[11] Andreev, O polozhenii pravoslavnoi tserkvi v sovetskom soiuze, op. cit., p. 9.
[12] Pol'skii, op. cit., II, 72.

With the increasing stringency of conditions in the camps, however, bishops became much less noticeable among the millions of prisoners. They continued to serve, sometimes in highly skilled capacities, as in the case of a prison surgeon who was a secret bishop.[13] It should be borne in mind, however, that bishops, even those secretly ordained, were limited in number and suffered an exceedingly high mortality rate. According to reports compiled by Nikita Struve, 24 bishops are known to have died in the period 1918–24, and 13 more in the period 1927–34. During the Great Purges, 52 bishops are known to have succumbed: 40 were shot, 5 died from other causes, and 7 were arrested and never heard from again. In this number were one bishop who had been in prison since 1918, and nine who had been at Solovky since 1923. Three of the members of Metropolitan Sergii's Synod (Archbishop Serafim, Archbishop Konstantin, and Metropolitan Anatolii) were among those who died, as were Metropolitan Iosif and six other bishops of the Josephite schism.[14]

Priests, of course, were much more commonly observed among the prison population. Many of them were sources of great comfort and encouragement to their fellow prisoners. Boris Shiriaev relates in considerable detail the story of a certain Nikodim, at Solovky during the twenties, who was a source of great comfort and encouragement to his fellow prisoners. A devout man, he 'observed the liturgy, rising earlier than anyone else and going to a secluded corner'. Shiriaev relates numerous conversations Nikodim had with his fellow prisoners, such as the following:

'And I hold services whenever possible.'
'Here? In the barracks?'
'Here, every third day. They haven't noticed yet. And when they brought us here I held services.'
'Didn't they bring you here in a "Stolypin" car? In three-man cages?'
'In the same.'
'How then did you hold service? In those cages you can't even stand up.'
'. . . There we held service. We were lying down. On one side of me was a swindler, and on the other a Tatar of the Caucasus, a Mohammedan. It was getting late, the train was swaying over the rails, the

---

[13] Ibid., pp. 25–6.
[14] Struve, op. cit., French edition, pp. 354–7.

soldier went beyond the grating. Quiet. And I held vespers: "From my youth. . . ." And when I came to the great glorification (I was praying in a whisper, as was the Tatar also, quietly, and to himself), at the Glorification in a full voice I proclaimed: "Lord God, Lamb of God, who takest away the sins of the world, accept our prayer." Here even the swindler crossed himself. Every evening I held service thus, the entire nine days, while they brought us in the car. What do you mean I have no parish? The Lord promised, where in His name two or three are gathered together, He is there in their midst, and there were three of us together then.' . . .

'Here it is, my parish, unworthy priest that I am. His parish who loved man, the blind, the weak, the bleeding, the lepers, the raving, and all, all thirsting for His miracle, praying for His miracle.'

In the prison he regularly performed services in a whisper and even administered the Eucharist, using cranberry juice instead of wine on the theory that wine being unavailable, the cranberry also was grown by the same Gardener.

In another conversation Nikodim was told that in view of the prison conditions, he was worthless, *nihil*.

'I, *nihil*!' Father Nikodim jumped up off the plank-bed. 'Who is this who can turn me, a son of the Lord, his creature and besides that a priest, into a *nihil*. I was a priest, a priest I am. Look, by my entire form a priest!' . . .

'In what respect am I not a priest? And again, I am a man, created in the image and likeness of God, and you say *nihil*, a void!' Father Nikodim even spat to one side. 'And my parish has not been taken away. Who deprives me of my parish? Here it is, my parish, see how it is, . . . three layers on both sides, what a rich parish!'

An accomplished raconteur, he regaled the prisoners with biblical stories. On one occasion when he was discovered by the guards during a Christmas service, he refused to break the rule that a service once begun may not be interrupted, and only gestured with his hands, persuading the guard to postpone the interruption.[15]

With the expansion of the prison system into a fully developed forced labour population, priests became a concomitant part of the system. They were variously treated. Tchernavin reported that priests 'form a special class; according to special instructions from the G.P.U. they are sent only to hard manual labour or, in

[15] Shiriaev, op. cit., pp. 248–63.

cases of complete disability, are appointed night watchmen'.[16] In other cases, priests served as barracks orderlies.[17] Incentives were sometimes offered (e.g., false promises of reduction of sentence) to clergy in order to elicit more work from them.[18] One elderly priest was observed to have a comparatively desirable job in the bath house.[19] In another case, a criminal reproached an old priest, 'You gents of the clergy have it easy; they make watchmen of you, for you are known to make the very best watchmen.'[20]

Despite the relatively relaxed conditions at Solovky during the early period, there were many burdensome aspects of the prison which priests had to endure.

The confinement of Russian priests at Solovky was an elaborate blasphemy. Detention in a monastery which from time immemorial had attracted numerous pilgrims and had now been converted into a concentration camp must have been felt by the priests as a special insult. The administration, far from sparing their feelings, compelled them to witness the profanation of former churches. Along with other prisoners, the priests were housed in the Troitskii and Preobrazhenskii Cathedrals. They were subjected to studied humiliation. In the middle twenties the commandant of the Kremlin division ordered forced hair cuttings for them.[21]

Apropos of the latter, George Kitchin reports an incident of shaving necessitated by a typhus epidemic:

The unfortunate priests wept as they parted with their luxuriant hair and beards. They exhorted the commanders and sent them petitions explaining that their religious order forbade them to cut off their beards. It was to no avail; all of them were shaved clean and deprived of their marks of distinction from other prisoners.[22]

Because of the critical need for some sort of consolation and encouragement, priests were often held in special esteem by fellow prisoners, and great energies were expended to protect the priest as much as possible from the harshest aspects of prison life. On

---

[16] V. Tchernavin, op. cit., p. 262.
[17] Gustav Herling, *A World Apart* (London: William Heinemann, 1951), p. 35.
[18] V. Tchernavin, op. cit., p. 307.
[19] Herling, op. cit., p. 138.
[20] George Kitchin, *Prisoner of the OGPU* (New York: Longmans, Green, 1935), p. 31.
[21] Dallin and Nicolaevsky, op. cit., p. 175.
[22] Kitchin, op. cit., p. 237.

one occasion a near riot occurred when prisoners had taken measures to protect a priest from the rancour of the guard, but to no avail.[23] Indeed, very little could be done, even with the best intentions of fellow prisoners, to ameliorate the harsh conditions of camp life.

A large number of monks were also included among the prison population. Kitchin noticed one in a convoy of prisoners: 'At the head of the column marched a monk in his long cassock with a rope around the waist.'[24] In one piquant scandal in the twenties the prisoner placed in charge of giving anti-religious lectures was himself secretly a monk.[25] Nuns enjoyed special stature in the female prison:

All the criminals are intensely superstitious. All of them also make a great to-do over their religion, which does not stop them from committing horrible crimes. For that reason they are generally somewhat restrained in their behaviour toward the nun prisoners.[26]

Many such female prisoners, together with women who had been arrested for helping churches or priests, dependents of clergy, etc., were inclined to view their personal sufferings in apocalyptic images.[27]

Even among the camp guards, occasional indications of religious sentiments could be observed. John Noble noticed a communist official in Vorkuta who crossed himself and said, 'Thank God!' when he was able to find a vacant seat at the camp's movie theatre.[28] Another ex-prisoner reported on a conversation with one of the camp guards:

'An unclean power has fallen on me here, chief.' The guard looked at me in fear.
'A plague on you for saying such things; as though devils existed.'
'They began to exist once they swiped me from bed.'
'Cross yourself, Tregubov!'

[23] Ibid., pp. 52–3.
[24] Ibid., p. 142.
[25] Shiriaev, op. cit., pp. 108–9.
[26] Elinor Lipper, *Eleven Years in Soviet Prison Camps* (London: Hollis and Carter, 1950), p. 189.
[27] Tatiana Tchernavin, *Escape from the Soviets* (New York: Dutton, 1934), p. 121.
[28] John H. Noble, *I Found God in Soviet Russia* (New York: St. Martin's Press, 1959), p. 190.

'And do you cross yourself, citizen chief?'
'When nobody is looking—I cross myself, I remember mother.'[29]

Devotional exercises were not at all uncommon in the prison camps. Individuals of deep religious convictions would perform devotions alone, heedless of who might be watching. For example, one frail, aristocratic old lady in the women's barracks 'had an indomitable faith: not showing the indubitable weariness, she worked on to the finish, and in the evening, as always, prayed for a long time, kneeling erect in front of a small icon'.[30] In another case, an old convict every night would spend several hours at prayer, covering his face with his hands.[31]

Believers usually made no secret of their faith. John Noble, an American imprisoned at the end of World War II, almost immediately upon his arrival at Vorkuta was asked by a group of Ukrainians whether he was a believer.

I had no idea what they were saying, for I knew neither Ukrainian nor Russian. One of them then took a scrap of paper and drew two symbols on it, a cross and a Buddha. I pointed to the cross and they murmured and nodded, obviously pleased, and one of the men made the sign of the cross. This was my first communication with my fellow prisoners, and their very first question had brought us the common bond that transcends race or nationality, the Cross of Christ.[32]

In a camp at Norilsk, some 200 miles north of the Arctic Circle, religious prisoners were observed to cross themselves quite openly before meals and to pass around scraps of paper on which prayers had been copied so that the prayers might be read in the barracks at night.[33] In some camps prisoners made no attempt whatsoever to conceal their faith from their fellow prisoners and quite openly conducted devotional services in a corner of the barracks, trusting on the general noise and confusion to prevent the guards from overhearing them.[34] One report from Vorkuta described a group

[29] Iu. A. Tregubov, *Vosem' let vo vlasti lubianki* ('Eight years in the power of the Lubianka') (Frankfurt: Posev, 1957), p. 160.
[30] Shiriaev, op. cit., p. 280.
[31] Herling, op. cit., p. 141.
[32] Noble, op. cit., p. 107.
[33] Judith Listowel, 'Is Soviet Youth Becoming Religious?', *Catholic World*, No. 180 (November 1954), p. 108.
[34] V. Tchernavin, op. cit., pp. 147–8.

of believers who had formed themselves into a non-denomina-
tional, Christian group which engaged in vigorous proselytizing
among the other prisoners, copied out biblical passages by hand
and distributed them, and, *inter alia*, considered the Moscow
Patriarchate the anti-Christ.[35]

Organized worship services were held throughout the labour
camp system. After his escape, one prisoner reminisced:

There, in the polar regions, how beautiful nature was! And people?
Unlimited possibilities, from the most disgusting traitor to the highest
flight. And secret services in the rock quarries or coal mines. I myself
confessed and received the Eucharist at 4.30 a.m. in the 'surgery' of a
doctor. The liturgy was conducted in whispers—a picture straight
from the first centuries.[36]

In Vorkuta, services were held at the bottom of mine shafts,
utilizing water and bread for the Eucharist, wooden crosses, etc.[37]
According to Walter Ciszek, after the death of Stalin, Uniates,
Orthodox, and Baptists were each able to arrange to have a
barracks to themselves for services on major holidays.[38] But
attendance at the services held in the prisons was by no means
denominationally exclusive: at one Christmas service an atheist
and a Jew were observed in attendance. When this particular
service was discovered by the prison guards, they themselves
joined in.[39] When possible, impromptu services would be held.
On one occasion a marching convoy stopped for the night in a
crowded auditorium, and 'a priest asked for silence and asked us
to pray. We all joined in the prayers, even those of us who had
never prayed in their lives.'[40]

Protestant believers tended to be somewhat more active in the
organization and conduct of worship in the labour camp
environment. According to Noble,

The Greek and Russian Orthodox believers at our camp had been
terrorized so long in their homeland and had been so miserably treated

[35] Listowel, op. cit., p. 108.
[36] Pol'skii, op. cit., II, xiv-xv.
[37] Noble, op. cit., pp. 120-2.
[38] Walter, J. Ciszek, S.J., *With God in Russia* (New York: McGraw-Hill, 1964),
p. 212.
[39] Shiriaev, op. cit., pp. 233-41.
[40] C. A. Smith, ed., *Escape from Paradise* (London: Hollis and Carter, 1954), p. 134.

in prison that they did not have quite the same spirit of resistance as did the Latvians, Poles, and Ukrainians. They did not worship together as often, although one group did have a little Church sanctuary set up in an abandoned coal gallery deep in the mine, complete with two-by-fours on which they knelt, and an altar with a rude crucifix cut out of tin sheathing.

The Ukrainians conducted their services in the Ukrainian language but when the meeting broke up and they returned to their bunks, they began speaking Russian again, using all the curses common to the Russian vernacular. I did not see how they could worship God one moment and revile His name the next, even though they explained that these phrases in Russian are never taken literally.[41]

Despite all the difficulties attendant on worshipping in prison camp conditions, the contrast between religious life in confinement and that in the free sector of society was not as great as might be imagined, especially before the moderate expansion of the legalized Church allowed by the State during the waning years of World War II and in the immediate post-war years. The number of open churches in Russia was so small and so inadequate for meeting the needs of that majority of the population which still considered itself religious that organized worship was exceedingly infrequent for most of the inhabitants of the U.S.S.R. Indeed, during the years immediately prior to World War II worship services and the sacraments were more frequently available to the prison population than to the members of the free sector of society.[42]

Nor was the chasm between the convicts and the rest of society quite so deep as might be thought. While it was infrequent to be sure, there were numerous instances of religious contact and interchange between prisoners and non-prisoners of the surrounding world. In one camp a church building existed in close proximity to the camp boundary:

On Sundays the villagers came here to worship. The doors of the church remained open and the singing could be heard outside. The few prisoners who were not at work gathered around the barbed-wire enclosure and listened to the singing. They were not permitted to enter the church but no objection was made to their standing around and listening.[43]

[41] Noble, op. cit., pp. 144–5.
[42] Andreev, *O polozhenii pravoslavnoi tserkvi v sovetskom soiuze*, op. cit., p. 11.
[43] Kitchin, op. cit., p. 289.

Contact with the surrounding population was somewhat more prevalent when prisoners were marching in convoys to the labour camp which was their destination. Material aid was not infrequently given to such convicts by the villagers as they passed through, which was on occasion taken as an example of divine providence.[44] George Grabbe cites reports to the effect that

in two camps peasants from surrounding villages repeatedly gave the prisoners pieces (and sometimes whole special loaves) of black bread which were the sacrament from the liturgy performed secretly by wandering priests who did not accept the Soviet Patriarch. Often they gave them holy water in bottles. Both sectarian leaflets and tracts of transcribed Orthodox prayers came into the prisoners' hands.[45]

On relatively infrequent occasions, imprisoned priests were able to serve the religious needs of free citizens with whom they came in contact. For example, a convicted priest was allowed to enter a village in search of food for a convoy of prisoners; he returned successfully.

We lifted the hero in our arms and tossed him up to the ceiling again and again in grateful triumph. He humbly accepted our exultation. It appeared that he owed his success to the fact that the local priest had been deported and the village was left without a spiritual head. The peasant women prevailed on our cleric to read the evening service in church, to christen two babies and to wed a young couple whose parents had forbidden any but a church wedding. The newly-weds, overjoyed at the unexpected stroke of luck, were the principal donors to our fund of supplies.[46]

A degree of clandestine contact was somehow maintained between banished and imprisoned leaders and their congregations and organizations from which they had been separated. That such communications could be maintained despite the intensive efforts of the police to frustrate these underground processes testifies to the ingenuity of the practitioners of clandestine religious life within the country. A Soviet commentator mentioned this sort of activity of a religious leader who was in Siberian exile:

---

[44] Ibid., p. 174.
[45] Grabbe, op. cit., p. 184.
[46] Kitchin, op. cit., p. 175.

I. K. Bukhanets, one of the banished, writes this in the name of 'all who are with him', namely, I. I. Brykov, N. K. Chernikov, I. Y. Romanov: 'Do not pay any attention to threats and obstacles. Do not give up your meetings. Whom would you rather obey—them (i.e. the Soviet Government) or the word of God?'[47]

Apparently this was a fairly common expression of the local loyalty to imprisoned leaders, and was made possible by the continuing interest of parishioners in those who had been arrested or had disappeared.

Imprisoned bishops and priests established bonds with their flock by various unknown means, of which the Government had not the slightest idea. . . . Some form of dissemination of epistles and letters of imprisoned archpastors was carried on among the believers despite the physical impossibility of receiving them by usual, normal means. . . . Someone sitting in a restaurant would be conducting a lively and entirely harmless conversation with two other persons, gaily mentioning Vasia, Misha, Kolia, etc. In fact, an exchange of information was taking place concerning the situation of certain people who were in the concentration camps.[48]

Despite such indications of religious life among the prisoners, exposure to the environment of the labour camps was an almost inexpressibly degrading experience. Primitive conditions, overwork and under-nourishment, the very real possibility of death and the extreme difficulty of mere physical survival, the indiscriminate inclusion of all sorts of prisoners in the overcrowded living conditions, and the complete lack of privacy—all these contributed to the extreme degradation of life in the camps. Moral standards disappeared entirely among the great majority of the prisoners. Life in the camps was a jungle, an illustration of the Darwinian thesis of the survival of the fittest. The primitive level of life emphasized the more bestial aspects of human nature, and it was difficult indeed to avoid succumbing to the debilitating effect of the surroundings. Only the deepest of religious convictions were able to withstand the onslaught of degradation. Such few religious prisoners as were able to resist 'are distinguished by their high moral standards and the firm strength of their conviction. Against the background of demoralization and mutual

[47] *Bakinski Rabochii*, 7 April 1963.
[48] Konstantinov, *Gonimaia tserkov'*, op. cit., p. 22.

enmity prevalent in the camps, these people shine like beacons in the dark.'[49] Despair was an ever-present danger, bringing with it the temptation to give up all attempt at maintaining some form of individual humanity and personal integrity.

In that land where I lost three years, but found new life, in that cursed part of the world where human beings are degraded to raw materials, where words like family life, morals, virtue, mutual respect, parents, mother or even life lost their true meaning long ago, God, prayer and hope were all I had left.
I was fortunate, I still had hope, prayer and God. Around me these also had lost their meaning: death was the only hope of millions.[50]

The most effective defence against this temptation to succumb to the depravity of camp life was a silent, almost stoic endurance on the part of the individuals subjected to these conditions.

People of simple faith found life in the camp somewhat easier to accept, for they looked upon it as the natural culmination of their previously hard existence and with humbleness in their hearts awaited heavenly reward for their patience in suffering.[51]

Those who were successful in resisting the prevailing atmosphere in the prisons and the camps were conspicuous for their fortitude, and often this was the chief distinguishing feature of the depth of religious convictions of those who could resist.[52]
Despite the degrading conditions of life in the camps, some among the prisoners were able to resist and preserve their own personal integrity. Unto Parvilahti observed a Russian Orthodox convict whose faith was preserved intact despite twenty years of imprisonment in the camps.[53] Clergymen developed a reputation for ability to withstand the cruellest challenges without breaking down mentally or emotionally.[54] So unyielding was the faith of some that ultimately they succeeded to a degree in forcing the system to conform to them, rather than the other way round. Noble observed a Russian Orthodox monk who was so stubborn

[49] Dallin and Nicolaevsky, op. cit., p. 6.
[50] Smith, op. cit., p. 156.
[51] Herling, op. cit., p. 98.
[52] V. Tchernavin, op. cit., p. 147.
[53] Unto Parvilahti, *Beria's Gardens: A Slave Laborer's Experiences in the Soviet Utopia* (New York: Dutton, 1960), p. 151.
[54] Noble, op. cit., p. 119.

that at last the guards simply let him alone.[55] Similarly, three nuns categorically refused to work for 'Satan' and, surviving torture and extreme forms of brutal persuasion, they were finally let alone, free to live according to the monastic rule without participation in the normal work of the labour camp.[56] Other instances of such fortitude among monastics were also observed.[57]

The stern lessons learned by those who did survive the prison experience were not easily forgotten, and upon completion of terms or on emancipation from the camps, the subsequent life of such individuals outside confinement continued to show the effect of the fortitude which they had learned in the prisons. The case of a priest who had served three years in a labour camp for participation in religious activities in opposition to the legalized Church is illustrative:

After release he, together with his wife and children, moved into an illegal position. His wife, having grown tired of constant hiding, told him that she would no longer endure such a life. But the Rev. ———— continued his secret sacerdotal activities. In 1937 he was arrested ane sentenced to ten years of forced labour, and in 1947, as an incorrigibld he was condemned to ten more years of the labour camps. . . . In the same camp there was one hieromonk of the Tikhonite church.

Freed before the end of his term, the Rev. ———— and this hieromonk lived together and secretly continued to serve. The Rev. ———— while in camp received the Holy Sacraments in a parcel from secret priests—Tikhonites. He also had a hand-made stole with which he conducted the service.[58]

Not unexpectedly, the severe crisis of camp life resulted in numerous conversions to religion—some of them dramatic.

The hospital was the only place, in camp and prison alike, where the light was extinguished at night. And it was there, in the darkness, that I realized for the first time in my life that in man's whole life only solitude can bring him absolute inward peace and restore his individuality. Only in all-embracing loneliness, in darkness which conceals the outlines of the external world, is it possible to know that one is oneself, to feel that individuality emerging, until one reaches the stage of doubt when one becomes conscious of one's insignificance in the

[55] Ibid., pp. 175–6.
[56] Ibid., pp. 113–17.
[57] Lipper, op. cit., p. 80.
[58] Grabbe, op. cit., p. 185.

extent of the universe which grows in one's conception to overwhelming dimensions. If this condition savours of mysticism, if it forces one into the arms of religion, then I certainly discovered religion, and I prayed blasphemously: 'O God, give me solitude, for I hate all men.'[59]

A fictional conversation with a priest in a Soviet novel of 1966 gave a persuasive illustration of this phenomenon. The priest is explaining his religious convictions to an atheist:

My way to God was complicated. I hesitated, believed and then fell into unbelief again and thought of becoming a doctor. Then, when I became a priest, I did not deceive people. I believed that the Christian religion strengthens ethical behaviour and that through the usages of the Orthodox Church the human soul could be disciplined. I discharged my religious duties, even if I sometimes had moments of doubt.

And to-day?

To-day I believe.

How did that come about? Through a shock?

How can I explain it to you? One day I was arrested and accused of anti-Soviet agitation.

And in reality?

I never engaged in any such agitation.

And then?

Then I was sent to a corrective labour-camp. Not a nice life. The heaviest work, hunger, cruel treatment. Among the people in charge at the top, there were some good ones. The cruel treatment of the prisoners was ordered from above. Men became depraved and mean, they denounced one another. I survived because of my belief. I would divide believers into two categories, communists and Christians. For the true communists also believed, after their fashion. But they believed in truth, in the victory of justice. They died. But they did not allow anybody to say anything against the government, because even in the camp the Soviet government remained their government. In the camp I got to know God afresh, as it were. If I had not believed in eternal salvation, I would have been lost.

What did you do to hold out?

I waited and believed: Untruth will pass away and truth will conquer.

How can we hasten the victory of truth?

We must know how to wait.

Better to die.

Taniushka, that is a great sin in the sight of God. Our life is not in our hands.

<hr/>

[59] Herling, op. cit., p. 103.

Then we must come to terms with untruth, make our peace with it. So it would seem.[60]

Not all such conversions were marked with the degree of lasting stability as that in the above illustration. One atheist who had broken with religion wrote in the report he gave to an Academy of Sciences field expedition concerning his experiences in prison (in 1945 at the age of eighteen he had been convicted of hooliganism):

At the colony I met one old Baptist. He spoke softly, in an ingratiating voice. He cleverly brought this divine saying to my corrective labour: 'This is God's sentence on you,' he whispered to me, 'It is necessary first of all to take care of life beyond the grave, to save your soul.' How could I object, with my third grade education? I fell under the influence of this old man, began to read the verses which he thrust on me, to pray soundlessly. Then they transferred me to another place, and I almost forgot about the sermons of the Baptist and his admonitions. But to my misfortune an Orthodox priest met me on my path, who was serving a sentence for theft. He found out about my thoughts on God and began to persuade and to show that the sectarian faith is false and that righteous life is only in Orthodoxy. And again I began to accept God. But this influence was also of short duration.

He later became a Jehovah's Witness, then a Baptist, Molokan, Baptist, Pentecostal, and finally gave up religion entirely and converted to atheism.[61]

Not all prisoners, of course, reacted positively to religion as a result of the trauma of conditions in the camps. Some reacted negatively and indeed participated in official anti-religious propaganda campaigns.[62] In one curious case, a prisoner was allegedly won away from religion by his prison experiences; a True Orthodox Christian some years later reported,

Believers who dropped by would say various things, the first one thing, the second another, the third a third thing. It ended that for what I did 'in the name of God' I wound up in prison.

[60] Lev Ovalov, 'Pomni obo mne' ('Remember me'), *Nauka i Religiia*, No. 4 (April 1966), p. 82, translation from *Current Developments in the Eastern European Churches*, No. 3 (August 1966), p. 28.
[61] 'Materialy k kharakteristike sovremennogo sektantstva v Tambovskoi oblasti' ('Materials characterizing contemporary sectarianism in Tambov oblast'), in AN SSSR, *Sovremennoe Sektantstvo*, op. cit., pp. 213, 217.
[62] Dallin and Nicolaevsky, op. cit., p. 236.

There I met people who believed variously. There were believers who called Saint Nikolai a Hetman, they did not acknowledge the cross. They said that one cannot acknowledge the cross, they crucified Christ on it; but we acknowledge both Saint Nikolai and the cross.

Others who believed in Christ denied the Holy Spirit.

And each says that he suffers for God, and all believe differently. This led me to doubt. There were also such believers in prison who had food. The food rotted, but these people nevertheless did not share it with their neighbours.

The unbelievers conducted themselves better. When I connected all this together it came out strangely: we had gathered together a small group of believers and we thought we would go to paradise. And where then would all the other believers go? And the unbelievers?

And I united myself, not to believers, but to the unbelievers.[63]

(As will become apparent below, there is some reason to doubt the validity of this alleged conversion.)

Not all the religious conversions in the camps were free from aberrations, and some of them obviously bore traces of irrational reaction to crisis and despair. In one case, for example, a prisoner became convinced that he was under the domination of an evil spirit.[64] In another instance, a prisoner convicted of murder and theft had a series of religious visions of Christ and the Virgin Mary; 'Up to the last breath of his death throes he prayed for forgiveness of his many crimes.'[65] Such outbursts were especially characteristic of the 'mortuaries', or barracks in which terminal cases were placed to await death.

Many storms troubled the peaceful course of life in the mortuary. One evening an old collective farmer from the region of Kalouga jumped down from a bunk, and frantically beating with his fist on the bottom of an empty tin, proclaimed 'the end of all this suffering', with his own Second Coming—'I am Christ in the rags of a prisoner.' When this was greeted with derisive laughter, he stood with his face to the bunks and his back to the fire and looked at us for a moment—imposing, tall, almost splendid with his outstretched arms and the blunted face of a madman—then rapidly turned round and jumped into the open fire.[66]

[63] 'Materialy k kharakteristike sovremennogo sektantstva v Tambovskoi oblasti,' op. cit., p. 220.
[64] Tregubov, op. cit., p. 160.
[65] Parvilahti, op. cit., p. 110.
[66] Herling, op. cit., p. 226.

Large numbers of people, of course, were broken by the bitter hopelessness of life in the camps. Despair was an ever present threat, as the intensity of the struggle for mere survival quickly burned up those whose resources were not adequate to the challenge. Bernhard Roeder quotes a Russian Orthodox priest:

I wanted to force martyrdom on myself. I have tempted God. But in His unfathomable decision God has refused me. There is no martyrdom in the camp, at least not the martyrdom suffered by the great saints of our Church. Here there is only work, work for the Bolshevik system in which man is gradually consumed like a candle that burns until it is extinguished. By martyrdom the man of faith can conquer Satan, and if his sacrifice is pleasing to God, he will enter the ranks of the saints. But by labour Satan can conquer the man of faith, enslave him, make use of him, exploit him to the bitter end for his own satanic aims. This knowledge is the most terrible temptation that Satan has so far set before me. Pray with me that this satanic despair will depart from me.[67]

Once a prisoner's spirit had been broken, his thoughts often turned to death with avid anticipation even if he were religious. Nor could force of argument often prevail in such cases: 'How could I have convinced this fundamentally religious man, who prayed for a speedy death as for God's greatest blessing, that man's greatest privilege is free will in slavery?'[68] Even clergy who devoted themselves to pastoral work among their fellow prisoners were not exempt from being broken, and a relatively short time could effect a radical transformation, replacing good cheer and optimism with indifference, pessimism, and despair.[69] For such unfortunates,

their Christianity is not a belief in the mystical redemption of souls wearied with earthly wandering, but only gratitude to a religion which promises eternal rest. They are religious suicides, worshippers of death for whom the release of the grave is the ultimate end, not the means to a life after death. . . .
. . . 'What is there left for me,' he said, 'besides death? I've no family, I'm too old to go back to the *kolkhoz*, I'll never see the mountains again. Every day I pray for death.' . . . And the curious thing was that he, whose guts had been 'knocked out', never shrieked or moaned in the

[67] Bernhard Roeder, *Katorga: An Aspect of Modern Slavery* (London: Heinemann, 1958), p. 170.
[68] Herling, op. cit., p. 145.
[69] V. Tchernavin, op. cit., pp. 237–8.

night; only occasionally he groaned quietly with the pain as he turned over on his side, or whispered deliriously in his sleep of death and God.[70]

This sort of despair was especially prevalent among those who upon completion of their sentences discovered that they had arbitrarily been given another long sentence, and that there was no escape for them from the camp. One such prisoner, on hearing of his re-sentencing instead of release,

lay down on his bunk without a word, and to all questions would answer only: 'My life is finished, it's all over'; and he, an old Bolshevik, alternately prayed soundlessly or beat his grey head against the planks of the bunk. He died between four and five in the afternoon. . . .[71]

To some degree the despair which so often caught up inmates of the penal system was operative throughout Soviet society. The Terror of the thirties and the post-war period served to introduce a large measure of insecurity into the lives of every citizen, for none could be sure that the terrors of the labour camps would not be his, suddenly and without warning. In a sense, the individual citizen is tempted to feel himself alone and defenceless in such conditions, with no visible means of ensuring his own safety.

Mikhail Pol'skii, indeed, suggests that this phenomenon is characteristic of all the churches which have accepted governmental legalization. He sees the Orthodox Church as composed of people whose spirits have been broken in ways analogous to those described above. In particular, its leaders, most of whom have themselves suffered imprisonment at one time or another, and very few of whom can feel absolutely certain that this fate does not await them in the future, are broken men according to Pol'skii.

If terror has such a huge influence on the conduct of the Moscow Patriarch, then it is vain to speak about consideration of the Church's profit and to see in this wisdom, politics, gain, hope. Nothing of the sort. It does not sell all of its positions, it gives them away, as a man gives them away who signs his personal death sentence. He is informed about the sentence and he signs what he reads. If he remains yet alive, then he lives each day on the mercy of his conqueror and does everything which is ordered. He works like a slave doomed to death, who has had everything taken out of his soul and for whom there is no case

---

[70] Herling, op. cit., pp. 146–7.
[71] Ibid., p. 33.

at all for morality and shame. It has all long since been destroyed. The death sentence may be executed and fulfilled on any day. Work for each day. If not one person in Russia has the guarantee of existence for one day, and finds himself not under law, but under dictatorship which knowingly breaks the law, then what are they who beforehand have been condemned to death, like the official Church in Russia, which continues its existence in conformity to the requirements of the general policy, and to what extent is it necessary that the Church pour water on the mill of world revolution. It is a temporary fellow traveller which was long ago decided to be considered as a passing necessity.[72]

In support of his hostile interpretation, Pol'skii adduces the consideration that especially during the period when he was writing churchmen were only infrequently (or, according to Pol'skii, never) released from confinement unless they had compromised their independence enough to satisfy the regime.[73]

It would appear that Pol'skii is too sweeping in his pessimism. Certainly the subsequent history of the legalized Church has given some evidence that not all of its adherents are so severely broken. Even among those of the clergy who did find it expedient to yield to the demands of the regime in one particular or another, in many cases such decisions were made not out of despair but for considerations (such as the need of the Church) which to the individual in question seemed sufficiently important to justify the concession.

Nor, of course, would Pol'skii's interpretation apply to the members of the underground Church who upon release from confinement reverted again to their preferred form of religious activity. So far from being broken by the prison experience, the effect on this group of former prisoners would be just the opposite.

There is one element, though, to whom it would appear justifiable to apply Pol'skii's interpretation. This would be that unknown number of former members of underground Orthodox groups who either through prison or threat were coerced into abandoning further participation in clandestine religious life. Some, of course, over a period of time became sincerely convinced that they no longer wished to participate in such dangerous activity. For others, however, whom coercion, threat, and fear

---

[72] Mikhail Pol'skii, *Kanonicheskoe polozhenie vysshei tserkovnoi vlasti v SSSR i zagranitsei* ('The canonical position of the supreme church government in the U.S.S.R. and abroad') (Jordanville, New York: Holy Trinity Monastery, 1948), p. 100.

[73] Ibid., p. 99.

had led to such a renunciation of clandestine activity without any accompanying conviction of their own persuading them against such a step, Pols'kii's judgement might indeed be fairly accurate description.

A curious case presented by Soviet scholarship might perhaps allude to such a phenomenon. This is the case of Vladimir Umrikhin, the True Orthodox believer cited above, who at the age of eighteen had been incarcerated and had renounced further participation in the movement.

For activity by no means of a religious character, Umrikhin ended up in confinement. But even here, what he met, discovered, and learned while in confinement showed him the gloom and horror of the spiritual prison into which his family had cast him and which was called 'True Orthodox Christianity'.

In confinement, Umrikhin began to 're-evaluate values' which formerly had seemed to him to stand outside human judgement, and gradually arrived at an understanding of his religious and social duties.

We visited Vladimir Umrikhin in his spacious and clean home, in the society of his wife and his baby in the cradle. In the home there was a feeling of well being and familial agreement. The wife spoke with pride of the modesty and love of labour of Umrikhin. And, nevertheless, both of them (the wife in the past had also been an adherent of the True Orthodox Christians) gave the impression of people who have not yet completely recovered from the spiritual traumas endured. In conversation they were somewhat reserved; they live secluded, satisfied with the society of each other only. Umrikhin works in the factory (he is a qualified cabinet-maker) but performs only temporary work. In order to turn Umrikhin to real, fundamental atheism, he should be tightly linked to the working collective, enticed to participation in social life.[74]

In view of the fact that those interviewing him were members of an investigatory team—academic, to be sure, but nevertheless

[74] 'Materialy k kharakteristike sovremennogo sektantstva v Tambovskoi oblasti, op. cit., pp. 214–15. It is possible that the case of Vladimir Umrikhin was by no means representative, for he may have been the son of one of the True Orthodox Christians' wandering leaders, Aleksei Umrikhin, described by Nikol'skaia (op. cit.) in the same volume, p. 179. Curiously, the compilers of these materials, ordinarily scrupulous in such matters, have neglected to include Vladimir's middle name, or patronymic (see pp. 214–15, 219), and hence it is not possible to establish a filial relationship with Aleksei. If, however, Vladimir Umrikhin was the son (or even a near relation) of one of the active True Orthodox leaders, his case would scarcely be typical.

investigatory—sponsored by the Soviet State, the hypothesis must arise that perhaps the subject of the interview was not replying with perfect candour. In many respects, his situation as described above would be fully compatible with someone who had broken with the clandestine movement not out of conviction as claimed, but out of fear of being subjected once again to the bitter experience of prison life.

The impact of the prison system, however, was not always so successful in persuading former members of the underground to abandon such activities upon their release. In some cases quite the opposite happened and those who returned from the camps redoubled the intensity of their underground efforts, at times in even more extreme forms. Soviet scholars discovered one leader of an underground group who after his release from prison had reverted to his activities in an extreme form, abandoning all contact of any sort with society.[75] In 1964, an active underground Orthodox group was discovered in Temirtau, some ten miles from Karaganda, which was the site of one of the largest of the labour camp complexes.[76] It seems quite possible that the members of this underground group were drawn from those who had been released from the camps after the running down of the forced labour system but who were still required to live in the area in strict exile.

Of considerable interest in this regard were studies in religious sociology conducted in Komi Republic of the far north, which had active groups of several different branches of underground Orthodox organizations.[77] This area has been widely used as place of exile for those who have completed their sentences of forced labour. Among this 'immigrant population' there are strong movements of underground Orthodoxy[78] which proved to be exceedingly resistant to State efforts to reduce their numbers.[79]

In most of the evidence, religious life in the prison system tends to take on the same colour, with differences of denomination much less prominently observable than in the world outside.[80] Nevertheless, members of the underground did make their contribution to the population of the camps and were in turn influenced by the

[75] Milovidov, op. cit., pp. 218–19.
[76] *Komsomol'skaia Pravda*, 22 May 1964.
[77] Krasnikov, op. cit., p. 186.
[78] Ibid., pp. 173–4.
[79] Ibid., p. 185.
[80] Noble, op. cit., p. 123.

peculiar experiences of prison life. As has been noted, John Noble knew of a priest in Vorkuta who had been apprehended for conducting rites in secret.[81] Parvilahti observed one old man who had already served twenty years merely for attending catacomb services.[82] In another case,

right up to the war the Bolsheviks occasionally closed the still remaining monasteries and exiled all the monks. The local archbishop of the Sergiite Church, himself soon to be arrested, ordained more than ten monks as priests by secret ordination, so that they, while they were in prison, might celebrate the mysteries of the divine service and ceremonies.[83]

Among the prison population could be found prisoners whose sects held that they could not even give their names to anti-Christ, sectarians who refused contact with any official documents and hence refused the certificate of release when the term was up and were soon returned to the camps.[84] All of these strange convictions observable among prisoners, and many more, were widely followed in the Orthodox underground throughout the Soviet period.

Thus the prison system of the U.S.S.R. had a considerable impact on the character and development of underground Orthodox movements. The extreme conditions of prison life formed the endemic, inescapable background for the underground Orthodox believers, representing a very present possibility of what awaited them in the future and, for those who survived the experience, exercising a continuing impact on their subsequent activities in the underground Orthodox movements.

[81] Ibid., pp. 143–4.
[82] Parvilahti, op. cit., pp. 158–9.
[83] Alexeev, op. cit., p. 83.
[84] Lipper, op. cit., pp. 143–4.

VI

War and the Ukraine

22 June 1941 marked the beginning of a new era for religious life in the U.S.S.R. The German invasion which brought the U.S.S.R. into World War II put an end to the previous State policy of open, adamant hostility towards religion, and in its place a new policy was begun which soon developed into a negotiated *détente* between Church and State in which the anti-religious aspirations of the regime were muted. Subsequent history has shown that this was by no means a profound conversion away from militant atheism on the part of the regime, but was more in the nature of a tactical compromise, postponing the implementation of the anti-religious designs of Marxism-Leninism. It was not a permanent change of policy, but nevertheless for almost two decades life was considerably easier for believers of all religions, including members of underground Orthodoxy. To be sure, such clandestine groups benefited perhaps least of all from the new religious policy, but, nevertheless, under the more relaxed State approach to religious affairs underground Orthodoxy was able to revive significantly and to experience its most flourishing period.

For the patriarchal Church, the new day had begun to dawn almost two years previously. Until 1939, despite its vigorous attempts to demonstrate political loyalty and willingness to co-operate with the regime, the legalized Church had been considered by the regime as an annoyance at best, and particularly towards the end of the decade had received such harsh treatment as to obliterate almost completely the distinction between legal and illegal Orthodoxy in society. The attempt to trade political loyalty for concessions from the State which would allow the Church to survive was proving an abysmal failure.

In September 1939, however, the Soviet Union suddenly found itself heir to large areas of what had formerly been Poland (and shortly thereafter the Baltic States as well). According to a secret protocol of the Nazi-Soviet pact of non-aggression and neutrality signed the month before, the U.S.S.R. acquired the eastern areas of Poland when Hitler invaded the country. In the new conditions, the Soviet regime felt constrained to exert every effort to transform the newly acquired areas according to the Soviet pattern as rapidly as possible, and in these conditions for the first time the patriarchal Church could be of significant service to the regime. Two of its remaining four bishops were quickly dispatched to the newly acquired areas in an attempt to neutralize the large Orthodox populations there.

The concessions gained by the Church in return for this collaboration were miniscule at first, consisting primarily of the negative concession of an immediate relaxation of anti-religious pressure directed against the patriarchal Orthodox Church. The Moscow Patriarchate was able, none the less, to make an exceedingly modest beginning of the arduous process of resurrecting and reconstructing its shattered institutional existence.

The breathing-space was of exceedingly short duration, however, for on 22 June 1941 the Nazis invaded the U.S.S.R. Immediately, Metropolitan Sergii declared the Church's patriotism and loyalty in the strongest possible terms. For the Moscow Patriarchate, the invasion seemed a catastrophe of first magnitude, bringing a very real threat that these modest efforts at resuscitation of the patriarchal Church would immediately come to naught, and the Church itself might receive that *coup de grâce* which it had been awaiting since the Great Purges ended in 1938. If the Church was considered potentially inimical in time of peace, there was every chance that in time of war this potential enemy from within would be liquidated summarily. Nor was the precarious situation of the Church rendered any less dangerous by the hope that those four bishops who survived the thirties in office would *ipso facto* be considered of unimpeachable loyalty, for on the first day of the war one of the two trusted bishops who had been sent to the newly acquired areas, Metropolitan Sergii (Voskresenskii), refused to evacuate Riga with the governmental party and defected to the Germans.

When the German armies reached the outskirts of Moscow in October 1941, the Soviet regime elected to evacuate the Moscow Patriarchate rather than find some more drastic means of insuring against their defection to the enemy. From this time forward the Government's willingness to utilize the services of the Church in promoting the war effort increased at a rapid rate. On 4 September 1943, a new relationship between State and Church was formalized when Sergii, Nikolai, and Aleksii were granted a private audience with Stalin. Three days later a Sobor—the first since 1917—was convened and Sergii was duly elected Patriarch by the nineteen bishops assembled. Thereafter, the fortunes of the Moscow Patriarchate rose rapidly, and for the next two decades the patriarchal Church was to enjoy limited but marginally adequate freedom, sufficient to ensure continued viability within Soviet society. The limited *détente* between Church and State, in which the State sublimated the more militant side of its atheistic commitment, began.

Naturally, the change in State policy which was ushered in by the beginning of World War II affected the underground Orthodox as well. If the enthusiasm of subsequent historians of the Moscow Patriarchate is accepted, the great wave of patriotism, which allegedly engulfed all religious people, swept over the underground Orthodox as well and caused a mass movement back to the patriarchal Church of holy Russia.

The first days of the war demonstrated the very great moral unity and highest patriotism of the peoples of the U.S.S.R., and simultaneously showed not only that the loyal children of the patriarchal Russian Church were stronger than ever before, rallying round their archpastors, pastors, and wise president Metropolitan Sergii, but also the absolute majority of the flock which hitherto had been in the schisms, voted against them, so to speak, with their feet; the temples of the renovators and 'right' schismatics were empty, the temples and prayer houses of patriarchal orientation were filled to capacity.[1]

According to another Orthodox historian, no sooner had Metropolitan Sergii been raised to patriarchal rank than 'the remainder of all the schisms ceased to exist and the divisions within the Church were overcome'.[2]

As will be demonstrated below, it is difficult to believe that these irenic descriptions are entirely candid. It is true that there was an immense resurgence of Orthodoxy, and indeed of religion

[1] Shabatin, op. cit., p. 44.
[2] Glukhov, op. cit., p. 68.

in general, during World War II. Even anti-religious authors hostile to religion frankly admit this war-time revival of religion.[3] In large measure, of course, this was doubtless due to the crisis of war. In his sermon of 12 August 1941, Metropolitan Sergii pointed out,

The important thing, though, is that we must not overlook the profound difference between a man's attitude when he is in his everyday circumstances and the same man's attitude in the hour of death. . . . The last few minutes and even seconds of his life sometimes are incomparably more significant for the fate of a man than the whole life he has lived on earth.[4]

In part, this renewed interest in religion was a concomitant of the increase of patriotism during the war. Particularly as the war progressed and the brutality of the invading forces became apparent, there was a revival of traditional Russian patriotism, in which religion and the Orthodox Church had always played a significant part.

No less significant, however, as a factor contributing to the revival of interest in religion during World War II was the almost immediate reduction of State pressure against religion. The extreme crisis of the war severely inhibited the regime's ability to maintain the measure of totalitarian control over the countryside which had been enforced during the latter thirties. With its very survival at stake the regime had little inclination to divert any significant part of its attention to the less immediate problem of suppression of religious activity among the population. With the concordat of 1943 this more relaxed approach to religion in local administration became institutionalized, and two decades were to elapse before local control over religious activities began to assume the comprehensiveness and effectiveness of the pre-war period.

This relaxation of social controls, of course, affected all religious believers, but particularly those who had been practising their

[3] E. F. Murav'ev and Iu. V. Dmitrev, 'O konkretnosti v izuchenii i preodolenii religioznykh perezhitkov' ('Concreteness in studying and overcoming religious survivals'), *Voprosy Filosofii*, No. 3 (March 1961), p. 64; F. Oleshchuk, 'Za konkretnost' nauchno-ateisticheskoi propagandy' ('For concreteness in scientific atheistic propaganda'), *Kommunist*, No. 5 (April 1958), p. 113.

[4] Orthodox Eastern Church, Russian, *Pravda o religii v Rossii* ('The truth about religion in Russia') (Moscow: The Patriarchate, 1942), pp. 96–7.

faith in secret, for it provided them with the possibility of renewing their activities.[5] Many of these believers had managed to continue clandestine religious activities through the worst periods, despite the intensive efforts of police and investigatory units to discover and obliterate such activities. No sooner was the regime's attention diverted into other areas than such believers could resume activity on a much larger scale, and throughout the war believers of all persuasions took independent action to resume full religious activity. In the Riazan area, for example,

believers of the city of Mikhailov (Riazan oblast) wrote to the City Soviet in 1944: 'We ask you to open the Mikhailovskaia Church, inasmuch as for believers in these days of Patriotic War there is so much grief that it is difficult to bear, and consolation is needed.' In a series of regions . . . house churches began to function. Priests of the Riazan area, giving up canonical rule as hopeless, encouraged the opening of such churchlets, seeing in them a supplementary channel for religious influence on the population. Mass, public divine services at fraternal graves, cemeteries, and squares, were also performed for various reasons: for 'granting victory', on 'saving the Motherland', and the like.[6]

N. Timasheff raised the attractive hypothesis that the surprisingly large figure of 30,000 religious communities officially listed by the Soviet Government in 1941 (if it had any relationship to reality whatsoever) may be explicable in part by 'the renewed registration of some religious communities which in 1927–38 went to the "catacombs" '.[7]

Especially during the early years of the war, the general resurgence of Russian patriotism was not necessarily universal. This was particularly evident among religious believers, who had not been treated with any noticeable delicacy by the regime. The patriarchal Church itself experienced considerable difficulty in overcoming unpatriotic and anti-patriotic feelings in the Church in 1941.[8] This was frankly admitted by Sergii himself in his proclamation delivered during the 'panic of Moscow' on the very eve of his evacuation:

[5] Thomas Fitzsimmons, Peter Malov, and John C. Fiske, *U.S.S.R.: Its People, Its Society, Its Culture* (New Haven, Connecticut: HRAF Press, 1960), p. 127.

[6] V. Zybkovets, 'Put' sovetskogo ateizma' ('The path of Soviet atheism'), *Nauka i Religiia*, No. 9 (September 1967), p. 14.

[7] Timasheff, op. cit., p. 92 n. 16, citing *Soviet War News*, 22 August 1941.

[8] Cf. Orthodox Church, *Patriarkh Sergii i ego dukhovnoe nasledstvo*, op. cit., p. 81.

Rumours are flying, which one would not like to believe, that there may be people among our Orthodox pastors who are ready to enter into the service of the enemy of our native land and Church, to be overshadowed by the pagan swastika instead of by the Holy Cross. One does not want to believe this, but in spite of all such pastors are found. I remind them that our Holy Church, in addition to the word of admonishment, is also given by the Lord the spiritual sword, punishing those who break oaths.

In the name of this authority given me from God I, as bishop, having the power to bind and to loose, call to repentance all who have wavered from fear or for other reasons; but those who do not wish to repent I declare deprived of divine services and I deliver to church judgement for even sterner decision. Let God not be outraged.[9]

There are hints that those Orthodox believers who were disaffected—and perhaps already experienced in underground Orthodoxy—categorically refused to contribute to the war effort, going so far as to refuse induction into the armed services. In one case, a Soviet author writing twenty years later about a leader of one of the contemporary underground groups states that during World War II he 'deserted and from that time on he hid from justice'.[10] S. D. Bailey, an American Quaker, reported in 1958 on an interview with Gostev, Deputy Chairman of the Government's Council for the Affairs of Religious Cults, in which he specifically raised the question of conscientious objection:

Mr. Gostev was not very precise, but I gather that objectors to combatant service are put in medical or catering units. Those who refuse all service, such as Jehovah's Witnesses, are apparently treated as deserters and tried in military courts.[11]

Informal, independent, and clandestine Orthodox activity flourished during the war. It assumed sufficiently large proportions as to become of direct concern to Patriarch Sergii himself. In October 1943 he warned against the use of unordained people for performing the Orthodox liturgy, citing a report that in Central Asia a local church had engaged the services of a man who frankly

---

[9] Orthodox Eastern Church, Russian, *Russkaia pravoslavnaia tserkov' i velikaia otechestvennaia voina* ('The Russian Orthodox Church and the Great Patriotic War') (Moscow: Standard Press of the Unified State Publishing House, n.d. [1944?]), p. 6, and in Orthodox Church, *Pravda o religii v Rossii*, op. cit., p. 410.

[10] Il'ia Okunev, 'Konets sviatoi muzy' ('The end of the holy muse'), *Sovetskie Profsoiuzy*, No. 1 (January 1965), p. 31.

[11] S. D. Bailey, op. cit., p. 306.

admitted that he was not a believer.[12] The Sobor of 1945, which elected Aleksii as Patriarch, specifically alluded to this problem in its general address to the Church:

We note with particular distress how in some places, owing to the negligence of the pastors towards the instruction and edification of their flock, the sheep of their pastures in their ignorance are unable to distinguish the pastors appointed according to the canons and clothed in grace, from impostors, alien to God's grace, self-appointed, who officiate at Christian rituals, sacrilegiously daring to administer even the Holy Sacraments.[13]

Obviously, such concern reflects the inability of the patriarchal Church, even with the limited approval which it had won from the Government, to supply clergy in sufficient numbers to ensure that underground clerics would not make inroads on the congregations. So great was the desire for a resumption of religious life that local believers appeared perfectly willing to improvise, using whatever resources were available to continue their religious worship.

It would appear that nearly every type of underground Orthodoxy was able to increase activities during the war. As might be expected, the predominant reaction even in the crisis of war was a continuation of hostility to that Government which had caused so much dislocation in the lives of those who went underground to preserve their faith. In common with a great number of other citizens of the U.S.S.R., they initially looked on the war with eager anticipation that the invaders might liberate them from the excesses of the regime. Referring to those in the underground who had broken all contact with society and entered a life of complete social alienation, of vagrancy and hiding, one Soviet scholar notes:

The eschatological mood in the ranks of the Wanderers especially revived in connection with the Great Patriotic War. In this period their leaders in their 'prophecies' predicted the destruction of the Soviet Government, and called on 'true Christians' to save themselves in the wilderness and in hiding places.[14]

---

[12] *ZMP*, No. 2 (1943), pp. 3–5.
[13] Orthodox Eastern Church, Russian, *The Call of the Russian Church* (London: 'Soviet News,' 1945), p. 20.
[14] Milovidov, op. cit., p. 218.

Information on the wartime activities of the large number of discrete underground Orthodox sects which had arisen during the Soviet period is exceedingly incomplete. Certain of the groups appear to have maintained their identity without major change and, predictably, reacted negatively to the Soviet war effort. For example, the syncretistic sect of the Apokalipsisty continued their activity through World War II and beyond.

In 1941, underground groups of the Apokalipsisty were discovered in the Kiev, Vinnitsa, and Zhitomir areas. During the occupation the members of the sect at once came up to the surface from the underground and became active accomplices of the Hitlerites.[15]

Most of the underground Orthodox groups, however, seemed to have experienced a diffusion of identity during the difficult decade of the thirties. By the advent of World War II, the constant police pressure, together with the near total elimination of churches and the resultant large number of potential recruits for the various types of underground Orthodoxy, had apparently served to blur the differences between the various underground groups and organizations. By the end of the war, at least—and perhaps considerably earlier—the former practice of each group referring to itself by the name of its leader or founder had almost completely disappeared, and instead the various groups tended to amalgamate in two broadly-based, nation-wide movements calling themselves the 'True Orthodox Church' and the 'True Orthodox Christians'. These two movements enjoyed a period of great success after the war, and even during the war the various smaller organizations out of which these large movements were formed had begun to coalesce and represent identifiable movements within the Orthodox underground.

Subsequent years would demonstrate that the 'True Orthodox Church' was the more coherent and better organized of the two movements. According to a Soviet scholar,

The preaching of the True Orthodox Church did not have success in the Riazan area. However, small groups preserved themselves during the course of the thirties and even the beginning of the forties, when in connection with the war the hopes of these groups for the restoration of the old order revived.[16]

[15] Fedorenko, op. cit., p. 217.
[16] Iankova, 'Sovremennoe pravoslavie,' op. cit., p. 69.

The belief that the Soviet Government had finally reached the point of collapse was widespread, and the various adherents of the True Orthodox Church even went so far as to predict the specific dates of its destruction.[17] Very quickly after the appearance of the True Orthodox Church movement, attempts were made to set up a single, centralized organization; it is uncertain, however, whether this attempt was begun during the wartime period itself, or immediately after the war's conclusion.[18]

The True Orthodox Christians, a much more diffuse grouping of disaffected Orthodox, also can trace their beginnings to World War II.[19] In the Tambov area the social instability of the wartime crisis created conditions in which these underground groups could flourish.[20] Similarly, in the Riazan area, the underground Orthodox were able to revive at this time under the name of True Orthodox Christians.[21] Like the True Orthodox Church, this movement also expected the imminent end of the Soviet regime.[22]

Soviet scholarship has dated the rise of the True Orthodox Christians in the Tambov area fairly precisely:

In a hand-written address to adherents by one of the leaders of the True Orthodox Christians, V. Titov, in the so-called 'Talks on Various Questions to Those Who Are in Doubt about the Path of Salvation', dated in the mid-forties, we read: 'We have received the words of exhortation from our pastors of the Holy Orthodox and Apostolic Conciliar Church. The preached word was spoken in the temples to Christians from the mouths of Bishop Uar and Archimandrite Mitrofan.' In other words, the True Orthodox Christians consider Bishop Uvarov (Uar) and Archimandrite Mitrofan as their pastors, priests who served in the Lipetsk Cathedral Church until 1943 exclusively and were arrested for anti-Soviet preaching among believers. All instructions, and also the texts of sermons and proclamations of leaders of groups of True Orthodox Christians in the Tambov area originated with V. Titov. Titov was directly linked with Uvarov and Mitrofan.[23]

---

[17] Vasin, op. cit., p. 21.
[18] Fedorenko, op. cit., p. 213.
[19] Klibanov, 'Sovremennoe sektantstvo v Tambovskoi oblasti,' op. cit., p. 296.
[20] Nikol'skaia, op. cit., p. 167.
[21] Iankova, 'Sovremennoe pravoslavie,' op. cit., p. 72.
[22] Vasin, op. cit., p. 21.
[23] Nikol'skaia, op. cit., pp. 166–7.

Apparently the True Orthodox Christians enjoyed great success in Lipetsk province at this time, reaching their peak of activity during the war years.[24]

The reaction of the True Orthodox Christians to the war effort was sharply hostile. 'They prayed to God, awaited the destruction of the Soviet Government, disseminated lying rumours, sowed panic, and sat it out in the *taiga*. This was perfidy, treason.'[25] The more extreme of them advocated complete renunciation of society and went into hiding to await the collapse of the Soviet regime.[26] Many of their followers categorically refused to take up arms in the defence of the country against the enemy.[27] In one reported case, a woman had 'moved to Siberia' with her family.

She refused to work in the *kolkhoz* for religious motives, referring to the fact that 'in the Bible nothing is said about *kolkhozes*'. After long persuasion she agreed to be a cleaning lady in the school. The time was difficult, war, there was no bread, clothes, shoes. Ivanova was unwilling to recognize the reason for these difficulties. She blamed everything on the Soviet Government. She considered the war unleashed by the German fascists as a punishment levied by God on the communists, and hour by hour she awaited the demise of the 'anti-Christ'.[28]

The overt activities of such underground groups within the country, however, by no means represented the greatest challenge to Soviet religious policy during World War II. Far more important was the revival of religion which began with the arrival of German troops in occupied areas. Immediately upon the departure of Soviet authorities, believers were quick to organize churches and attempt to regain ground lost during the preceding years. A large proportion of the increase in the number of open churches, from 4,000 or fewer in 1941 to 15,000 or 16,000 in 1945, was due to the churches which had been re-opened under the German occupation and which resisted immediate closure when the Soviets reoccupied the area.

Soviet scholarship on occasion quite frankly admits that the

---

[24] I. A. Malakhova, 'Historians are studying present-day religious movements', *Istoriia SSSR*, No. 2 (March-April 1961), translated in *Current Digest of the Soviet Press* (Hereafter *CDSP*), 24 May 1961, p. 16.

[25] Vasin, op. cit., p. 21.

[26] Milovidov, op. cit., p. 218.

[27] *Komsomol'skaia Pravda*, 22 May 1964.

[28] Vasin, op. cit., pp. 17–18.

reopening of churches in occupied areas was due to the fact that these churches had been closed without the consent of the believers, thereby implying that even through the hard years of the twenties and thirties many of the Orthodox remained true to their faith despite all the pressures.[29] Church buildings were restored, new buildings were erected, and in many of the occupied areas 'the number of parishes more than doubled in 1941 to 1945'.[30] The revival of religion was a normal concomitant of the arrival of the Germans.[31]

Orthodox who had gone underground, either individually in hiding their faith or priestly ordination, or who had maintained their activities in underground groups, were exceedingly valuable in the new conditions ushered in by the German occupation. These individuals, who had managed to survive the years of Soviet pressure, provided the basis on which religious life could be reconstructed:

In the southern provincial city where I lived, at the time of the arrival of the Germans there remained only one church, a cemetery church behind the road-bed of the railway. Only those who had nothing to lose or who could not be threatened because of advanced age attended it.

In the course of the first two weeks after the arrival of the Germans, four churches were opened in the city. At the end of the month, there were already sixteen church congregations in the newly formed diocese. They were already formed but there were not enough priests; the reserves, who had concealed themselves as office accountants, behind the counter of bread stalls, and even with the sanitation carts, had been exhausted. All of these parishes rose 'from below': a group of believers would gather, would seek and find a priest, would clean out a temple which had been turned into a warehouse or a club, decorate it with icons which had been preserved in attics and basements, dedicate it, and gather a choir. Nor were there enough half-destroyed former churches. Vacant clubs and halls of institutions were adapted as temples.[32]

Large numbers of baptisms were performed in the early days of the occupation, as great masses of believers who had not dared to have their children baptized or who were unable to because of the lack of available churches sought to make up for lost time.[33]

---

[29] Iankova, 'Sovremennoe pravoslavie,' op. cit., p. 72.
[30] Shabatin, op. cit., p. 44.
[31] Iankova, 'Sovremennoe pravoslavie,' op. cit., p. 72.
[32] Shiriaev, op. cit., pp. 362–3.
[33] Davis, op. cit., p. 272.

This revival of religion represented a real problem to the Soviet Government after the Red Army had driven out the Germans and the occupied territories were returned to Soviet rule. The initial re-establishment of Soviet social control was generally so incomplete as to preclude any attempts summarily to close down the reopened churches. In view of the change in the regime's policy brought about by the limited concordat with the Moscow Patriarchate, most of these churches were transferred intact to patriarchal administration, and Soviet authorities limited themselves to the formidable enough task of overcoming the more extreme religious groups (Pentecostals, Jehovah's Witnesses, etc.) and of purging the Orthodox churches of their more hostile elements.[34] The magnitude of the problem of restoring some form of control over religious life in the newly occupied areas is reflected in the deployment of the small number of bishops which the Moscow Patriarchate possessed. During the first part of the war, of the twelve known bishops only one was in the eastern areas, and as the Nazis retreated five were immediately transferred to the liberated areas. Of the 21 bishops appointed in 1944, 14 went to the liberated areas, 6 to European Russia, and only 1 to the Urals. Of the 35 appointed between 1945 and 1950, 28 went to the formerly occupied areas, 4 to European Russia and only 3 to Siberia and Soviet Central Asia.[35] In view of the fact that this deployment of the episcopal corps of the Moscow Patriarchate was directly opposite to the general wartime and immediate post-war eastward migration of the population, it seems apparent that the revival of religion during the German occupation represented a considerable problem for the authorities and exercised an important influence on the activity of the Moscow Patriarchate for some time to come.

The revival of religion in the occupied areas was a complex phenomenon, reflecting a number of motivations in addition to purely religious aspirations. In the Ukraine, which came under German occupation almost entirely, religion was deeply intertwined with Ukrainian nationalism. Resentment against domination by the Great Russians had roots which were already deeply embedded in the Ukraine long before the Revolution. During the brief period in the Civil War when an independent Ukrainian

[34] Fireside, op. cit., p. 366.
[35] Alexeev, op. cit., pp. 10–36.

Government was established by Simon Petliura, the Ukrainian National Republic's first directive of 1 January 1919 laid down guide lines for the establishment of a national Ukrainian Orthodox Church. Such a Church was actually created after the Ukraine had been recaptured by the Red Army. In October 1921, an All-Ukrainian Church Assembly in Kiev established the Ukrainian Autocephalous Orthodox Church.[36]

From a canonical point of view this was a somewhat uncertain procedure, for no means could be found to acquire apostolic succession from a previously ordained bishop, and instead the Assembly itself consecrated V. K. Lipkovskii as 'Archbishop and Metropolitan of Kiev and All the Ukraine'. He, together with the Assembly, consecrated five more bishops, after which additional bishops could be appointed in the normal, Orthodox manner. However, this independent consecration of a bishop, together with the proclamation of autocephaly without permission from any previously existing Orthodox Church—neither Moscow, Georgia, nor Constantinople would sanction the new group—was directly contrary to Canon Law. Thus the Ukrainian Autocephalous Orthodox Church lacked a stable basis for its existence.

In addition, the new Church was infected with that same enthusiasm for reform which the Living Church groups were soon to display. By introducing such novelties as a married episcopate, lay preachers, and the transformation of monasteries into working collectives, the Ukrainian Church further diluted its claim to status as an autocephalous Orthodox Church. In its attitude towards the Soviet Government the Ukrainian Church displayed enthusiasm similar to that which was rampant in the Living Church Adventure, seeking to demonstrate loyalty to the Soviet Government and a willingness to co-operate, in return for which legal status might be granted.

Nationalism was a dominant force in the Ukrainian Autocephalous Church. The Ukrainian language was mandatory in all services, and loyalty to the Ukrainian nation was required of its clergy. In fact, the willing acceptance of the Soviet regime itself was dictated primarily by nationalistic sentiments. Taking

[36] For a detailed analysis of the history of the pre-war Ukrainian Autocephalous Orthodox Church, see Bohdan R. Bociurkiw, *Soviet Church Policy in the Ukraine, 1919-1939* (Unpublished Ph.D. dissertation, University of Chicago, 1961), pp. 186-97.

literally the early Leninist doctrine of national independence within a community of nations united by the working class in the Communist Party, the adepts of the Ukrainian Autocephalous Church saw themselves as the vanguard of a free Ukraine. By proclaiming independence from the Moscow Patriarchate, this Church felt that it was working in line with Party doctrine concerning national independence, and therefore welcomed the advent of Soviet power as the harbinger of a new, independent freedom which would replace the centuries of domination by Great Russians under the Tsars.

History was soon to prove, however, that these hopes were too sanguine. In the later twenties the Soviet regime became ever more suspicious of nationalistic sentiments within the U.S.S.R. In 1929, a purge was conducted against Ukrainian nationalists, which reached its peak in a trial of forty-five leaders of a Ukrainian nationalist movement in March 1932. Two of the clergy (one of them a founder) of the Ukrainian Autocephalous Orthodox Church were among those condemned in this trial, and the Church as a whole came under vigorous attack as a seed-bed of nationalism.

The activists of the Ukrainian Autocephalous Orthodox Church ('self-ordained Lipkovtsy') used the pulpit for anti-Soviet propaganda preaching a hostile relationship to the Russian people, and fought for the withdrawal of the Ukraine from the composition of the Soviet Union.[37]

The Church itself had foreseen the attack, and in a vain attempt to forestall it had met in January 1930 and decided to disband the organization. According to a subsequent Orthodox historian,

The motives for self-liquidation were: the fact, established by revision commission of clergy and laymen, of widespread use of the church pulpit, especially by 'bishops' of the Ukrainian Autocephalous Orthodox Church, both for instilling a hostile attitude in the masses of the Ukrainian people towards the Russian people, who were of one blood and one faith with them, and for propaganda for withdrawing the Uk.S.S.R. from the composition of the Soviet Union and uniting it with the Western Ukraine under the protectorship of Poland and Germany; the ranks of the clergy (especially the higher clergy) were

[37] Kurochkin, op. cit., p. 50; cf. Sheinman, 'Obnovlencheskoe techenie v russkoi pravoslavnoi tserkvi posle oktiabria,' op. cit., p. 62.

progressively being filled with non-church and theologically un-educated people; priests had been removed from the ranks of the clergy because they had dared, either on demand of their parishioners or on their own authority, to conduct services in Church Slavonic and had tried to establish relationships with the patriarchal Russian Church.[38]

It seems odd, however, that this Orthodox scholar (as well as a contemporary Soviet author[39]) places this event in the following year, when actually this action was taken in 1930 in direct pre-monition of the anti-nationalist attack which was soon to come.

By the end of 1930 the Ukrainian Autocephalous Orthodox Church was defunct. The majority of the parishes reaffiliated with the Moscow Patriarchate, while some united themselves to the various Living Church groups then active in the Ukraine.[40] It would appear, however, that a number of parishes attempted to maintain an independent existence, forming such organizations as the times would permit.[41] According to Walter Kolarz, 'The evidence suggests, nevertheless, that the Ukrainian Autocephalous Church was never completely vanquished and that it continued to exist as a Church of the catacombs in some rudimentary form until the beginning of World War II.' He cites in evidence a report of an atheist in 1939 that Ukrainian Autocephalous priests continued to be active, and in many churches the Ukrainian language was still used for the liturgy; affiliation with the Moscow Patriarchate was only a sham.[42]

Thus, when the Germans arrived in the Ukraine there was a considerable fund of nationalistic and independent Orthodox sentiment which might be unleashed. Despite the attempts of the Soviet Government to suppress such Ukrainian particularism, in the field of religion it remained a viable force and could revive almost immediately on the termination of Soviet governmental control.

Under the German occupation, the Ukrainian Autocephalous Church was revived and enjoyed a brief period of renewed life. The Autocephalous Church under the Germans differed from its

---

[38] Shabatin, op. cit., pp. 42–3.

[39] Kurochkin, op. cit., p. 50.

[40] Shabatin, op. cit., p. 43.

[41] Sheinman, 'Obnovlencheskoe techenie v russkoi pravoslavnoi tserkvi posle oktiabria,' op. cit., p. 62.

[42] Kolarz, op. cit., p. 113, citing *Antireligioznik*, No. 5 (1939).

predecessor of the twenties in two important details: it had a fully canonical episcopate, with apostolic succession guaranteed in the person of its leader, Metropolitan Polycarp (Sikorskii); and in the wartime Autocephalous Church there was no question of tampering with the traditions and canons of the Church.

The Ukrainian Autocephalous Orthodox Church during the war shared with its predecessor a vehement commitment to Ukrainian nationalism. This Church organization very quickly became a rallying point for the most ardent of the Ukrainian nationalists, and as such, whatever its numerical size, it represented a clear and present danger to the Soviet regime even though the Soviets had been driven out of the territories on which it operated. Should this Ukrainian Church successfully challenge the Moscow Patriarchate, a Pandora's Box of nationalistic troubles might be opened, and for this reason the Soviet regime was more than pleased with the Moscow Patriarchate's ecclesiastical hostility to the new group.

On 27 March 1942 the Moscow Patriarchate convened a small sobor of bishops and condemned Metropolitan Polycarp.[43] The following day Metropolitan Sergii proclaimed:

Now I have the information that in answer to my address Bishop Polycarp calls me an imposter, as though I had uncanonically occupied the position of patriarchal locum tenens, and he is continuing his evil affair. However that may be, I now know that my address, published in the foreign press, came to Bishop Polycarp. . . .[44]

It is interesting, however, that in this early attempt to condemn the Ukrainian autocephalous movement Metropolitan Sergii really had no persuasive answer to any slurs on his canonical authority which might be raised in defence of Polycarp's assumption of such authority in the Ukraine. It is not unlikely that the canonical weakness of Sergii's position in dealing with challenges in the occupied territories was one of the considerations which persuaded Stalin to permit a Sobor to be held in 1943 which could elect Sergii Patriarch. This Sobor, of course, brought the full weight of its authority to bear on the problem, and declared Polycarp excommunicate forthwith.

---

[43] Orthodox Church, *Patriarkh Sergii i ego dukhovnoe nasledstvo*, op. cit., p. 47.
[44] Orthodox Church, *Pravda o religii v Rossii*, op. cit., p. 137.

It is difficult to determine in retrospect just how successful the Ukrainian Autocephalous Orthodox Church was during the years of German occupation. It would not appear to have won universal support even among the Ukrainian people. Alongside of it a second organization, the Ukrainian Autonomous Orthodox Church, sprang up, and it would appear that this latter had a somewhat broader appeal among the population.[45] The autonomous group continued to recognize the jurisdictional authority of the Moscow Patriarchate, but this was declared to be held in abeyance for so long as the Moscow Patriarchate was under communist domination. Most of the Russian minority in the Ukraine belonged to this Church, and in general it would appear that Ukrainian nationalism played a very small role indeed in the Autonomous Church, as compared with the overt and outspoken nationalism in the Autocephalous Church.

Immediately upon the formation of the Ukrainian Autonomous Church it enjoyed a mass enrolment of believers who had previously been in the Orthodox underground, who welcomed it as a sign of their emancipation from atheistic rule.[46] If, as seems probable, the Autonomous Church, with its refusal to sever canonical relations with the Moscow Patriarchate, did succeed in attracting the great majority of the population, it would not seem correct to interpret the mass movement into these religious organizations in the Ukraine as a sign of disaffection with the Muscovite jurisdiction.[47] Certainly the success of the Autonomous Church would imply that nationalistic sentiments were somewhat less widespread among the believing population of the Ukraine than was the simple desire to be able to worship freely and without fear of reprisal.

Faced with the relatively good success of the competitive autonomous organization, the Ukrainian Autocephalous Orthodox Church had a very uncertain status in the occupied areas. Polycarp and his bishops enthusiastically welcomed the occupation forces as liberators and displayed great willingness to co-operate with them in any way possible. The German authorities,

---

[45] Spinka, *The Church in Soviet Russia*, op. cit. More detailed treatment of both the Autonomous and the Autocephalous wartime churches may be found in John A. Armstrong, *Ukrainian Nationalism* (New York: Columbia University Press, 1955), pp. 187–209 *et passim*.

[46] S. Raevskii, *Ukrainskaia avtokefal'naia tserkov'* ('The Ukrainian autocephalous church') (Jordanville, New York: Holy Trinity Monastery, 1948), pp. 11–12.

[47] So Teodorovich, 'The Catacomb Church in the U.S.S.R.,' op. cit., p. 4.

however, did not seem particularly impressed and showed no enduring friendship to this Ukrainian nationalist religious group. In large measure this failure on the part of the Germans to capitalize upon the warm welcome they received (in the Ukraine, not only the nationalistically inclined, but almost the entire population defected to the German side *en masse* and welcomed the arriving *Wehrmacht* with enthusiasm) was due to the peculiar inability of the Nazi leadership to see beyond their own ideological presuppositions. Considering all Slavs as *untermenschen*, the occupying authorities usually were sublimely indifferent to the desires of the conquered population, and those officers who did attempt a sympathetic understanding of the needs and aspirations of the people under their administration were rare exceptions.

Furthermore, it soon became apparent that the German authorities were no more enthralled with the prospect of a vigorous Ukrainian nationalism than the Soviet authorities had been. The sword cut both ways, and if the desire for national independence had been a threat to Soviet rule it also represented a potential danger for German rule over the Ukraine. In consequence, the German authorities did not offer to Polycarp's Church anything like that degree of conniving support which subsequent Soviet scholarship has seen in the history of the Ukrainian Autocephalous Orthodox Church. Quite the contrary: the German policy towards the Orthodox churches in the Ukraine seemed to be somewhat ambivalent, designed primarily to play off one group against another. There was great inconsistency in the religious policy of the occupying forces, and support would be given now to the Autonomous Church, now to the Autocephalous Church, in the attempt to minimize the problem of religious and national resurgence in the Ukraine.

In any event, the history of the Autocephalous Church in the Ukraine was not completely smooth. While some of the leaders of this organization elected to emigrate when the Germans retreated others were executed by the Germans for partisan activities. Naturally, when the Red Army reoccupied the area the Ukrainian Autocephalous Orthodox Church was immediately suppressed with its leaders arrested or going underground to escape the reprisals carried out by the returning Soviet authorities.

Similar autocephalous churches sprang up in a number of areas of the German occupation outside the Ukraine. Perhaps the most

important was the evanescent Belorussian Autocephalous Orthodox Church founded in 1942. This group also welcomed the
Germans enthusiastically, expressing desires for great success for
their liberators. Unlike the Ukrainian Autocephalous Church,
the Belorussian Church enjoyed the fairly consistent support of
the occupying authorities. It proved no more able to survive the
German retreat than had the Ukrainian Church, however, and
with the reoccupation by the Red Army it was liquidated entirely.[48]

These short-lived experiments in nationalistic Orthodox
organizations thus proved unable to survive the reassertion of
Soviet control, and at least from a formal point of view may be
considered temporary aberrations in the life of the Orthodox
Church in the U.S.S.R. Nevertheless, they vividly illustrated the
depth of religious feeling, even in a population which had been
thoroughly suppressed by the application of a decade of terror and
strict control over every aspect of social life. As such they served
to warn against too facile an assumption of victory over religion,
even when all or nearly all of the active churches were defunct.
The ability of the population which came under German occupation to maintain their religious identity, and of the clergy and
active laity to survive the preceding decade of extreme difficulty,
gave evidence of the effectiveness of clandestine and underground
means of preserving the faith, at least over the short term. Furthermore, the immediate resurgence of Ukrainian nationalism, despite
its total suppression ten years previously, provided a background
for the religious life in such areas. Particularly when conditions
are sufficiently severe to cause large-scale application of clandestine and underground methods of worship, there is always the
possibility that nationalism will become inextricably interwoven
with religion in the minds of the believers.

These elements were vividly expressed in a second problem
which confronted the Soviets upon their victory over the German
forces. Particularly in formerly Polish Galicia, Roman Catholicism
of Byzantine Rite, or Uniatism, was widespread. Suppression of
the short-lived autocephalous Orthodox churches in the occupied
areas apparently caused the Soviet authorities no particular
problems, even if it did take some years to effect the complete
liquidation of underground nationalist partisan organizations.

---

[48] Ladorenko, op. cit., p. 121; cf. Teodorovich, 'The Belorussian Orthodox Church,'
op. cit.

Suppression of the Uniates, however, proved to be a much more difficult matter.

Soviet hostility towards the Uniates did not originate with the acquisition of these new, predominantly Uniate territories. In the thirties, professional atheists had testified with horror that Roman Catholic Uniates were infiltrating into the Soviet Ukraine in an attempt to arouse nationalistic sentiment against the Soviet Union.[49] Ever alert to the danger of the Catholic menace, the Moscow Patriarchate late in the war also warned against the aspirations of the Vatican to gain influence among the Slavs, particularly in the Western Ukraine.[50]

Apparently the Germans were not particularly sympathetic to Uniate aspirations and refused to allow the Roman Catholic Church to accompany the occupying forces in these areas.[51] Nevertheless, it was patently impractical to attempt to suppress the Uniate faith during the early years of the occupation, and when the process of history abruptly terminated German rule over the Western Ukraine, the Uniate Church had survived the war successfully and maintained a strong position among the population.

In large measure, the religious loyalties of the Uniate population were focused in the person of Metropolitan Szeptycki. Granted extraordinary powers by Pope Pius X, Szeptycki served as the virtual Patriarch of the Uniates. An able organizer, he was universally admired and revered in the Uniate population to which the Soviets fell heir. Exercising an intelligent measure of prudence, the Soviet regime refrained from taking action with regard to the Uniate problem until Metropolitan Szeptycki's death on 1 November 1944—indeed, the Prime Minister of the Soviet Ukraine, N. S. Khrushchev, attended the funeral.[52]

Even after the death of Metropolitan Szeptycki, the Soviet regime continued to act circumspectly with regard to this powerful Church. It soon became obvious, however, that the problem could not be ignored indefinitely. The suppression of nationalist organizations in the Western Ukraine immediately raised the threat of a

---

[49] 'II Vsesoiuznaia antireligioznaia konferentsiia' ('II All-Union anti-religious conference'), *Pod Znamenem Marksizma*, No. 5 (September-October 1934), p. 178.

[50] *ZMP*, No. 4 (April 1945), pp. 20–1.

[51] M. Sheinman, *Vatikan vo vtoroi mirovoi voine* ('The Vatican in the Second World War') (Moscow: AN SSSR, 1951), pp. 179–80.

[52] Lino Gussoni and Aristide Brunello, *The Silent Church* (New York: Veritas, 1954), p. 25.

transference of nationalistic sentiment to the Uniate Church. And this, of course, was considered intolerable by the Soviet authorities. On 11 April 1945 the successor of Szeptycki, Metropolitan Slipiy, and four other bishops were arrested.

With 3,500,000 members, the Uniate Church of Galicia represented a formidable problem to the regime, and rather than risk an outright confrontation through naked use of force the regime elected to utilize a somewhat more indirect approach. If the Uniates could be brought under the wing of the Moscow Patriarchate, which already was sufficiently reliable from the regime's point of view, control could be established much more easily. Particularly in view of the exhausted state of the Soviet Union, this procedure held great promise for an easier transition from independence (and hence a threat to the regime) to docility.

Accordingly, in March 1946, a group of priests representing some ten per cent of the Uniate clergy gathered in L'vov and proclaimed themselves a Synod. A 'Committee of Initiative for the Transference of the Greek Catholic Church to Orthodoxy' was endorsed, under the leadership of three priests, Kostelnyk, Melnyk, and Pelvetskii. With rare candour, Corliss Lamont notes that 'Premier Stalin and his associates undoubtedly welcomed the announcement in 1946 that the Greek Catholic or Uniate Church of the Western Ukraine had broken its centuries old union with the Vatican, and returned to the Russian Orthodox fold'.[53]

The ground had been well prepared. There had been mass arrests of Ukrainian churchmen in the preceding year,[54] and there could be little doubt that refusal to submit to the russification movement would court a similar fate. The regime had used the preceding months to good advantage in gaining knowledge necessary for enforcing the transference. According to a directive of the Supreme Soviet of the U.S.S.R. of June 1954,

While proceeding with the registering of Greek-Catholic deaconships, parishes, and convents, the Initiating Committee must send to the Department of Orthodox Church Affairs of the Peoples Commissars of the U.S.S.R. a list of the deaconships, parishes, and respectively of the deacons, parish priests, and superiors of convents who refuse to

[53] Corliss Lamont, *Soviet Civilization* (New York: Philosophical Library, 1952), p. 152.
[54] U.S. Congress, House, *The Crimes of Khrushchev* (Washington, D.C.: U.S. Government Printing Office, 1959), Part 2, pp. 51–4.

submit to the Initiating Committee for the passage of the Greek Catholic Church to the Orthodox Church.[55]

No such elaborate mechanism was employed to engineer the transfer to Orthodoxy of the 350,000 Uniates of formerly Czecho-slovak Transcarpathia. In this area, which a year previously had been declared hopeless by the Moscow Patriarchate, the transfer was simply proclaimed as a *fait accompli* during a church ceremony in August 1949. Such a move had become possible because of the death of the head of the Catholic Church of Byzantine Rite of Transcarpathia, Romzha, in a 'mysterious accident' in November 1947. According to Kolarz,

The death of this young and popular bishop became the object of pious local legends which in themselves proved the survival of his Church in the hearts of the people. Later it became known that Mgr. Romzha, in premonition of his death, had appointed a successor, Mgr. Chira, whom he had secretly consecrated Bishop. Chira was arrested in 1948 and spent ten years in a Siberian camp.[56]

Thus the simple transfer of the Uniate population into the jurisdiction of the Moscow Patriarchate afforded a convenient means of bringing them under control. The arm of the regime was openly visible in the entire operation, and in view of the curious means employed to effect the jurisdictional transfer it would be difficult to presume that such a move was universally desired by the Ukrainian population. Nevertheless, in a strange interpretation of history, the Moscow Patriarchate has persisted in referring to the event as the liberation of the Orthodox populations of these areas, who had been suffering under the enforced rule of the Vatican. That such enslavement had persisted largely unchanged for the three and a half centuries since 1596 was apparently of little importance in the Moscow Patriarchate's interpretation of the event.

Not all the Uniates, however, appeared to agree with this interpretation of the process of forcible russification. Patriarchal authorities themselves admitted that there were some, primarily monks, who refused to acquiesce to the jurisdictional transfer and went into secular occupations rather than continue to serve the Church.[57] Further events were to show that Uniate sentiments by

[55] Cf. Gussoni and Brunello, op. cit., p. 28.
[56] Kolarz, op. cit., p. 235.
[57] *One Church*, XII, 7–8 (1958), p. 261.

no means perished with the transfer of the Uniate churches to Muscovite jurisdiction.

A number of imprisoned Uniate clergymen were released in the general amnesty of the mid-fifties. Their re-entry into society precipitated a considerable revival of Uniate sentiment, either in maintaining the Uniate tradition within open churches formally affiliated with Orthodoxy or in clandestine and semi-clandestine activities.[58] A cult of veneration for Szeptycki also became evident.[59]

An alleged miracle of great importance to the Uniate population took place during this period. As early as 1947 the Blessed Virgin was said to have appeared in the Eastern Ukraine.[60] After the emancipation of the prisoners, however, two priests were accused of fabricating a miraculous appearance of the Mother of God at the village of Serednye, in which she promised that the Uniate Church would soon be re-established.[61] According to an atheist writer in 1967,

The 'Serednye miracle', fabricated in 1954 near the village of Serednye, ... is one of the grossest examples of swindle which the Uniate and nationalist leaders have perpetrated in recent decades.

Ignatii Soltys, a pupil of the monks, initiated the 'Serednye miracle'. He spent the years from 1941 to 1945 in the Stanislav Theological Seminary. Anyone who studied there was methodically infected with a hatred for the Soviet people.[62]

A somewhat more complete report of the miracle had been published the previous year, apparently based on the evidence of a court process against the leader of an underground organization, the 'Penitents', which had grown up as a result of this miracle.

The founder of the group of 'Penitents' was a former Uniate priest, Ignatii Soltys, who proclaimed himself the 'plenipotentiary of the Vatican' who allegedly had been commissioned by the Pope of Rome himself to head the church in the Ukraine; a few years ago he disseminated the rumour about the 'Great Miracle'. Allegedly, on High Mountain, near to his home, the Virgin Mary, turning to Ignatii Soltys

[58] Struve, op. cit., p. 264.
[59] Kolarz, op. cit., p. 241.
[60] A. Shysh, 'The end and the means,' *Liudyna i Svit*, No. 4 (April 1967), pp. 46–8, as translated in *Digest of the Soviet Ukrainian Press*, No. 7 (July 1967), p. 23.
[61] Kolarz, op. cit., p. 241.
[62] Shysh, loc. cit.

and his followers 'who just happened' at that moment to be on High Mountain, informed them in confidence that 'the end of the world is coming soon' and only true believers would get to the kingdom of heaven. As for other people, the Mother of God consigned them all to 'the devil' and doomed them to 'death and eternal torment in the hell of fire'. Only those who made a clean break with all connection to the world and devoted themselves to repentance would be accounted true believers.[63]

By the end of the fifties the Uniate underground movement was beginning to reach serious proportions.[64] Chira, the secretly consecrated successor of Metropolitan Slipiy, had been released during the amnesty but was assassinated in 1958,[65] further exacerbating the tensions.

During the sixties, the underground Uniate movements reached sufficiently serious proportions as to draw on themselves the wrath of the State. In a trial in L'vov in 1964, it was revealed that a complex operation had been discovered in the city. A group of underground Uniates, led by a priest, was operating a well-equipped photographic studio for the production of religious pictures. In addition, a foundry had been secretly built in an apartment and was used to cast crucifixes, again for sale to the believers. This organization, in addition to its commercial activities, was exerting great efforts to train and prepare candidates for secret Uniate priesthood.[66]

Another trial during the same year was directed against the 'Penitent' organization mentioned above. An interesting extract from the interrogation of the members was quoted:

'Your name?'
'Penitent.'
'First name?'
'Elect.'
'Your age?'
'Three years.'
'Where are you employed?'
'In God's field.'

[63] L. Smirnov, 'Iavlenie bogomateri—s pomoshch'iu nozhits i kleia' ('The appearance of the Mother of God—with the help of scissors and paste'), *Nauka i Religiia*, No. 1 (January 1966), p. 95.
[64] *Sovetskaia Kultura*, 5 September 1959.
[65] Kolarz, op. cit., p. 242.
[66] *Molod' Ukrainy*, 11 September 1964.

'Place of employment?'
'On the Holy High Mountain.'[67]

At this trial, the leader, Soltys, was convicted of 'banditry', having allegedly seized and burned the personal property of a member who had expressed a desire to leave the sect.[68] There were numerous other reports of the activity of underground Uniates during the sixties.[69]

Apocalypticism was apparently very strong among the 'Penitents'. The date of the end of the world was set originally for 1 April 1962,[70] and subsequently revised to 1964.[71] Their worship was conducted in deep secrecy.

In the middle of the night a small room is filled with middle-aged and elderly people. They are all on their knees, heads are humbly bowed, the air is heavy with the smell of incense and candle smoke. Over all this comes the commanding voice of a young priest with a gleam of fanaticism in his eyes.

The second mass . . . was conducted at the home of Mikola Virsta. It was there that I saw the 'Mother of God' in the person of Anna Kuzminskii, sister of Ignatii (Soltys). I discovered later that this sickly, hysterical woman was and remains merely a mouthpiece for all the acts of her shrewd brother. Between 1954 and 1958 she allegedly had sixteen visions of the 'immaculate Mother of God', and prophesied 'quick perdition' to all the 'unfaithful'. Dressed in black, with an unhealthy flush on her cheeks, this 'virgin' enthusiastically related her latest conversation with the 'Mother of God'.[72]

Ukrainian nationalism was a prominent feature in the 'Penitent' movement,[73] as was alienation from society and refusal to participate in collective farms, industry, or education.[74]

Numerous other Uniate movements in addition to the 'Penitents' apparently were active in the Ukraine in the latter fifties and early sixties.[75] The shrine of *Iasnaia Gora* (Bright Mountain)

[67] Smirnov, op. cit., p. 95.
[68] Ibid.
[69] Teodorovich, 'The Catacomb Church in the U.S.S.R.,' op. cit., p. 13.
[70] Shysh, op. cit., p. 24.
[71] Smirnov, op. cit., p. 95.
[72] Shysh, op. cit., p. 24.
[73] Ibid.
[74] *Molod' Ukrainy*, 12 November 1965.
[75] Cf. Struve, op. cit., p. 264.

was widely popular as a place of pilgrimage.[76] In another case, a group was forcibly taken by truck sixty miles away from the sacred well at which they were praying and made to walk home.[77]

Thus the dislocations caused by the German occupation, together with the acquisition of new territories in the Western Ukraine, added a new dimension to the underground Orthodox milieu of the post-war period. The war demonstrated convincingly that even if churches are closed religion retains its potential for a considerable period of time, and so soon as conditions permit, will revive and resume activity. The immediate resurrection of Orthodoxy during German occupation demonstrated that clandestine measures and underground activity can, over a period of a number of years, preserve the religious capability of the population.

Furthermore, the overt and outspoken attitudes of nationalism prevalent in the Ukrainian Autocephalous Orthodox Church during the period of the German occupation demonstrated that nationalism remains a potentially important adjunct to religion in those areas where both the religious and the national aspirations of a minority group are repressed by force. The nationalistic dimensions of the religious temperaments of the national minorities were not especially evident during the difficult pre-war years. Underground conditions of religious life would not seem to be conducive to an overt alliance between nationalism and religion. Nevertheless, the war demonstrated that nationalism remains a background factor, and, indeed, in understanding the underground Orthodox movements among the ethnic minorities it might be well to consider nationalism an important aspect in the motivations which induce individuals to participate in underground religious worship.

In the case of the Uniates, this nationalistic dimension was especially evident, for in the revival of Uniate sentiments following the emancipation of the mid-fifties, Ukrainian nationalism was often a concomitant factor. The activities of such underground movements as the Penitents would exercise an attraction not only on religious grounds but also among those who yearned for some

[76] D. Koretskii, 'Iasna Hora' ('Bright Mountain'), *Liudyna i Svit*, No. 1 (January 1967), pp. 28–32.

[77] O. Chaikovskaia, 'Pochemu ushel topol'' ('Why the poplar tree went away'), *Nauka i Religiia*, No. 6 (June 1966), pp. 5–6.

expression of their national identity, which was felt to be in danger of suppression by Great Russian imperialism.

To some extent, of course, the activities of the Uniate underground organizations are to one side of the proper subject of this study. These, after all, were not, strictly speaking, Orthodox underground movements but Catholic activities. Nevertheless, the regime's policy of including the Uniates in Russian Orthodoxy meant that the Moscow Patriarchate fell heir to a number of problems which could only exacerbate the difficult enough challenge of underground schismatic movements within its ranks. After World War II, not only was Orthodoxy threatened by fissiparous tendencies within its ranks, it also had to contend, at least in formerly Uniate areas, with schismatic movements leaning towards Roman Catholicism. Hence the post-war problem of underground movements was even more complex than the pre-war situation had been.

VII

The True Orthodox Church

With the waning of World War II, a period of intense activity began for underground Russian Orthodoxy. The large number of individual local groupings coalesced during this period into underground Orthodox movements which exerted a considerable influence throughout the country. The more highly organized of these movements was the 'True Orthodox Church', which during the latter forties was able to play an influential part in the somewhat chaotic post-war conditions. It was only towards the end of the decade that the regime, which had been forced to concentrate almost its entire attention on surviving the challenge of war, was able to reconstruct its facilities for social control. In the absence of this control over society, conditions were sufficiently relaxed in many areas of the country to allow the formation of a well-organized, clandestine church structure.

The direct antecedents of the True Orthodox Church can be traced back at least as far as the immediate post-revolutionary period. In the Tambov area, for example, the city of Michurinsk (formerly Kozlov) was one of the most active centres of the True Orthodox Church during the forties. This city had long been a point of active Orthodox dissent, dating back to the immediate post-revolutionary period when twelve of the fourteen churches and both monasteries of the city were closed. This had forced believers to make use of whatever expedients were possible for continuation of their religious life, and, during a major uprising against the fledgling Soviet regime, the clergy played a prominent role. When the Living Church Adventure further exacerbated the situation, an organized movement appeared in response to Tikhon's censure of innovations in the Church, as has been noted above. These early resistance movements in the Church were of direct influence on the underground formations of later years.

The controversy surrounding Metropolitan Sergii's declaration of 1927, however, had a much more direct impact in preparing the soil from which the True Orthodox Church sprang. Mitrokhin reported on his findings during the field study of 1959 as follows:

One of the followers of the True Orthodox Church, S., related: 'In the initial years of Soviet rule the clergy of the churches in the city of Kirsanov split into Tikhonites and Sergiites. . . . Since the Tikhonites preserved all that was old and pre-revolutionary in their services, a certain part of the believers, who were dissatisfied with the Soviet Government, from the ranks of kulaks, traders, and other people, joined the Tikhonite movement. At this time the Tikhonites in Kirsanov were led by Archpriest Aleksandr, who, in his sermons, called believers to support the Tikhonite movement.' Both in Kozlov, in Kirsanov, and in other cities there existed a series of smaller organizations. On their base the church monarchistic movement led by Aleksei Bui also sprang up in the twenties, which had links in many oblasts.[1]

The vicissitudes of such organizations as these during the following decade have been described above. The intimate relationship of these schisms and the post-war True Orthodox Church, both in terms of personnel and of general approach, has led certain Soviet commentators to date the latter's rise in 1927.[2] The Josephite schism served as a direct precursor of the later True Orthodox Church,[3] and the leading Soviet authority, L. N. Mitrokhin, dispenses entirely with the term, 'Josephites', and refers to Metropolitan Iosif by his secular name when speaking of the origins of the True Orthodox Church, 'which was founded at the end of the twenties by Metropolitan F. Petrovykh in Leningrad'.[4]

The social turmoil of the collectivization campaign was also of considerable impact in preparing the way for the subsequent development of the True Orthodox Church.[5] During the thirties, when the regime had successfully disrupted the organized Josephite movement, many of the local underground Orthodox groupings which developed were direct predecessors to the True Orthodox Church.[6] The Buevtsy organization, for example, embraced a

---

[1] Mitrokhin, op. cit., p. 151.
[2] Filippova, op. cit., p. 92.
[3] Fedorenko, op. cit., p. 211.
[4] Mitrokhin, op. cit., p. 148.
[5] Fedorenko, op. cit., p. 211.
[6] M. Hordienko, 'Is Orthodoxy Changing?', *Liudyna i Svit*, No. 3 (March 1969), pp. 18–23, as translated in *Digest of the Soviet Ukrainian Press*, May 1969, pp. 16–17.

number of people who subsequently became leaders of the True Orthodox Church,[7] and even after this movement had been liquidated as an organization, these members continued their underground Orthodox activity throughout the decade of the thirties.

This very organization served both in idea and in its organizational relationship as the starting point for the followers of the True Orthodox Church in 1946–1952. Among the workers of the True Orthodox Church at this time we continually meet either active Buevtsy or people who at one time had been connected with them.[8]

In addition, the True Orthodox Church utilized the experiences of other, allied Orthodox and semi-Orthodox underground groups, such as the Fedorovtsy, Imiaslavtsy, etc.[9]

The regime's diminished capacity to control society during the war and the immediate post-war period allowed underground Orthodoxy to enjoy a period of intense activity.[10] Between 1943 and 1952 non-Orthodox religions in general enjoyed considerable revival.[11] This, of course, was a part of the general resurgence of religion during this period.

The post-war years saw a revival of religious moods and prejudices among some of our people. Increased activity on the part of the religious people and decreased attention to atheistic propaganda resulted in a relative rise in the number of members of sects (chiefly at the expense of the Orthodox Church, but also from among persons of vacillating views) in certain portions of our country.[12]

The field study conducted by the Academy of Sciences of the U.S.S.R. discovered that the True Orthodox Church had been active during this period throughout the Tambov area,[13] as did a similar study conducted in the Lipetsk area.[14] It would seem that these were not isolated cases, but were indicative of the spread of the True Orthodox Church throughout the country.

[7] Mitrokhin, op. cit., p. 151.
[8] Ibid., p. 154.
[9] Klibanov, 'Sovremennoe sektantstvo v Tambovskoi oblasti,' op. cit., p. 95.
[10] Ibid.
[11] A. I. Klibanov, 'Sektantstvo v proshlom i v nastoiashchem' ('Sectarianism in the past and in the present'), in AN SSSR, Sovremennoe Sektantstvo, op. cit., p. 30.
[12] Muraviev and Dmitrov, op. cit., p. 64.
[13] Klibanov, 'Sovremennoe sektantstvo v Tambovskoi oblasti,' op. cit., pp. 95–6
[14] Klibanov, 'Sovremennoe sektantstvo v Lipetskoi oblasti,' op. cit., pp. 157, 159 160.

It is fully possible that in other oblasts the concrete history of groups of the True Orthodox Church was different, that their bonds and intermediate ties were different. But we think that in general the principal evaluations of the substance of the True Orthodox Church will preserve their full significance for any adherents of the True Orthodox Church, wherever they may be found.[15]

It is difficult to determine the strength of the True Orthodox Church during this period. Geographically, the movement was widespread.[16] According to Konstantinov, 'There are assertions that it united millions of believers, but no factual data have been published in the press'.[17] Despite Konstantinov's well merited caution, these estimates may not be unduly inflated, for according to I. Klibanov, in the two areas intensely studied by the Academy of Sciences the Orthodox underground groups were the predominant factor in the general rise of non-Orthodox religion during the post-war period, and indeed formed the basis of that revival of sectarian religion.[18] In one of these areas, at least, the underground Orthodox enjoyed greater success than all other non-Orthodox religious groups.[19]

The True Orthodox Church was a highly organized, clandestine movement, which attempted to duplicate, secretly and in competition with the legalized Orthodox Church, an institutional Orthodoxy which was liturgically as complete as possible. There is no evidence that it enjoyed the services of an episcopate. The institution of the priesthood, however, was preserved and, indeed, formed the basis for the organization of the True Orthodox Church. When possible, they utilized duly ordained Orthodox priests who had broken with the legalized Church.[20] In addition, they were able to enjoy the services of those priests who had temporarily abandoned the active ministry and had successfully concealed their ordination during the thirties.

The large number of priests who had been incarcerated during the pre-war period, however, were not available during the post-war period, for it would not seem that any considerable number of

---

[15] Mitrokhin, op. cit., p. 145.
[16] *Soviet Agricultural and Peasant Affairs* (Lawrence, Kansas: University of Kansas Press, 1963), p. 90.
[17] Konstantinov, *Gonimaia tserkov'*, op. cit., p. 57.
[18] Klibanov, 'Sovremennoe sektantstvo v Lipetskoi oblasti,' op. cit., p. 167.
[19] Klibanov, 'Sovremennoe sektantstvo v Tambovskoi oblasti,' op. cit., p. 91.
[20] Ibid., p. 95.

13

such prisoners were released from the prison system unless they agreed to accept the legalized Orthodox Church.[21] There were attempts to train priests clandestinely and to organize secret theological schools, but it would not appear that new initiates to the priesthood were sufficiently numerous to have a great impact on the True Orthodox Church.[22] Women, many of them secretly nuns, were widely utilized to augment the inadequate number of active priests.[23]

The True Orthodox Church was attempting to establish a centralized organization immediately after World War II.[24] Apparently these attempts, which continued until 1950, were unsuccessful in establishing a nation-wide organization—subsequent Soviet scholarship, at least, was unable to detect a successful, nation-wide organization.[25]

The basic organizational unit of the True Orthodox Church was the home monastery, usually headed by a nun.[26] Some of these monasteries had several dozen adherents and sympathizers. Prayer meetings with ten to twelve people in attendance were held, and individual conversations between leaders and members were also conducted.[27] Great care was exercised in admitting new members, generally after strict examination and on the personal recommendation of another member.[28] Strict, solemn oaths were taken by all members to avoid participation in Soviet society and the patriarchal Orthodox Church,[29] and of strict obedience to the leaders of the movement and refusal to divulge its secrets.[30]

The activities of the True Orthodox Church utilized a broad range of highly conspiratorial methods. Strictest secrecy was maintained concerning meetings and gatherings. Secret codes and ciphers were used in correspondence and communications between members and among the leaders of various local and regional groups. Couriers, as well as false identifications for non-existent persons, were used in the communications network. The activity

[21] Konstantinov, *Gonimaia tserkov'*, op. cit., pp. 48–9; but cf. Roeder, op. cit., p. 167.
[22] Ibid., p. 57.
[23] Andreev, *O polozhenii pravoslavnoi tserkvi v sovetskom soiuze*, op. cit., pp. 10–11.
[24] Fedorenko, op. cit., p. 213.
[25] Mitrokhin, op. cit., p. 155.
[26] Ibid., p. 156.
[27] Klibanov, 'Sovremennoe sektantstvo v Tambovskoi oblasti,' op. cit., p. 95.
[28] Mitrokhin, op. cit., p. 155.
[29] Klibanov, 'Sovremennoe sektantstvo v Tambovskoi oblasti,' op. cit., p. 95.
[30] Fedorenko, op. cit., p. 212.

of the leadership was conducted in deepest secrecy, and not even the members of the group were informed of such matters.[31] Clandestine methods were even used for the sacraments of the church:

They have gathered a special institution of priests of the 'True Orthodox Church' and a particular form of an institution of 'links': adherents of the True Orthodox Church put down a confession in written form and a 'link' gives these to a priest, who orally prescribes penance for those confessing so that the 'link' can give them back to those confessing.[32]

Many of the leaders of the True Orthodox Church maintained no permanent address and wandered from group to group in order to exercise their ministry. This was comparable to the practice developed earlier by one of the branches of the Old Believers, the *Beguny*,[33] and was destined to become especially important in underground Orthodoxy a decade later (see below). It was not unusual for such wandering leaders to take apprentices with them on their illegal travels.[34]

Like the earlier Josephite movement, the larger organization of the True Orthodox Church embraced a number of discrete, identifiable sub-groupings, even though after World War II it was no longer the common practice for local groups to maintain their own, particular identity, but instead they tended to merge themselves into the True Orthodox Church without local or peculiar distinctions. Nevertheless, there were identifiable sub-groupings in the True Orthodox Church, such as the Leontevtsy, formed by Leontii Gritzak, who refused to accept the limited concordat of 1943 and formed his own Church.[35] Other groups within the True Orthodox Church, such as the Mikhailovtsy, the Podgornovtsy, and the Agapitovtsy, had originally been able to form themselves in the confusion of the war and the German occupation.[36] Little more than the name is known of other sub-groupings,

---

[31] Mitrokhin, op. cit., pp. 155–6.

[32] Klibanov, 'Sovremennoe sektantstvo v Tambovskoi oblasti,' op. cit., p. 95.

[33] Milovidov, op. cit., p. 218.

[34] S. V. Koltuniuk, 'Dokhodit' do kazhdogo—znachit uchityvat' osobennosti kazhdogo' ('To approach each means to study the peculiarities of each'), in N. I. Gubanov, et. al., *Induvidual'naia rabota s veruiushchimi* ('Individual work with believers') (Moscow: 'Mysl' ', 1967), p. 91.

[35] *Sovetskaia Kultura*, 13 January 1959.

[36] Ibid.; *Z.M.P.*, No. 1 (January 1948), p. 77.

such as the Iovtsy and the Solianovtsy (the latter perhaps being an alternate designation for the Leontevtsy).[37]

It seems unlikely that the True Orthodox Church had any relationship whatsoever with Orthodox Churches in the Russian emigration. A Ukrainian journal, however, a decade later made the accusation that 'the stinking corpse of the True Orthodox Church is being galvanized from abroad by the Russian Orthodox Church Synod [Abroad] headed by Metropolitan Anastasii'.[38] In 1958, a local remnant of the True Orthodox Church was found to have composed an 'address to Orthodox Christians abroad'.[39] It is not clear whether this represented an attempt to establish ecclesiastical relationships or whether, as seems more likely, it was an early example of that practice of appealing to the world for support which would soon become widespread among Baptists, Orthodox, and the intelligentsia at large. In general, however, it would not appear that there were any significant ecclesiastical or jurisdictional relationships between the True Orthodox Church and Orthodox organizations abroad.

The True Orthodox Church was exceedingly hostile to the legalized, patriarchal Orthodox Church. The dispute was not based on doctrinal, liturgical or other clearly religious grounds, for there were no significant differences between the two organizations in these matters; 'the True Orthodox Church basically preserved the doctrine and ritual of Orthodoxy'.[40] Although such matters were largely irrelevant in areas in which even during the relatively relaxed post-war period there were no open patriarchal churches, the primary cause of the hostility of the True Orthodox Church towards the patriarchal jurisdiction would seem to have been the latter's acceptance of the Soviet regime. The regime itself contributed to the exacerbation of this disagreement by making acceptance of the Moscow Patriarchate a condition for religious activity—especially in the prison system, this became the criterion which determined whether a clergyman would be released.[41]

For its part, the Moscow Patriarchate definitely felt the under-

---

[37] Ibid. Struve classifies the Solianovtsy as a sub-grouping of the Imiaslavtsy (op. cit., p. 230).

[38] *Voiovnychy Atheist*, No. 4 (1961), p. 34.

[39] Fedorenko, op. cit., p. 213.

[40] Ibid., p. 212.

[41] Andreev, *O polozhenii pravoslavnoi tserkvi v sovetskom soiuze*, op. cit., pp. 9–10.

ground groups to be competitors for the religious affections of the people. The 'Journal of the Moscow Patriarchate' in 1948 frankly noted that the Krasnodar diocese was 'grieving under the onslaught of Baptist agitators and of every sort of underground, anti-patriarchal agitators . . . and other sectarians'.[42] The inclusion of the word 'anti-patriarchal' seems a direct reference to underground Orthodoxy as contrasted with Protestant sects.[43] In 1948 the 'Journal' presented a speech of Ioasaf, Bishop of Tambov, in which he frankly stated:

Your sincere prayers in the temple and love for it are comforting, but my joy is tempered by the fact that among you there are people who call themselves Christians but in fact these people are self-ordained. They deny the temple of God, do not accept it and even mock this sacred place. The self-ordained slander the contemporary Orthodox Church and spread obloquy on the Holy Patriarch and on the entire priestly rank, and to themselves they arrogate the function of meeting the needs of Orthodox Christians: they baptize infants, conduct funerals, administer extreme unction, and even conduct the Eucharist. They consider only themselves to be Orthodox Christians.[44]

Some months later the 'Journal', in denying the existence of underground Orthodoxy, equated 'self-styled priests' with the émigré Synod Abroad.[45] A year earlier, the 'Journal' had accused such priests of undermining the work of the churches in the dioceses.[46]

Such 'prohibited priests' were a major source of clergy for the True Orthodox Church. Only ordained priests were used, but these must be of Tikhonite persuasion, and as the war years receded into the past it became more and more difficult to acquire such priests.[47]

In all other respects, the True Orthodox Church was bitterly hostile to patriarchal Orthodoxy, particularly to its leaders.[48] Andreev, utilizing the testimony of émigrés from this period, illustrates the prevalent attitude as follows:

[42] Z.M.P., No. 1 (January 1948), pp. 76–7.
[43] Alexeev, op. cit., p. 61.
[44] Z.M.P., No. 2 (February 1948), p. 65.
[45] Ibid., No. 12 (December 1948), p. 25.
[46] Ibid., No. 3 (March 1947), pp. 52–4.
[47] Mitrokhin, op. cit., p. 158.
[48] Fedorenko, op. cit., p. 211.

'I cannot live without the Church,' say several rank and file, 'but I do not accept the Soviet Patriarch.'

Many attend Soviet temples only because they have honoured or miraculous icons there.

'We go to church when there is no service there, to be close to the icons,' say others. 'We often leave the service when they praise Stalin in the sermons,' say others.

'I go to church, but I do not confess and I do not participate, because the bishops and priests serve the Soviet Government,' relate others.

There are priests who weep and repent at home that they serve in the Soviet Church, but there are also other priests and monks who say that 'lying in church now is to salvation', but the main thing is 'preservation of the canons'. Very few approve the words and deeds of Patriarch Aleksii wholly, primarily among the intelligentsia and professors who are useful to the Soviet Government. The more simple the people, the more clearly they see the falsehood in the Church and mourn over it.[49]

It is possible that Andreev's evaluation was unduly pessimistic, inasmuch as his evidence is from hostile sources. Nevertheless, where such sentiments were prevalent the True Orthodox Church could enjoy considerable success.

It is important to note, however, that such hostility to the patriarchal Church was only one—and perhaps not even the most important—reason for participation in the True Orthodox Church. Of great importance is the paucity of active churches even during the post-war period. Great masses of the population who still desired to worship in the Orthodox manner and to receive the various sacraments of the Church were unable to be satisfied because of the great distances between churches and the limited capacity of the understaffed and overworked clergy to administer to their needs.[50] Given such conditions, the appearance of priests claiming to be truly Orthodox and capable of administering the sacraments could be expected to have a considerable response.

The True Orthodox Church was deeply imbued with hostility towards the Soviet regime and, indeed, towards almost every aspect of contemporary Soviet society. This thorough alienation from society necessarily attracted elements of the population which were not happily integrated into society, and was reinforced by their negative experiences. By and large, the leaders of the True

---

[49] Andreev, *O polozhenii pravoslavnoi tserkvi v sovetskorn soiuze*, op. cit., pp. 11–12.
[50] Ibid., p. 10.

Orthodox Church 'could count on the belief only of the most ignorant, backward people in order to exploit their ignorance and backwardness to their own ends, which were often openly anti-Soviet, hostile to that grand construction of a new life which is being established in our country'.[51] Everything remotely connected with the Soviets was considered 'godless' and anti-Christian. Self-denial on earth was the path to 'eternal bliss in heaven'. Soviet laws were invalid and need not be observed.[52]

The leaders of the True Orthodox Church rigidly required the follower to refrain from participation in elections, not to sign for loans, and not to participate in social actions in order that they might boycott all Soviet life. In this regard, one of the active partisans of the True Orthodox Church gave such 'instructions' as these to a young woman: 'Under no circumstances may one go to their idolatrous festivals, and celebrate the revolutionary holidays with them—October day, New Year, etc. These days must be spent in prayer and work and not in joy or, especially, demonstrations—a single word for "demons' straits".[53] Do not go to the theatre or to the cinema, nor to any drinking party or feast. Have nothing to do with your godless neighbours, read God's books. Throw out the radio so that it won't play, and tell him [the husband—L.M.] that it breaks your heart that the children are being educated in the godless education.'

Membership in the True Orthodox Church signified a hostile relation to all the good things of our culture, to science, and to the very spirit of our life. The immutable condition for each member of the True Orthodox Church was non-participation in the work of the *kolkhoz* or of Soviet institutions.[54]

According to one of the leaders, 'Our business is monastic, to be in cells and not to participate in any worldly affairs'.[55] Thus by capitalizing upon the strong theme of the idealization of asceticism, the True Orthodox Church achieved an almost theological basis for social alienation. Alienation from society was elevated to a theological requisite in the doctrine of sin; according to a former member of the True Orthodox Church,

The basic thought of repentance implies that the people entering into the organization had repented of sins which, in our opinion, they had

[51] Klibanov, 'Sovremennoe sektantstvo v Tambovskoi oblasti,' op. cit., pp. 90–1.
[52] Fedorenko, op. cit., p. 211.
[53] The pun in Russian is literally 'demons' passions'.
[54] Mitrokhin, op. cit., pp. 157–8.
[55] Ibid., p. 159.

committed against the Orthodox faith. Besides personal sins, we also considered it a sin when persons entering into the True Orthodox Church had participated in voting, had worked in *kolkhozes* or other social organizations; i.e. we did not receive those people who according to their own persuasion were Soviet people, but we accepted, on the contrary, those who were inimically disposed towards the Soviet Union.[56]

The confessional was widely used to reinforce this particular aspect of the doctrine of sin.[57] Understandably enough, rank and file members displayed a lesser degree of social alienation than did the clergy.[58]

In view of how deeply the True Orthodox Church was alienated from society, it is scarcely surprising that apocalypticism played a dominant role in the movement. Special emphasis was placed on the Orthodox doctrine that the world would be conquered by the anti-Christ immediately prior to the Second Coming of Christ.[59] Anti-Christ was held to have assumed power in 1917, and since that time the only way to avoid his clutches was through asceticism and much prayer.[60] The end of the world draws near, and only the righteous 'will be saved from the "terrible judgement" and will be received by Christ into the kingdom of heaven'.[61] Every care must be taken to avoid the 'seventy-seven nets' of the anti-Christ.[62] According to Mitrokhin, the members of the True Orthodox Church

disseminated their blind and fanatical rumours by every means, 'testifying' to their prophecies. The very character of these rumours makes it possible to make a direct evaluation of the squalid clerical lives of these spiteful people, who were ready by any means to slander socialism. 'The earthquake in Ashkhabad was sent expressly,' whispered the True Orthodox Church in 1948, 'and soon Moscow will tremble just as Ashkhabad did.' When as a consequence of underground volcanic activity in the Kuril Islands a gigantic tidal wave (the so-called *tsunami*) appeared, the religious fanatics began to say: 'Fiery lava is coming from Kamchatka, and everything will be burned up. One woman has come from there.' In connection with the elections it was

---

[56] Quoted in ibid.
[57] Fedorenko, op. cit., p. 212.
[58] Klibanov, 'Sovremennoe sektantstvo v Tambovskoi oblasti,' op. cit., p. 95.
[59] Mitrokhin, op. cit., p. 156.
[60] Fedorenko, op. cit., p. 212.
[61] Klibanov, 'Sovremennoe sektantstvo v Tambovskoi oblasti,' op. cit., p. 95.
[62] Teodorovich, 'The Catacomb Church in the U.S.S.R.,' op. cit., p. 9.

said: 'Three elections yet remain; two will be Soviet elections, but the third time we will elect the Pope of Rome. We must keep hands off all elections,' and the like. The conclusively anti-social character of the ideology and practice of the True Orthodox Church is seen in the fact that some of its leaders, powerless to find support among the Soviet people, linked the realization of their plans with imperialistic aggression, spreading in 1950 rumours about the inevitability of World War III.[63]

It is interesting that with regard to the rumours of the imminence of war, the True Orthodox Church could draw directly on Soviet propaganda, which had been increasingly strident in its utilization of the threat of war to encourage the population to greater efforts, and with the beginning of the Korean War such predictions as these might have seemed very credible indeed to the Soviet population.

To some degree it would seem that the apocalypticism of the True Orthodox Church at times was predicated on a restoration of the monarchy. This, of course, is a theme which has been connected fairly intimately with eschatological doctrines throughout Russian history. Occasionally, True Orthodox Church leaders would claim to be members of the Tsar's family.[64] Especially in the Tambov area, the cult of Saint Serafim of Sarov had monarchistic overtones.

It is well known that Serafim of Sarov was elevated to a 'Saint' by the direct order of Nicholas II, and in the mind of the monarchistic churchmen he was 'their own' authoritative preserver of the monarchistic legacies. That same reason explains why among the followers of the True Orthodox Church there existed the cult of the Archangel Michael. It was not only that this Biblical personage 'fights with the devil' and according to the assertions of the True Orthodox Church he is the harbinger of the hour of retribution of the anti-Christ and sinners. In the thought of the followers of the True Orthodox Church, the name Michael is connected with the brother of the Tsar, Michael Romanov. Many uprisings were instigated for the surviving members of the tsar's family.[65]

The apocalypticism of the True Orthodox Church was reinforced and in large measure inspired by the literature which they

[63] Mitrokhin, op. cit., p. 157.
[64] Fedorenko, op. cit., p. 211.
[65] Mitrokhin, op. cit., p. 159.

utilized. In addition to the biblical books of *Daniel* and *Revelation*, which have always been popular in chiliastic movements, the 'Collection from the Transcripts about the Holy Serafim of Sarov', and the 'Visions of John of Kronstadt' enjoyed wide popularity.[66]

The 'Collection from the Transcripts about the Holy Serafim of Sarov' was attributed to the pre-revolutionary saint but deals with conditions in the Soviet period. According to one of its prophecies,

Heretics will assume power over the churches, will found a religion of their servants. The first act of their persecution will be against the true pastors, imprisoning, exiling them. There will be great vilification of the monks, and the life of the monks will be in vilification. But God is stronger than the enemy and will never ravish his servants. The true monasteries will survive to the end of the age, only for this there will be solitary places.[67]

Especially because of the passages referring to monasticism in the above prophecy, it would seem highly probable that this tract was composed in response to the challenge of the Living Church, which, as has been noted above, bitterly attacked the institution of monasticism, and therefore Soviet scholars are probably correct in their assumption that it was composed during the early twenties and back-dated to Saint Serafim of Sarov.[68]

Similarly, the 'Visions of John of Kronstadt', according to Mitrokhin,

was fabricated, judging by its composition, in the years of Soviet rule as a manifesto of the church monarchists. Its date can be given approximately. On the one hand, the Renovating Church is mentioned in it. Its partisans are evaluated as direct 'servants of anti-Christ'. On the other hand, this document was already known in 1926–28. It is full of bitter hatred towards the Soviet Government, and was written in an openly monarchistic spirit. The 'anointed Nicholas' was here spoken of unctuously and with tender passion. In the 'Visions' there are pictures of the burning of the books of the 'godless, the heretics'.

The text of the 'Visions' continually calls on the ideas of *Revelation*, on the prophecies of *Daniel*, and others. Serafim of Sarov comes out in the document as the bearer and commentator on all these 'visions'.[69]

Soviet scholarship has not yet clarified whether the 'Visions of

[66] Fedorenko, op. cit., p. 212.
[67] Mitrokhin, op. cit., pp. 156–7.
[68] Ibid., p. 156.
[69] Ibid., p. 153.

John of Kronstadt' and the 'Collection from the Transcripts about the Holy Serafim of Sarov' are two separate compositions or represent instead two different recensions of the same source document. Nor is it clarified what connection, if any, the 'Visions of John of Kronstadt' has with the Ioannity, who claimed to be his direct progeny.

In addition to these works, the 'Protocols of the Elders of Zion' allegedly enjoyed some popularity in the True Orthodox Church.[70] While the 'Protocols' are not directly applicable to the stimulation of eschatological moods, this viciously anti-Semitic product of the late tsarist period could be used indirectly in evoking hostility towards the Soviet regime. Especially during the first years of Soviet rule, there was a widespread suspicion that communism was a Jewish conspiracy, and this suspicion has remained a latent option among those bitterly hostile to the regime, especially in areas of the country where anti-Semitism is endemic.

In view of the effective controls imposed by the State on printed works, it is not surprising that members of the True Orthodox Church made extensive use of hand-copying, not only for such works as those described above, but also for private devotional materials. Klibanov reported on one conversation with a former leader of the True Orthodox Church in 1959:

Behind the image case I note a student notebook. I pull it out. On individual pages in the notebook I read: 'Prayer to the Cross of Honour.' This prayer, which is used in the Church, is 'Let God arise and scatter His enemies.'[71]

The worship of the True Orthodox Church generally followed the normal Russian Orthodox pattern. The liturgy was conducted without important innovations. The Eucharist was often celebrated, prayers were used without modification, and the normal Church holidays were observed. Special emphasis was placed on monasticism and the rites connected with repentance.[72] All of the sacraments of the Church, especially those dealing with the family (baptism, extreme unction, funerals, etc.) were often performed.[73] The confessional was widely utilized by the leadership of the True Orthodox Church, both as a means of enforcing

[70] Ibid.; Fedorenko, op. cit., p. 212.
[71] Klibanov, 'Sovremennoe sektantstvo v Tambovskoi oblasti,' op. cit., p. 94.
[72] Mitrokhin, op. cit., p. 158.
[73] Z.M.P., No. 2 (February 1948), p. 65.

discipline (by granting absolution only upon satisfactory fulfilment of specified obligations) and as a means of counselling individual believers.[74] The more mystical elements in Orthodox worship were strongly emphasized, and indeed, some of the practices of the True Orthodox Church at times approached the realm of magic, especially with regard to rites and practices designed to protect the believer from the power of the anti-Christ.[75]

In addition to the house churches and monasteries in which services were conducted, the True Orthodox Church made widespread usage of informal shrines, usually consisting of a spring, lake, tree, or the like, which was considered to be especially holy.[76] Inasmuch as the use of Church buildings was unavoidably precluded to such a clandestine group and house churches and monasteries were always threatened by exposure, use of such shrines was a logical development in the attempt to acquire stable and enduring places of worship.[77] This usage of natural shrines for worship was much more widely practised among the parallel underground movement, the True Orthodox Christians, as will become apparent below.

In their private lives the members of the True Orthodox Church maintained the maximum possible distance between themselves and Soviet society.[78] They refused to participate in industrial labour, and in their great majority consisted of those elements in the population classified in the Soviet lexicon as 'former' people.[79] Klibanov describes the abode of one True Orthodox Church leader:

A spacious room. Little furniture. In the corner an image case with twenty or thirty icons. They gleam with gold, evidently prepared quite recently. A small shelf in front of the image case. Three dyed eggs and books on it—two Gospels in Russian and a psalter.[80]

Very little evidence is available concerning the social composition of the membership of the True Orthodox Church. According to Mitrokhin,

---

[74] Mitrokhin, op. cit., p. 158.
[75] Klibanov, 'Sovremennoe sektantstvo v Tambovskoi oblasti,' op. cit., pp. 90–1.
[76] Fedorenko, op. cit., p. 212.
[77] Mitrokhin, op. cit., p. 154.
[78] Fedorenko, op. cit., p. 212.
[79] Mitrokhin, op. cit., p. 155.
[80] Klibanov, 'Sovremennoe sektantstvo v Tambovskoi oblasti,' op. cit., p. 93.

We were able to gather data on 98 of the most active members of the
True Orthodox Church who were operating in 1949–50 in Michurinsk.
We were interested first of all in such factors as occupation, age and
sex. The collected material, unfortunately, permits an unequally complete answer to all the questions which interested us. While there are
data on the gender of the composition of all the indicated groups of
people, in which there were 94 women and only 4 men, data on the age
composition cover only 65 people, and data on occupation 62. However,
even these incomplete data paint a most characteristic picture. In the
number of 62 people on whose occupation there is information, there
were: former merchants—8; nuns—45; persons existing on indeter-
minate sources of income—9. Among these 65 activists of the True
Orthodox Church, there were 8 persons under 40 years of age; from
40 to 60—32; over 60—29 [*sic*].[81]

It is difficult to determine how representative these data are.
Mitrokhin does not indicate specifically how this information was
acquired. If, as does not seem altogether improbable, such data
were derived primarily from court records concerning people who
were brought to trial and records kept by the investigatory organs
of the Ministry of Internal Affairs, these data may not be completely representative of a composition of the True Orthodox
Church during the forties, but may be applicable merely to that
portion of membership which the investigatory and judicial
organs of the State were successful in discovering.

Despite the use of informal shrines in the countryside, a relatively unsophisticated approach to life, and the refusal to participate
in society, the True Orthodox Church apparently was not a predominantly rural phenomenon. Most of the members were to be
found in the cities.[82] Such an orientation would be explicable by
the degree of anonymity which can be achieved in a city, as
contrasted with the greater difficulty of maintaining a highly
organized clandestine life in the more intimate circumstances of
the village.

Despite the relatively higher proportion of the elderly in the
figures cited above, the True Orthodox Church devoted considerable energy to influencing the younger generation.[83] 'It is to be
noted that the leaders of the True Orthodox Church devoted
special attention to enticing the youth, forming, for example,

[81] Mitrokhin, op. cit., p. 155.
[82] Klibanov, 'Sovremennoe sektantstvo v Tambovskoi oblasti,' op. cit., pp. 95–6.
[83] Fedorenko, op. cit., p. 213.

special youth evening parties and putting together, if successful, youth circles'.[84] Children of members generally were allowed to attend public schools for primary education only.[85] The reason for this, according to one of the leaders, was as follows: 'Up to the fourth grade only general science is conducted in the schools, but beginning with the fifth grade they teach godlessness.'[86]

The period of intense activity of the True Orthodox Church was relatively brief. To a large degree, the regime's inattention to religious matters was the product of the concordat worked out between the patriarchate and the regime in 1943. Because of the almost overwhelming magnitude of wartime and immediate post-war problems facing the regime, there was little energy which could be devoted to the problem of religion, and in view of the highly publicized concordat and the considerable (if still limited) latitude which the patriarchal Church had been granted as a result of the meeting with Stalin, local authorities seemed little inclined to devote much attention to religion. For a brief period, pressure against religion was minimal, and in these conditions the True Orthodox Church was able to achieve a relatively high degree of organized clandestine life. In 1948, however, conditions began to revert to the pre-war pattern of pervasive social control, and the regime began to reassert its hold on the life of the people. The repressions of the *Zhdanovshchina* in 1948 first focused upon the intellectuals in restoring control, and then spread into other areas of society. Anti-religious propaganda, which had been suspended during the war, recommenced in a desultory fashion even before the end of the war, but in 1948 and subsequent years was again emphasized energetically. Those religious groups which were not direct parties to the concordat between Church and State found themselves under increasing pressure after 1948.

By 1950–1, the most active elements of the True Orthodox Church had been discovered and suppressed.[87] In the Tambov area the True Orthodox Church had ceased to exist as an organization by 1952. By 1959, when the expedition was working, 'only individual fanatics remained in the Tambov area, who formed closed circles in themselves'.[88] Their lives were conducted in great

[84] Mitrokhin, op. cit., p. 155.
[85] Fedorenko, op. cit., p. 212.
[86] Mitrokhin, op. cit., p. 158.
[87] Ibid., p. 160.
[88] Ibid., p. 144.

reticence, and 'as a rule they make no attempts to propagate their views'.[89] In the latter fifties, small groups of the True Orthodox Church which continued to function were occasionally discovered,[90] but it would seem that the force of law, together with intensive efforts of the atheist organizations, were quite able to render them inoperative.[91]

Thus by the early fifties it would appear that the True Orthodox Church no longer existed as an organized movement in the U.S.S.R. This complex and highly organized branch of underground Orthodoxy was able to enjoy considerable success in the forties owing primarily to social dislocations caused by the war, and the diminished ability of the regime to exercise social control. So soon as the regime was able successfully to reassert its control over society, however, it became apparent that this highly organized variant of underground Orthodoxy was poorly equipped for continued operation in the increasingly difficult circumstances. The centre of gravity in the underground Orthodox movement was located in the less highly organized, more flexible form of underground Orthodoxy which had sprung up concurrently with the True Orthodox Church, and which continued to be of considerable influence long after the organized, disciplined True Orthodox Church was defunct.

[89] Ibid., p. 160.
[90] E.g., Fedorenko, op. cit., p. 213; Skazkina, op. cit., p. 135.
[91] Cf. Koltuniuk, op. cit., p. 91.

VIII

The True Orthodox Christians

The True Orthodox Christians form a diffuse, flexible movement of considerable magnitude throughout the U.S.S.R. Indeed, this movement has dominated the world of underground Russian Orthodoxy during the entire post-war period, with the possible exception of the later forties when the True Orthodox Church was also exceedingly active. Unlike the latter, the True Orthodox Christians maintained few organizational encumbrances, and instead relied on an exceedingly flexible, almost spontaneous form of underground religious activity. Perhaps it would be more accurate to refer to the True Orthodox Christians not so much as a movement but rather as a broad congeries of similar but independent groupings scattered throughout the Russian countryside, exceedingly fluid in their interconnections. When opportunities permit, the True Orthodox Christians have demonstrated an ability to establish some evanescent organizational structures on a regional or even a nation-wide basis, but the groups seem fully able to function in their own locality in complete isolation if necessary. This extraordinary flexibility has enabled the True Orthodox Christians to survive numerous waves of intense pressure by investigatory and police organs of the State and indeed, some forms of the True Orthodox Christians movement have been able to thrive on the intense pressure which has been almost constant since the latter fifties.

It is difficult to determine precisely when the True Orthodox Christians appeared in Russia. One of the scholars participating in the Academy of Sciences field survey in the Lipetsk area discovered that the period of their greatest activity was during World War II. Without giving any figures, she stated that their numerical size in 1960 was less than one-sixth of the 1941–3 figure.[1] Z. A. Nikol'skaia

[1] Malakhova, op. cit., p. 16.

who, on the basis of a similar expedition in the Tambov area in 1959, has produced the most comprehensive study of the True Orthodox Christians, states that they were 'fully formed in the Tambov area in the beginning of the forties of this century'.[2] However, later in the same study she dates the rise of the movement in the mid-forties or, more precisely, 1944–7.[3] One of her colleagues in an earlier summary of the same expedition, stated that 'groups of "True Orthodox Christians" began to appear even in the period of the Great Patriotic War on the territory of Riazan and Voronezh *oblasts* and particularly since 1947 on the territory of Tambov *oblast'*.[4] Other evidence would also indicate that the rise of the True Orthodox Christians occurred during the immediate post-war period.[5]

In view of the diffuse and almost spontaneous nature of the movement, however, the question of their exact date of appearance is largely academic. Because a great many of the initial participants of the movement doubtless had had prior experience in some form of underground Orthodox life, the question reduces to the minor matter of determining when they began to designate themselves 'True Orthodox Christians' instead of whatever previous nomenclature they had attached to their own local group. Nikol'skaia discovered that the parents of one of the leaders of the True Orthodox Christians took part in a peasant insurrection as early as 1918, while another leader personally took part in the 'Walking Stick War' in his region during collectivization.[6] According to Klibanov, the True Orthodox Christians in the Lipetsk area

are one of the movements of Orthodoxy which have drunk the 'spiritual legacy' of the Church monarchist counter-revolution of the time of Tikhon, which, it appeared, had its nests on the territory of the Lipetsk *oblast* also. These were the groups which had drunk the kulak religious obscurantism of the 'Fedorovtsy', 'Imiaslavtsy', and 'Ioannite' movements . . . in the period of collectivization.[7]

At the very least, these earlier underground Orthodox and semi-Orthodox movements exerted an ideological influence on the True

[2] Nikol'skaia, op. cit., p. 161.
[3] Ibid., p. 166.
[4] Klibanov, 'Sovremennoe sektantstvo v Tambovskoi oblasti,' op. cit., p. 96.
[5] Iankova, 'Sovremennoe pravoslavie,' op. cit., p. 71.
[6] Nikol'skaia, op. cit., p. 164.
[7] Klibanov, 'Sovremennoe sektantstvo v Lipetskoi oblasti,' op. cit., p. 167.

14

Orthodox Christians.[8] The leader in the Lipetsk *oblast* claimed direct spiritual descent from two Orthodox hierarchs who were executed by the Soviet authorities in 1943.[9]

On the basis of the relatively scant data available it is difficult to determine the precise relationship between the True Orthodox Christians and the more highly organized True Orthodox Church which was extant during the same period. Soviet scholarship has discovered 'ideological and genetic links' between the two movements[10] and, indeed, to some degree the True Orthodox Christians may have resulted from the dissolution of groups of the more highly organized movement.[11] According to one Soviet scholar, the True Orthodox Christians are the direct successors of the True Orthodox Church, forming themselves after the latter's destruction.[12] Such an inference may also be possible from Klibanov's statement (above) that they began to appear 'particularly since 1947', when, as has been noted, the True Orthodox Church came under severe attack.

The True Orthodox Christians were widely disseminated throughout the Soviet Union. Nikol'skaia cites data concerning their activities in sixteen separate localities, ranging from the Donbas and the Kiev-Kharkov areas in the Ukraine, to the Moscow and Kirov areas in European Russia, to Novosibirsk in Western Siberia, and to Alma-Ata near the Sinkiang border and the Tashkent area in Kazakhstan.[13] And her list far from exhausts the data concerning the geographic extent of the movement.[14] In addition to many groups discovered in the Tambov area, field studies discovered numerous groups in widely scattered locations in the Voronezh[15] and Lipetsk areas.[16] So important was the movement in the latter area that, according to Klibanov, 'in the period of the forties to the early fifties on the territory of Lipetsk *oblast* the organizations of the so-called True Orthodox Christians

---

[8] Nikol'skaia, op. cit., p. 164.

[9] Ibid., pp. 166–7.

[10] Klibanov, 'Sovremennoe sektantstvo v Tambovskoi oblasti,' op. cit., p. 96.

[11] Nikol'skaia, op. cit., p. 167.

[12] Fedorenko, op. cit., p. 214.

[13] Nikol'skaia, op. cit., p. 162.

[14] Klibanov, 'Sovremennoe sektantstvo v Tambovskoi oblasti,' op. cit., p. 60; cf. the sources listed in Teodorovich, 'The Catacomb Church in the U.S.S.R.,' op. cit., pp. 10, 12.

[15] Aleksandrovich, op. cit., p. 63.

[16] Klibanov, 'Sovremennoe sektantstvo v Lipetskoi oblasti,' op. cit., pp. 166–7.

were more active and numerous than the sectarians'.[17] The centre of gravity of the movement was in rural areas and villages,[18] but groups were known to exist in the cities as well.[19]

The general historical pattern of the movement was marked by a peak of activity between 1945 and 1947. The Tambov expedition estimated their number as approaching 1,000 in the Tambov area alone during this period. The rise of pressure in 1948 and 1949 affected the movement, and by 1950–1 they had lost an estimated half of their followers and certain of their leaders were accused (and presumably convicted) of instigating bloody reprisals.[20] In the mid-fifties the movement revived,[21] only to come under intense pressure again in the late fifties and during the following decade. The movement has by no means succumbed to the pressure, however, for in Lipetsk *oblast* groups were still in existence in 1960.[22] In 1964 the movement was apparently considered a serious enough problem in Arkhangel'sk *oblast* (in which the Solovky and other camps are located, and which has served as a place of exile) to warrant a production of a documentary movie on the subject.[23] On 1 January 1965 there were 350 True Orthodox Christians known to be active in the Voronezh *oblast*,[24] and in April 1968 members of the movement in Kazakhstan drew the attention of the press.[25] The recent decade of pressure has, however, resulted in certain modifications and new movements within the True Orthodox Christians which will be discussed in the following chapter.

Even during the mid-fifties, after the collapse of the True Orthodox Church, there were priests who had renounced their position and were working in industry, and who collected around themselves groups of followers.[26] Such leadership would seem to be

[17] Ibid.
[18] Nikol'skaia, op. cit., p. 163.
[19] Aleksandrovich, op. cit., p. 63.
[20] Nikol'skaia, op. cit., p. 172.
[21] *Komsomol'skaia Pravda*, 18 September 1954.
[22] Malakhova, op. cit., p. 15.
[23] M. Semenov, 'Eto proizoshlo v Mud'iuge' ('This happened in Mud'iuga'), *Nauka i Religiia*, No. 2 (February 1966), p. 29.
[24] M. K. Tepliakov, 'Pobeda ateizma v razlichnykh sotsial'nykh sloiakh sovetskogo obshchestva' ('The victory of atheism in various social strata of Soviet society'), in AN SSSR, *Voprosy nauchnogo ateizma*, op. cit., IV, 156.
[25] *Kazakhstanskaia Pravda*, 28 April 1968.
[26] Pol'skii, op. cit., II, xiv.

atypical for the True Orthodox Christians, for in general they dispensed with the institution of the priesthood.[27] Instead,

in the position of pastors the True Orthodox Christians selected out of their midst organizers, calling them 'preachers' and 'elder brothers in the spirit'. As a rule, both the 'preachers' and 'elder brothers', according to their social precedents, were former kulaks or wealthy middle peasants. In a few cases they came from the families of former clergymen.[28]

Such children from clerical families might be eminently well qualified for leadership of underground Orthodox worship. It will be recalled that until the promulgation of the 'Stalin Constitution' in 1936 the clergy were disfranchised and their children barred from higher education. This inadvertent continuation of the earlier caste system with regard to clerical families may have contributed to the ranks of leadership of the True Orthodox Christians a decade later, for, with other occupations closed to them, children of these families might be expected to gravitate towards the Church. At least insofar as the liturgical and ritual practices of Orthodoxy are concerned, such people, and indeed almost any devout Orthodox, could become reasonably adept at the conduct of Orthodox worship provided only that they were sufficiently imbued with the major liturgical practices and had memorized them.

In general, the leadership of the True Orthodox Christians consisted mostly of men, although there were relatively infrequent exceptions to this rule.[29] According to Soviet sources, the leaders of the True Orthodox Christians at times resorted to somewhat bizarre practices.

These 'people of God' create popularity for themselves by all possible means. Thus the leader of a group of True Orthodox Christians, V. I. Gichev, according to the example of the 'holy saints', wandered about in the republic, wore torn, dirty clothes, went barefoot in winter time, and took a bath once a year. L. A. Sidorov hid himself as an anchorite in the basement of his house for three years, coming up only for participation in prayers in a specially equipped house church. The Ukhtin preacher, Vshivkov, who has now renounced religion, at the

[27] Gagarin, op. cit., p. 182.
[28] Nikol'skaia, op. cit., p. 168.
[29] Ibid., pp. 168-9.

time of the prayers dressed himself in a white shroud and gave the appearance that he was hearing the 'voice of God' which allegedly gave orders through him.[30]

Such leaders were not only able to exert an influence on their original group of followers, but also they often managed to extend their field of service to include a number of similar groups.

In individual organizations of the True Orthodox Christians up to 1950, leaders representing themselves as 'people of God' renounced earthly blessings and roamed from village to village 'according to the example of the apostles' and from house to house with the goal of 'strengthening' their followers 'in the faith'. Thus, for example, the leader of the group of True Orthodox Christians in the village of Staevo, V. Riakhovskikh, at first made the rounds of the Riazan *oblast*, then began to wander about the villages of the Machurin *rayon*, Tambov *oblast*, until at last he chose the village of Staevo as the centre of his preaching activity. Another leader of the True Orthodox Christians, Aleksei Umrikhin, wandered in the guise of a 'man of God' in Degtian, Sosnov, Pervomai, and Michurin *rayons* of the Tambov area. The True Orthodox Christian preacher, P. Polovinkin, went about in the Sosnov and Degtian *rayons*. The founder of the Silence Movement, L. Kisliakova, wandered in Sosnovka, Atmanov Ugol, Malye Pupki, and Degtianka, and A. Ermoshkin went about the Kirsanov *rayon*. A black, closed gown, a black headdress, knapsack, and staff sharply distinguished such 'wanderers' from the clergy of the active churches and symbolized their renunciation of earthly joys, emphasizing their special commitment to God.

The practice of wandering, which in no small degree was evoked by the hope of avoiding socially useful labour and of fleeing from accountability for their anti-social activity, was 'argued' by the leaders of the True Orthodox Christians as supporting the Gospel symbol of the 'birds of the heavens', who neither sow nor reap, but God feeds them.[31]

The need to escape the police and investigatory pressure of the regime doubtless was among the motivations of such wandering leaders,[32] but as subsequent developments were to demonstrate (see the following chapter) other motivations entered into the decision to undertake this practice. Many of these wandering preachers served to provide what little organizational intercom-

[30] Gagarin, op. cit., p. 182.
[31] Nikol'skaia, op. cit., pp. 179–80.
[32] Fedorenko, op. cit., p. 214.

munion the various groups of True Orthodox Christians might have with each other.[33] In Lipetsk *oblast*, one such leader served as the titular head of True Orthodox Christians in the entire *oblast*.[34]

In addition to such leaders, a considerable cult of charismatic figures quickly arose among the True Orthodox Christians. As one example, one such woman—allegedly an idiot—would often appear before believers and screech, 'Lord Jesus Christ, Wise One, forgive me'.[35] According to Nikol'skaia, hordes of the blind, cripples, beggars, and general rogues frequented the places of worship of the True Orthodox Christians. In one case, a mute

was accompanied by two 'lay sisters' who spread among the ignorant True Orthodox Christians a legend about his tsarist extraction ('of the blood of the Tsars') and his sagacity ('a man of God'). Several women who were convinced of his 'sanctity' harnessed themselves to a cart in place of the horses and drove this rascal from spring to spring. By gesticulations [he] gave 'counsels' and 'prophecies' which were elucidated by his lay sisters, for which he received money and food from the believers.

Other such charismatics practised faith healing, exorcism of demons, clairvoyance, and even merchandising of holy water.[36] In another case a six-fingered idiot, thought to be clairvoyant, led one group of True Orthodox Christians.[37]

In its attitude towards the patriarchal Russian Orthodox Church which was able to function openly and legally, this clandestine, highly illegal movement was sharply critical. The True Orthodox Christians rejected the patriarchal Church but only, as it were, temporarily; they maintained deep loyalty to Russian Orthodoxy itself.[38] Indeed, to some degree the True Orthodox Christians idealized pre-revolutionary Orthodoxy, but so far as the contemporary patriarchal churches were concerned they denied the canonicity of their activities, rejected the clergy, and renounced sacraments administered by them.[39] Apparently the reason for their rejection of the churches (other than general social and

[33] Nikol'skaia, op. cit., p. 169.
[34] Ibid.
[35] Klibanov, 'Sovremennoe sektantstvo v Tambovskoi oblasti,' op. cit., p. 97.
[36] Nikol'skaia, op. cit., p. 182.
[37] Klibanov, 'Sovremennoe sektantstvo v Tambovskoi oblasti,' op. cit., p. 97.
[38] Fedorenko, op. cit., p. 214.
[39] Nikol'skaia, op. cit., p. 161.

political alienation) was in large measure due to a profound dis-
trust of the integrity of the post-war churches which were able to
operate with little or no overt pressure from State authorities.

When in 1944–7 churches in a series of villages of the Tambov *oblast*
which had earlier been closed began to function at the request of
believing collective farmers, in the majority of cases their former priests
also returned to these churches and only in a number of churches did
new priests appear. A small number of non-collectivized people, who
gravitated to the kulak form of life, tried to make use of the latter cases.
They called the reopened churches 'heathen temples of anti-Christ',
and their priests the servants of anti-Christ. Renouncing the active
Church and its clergy, they countered it with the 'old Church' and those
of its priests who in the past had conducted anti-Soviet activity.[40]

Such suspicion of newly arrived, unknown priests who, unlike their
predecessors of the thirties, seemed able to maintain the best of
relationships with the State authorities, would not appear to be an
unnatural phenomenon, particularly in view of the considerable
social cohesion and resistance to innovation in the rural peasant
community. In addition, in view of their long experience with
various sorts of Party machinations, believers might well question
the personal integrity of the newly arrived priest. Patricia Blake
quoted a young Kiev Professor of Russian Literature who protested, 'How can I confess to a priest who, for all I know, might
report me to the Secret Police?'[41]

The rejection of the legalized Russian Orthodox churches would
not appear to have been uniform among the True Orthodox
Christians scattered throughout the Soviet Union. Varying attitudes were observable, ranging from outright, total, and even
bitter rejection to an almost congenial attitude of participation in
the clandestine movement merely from personal preference. There
was a widespread conviction that after the present 'time of
troubles' has passed a complete reconciliation between the two
forms of Orthodoxy will occur. According to one of the True
Orthodox Christians,

Earlier the Church was true, now anti-Christ makes an outrage of her.
The time will come and she will again stand on the former path, but

---

[40] Ibid., p. 166.
[41] Patricia Blake, 'Alliance with the Unholy,' *Life*, 14 September 1959, p. 126.

meanwhile we should pray at home and perserve the faith in our heart.[42]

Especially with the rise of the anti-religious campaign of the sixties, which placed all believers under great pressure and caused members of the legalized churches to experience the same insecurity long extant in the clandestine groups while the latter found it more and more difficult to organize meetings with impunity, there was a considerable tendency among the True Orthodox Christians to minimize the differences and many of them, while continuing to deny the validity of the open churches, would attend their services on major festivals.[43] Conversely, when True Orthodox Christians experienced periods of extreme difficulty it was not unusual for members of the legalized churches to render material aid to them.[44]

The True Orthodox Christians movement was predominantly spontaneous, with an exceedingly loose organizational structure. Indeed, in large measure the movement's extraordinary tenacity and ability to survive extreme pressure was due precisely to its lack of organizational complexity. By its very nature the movement was all but immune to large-scale roundups by the police, but instead the latter were reduced to seeking out the individual groups one by one. Furthermore, the lack of dependence on a priesthood made it possible for new groups to arise almost immediately after a particular group had been discovered and disbanded.

Nevertheless, there was a degree of liaison between the various groups of the movement. Wandering leaders provided one means of intercommunication.

In leading a wandering manner of life, the preachers of the True Orthodox Christians had (each of them) a special region for their wandering, on the territories of which they carried out the function of a link between the local adherents of True Orthodox Christians, giving them all sorts of instructions and supporting religious fanaticism in their spirits.[45]

Certain of the more stable house churches also served as points of contact for members of neighbouring groups,[46] as did various

[42] Gagarin, op. cit., p. 182.
[43] Iankova, 'O nekotorykh metodakh,' op. cit., p. 113.
[44] Nikol'skaia, op. cit., p. 174.
[45] Ibid., p. 180.
[46] Klibanov, 'Sovremennoe sektantstvo v Tambovskoi oblasti,' op. cit., p. 97.

shrines, at which large numbers of believers would gather from time to time.[47] Leaders would compose letters for distribution over a large area, using parabolic language.[48] Similarly, various sorts of chain letters were disseminated.

In the mid-forties the 'preachers' and 'elder brothers', in order to swell their ranks with new partisans, sent anonymous letters and proclamations into the villages and cities of the Tambov area. The letters were addressed not only to members and believers but even to unbelieving collective farmers, workers, and employees. The contents of these letters amounted to the following: the coming of anti-Christ into the world has taken place, the end of the world will soon come, people will be judged with terrible misfortune, poverty, and terror. Only the believers who have repented will be saved. In order to flee the misfortune and damnation, each recipient of the letter is invited in addition to repentance and salvation to spread his copy among not less than ten to twenty people.[49]

Such chain letters would appear to be a direct continuation of the 'letters from heaven' which were widespread in the thirties and which have continued to be distributed in the U.S.S.R. to the present. In 1966, the leading anti-religious journal presented photostats of two such letters, hand-copied in an almost illegible, cursive Russian:

A holy letter a 12 year old boy relates that he saw a man by the white sea in a white chasuble he was saying do not forget god copy to various sides One family copied 9 times and distributed after 36 days received great happiness but another did not copy and received an incurable disease pray to god in the name of the father amen Soon will come the judgement of the living and the dead the sun will grow dim and will stop shining the sea will flow with blood He who does not believe will see but it will be too late do not forget god the holy mother of god Children help your parents to copy the holy letter 9 times and after 36 days you will receive great happiness do not fear this letter it is entrusted to the whole world.

A 12 year old saw a man at the sea shore in white clothing he said do not forget god copy the letter it should go about the whole world to this end one family copied 9 times and after 6 days [he] received great joy another copied but did not send it out and after 36 days received an incurable disease pray to god in the name of the father and the son

[47] Nikol'skaia, op. cit., p. 180.
[48] Ibid., p. 169.
[49] Ibid., p. 171.

and the holy spirit and SOON WILL COME THE JUDGEMENT THE PEOPLE
LIVING AND DEAD WILL APPEAR THE SEA WILL FLOW WITH BLOOD he
who keeps this letter then it will be too late do not forget god he will
not forget you nor will the holy mother of god do not forget that this
letter has been Travelling around the world 12 years rejoice he said
for the judgement will come the living and the dead furthermore he saw
the mother of god on her breasts was written do not forget god copy
9 times spread it to various sides and you will receive great joy
the holy letter should go to the world to warn the sinners if you keep
the letter three weeks you will receive a great sin for in the name of
non-fulfilment towards god glory to the father and the son and the holy
spirit
    Amen.[50]

It would appear that these are extreme examples of the 'letters
from heaven'. Even in these examples, however, there are devotional and doctrinal suggestions which, given the proper circumstances, might be of some value in enriching the devotional life
of the recipient. In view of the insuperable lack of religious literature in the U.S.S.R., where Bibles, prayer books, and the like are
virtually unobtainable and even small portions of devotional
literature assiduously copied out by hand are immensely precious,
such 'letters from heaven' could fill a considerable need in providing the literature-starved believers with some form of aid in their
private or group devotional lives. Dmitry Konstantinov presents
the full text of a devotional tractate originating during World
War II which may represent the opposite extreme of this genre of
religious literature, samples of which have not been (nor are likely
to be) presented in the anti-religious propaganda.

THIS WAS FROM ME

Have you ever thought that everything which concerns you likewise
concerns Me also? Or that what concerns you simultaneously concerns
the apple of My eye? You are dear in My eyes, of much value, and I
have cherished you, and therefore to educate you is a special
comfort for Me.

When trials come upon you, if the enemy approaches like a river,
I want you to know that this was from Me, that your infirmity needs
My power, and that your danger exists in order to give Me the
opportunity to fight for you.

Do you find yourself in difficult circumstances among people who do not understand you, who do not consider what may be acceptable or unacceptable to you, who ignore you? This was from Me. I am God, who arranges your circumstances. You are not in your place by chance: this is that very place which I predestined for you. Have you not asked that I teach you humility? Behold: I have placed you in that very school where this lesson is learned. Your circle and those who live with you only fulfil my will.

Do you find yourself in financial difficulties, is it difficult for you to make ends meet? This was from Me. For I have arranged your purse. I want you to flee to Me, and to be dependent on Me. My wealth is inexhaustible; I want you to be convinced of My faithfulness and My promises—let it not be such with you that they might say to you in your need, 'You have not believed the Lord your God.'

Are you living through a night of sorrows? This was from Me. I am a man of sorrows, acquainted with grief. I have allowed this that you might turn to Me and find eternal comfort.

Have you been mistaken in your friend, in anyone to whom you opened your heart? This was from Me. I have allowed this disappointment to happen to you, that you might know that your best friend is the Lord. I want you to bring everything to Me and to prove Me.

Has someone slandered you? This happened to Me, and it rubs off on those who are close to Me your shelter. I will bring forth your truth and your righteousness like light, like the noonday.

Have your plans come to nothing? Are you crestfallen in spirit and tired? This was from Me. You made your plans and brought them to Me that I might bless them; but I want you to let Me arrange your circumstances—and then responsibility for everything will be on Me: for this is too heavy a burden for you, you are alone and cannot set everything right. You are only the instrument, not the person who is acting.

Have you dreamed to accomplish any special thing for Me, and instead languish on a bed of sickness and weakness? This was from Me. When you were engrossed in affairs, I could not attract your thoughts to Myself, and I want to teach you My very deepest thoughts, that you will be in service to Me. I want to teach you to recognize that you are nothing. Among My best co-workers are those who have been cut off from external activity, in order to learn to bear the arms of ceaseless prayer.

Were you unexpectedly called to occupy a difficult and responsible position? Go, lay it on Me. I entrust you with difficulties, for the Lord your God blesses you in all your affairs, in everything that will be done by your hands. In this day I give into your hands the vessel of My holy oil, My blessing: use it freely, My child. Every difficulty which arises, every word of sorrow to you, every revelation of your weakness and inability—let them be anointed with oil. Remember that every obstacle is a divine instruction. Every sorrow will be reduced if you learn to see Me in everything that happens to you—and therefore lay up for yourself in your heart all the words which I have given you today: this was from Me. For this is not an empty word for you, this is your life.[51]

The basic organizational unit of the True Orthodox Christians was the local group consisting of between ten and a maximum of fifteen people.[52] Worship was usually conducted in the various homes of the members rather than in a single house church.

The house meetings were conducted secretly, now in one, now in another house of the True Orthodox Christians. At them would gather not more than 10–15 people, inhabitants of one or two neighbouring population points and members of one society. Sundays and festival services would serve as the occasion for this. . . . The service in such a meeting house was surrounded in mystery and was conducted behind closed doors, curtained windows, and, chiefly, at a late hour.[53]

Many of the True Orthodox Christians turned their homes into chapels, with icons and the various utensils and decorations of the liturgy.[54] In 1962 an atheist author reported on a visit to the home of one member of the movement:

The house is divided into two parts. In one of them a kind of private church was built: an iconastasis, burning sanctuary lamps, communion bread, and self-made, miniature 'God's grave'. An icon of the mother of God took the central place. I recognized it right away after the description I saw in the *Atheist's Guide*: it was the same icon on which, at the order of the tsarist satrap, Arakchaev, his love, Mikina, was painted as the model. Now, people come to pray to this icon.[55]

These worship services in the home were complemented by a cult of natural shrines and holy places, which assumed major proportions among the True Orthodox Christians.[56] According to the study conducted by the Soviet Academy of Sciences,[57] such

[51] Konstantinov, *Gonimaia tserkov'*, op. cit., pp. 76–8.
[52] Nikol'skaia, op. cit., p. 168.
[53] Ibid., pp. 182–3.
[54] *Izvestiia*, 30 July 1960.
[55] *Ogonek*, 13 March 1962.
[56] Klibanov, 'Sovremennoe sektantstvo v Tambovskoi oblasti,' op. cit., pp. 96–7.
[57] Unless otherwise specified, data concerning the cult of natural shrines are drawn from the detailed study of Nikol'skaia, op. cit., pp. 180–3.

shrines were predominantly associated with natural springs (although one entrepreneur allegedly constructed his own as a profit-making example of private enterprise). More infrequently, cemeteries, oak trees, or other locations would acquire the sanctity of a shrine. Each shrine was generally associated with a particular saint, and services were held at the particular shrine once or several times a year, according to the Orthodox calendar.

There were exceptions to this rule, however, for certain of the shrines, such as the Spring of the 'Three Oaks', acquired sufficient reputation to attract an almost continual stream of the devout. In effect, they became more or less permanently functioning churches in the open air. At the 'Three Oaks' shrine a model of a wooden church would be used during the service, a practice which may reflect the influence of iconographic practices prior to the Old Believer schism of the seventeenth century, whereby events taking place within a church would be depicted on the icon as taking place outside, with the cathedral represented in the background— thereby suggesting that the depicted event had universal significance transcending its original setting.[58]

At the shrines no attempt was made to duplicate the whole liturgical practice of Russian Orthodoxy. Instead, worship consisted of those practices which could be performed by the laity without the intercession of a priest. Services generally consisted of several hours of congregational singing, followed by numerous sermons and exhortations, and more congregational singing. The services were extraordinarily long, generally ending just before dawn.

The congregational music consisted primarily of the *akafists*, which are songs of praise to Christ, the Blessed Virgin, or various saints. One of the most popular in the Tambov area was in honour of Saint Pitirim:

> Rejoice, strengthening by the weak.
> Rejoice, wisdom of the blind.
> Rejoice in the holiness of Pitirim,
> Revelation of the Tambov lands.

Prayers were generally read between the singing of the *akafists*.

Sermons were delivered by various leaders and charismatic figures of the movement. Such sermons were designed for the

---

[58] Cf. Sergei Hackel, 'New Perspectives and the Old Believers,' *Eastern Churches Review*, I, 2 (Autumn 1966), p. 115.

edification of those present and included various sorts of exhortations against sinful action or contamination with the world. Apocalypticism was a dominant theme and, at times, this part of the worship service might have anti-social or even overtly anti-Soviet overtones.

In addition to the worship functions, these convocations at various shrines served as a means of maintaining communications and intercourse between various local groups of the True Orthodox Christians. Leaders of various groups, or even regional leaders, could meet together at these festivals. In some cases leaders were able at these meetings at the shrines to render material aid to their less fortunate colleagues from other areas.

Participation in the cult of the shrines was by no means limited to the members of the clandestine movement. Some of the shrines frequented by the True Orthodox Christians had enjoyed a reputation for sanctity among the Orthodox for generations and would be visited by large numbers of members of the open churches, as well as by the True Orthodox Christians. Even at shrines which were predominantly used by the latter, and which were of relatively recent reputation, members of the open churches would come to attend the worship services. In this manner, then, the cult of the shrines also served as a means of dissemination of the clandestine movement, whereby its members could come into contact with fellow believers who had not joined them and could be proselytized.

There was great emphasis on the water of the sacred springs, which was considered especially holy. All through the meetings at the springs the participants would sprinkle themselves and one another with the water of the spring. Vials of the water were taken home by the participants and were considered particularly effective in guarding the True Orthodox Christians from contamination by the surrounding world.

Miracles were widely associated with the cult of the shrines. Under the influence of superstition, sick women and children bathed in the spring in the hope of being cured. They stood motionless for hours, hoping for the appearance of the 'divine image' on the surface of the spring. Here hysterical women would cry out and those present would again pray aloud. All this taken together created a mood of extreme religious exaltation, in the atmosphere of which the leaders of the True Orthodox Christians also conducted their preaching.

At one of the popular shrines, that of 'Mammoth Lake', there were legends that the wonder-working icon of Nikolai the Humble appeared on the surface of the lake and services were held in celebration and expectation of this miracle. At other springs the appearance of the Blessed Virgin was expected.[59]

Probably the most popular shrine in all of Russia was Lake Svetloiar, which drew large numbers of pilgrims throughout this period.[60] According to Old Believers, the holy city of Grand Kitezh, threatened by the Tatar invasion during the Middle Ages, had been miraculously preserved beneath the waters of the lake and would appear to those of particularly devout faith; in a variant of the legend, a hidden monastery would rise from the waters and the especially devout could actually see the monks and hear the ringing of the bells.[61]

In their general worship practice the True Orthodox Christians were exceedingly diligent in observing every event in the Russian Orthodox calendar, excepting only those subsidiary practices (such as carol singing) which involved contact with the outside world.[62] Easter, always the dominant celebration in Russian Orthodoxy, was exceedingly important to them. Prayers and the *akafists*, beginning and ending with the *akafist* to Christ, were conducted continuously for twenty-four hours, during which the participants drank holy water and ate only bread. Similarly, Pentecost was an especially important day of mourning to them.[63]

The True Orthodox Christians conducted *daily* prayer meetings.[64] Such devotion would be especially impressive in the environment of the rapidly secularizing Soviet society. In addition, they subjected themselves to frequent and prolonged fasts and often conducted prayer meetings of exceptionally long duration.[65]

Despite their inability to enjoy the normal worship life of

---

[59] Chaikovskaia, op. cit., pp. 4–6.
[60] *Komsomol'skaia Pravda*, 25 October 1959; *Nauka i Religiia*, No. 12 (December 1961), p. 32.
[61] V. N. Vasilov, 'O proiskhozhdenii kul'ta nevidimogo grada kitezha (monastyria) u ozera svetloiar' ('On the origins of the cult of the invisible city of Kitezh (monastery) at lake Svetloiar'), in AN SSSR, *Voprosy istorii religii i ateizma*, op. cit., XII, 150–69; N. Savushkina, 'Kitezh—byl' ili skazka' ('Kitezh—fact or tale'), *Nauka i Religiia*, No. 6 (June 1969), pp. 61–5.
[62] Nikol'skaia, op. cit., p. 183.
[63] Ibid., p. 184.
[64] Ibid., p. 168.
[65] Vasin, op. cit., p. 17.

Orthodoxy owing to their rejection of the institution of the priest-hood, liturgical practices were of considerable importance to the True Orthodox Christians.[66] Thus, although the sacraments of ordination, extreme unction, holy anointing, and, usually, paedobaptism were precluded, the Eucharist and penance received elevated emphasis. The Eucharist was celebrated in the home, administered by laymen using unleavened bread and water from a holy spring as the sacramental elements. Confession, which took place once or twice a year, was conducted collectively rather than in private, with each penitent reciting his sins aloud and receiving absolution or penance from the leader of the group.[67]

Perhaps inevitably, in view of the fact that the True Orthodox Christians allowed themselves the non-Orthodox innovation of lay administration of the Eucharist, further innovations and aberrations occasionally appeared in the ritual practice of certain of their groups. In the Komi republic in the far north, for example,

There is no uniformity of ritual among various groups of the 'True [Orthodox Christians]'. This is explicable by the fact that the preachers introduce certain flights of fancy, allegedly directed from above. Thus, for example, the Kerchomsk True Orthodox Christians, at the insistence of V. I. Gichev, renounced icons, candles, and icon lamps. However, this renunciation bore a temporary character, inasmuch as part of the above mentioned materials of the cult had been prepared by the 'anti-Christian' church and to use them was a grievous sin. When the Church is 'reformed' one can again return to them.[68]

If the Soviet press is accurate, such aberrations at times reached extreme degrees and, indeed, seemed to bear little relationship to normal Orthodox practice.

It was half dark behind the wooden partition. The window was tightly closed. It was here on a wooden floor covered with torn rags that 'God's servant', Arkhip, has passed ten years of his life, chained by his leg.

Arkhip was only 7 years old when his mother and his older sister—both religious fanatics—started to perform religious rites with the child. The boy was scared, cried, asked to be left alone, but they continued. They even started to 'treat' him for illness. They would put a basin filled with water on his head and pour melted wax into the water,

---

[66] Gagarin, op. cit., p. 186.
[67] Nikol'skaia, op. cit., pp. 178–9.
[68] Gagarin, op. cit., pp. 182–3.

with prayers accompanying the procedure. Naturally, such 'procedures' caused nervous disorders in the boy. He would escape to the woods, they would catch him and continue to 'cure' him. He started crying in his sleep and getting scared of other people, and the Lazarevs decided: 'Since his illness is pleasing to God it shows that he is God's choice.' A very simple and cruel approach: disabled people, and especially those with nervous disorders, enjoy special respect among the 'True Orthodox Christians,' to which the Lazarevs claim to belong. In order to make 'God's choice' submit to God's will without opposing it, he was put in chains. After that he first forgot how to read and write, and then ceased to speak and understand.

He sits in front of us, a lost man of 26. The expression on his face is dull and thoughtless; his dimmed eyes fix on one spot.[69]

In another instance reminiscent of the pre-war Cherdashniki, an infant was considered Christ and, suspended by a towel under the icons, was the object of prayer.[70]

The cult of the cross was especially prominent among the True Orthodox Christians. Many of them drew crosses with chalk or branded them over doors, windows, ceilings, etc., in order to ward off the power of the anti-Christ.[71] Many of them would continually make the sign of the cross on their foreheads, various parts of their bodies, objects surrounding them, and passers-by, for the same reason.[72]

When they were outside the house they crossed themselves incessantly. They kept looking downward, 'so as not to see the face of the cunning one'. They embroidered their head gear with crosses and covered a large part of their faces with it and, finally, they tied a woollen thread to their right hand which, according to their magical ideas, protected the hand from the blow of the anti-Christ while it was making the sign of the cross.[73]

One group, following a divine order received by its leader, crossed themselves with both hands, one for each of the two advents of Christ.[74]

While the True Orthodox Christians rejected the rite of infant baptism, they did practise adult baptism, generally with allusions

[69] *Ogonek*, 13 March 1962.
[70] Klibanov, 'Sovremennoe sektantstvo v Tambovskoi oblasti,' op. cit., p. 94.
[71] Nikol'skaia, op. cit., p. 186.
[72] Fedorenko, op. cit., p. 215.
[73] Nikol'skaia, op. cit., p. 186.
[74] Gagarin, op. cit., p. 183.

to the baptism of Christ in the River Jordan. The candidate would immerse himself three times in a special, cross-shaped hole cut in the ice of a river in winter in the presence of all members of the group. Apparently this rite was universally practised among the True Orthodox Christians during the forties.[75]

Doctrinally, the True Orthodox Christians adhered to the traditional tenets of the Orthodox faith. Naturally, the inability to follow the canons concerning ecclesiology did lead to certain innovations, particularly in regard to the believer's relationship to God. According to the True Orthodox Christians, God the Son is able to meet directly with believers without the mediation of priests or sacraments. Piety and prayer provide the believer with access to Christ, and He is present in response to such devotion, thereby obviating the role of the priest in traditional Orthodox worship. Furthermore, Christ is present during the Eucharist, despite the fact that it is administered by laymen. Similarly, the special presence of the Holy Spirit is not unique to churches but He is able to be present in an especially tangible way wherever exalted worship takes place. In particular, the cult of the shrines suggested that the Holy Spirit was present in a special way at the sites of the shrines and, similarly, in the premises of house churches, which became endowed with the special sanctity of the presence of the Holy Spirit traditionally associated with duly consecrated churches and cathedrals.[76]

A second doctrinal distinction between the clandestine movement and the traditional forms of Orthodoxy was to be found in the cult of the saints and charismatic leaders. This was primarily a matter of degree, for saints have always played a large role in Orthodox worship, as have various holy men, whether monastic or lay, and 'holy fools'. Among the True Orthodox Christians, however, the reverence of the saints, particularly those whom the participants felt congenial to their needs, was especially pronounced. Even more pronounced was the honour given to the various charismatic figures which operated within the movement. One Soviet scholar found this tendency so strong as to constitute, in his opinion, a transgression against the first commandment, 'Thou shalt have no other gods before Me': 'the consubstantial, biblical God not seldom moves to a secondary place, leaving the

---

[75] Nikol'skaia, op. cit., p. 183; cf. Fedorenko, op. cit., p. 214.
[76] Nikol'skaia, op. cit., pp. 178–9.

primary place to "other gods", in most cases, dead or living organizers, leaders, preachers of the sects, various "prophets" and "seers".[77]

In their religious literature, apart from the Bible (with special emphasis on the book of *Revelation*) the True Orthodox Christians apparently were primarily dependent on various formal and informal compositions of their leaders. V. Titov who, during the forties, was the leader of the True Orthodox Christians for the entire Lipetsk *oblast*, was apparently a prolific author of such devotional literature. His works were spread throughout the *oblast*. Of particular importance, according to subsequent Soviet scholarship, was his 'Talks on Various Questions to Those Who Are in Doubt About the Path of Salvation'. In other areas, texts of sermons and proclamations by leaders were circulated among the believers.[78]

A considerable degree of social alienation was naturally present in the movement of the True Orthodox Christians.[79]

Renunciation of the surrounding world as 'contaminated' by anti-Christ also finds its expression in asceticism, which constituted a characteristic trait of the life of the True Orthodox Christians. . . .

The use of meat and of grocery products and the wearing of manu-factured clothes are declared a 'temptation of the anti-Christ' by the True Orthodox Christians.[80]

Some of the more fanatic cut the electric wiring in their houses and removed the plumbing in order to avoid contamination with the surrounding society.[81] Especially as this social alienation was intensified by increasing pressure, the True Orthodox Christians tended to avoid outside employment and held that 'God would not permit children to attend the school of the "anti-Christ" because they did not teach "the laws of God" there.'[82] In response to the question, 'Do you consider that a man can have a social ideal to which he can devote his life?' one of the leaders of the True

---

[77] Onishchenko, op. cit., p. 98.
[78] Nikol'skaia, op. cit., pp. 166–7, 185.
[79] P. Vdovichenko, 'Reaktsionnaia sushchnost' religioznogo sektantstva' ('The reactionary essence of religious sectarianism'), *Kommunist Belorussii*, No. 11 (November 1964), pp. 56–62.
[80] Ibid., pp. 186–7.
[81] Ibid.
[82] *Komsomol'skaia Pravda*, 22 May 1964.

Orthodox Christians answered, 'No! If he proceeds from the teaching of the Gospel this cannot be. Why, you know the words of the Saviour that one cannot serve two masters.'[83]

To some degree this social alienation, which is not uncommon in particularly intense forms of Christianity, may have been coupled with a nostalgia for the past. One Soviet author, in describing a True Orthodox Christian woman, stated:

All happiness and good fortune was for her connected with the life long gone. At one time the family in which she grew up had a strong kulak farm, rights to a mill, horses, labourers. Ivanova did not cease asking God that all would be turned back to the old times, that on the Russian throne again there would be a tsar of the house of the Romanovs.[84]

In view of the communist predilection to regard everything in economic terms, together with the overt political motivation of most anti-religious authors, it is difficult to determine from Soviet sources to what degree this social alienation sprang from such reasons as these or whether other factors were operating which led the members to alienation from society. While there can be little doubt that the True Orthodox Christians did withdraw from social interests and often displayed a degree of hatred towards the surrounding world, when a Soviet researcher suggests that this social alienation also implies self-contempt,[85] it seems probable that the motivations behind such alienation have not been fully grasped.

In the mid-fifties the earlier social alienation of the True Orthodox Christians was ameliorated somewhat and the participants began to participate to a slightly greater degree in the life of society. The earlier, categorical refusal of work in collective farms was suspended and some of the members even engaged in work in industry.[86] In large measure Nikol'skaia may be correct in assigning this modification of the movement's practice to the changing economic conditions, for with the regime's increasingly comprehensive control over society in the later forties and early fifties it may indeed have become impossible to continue the former life of almost complete self-sufficiency without contact with society.

[83] Klibanov, 'Sovremennoe sektantstvo v Lipetskoi oblasti,' op. cit., p. 183.
[84] Vasin, op. cit., p. 18.
[85] Gagarin, op. cit., p. 183.
[86] Nikol'skaia, op. cit., p. 172.

Thus, increased participation in society may have been forced on the believers by economic necessity. In addition, however, particularly during the middle fifties with the relaxation of the secret police which followed the fall of Beria, a closer relationship to society may have seemed, for a time, somewhat less inimical to the conduct of one's preferred form of Orthodox worship.

In the later fifties, however, pressure against religion began to increase at an alarming rate, and the True Orthodox Christians, by and large, reverted to a steadily increasing degree of alienation from society. According to Soviet scholarship, some went so far as to advocate renunciation of life itself,[87] and extreme forms of social alienation began to appear in some of the new trends within the movement which will be discussed below. In the late fifties small, secluded monasteries were found in the vast forests of western Siberia, peopled by Orthodox who had fled entirely from society and who lived in exceedingly primitive conditions, subsisting on berries, nuts, mushrooms, etc.[88]

To a degree, the social alienation of the True Orthodox Christians spread over into political alienation, even though it would not seem that anti-Soviet sentiments occupied so large a position in their lives as in certain earlier forms of underground Orthodoxy. Many of the leaders were outspokenly anti-Soviet and urged their followers to shun all contact with anything connected with the Soviet regime. According to one True Orthodox Christian leader,

In the Gospel it is said that the existing authority is from God and therefore one must be subordinate to it, but the Soviet government is from anti-Christ, for it denies God. On the strength of this we do not recognize its laws and do not fulfil them. For these same reasons we consider that one must not enter into the *kolkhozes*, work in businesses or institutions, take part in elections, have Soviet documents, or educate children beyond the third/fourth classes. One also must not serve in the army.[89]

To some degree the True Orthodox Christians continued the earlier political hostility to the Russian Orthodox Church, calling themselves the 'Guardians of the legacy of Patriarch Tikhon' in

[87] Ibid., pp. 172–3.
[88] Aleksandr Shamaro, 'Kerzhatskie tropy' ('Kerzhat footpaths'), *Nauka i Religiia*, No. 4 (December 1959), pp. 68–76.
[89] Gagarin, op. cit., p. 183; cf. Vasin, op. cit., p. 17.

contrast to the patriarchal Church which had accepted the Government in 1927.[90]

Such political hostility towards the regime may be reflected in subsequent accusations that certain True Orthodox Christians had refused to contribute to the war effort,[91] although there are, of course, many other possible reasons for Christian pacifism. In 1968, one young True Orthodox Christian who refused to perform his military service was quoted as arguing,

'I am obliged to serve and be faithful to the motherland,' he pondered aloud. 'But where is my motherland? Where is my happy childhood? I had none. Whom will I defend? Those who oppress us believers?'[92]

In another case a mother destroyed her diploma, calling it 'a mark of Cain'.[93]

Anti-Soviet sentiments were reinforced by, and perhaps to some degree the product of, apocalypticism, which occupied a large place in the religious life of the True Orthodox Christians, as it had in the other forms of underground Orthodoxy.[94]

These ideas of the True Orthodox Christians about the anti-Christ, which were borrowed from Orthodox ecclesiastical literature, basically repeated the ideas of the active Church. However, in making the idea of the arrival of the anti-Christ the main point in their teaching and in transferring the apocalyptic signs of the 'end of the world' into the present, the leaders of the True Orthodox Christians gave detail to this idea and imparted to it a character which evoked hostility to society. The first 'evidence' of anti-Christ's presence in the world was, as the leaders of the True Orthodox Christians preached, the growth of civilization. 'Already the Russian land is covered, not by the fragrant smoke of the prayers of believers praying to the Lord,' says one of the leaflets disseminated among the True Orthodox Christians, 'but the coal stench of factories, plants, engines, the sickening stink of gasoline motors, hovering over the clouds, furrowing the land like lightning in all directions.' The development of industry, transport, and aviation were considered by the True Orthodox Christians as the 'fumes of human pride, as a challenge to God', and therefore as 'evidence' of the presence of anti-Christ. Such 'evidence' was also the development of

---

[90] Ibid.
[91] Aleksandrovich, op. cit., pp. 64–5.
[92] Vasin, op. cit., p. 20.
[93] *Izvestiia*, 12 December 1959.
[94] Nikol'skaia, op. cit., p. 171.

culture and literacy among the people, preached the leaders of the True Orthodox Christians, when not 'so much the divine word as the human word, the wisdom of this age . . . the science of evil . . .' began to be disseminated among the people.

Finally, 'abundance in everything', which also proved the 'approach of the end of everything', was explained as one more 'evidence' of the presence of anti-Christ in the world.[95]

As has been noted, apocalypticism played a considerable role in the worship practices of the True Orthodox Christians, particularly in their private, individual practices such as the almost mystical cult of the cross as protection against the anti-Christ. At least according to one Soviet author, the chiliasm of the True Orthodox Christians was reinforced by apocalyptic works composed in the twenties.[96] At one point True Orthodox Christians were predicting that the end of the world would coincide with the day the World Youth Festival was to open and the only safety to be found would be 'a small piece of land on the lower reaches of the Kama River where a certain "Grand Duke Mikhail", almost—but not quite—a reincarnation of Christ, would be ruler.'[97] Such monarchical overtones, while they were by no means a dominant theme in the apocalypticism of the True Orthodox Christians, nevertheless did appear from time to time. One group expected the world to end on 11 April 1964.[98] That same year,

the believers were told to abandon worldly life, to refuse to recognize the Soviet Government and its laws but, rather, patiently to wait for the return of the Emperor Nicholas II or his successor. 'God wanted' them to remain 'True Orthodox Christians', devoted with their bodies and souls to him alone and to his 'chosen' one—the Emperor of Russia.[99]

Similarly, certain of the leaders from time to time claimed to be relatives of the Tsar Nicholas II.[100] In one case a new-born son of a True Orthodox Christian family was announced to be the successor to Nicholas II and for the next seven years, until the group was discovered by the State, he was a considerable attraction for believers in a number of other cities in the area.[101]

[95] Ibid., p. 185.
[96] Fedorenko, op. cit., p. 215.
[97] *Sovetskaia Rossiia*, 7 September 1961.
[98] Semenov, op. cit., p. 29.
[99] *Komsomol'skaia Pravda*, 22 May 1964.
[100] Vasin, op. cit., p. 17.
[101] *Komsomol'skaia Pravda*, 22 May 1964.

With regard to the occupations of the True Orthodox Christians, Nikol'skaia was able to compile a considerable fund of data,[102] despite the fact that a similar scholar in another field study considered occupational data irrelevant because of their general renunciation of socially useful labour.[103] During the immediate post-war period the membership of the movement was predominantly to be found among the non-collectivized portion of the rural population. Some 10 to 15 per cent of the population in the areas of greatest activity of the True Orthodox Christians had managed to avoid conscription into the collective farm system and supported themselves independently from these State-oriented organizations. A number of such people among the True Orthodox Christians were home craftsmen (shoemakers, fullers, etc.) who made their living by providing services to the neighbouring population.

Probably the most important source of subsistence in the movement was the private farming activity of the members. In this period it was possible to maintain land holdings of 1–1·3 acres for private, family garden plots. Application of intensive farming methods made it possible to grow rye, wheat, potatoes, onions, cucumbers, tomatoes, garlic, etc. on these miniature farms. In addition, a cow, sheep, goats, swine, and chickens could be raised.

Another important source of income was seasonal labour. In the Tambov area, and particularly in the north-eastern regions of the area, there was a tradition of migratory, seasonal labour. Inhabitants would move to Moscow for four or five months of temporary employment as sawyers, plasterers, carpenters, stove-setters, etc. Such seasonal employment would earn as much as 4–5,000 roubles, which was marginally adequate for the year's support of the family.

Those who did not have private land holdings nor engage in seasonal labour often made their living by speculation, transporting produce to the cities and returning with manufactured items for resale to the rural inhabitants. In view of the immense scarcity of consumer goods resulting from the regime's almost exclusive concentration on heavy industry, together with the exceedingly primitive distributional system for these goods, such

---

[102] Unless otherwise specified, occupational data are drawn from Nikol'skaia, op. cit., pp. 167–71.

[103] Gagarin, op. cit., pp. 186–7.

private enterprise even on a miniscule scale could earn considerable profits. It is not unlikely that seasonal workers also augmented their income in this manner.

Particularly among the younger members of the movement, an important source of income for True Orthodox Christians was the preparation of religious articles which, for two generations, had been in increasingly scarce supply.

The preparation and embellishment of icons among the True Orthodox Christians was usually done as an artel: a few men and women of the group, more often young, would obtain 'divine images' from photographers. They would crudely colour them with aniline dyes, then the women would decorate them with tin foil and the men would make wooden frames (icon cases). Prepared in this manner the icons would be disposed of both in the Tambov *oblast* and outside it for 45 and 50 roubles each.

Neck crosses of celluloid were also made by the True Orthodox Christians at home and were sold by them for 5–10 roubles apiece, and also candles which, in contrast to the church candles which were moulded from wax and stearin by factories, were made exclusively from wax which was gathered on the farm by private people from the so-called 'wax of divine bees' and therefore were considered especially 'pure'. These candles were sold primarily at the 'holy springs' during pilgrimages there by believers.[104]

Those members of the movement who were relatively well off played a considerable role in the movement's religious life. Their homes would generally be utilized for divine services and for prayer meetings. The full-time leaders of the movement, of course, relied on the contributions and help of the members for their subsistence.

Particularly during the immediate post-war years, there was a marked contrast between the standard of living of such non-collectivized families and that of the members of collective farms. The extraordinary mismanagement and lack of proper equipment of the collective farms, together with exceedingly heavy State assessments on their product in order to provide the wherewithal for the reconstruction of the war-damaged industrial base—assessments which private individuals found much easier to avoid than did the collective farmers—combined to reduce the standard of living on the *kolkhozes* to the barest minimum. The higher standard of living of the non-collectivized families which formed the

[104] Nikol'skaia, op. cit., p. 170.

bulk of the membership of the True Orthodox Christians was seized upon by the movement in propagating their form of Orthodoxy and, in particular, was taken by them as a sign of God's blessing on their form of worship as contrasted with the poverty of members of the patriarchal churches. It was not long, however, before this situation was reversed, both by the recovery of the Soviet economy and by the increasingly strict controls applied against non-collectivized peasants. By the end of the forties it was becoming more and more difficult, if not impossible, to survive without joining the collective farms and, as has been noted, during the fifties and thereafter True Orthodox Christians began to be found on the collective farms and working in industry.

Even in such conditions, however, the True Orthodox Christians made little secret of their religious attitudes. In the field study conducted in 1960,

for example, we quickly learned to distinguish the residences of adherents of the True Orthodox Christians by means of the abundance of icons sparkling with new adornments, various cultic utensils, vestments, brass, foil. This was, as it were, a residence church.[105]

Little information is available concerning the membership itself. In the Tambov area, 60 to 70 per cent of the True Orthodox Christians were women,[106] while a subsequent study of two groups in the far north found that 78 per cent were women. Of 37 members of these groups, 33 had received four years' education or less, 2 had finished the seven-year elementary schooling, and 2 had a secondary education.[107] It would seem that a large proportion of the members are relatively young, which places the True Orthodox Christians in rather sharp distinction to all other (or at least to official data concerning all other) clandestine and, indeed, overt religious denominations in the U.S.S.R. Even though one Soviet scholar claims that not more than 15 per cent are under thirty years of age,[108] according to Klibanov,

The 'True Orthodox Christians' according to their age composition basically relate to the generation which was born after the Great October Socialist Revolution. . . . Of 65 people who made up the nucleus of the Michurin group of the True Orthodox Church at the

[105] Klibanov, 'Nauchno-organizatsionnyi i metodicheskii opyt,' op. cit., p. 19.
[106] Nikol'skaia, op. cit., p. 169.
[107] Gagarin, op. cit., p. 186.
[108] Aleksandrovich, op. cit., p. 64.

end of the forties and beginning of the fifties, there were a total of 8 people younger than 40 years old. Of 83 activists of the True Orthodox Christians (at the end of the forties and beginning of the fifties) 44 were younger than 30 years, 27 were between 30 and 50, and only 12 people belonged to the generation born before the October Revolution.[109]

In recent times the ability of the movement to attract former Komsomol members into their ranks has been of great concern to the regime.[110]

One curious reaction of the True Orthodox Christians to the increasing pressure they experienced in the latter forties and again when the anti-religious pressure began to be resumed the following decade, was the renunciation of marriage.

The True Orthodox Christians, since they do not wish, as they say, to increase the number of servants of the anti-Christ, preached renunciation of the continuation of the human race. In the mid-forties when, according to the ideas of the True Orthodox Christians, they were 'covered by darkness unto the time appointed by God', when there was no true Church, when the continuity of the clergy was broken, and 'the voice of the archangel has become silent', a relationship of 'brother and sister' began to be preached among the young men and women. Young women were proclaimed 'brides of Christ' following the 'unblemished path of the earthly life of the Mother of God'. Young men were called to become like Christ, also to follow this earthly 'sinless path'. The virginal form of life allegedly brought together the 'true believer' 'with God'.

Beginning in 1955, the preaching of celibacy spread over the entire organization as a whole. From this time on the birth rate among the True Orthodox Christians declined sharply. Children, when they appeared, usually from the preachers, whose personal lives did not correspond to their preaching, were proclaimed 'the womb of divine incarnation. . . .' Awaiting the return of Christ in the course of the years immediately to come, they 'based' the requirement of celibacy on a gospel text: 'Woe to them that are with child and give suck in those days.'[111]

---

[109] Klibanov, 'Sovremennoe sektantstvo v Tambovskoi oblasti,' op. cit., p. 96.

[110] Aleksandrovich, op. cit., p. 66.

[111] Nikol'skaia, op. cit., p. 187. It should be noted that the pre-revolutionary Old Believers were persistently, and usually wrongly, thought to be celibate because of their peculiar definition of the term 'virgin' to mean, not celibate, but unmarried, according to the church classifications of 'married' or 'virgin' (cf. the French usage of 'célibataire'). In this usage, conjugal relations, if outside sacramental marriage, are irrelevant to 'virginity'.

To some degree this may reflect, in part, the high esteem for monasticism, which has always been one of the features of underground Orthodoxy and which, in subsequent developments within the movement, was to assume increased importance. In addition, the practice begun by the regime in the latter fifties of forcibly separating True Orthodox Christians from their children (see below) may have contributed to the idealization of celibacy.

The influence of the prison system played a considerable role in the history of the True Orthodox Christians. After the emancipation from the labour camps in the mid-fifties the movement enjoyed a revival.[112] 'Former leaders of the True Orthodox Christians who were returning from confinement became the closest helpers' of the newly revived leadership.[113] Furthermore, the prison system itself and, in particular, the practice of subjecting prisoners to a further period of exile in the same area upon their release from the labour camps, served to expand the geographic area in which the movement was active. For example, according to the 1967 report of the field study in the far north which discovered active groups of True Orthodox Christians,

It is necessary, furthermore, to bear in mind that the Komi *oblast* served at one time as a place for administrative exile of former kulaks and persons engaged in counter-revolutionary and anti-Soviet activity. Among this category of people the percentage of sectarians (Baptists, Evangelicals, Pentecostals, Churikovtsy, Fedorovtsy, and others) was higher than in other groups of the population.[114]

In Soviet Central Asia, the movement was discovered in Temirtau, some ten miles from Karaganda, which had been the location of one of the major labour camps.

God had made dozens of people, who had built their mud houses on the banks of the Temirtau reservoir, to separate themselves with walls of icons from the outer world. A few kilometres away from these mud houses nightly fires were burning in the first furnaces of the Kazakhstanskaia Magnitka plant, but here, crowded in tight groups, people were praying by the flickering light of small candles.[115]

Apparently the closing of this group of True Orthodox Christians in 1960 had only limited success, for eight years later it was again

---

[112] Ibid., p. 172.
[113] Ibid., p. 173.
[114] Gagarin, op. cit., p. 168.
[115] *Komsomol'skaia Pravda*, 22 May 1964.

announced that a prayer house and home monastery had been closed in Temirtau.[116] Furthermore, as was noted in the case cited in an earlier chapter, even a member of the True Orthodox Christians who had been persuaded during his years in prison to leave the movement, displayed sufficient social alienation and reticence when interviewed by an atheist author to raise serious questions as to how effective his conversion away from the movement had been.[117]

The True Orthodox Christians have shown a considerable tenacity and ability to recover from intense attack by the regime. The severe campaign against underground Orthodoxy by investigatory and police powers of the State in the late forties, while it disrupted other forms of underground Orthodoxy completely, was able only to cause a reduction in membership, but not a collapse, of this movement. The True Orthodox Christians still retained approximately half of their peak membership by the end of the campaign and were, in some respects, even more active than they had been previously.[118] After the middle of the fifties they again came under pressure and their membership began to decline.[119] In the waning years of the fifties an intensive campaign against underground religion began, which very quickly expanded into the general campaign of the 1960s against all religions. Antireligious propaganda against the True Orthodox Christians was intensified.[120] Numerous lectures were organized, dealing with such themes as 'The Reactionary Essence of the Sect of True Orthodox Christians'.[121] Plenary meetings in *kolkhozes* were held to discuss what further action should be taken against this movement.[122] It was discovered that the practice of assigning an individual atheist propagandist to known members of the movement was particularly effective, even though it was not always successful. In one such case,

the local atheists knew this family well. They came to Ivanova during the election campaign, trying to establish normal relations with the members of the family but without result. On election day Ivanova

---

[116] Ibid., 27 February 1968.
[117] 'Materialy k kharakteristike sovremennogo sektantttvo v Tambovskoi oblasti,' op. cit., pp. 214–15, 219–20; see above, p. 150.
[118] Nikol'skaia, op. cit., pp. 171–2.
[119] Klibanov, 'Sovremennoe sektantstvo v Tambovskoi oblasti,' op. cit., p. 97.
[120] Ibid., p. 98.
[121] Aleksandrovich, op. cit., p. 71.
[122] *Nauka i Religiia*, No. 4 (April 1961), p. 84.

drew a cross on the door of their house and together with the children went into the *taiga*.[123]

According to Klibanov, by 1959 the campaign had succeeded in liquidating the True Orthodox Christians as a movement in the Tambov area, even though they could still be met on occasion.[124] A year later he discovered in the expedition to the Lipetsk area that 'there remained only small numbers and individual partisans of the True Orthodox Christians, many of whom are already wavering in their religious views and decisively condemn the disloyal position of their former leaders'.[125]

Probably the most effective of the measures taken against the True Orthodox Christians, short of outright arrest and imprisonment, was a new innovation which was exceedingly severe and had no precedent in Soviet history. This was the denial of parental rights, whereby the children would be forcibly removed from their parents and placed in atheistically oriented State boarding schools. Early in 1959, authorities discovered True Orthodox Christian parents subjecting their children to three or four hours of prayer daily, and deprived them of parental rights, removing the children to a State boarding school.[126] In 1960, a Comrade's Court sentenced six active leaders of a True Orthodox Christian group to deportation, and sentenced the parents of a seven-year-old boy to deprivation of parental rights.[127] In 1962, one of the major national periodicals reported two cases of deprivation of parental rights and made much of the happy results obtained with the children after they had been placed in State boarding schools.[128] The results were not always so felicitous, however, for in one case, at least, a child of parents who had been deprived of parental rights continued to attend meetings of the True Orthodox Christians, and it required considerable effort to win her away from the faith.[129]

---

[123] Vasin, op. cit., p. 18; cf. Aleksandrovich, op. cit., p. 74.

[124] Klibanov, 'Sovremennoe sektantstvo v Tambovskoi oblasti,' op. cit., p. 98.

[125] Ibid., p. 167.

[126] Aleksandrovich, op. cit., p. 67.

[127] *Komsomol'skaia Pravda*, 22 May 1964.

[128] *Ogonek*, 13 March 1962.

[129] M. K. Tepliakov, 'Sostoianie religioznosti naseleniia i otkhod veruiushchikh ot religii v Voronezhskoi oblasti (1961–1964 gg)' ('The condition of religiousness of the population and the departure of believers from religion in Voronezh oblast (1961–1964)'), in N. P. Krasnikov, ed., *Voprosy preodoleniia religioznykh perezhitkov v SSSR* ('Problems of overcoming religious survivals in the U.S.S.R.') (Moscow: 'Nauka,' 1966), pp. 44–5.

Despite the severity of the measures applied against them, however, the True Orthodox Christians have demonstrated a considerable ability to survive harsh pressure. That the movement has continued more or less intact for a quarter of a century indicates its resilience and capacity for survival. Particularly during the sixties, as will become evident below, the movement has been able to modify itself, taking whatever forms seem necessary to its continued existence. In the True Orthodox Christians underground Orthodoxy appears to have discovered a form of clandestine life which is sufficiently flexible to allow it to survive the worst measures undertaken against it by the regime. Groups of True Orthodox Christians continue to be discovered maintaining the movement's rites and practices more or less unchanged and, in addition, in response to the extreme pressure of the past decade new variants of the movement have arisen which seem all but immune to the State's attempts to liquidate underground Orthodoxy.

IX

Innovations

With the waning of the fifties, the period of relative tolerance of religion in the U.S.S.R. drew to a close. For almost two decades the Soviet regime had indulged religious people with a degree of permissiveness. The rather desultory anti-religious campaign begun in 1948 had been abruptly terminated on the death of Stalin in 1953. A similar attempt to revive militant atheism in 1954 was personally stopped by Nikita Khrushchev in his struggle for power.[1] But this hiatus was short-lived, for as early as 1957 pressure began to increase against illegal religions, and by 1960 this modest beginning had spread over into the general anti-religious campaign which was to become the dominant feature in the lives of all denominations, legal and illegal, throughout the succeeding decade.[2] In the new conditions of extreme tension, underground Orthodoxy, and, in particular, the True Orthodox Christians, were faced with an immediate and immense challenge to their continued existence, and new approaches were tried within the movement as conditions became more difficult.

One of the early variants, which developed in the latter part of the fifties, was the 'Silence' movement (mol'chalniki).[3] True Orthodox Christians entered this sub-grouping by taking a vow of total silence, never on any occasion speaking again, even to other members of the movement. According to the Soviet re-

[1] *Pravda*, 11 November 1954. For the significance of this pronouncement in Khrushchev's struggle for power, see William C. Fletcher, *Nikolai: Portrait of a Dilemma* (New York: Macmillan, 1958), pp. 154–5.

[2] As yet no single, convenient source adequately covers the anti-religious campaign of the sixties, although numerous brief treatments are available. See Donald A. Lowrie and William C. Fletcher, 'Khrushchev's Religious Policy, 1959–1964,' in Richard H. Marshall, Jr., ed., *Aspects of Religion in the Soviet Union, 1917–1967* (Chicago: University of Chicago Press, 1971), pp. 131–55.

[3] Data on the Silent ones are drawn from Nikol'skaia, op. cit., pp. 173–7, except as otherwise specified.

searchers in the Tambov area, this movement was begun as early as 1955 by a certain L. Kisliakova. Attaching herself to an alleged lunatic, she had served as interpreter of her prophecies before becoming an advocate of Silence. In 1955, she

performed the rite of baptism in Tambov, in the river Studenets. In the presence of a large group of True Orthodox Christians of Tambov she ostentatiously tore her town clothes off, destroyed her passport, and with the reading of prayers she performed the rite of baptism in the ice hole. At the time of the rite a dove was released from her hand into the sky, which was to symbolize for the believers the descent of the grace of God—the Holy Spirit—onto her.[4]

Thereafter she began to wander about the region, seeking converts to the new practice of total silence. The movement apparently expanded fairly rapidly, until by the end of the decade it was widespread throughout the area.

In their daily lives the Silent ones apparently represented a fairly extreme development of the social alienation which was characteristic of the True Orthodox Christians movement.

Representatives of this religious group have destroyed their personal documents, have refused to accept all types of state permits and money in general. The Silent ones did not acquire fabricated articles and wore home-spun clothes, home-made footwear. They did not participate in any form of collective labour and made a minimum wage necessary for a marginal, hungry existence. They bricked up the window openings of their residences and put heavy locks on the entrance doors. They speckled the walls, ceilings, and floors of their residences with crosses, counting on the magical power of these signs as barriers to the access of all influences of the external world.[5]

Composed predominantly of women (according to data from the Tambov expedition only some thirty per cent were men), the Silent ones made every attempt to avoid all contact whatsoever with the surrounding society. Naturally, they would refuse to answer any questions put to them and, according to Nikol'skaia, they would make the sign of the cross before their eyes 'as a sign that they had seen nothing and their mouth as a sign that they never will say anything'.[6] (Klibanov makes an intrinsically more probable suggestion that these responses were designed as a defence against

[4] Ibid., p. 183.
[5] Klibanov, 'Nauchno-organizatsionnyi i metodicheskii opyt,' op. cit., pp. 19–20.
[6] Nikol'skaia, op. cit., p. 186.

16

the surrounding world, rather than, as here implied, a means of communication.)[7]

In their religious practices, it would not seem that the Silent ones differed markedly from other True Orthodox Christians, except, of course, for those practices which require vocal communication. Talismanic practices, such as the wearing of prayers to the Virgin Mary under their scarves when outside the house, were widespread among them.[8] For reasons which remain unclear, the Silent ones apparently renounced the sacrament of baptism in any form (with occasional exceptions).[9] Idealization of celibacy or even its compulsory practice were widespread among them.[10]

Because of their strictly ascetic form of life, the Silent ones were able to live on exceedingly small incomes. Economically, there were three different gradations within the movement. First there were those who had the foresight to lay in considerable stores of food prior to taking the vow of silence. A second group was supported by relatives who were not members of the movement and hence still had incomes. The third classification within the movement had no source of income whatsoever, and were able to survive only through the help of members who were better off. On occasion, members of the open churches would feel sympathy for these latter unfortunates and would donate food to help them out. Naturally, the Silent ones refused all medical aid or any articles which might bear the 'seal of the anti-Christ'.[11]

It was not long before the Silent ones attracted the attention of the regime and stern counter-measures were instituted against this development among the True Orthodox Christians. The first blow fell against the founder and leader of the movement, Kisliakova. In 1957 she was discovered to be schizophrenic and was committed to a mental hospital, which effectively decapitated the movement.[12] Action against the Silent ones followed in a number of the villages of the area. One enlarged conference of the government of a collective farm passed a resolution asking the Village Soviet

[7] Klibanov, 'Nauchno-organizatsionnyi i metodicheskii opyt,' op. cit., pp. 19–20.
[8] Nikol'skaia, op. cit., p. 186.
[9] Ibid., p. 183.
[10] Ibid., p. 187.
[11] Interestingly enough, the Russian word 'seal' also is used for 'press', and hence the phrase would naturally associate with the Soviet press.
[12] Ibid., p. 180. This expedient was to become widely used in coming years, as a convenient alternative to arrest and trial—the individual was effectively removed from society by either method.

to institute a petition in the name of the *kolkhoz* 'Proletarian Victory' to apply strong measures, up to expulsion from the territory of the *kolkhoz*, against that group of the True Orthodox Christians who do not converse with the people and who do not participate in the activities of the Soviet Government.[13]

Similar resolutions were passed in numerous other collective farms, and a well conceived and exceedingly effective campaign was instituted against the Silent ones.

Three different methods were employed against the movement. In some cases special loans, grants, or gifts were made by the authorities to known Silent ones. In at least two of the eight cases described by Nikol'skaia, this method was sufficient to achieve the desired results. In other cases, this method was used concurrently with one or both of the other forms of attack.

The second approach was to assign atheistic propagandists to conduct individual work with Silent ones. This was an exceptionally difficult assignment, for naturally the individual agitator had to exercise his persuasion on the member against the latter's wish and initially, at least, had to effect some sort of invasion of privacy to establish any contact at all. Nevertheless, persistent employment of this tactic, carried out vigorously and over a period of time, did produce some results.

The most effective method, however, was deprivation of parental rights. By court order, parents belonging to the Silence movement were deprived of parental rights and their children forcibly removed to atheistic State boarding schools. This approach, which had an immense impact, both on the parents and on the children involved, proved eminently effective and it was quickly applied against other denominations as well for the next several years.[14] The severity of

---

[13] Ibid., p. 175.

[14] For examples of deprivation of parental rights, see *Sel'skaia Zhizn'*, 14 June 1962, and 20 June 1962; *Izvestiia*, 28 June 1962; *Pravda*, 3 October 1964; *Kazakhstanskaia Pravda*, 24 June 1964; and cf. Harry Willetts, 'De-opiating the Masses,' *Problems of Communism*, November–December 1964, p. 37. Ideological basis was provided by an explanation in *Izvestiia*, 17 April 1962, that no parent should be allowed spiritually to cripple a child, and legal basis was supplied by *Sovetskaia iustitsiia*, No. 21 (1962) (translation in *Soviet Law and Government*, Spring 1963, pp. 6–7), in asserting that the State, because it grants parental rights in the first place, has the power to withdraw them, even without due process at law if need be. According to *Kazakhstanskaia Pravda*, 24 June 1964, parents must continue to pay for their children's upkeep even after deprivation of parental rights.

this attack, especially when coupled with the lesser forms of pressure described above, would appear to have disrupted the movement almost entirely.

Nevertheless, the Silence variant of the True Orthodox Christians has remained a live option in the movement to the present, even if, because of the severe counter-measures employed by the State, it has never approached anything like the widespread movement promised by its initial success. Even after two years of such attack, Silent ones were still to be found in the Tambov area in 1959.[15] In 1964 they were again attacked,[16] and in 1966 a newspaper article commented on two female Silent ones who had been sent to a *kolkhoz* for corrective labour; only after a long struggle had they been persuaded to start speaking.[17] Thus it would seem that the vow of silence continued to be utilized, if only infrequently, despite the severity of the counter-measures instituted by the regime against it.

Soviet scholarship has not been especially successful in elucidating the motivations which prompted True Orthodox Christians to take a vow of silence. Nikol'skaia simply describes the phenomenon as based on 'the principle of renunciation of life itself': 'They proclaimed death a blessing, "God given" to man. They conducted themselves in a mode of life as living corpses, uniting on the basis of a vow of silence.'[18] The possibility that the movement was inspired by a symbolic enactment of a suicidal tendency on the part of the individuals involved, however, would scarcely seem to exhaust the range of possible motivations. At the very least, religious and devotional aspirations could have been involved, particularly in view of the similar phenomena in other countries (such as the Trappists in Roman Catholicism).

There are some indications that the Silence movement may have represented a much more concrete reaction to surrounding events. In some cases, at least, this extreme form of social alienation may have been embraced in conscious desire to frustrate attempts by the State to induce self-incrimination or incrimination of others among the True Orthodox Christians. In this regard, it is interesting that two earlier instances of Silence had appeared in 1948,[19]

[15] Klibanov, 'Sovremennoe sektantstvo v Tambovskoi oblasti,' op. cit., p. 98; cf. Aleksandrovich, op. cit., p. 63.

[16] Teodorovich, 'The Catacomb Church in the U.S.S.R.,' op. cit., p. 11.

[17] *Sel'skaia Zhizn*, 13 July 1966.

[18] Nikol'skaia, op. cit., pp. 172–3.

[19] Ibid., p. 173 n. 47.

which, as has been noted, was a year of severe attack against underground Orthodoxy by the regime. Furthermore, the initiator of the movement, in 1955, was aided by former prisoners who had been released in the emancipation, which might suggest a reaction to State pressure supported by the experience of those from the underground Orthodox movements who had already suffered from the investigatory and police actions of the State.[20] Hence in many instances, the Silence movement may have represented (and may still continue to represent) an attempt to maintain secrecy when under State pressure.

Obviously enough, this counter-measure (if such it was) to the increasing menace of the rising anti-religious campaign was inadequate to insulate its members from reprisal, and the movement very quickly collapsed. In its place, however, a second variant appeared among the True Orthodox Christians, which has proved itself exceedingly competent in surviving the most extreme of pressures.

This new variant of modern underground Orthodoxy is generally referred to by the name 'True Orthodox Christian Wanderers' although, as will become apparent below, there are many local variants of nomenclature. Essentially, the Wanderers carry their alienation from society to its logical conclusion. Destroying all documents, they renounce all contact with normal society and lead a life of complete secrecy. Often they have no permanent abode, and spend their lives wandering from place to place, practising their religion as secretly as possible. With the mounting vigour of the anti-religious campaign, which has been dominant in the U.S.S.R. for the past decade, the Wanderers have become an increasingly important phenomenon in clandestine religious life, for naturally enough the absolute secrecy necessary to such an existence in a controlled society is ideally suited to allow its members to avoid detection by even the most vigilant efforts of the regime.

New members of the movement make a complete break with society, and are initially subject to considerable discipline.

The leaders of the sect required them to destroy their documents which were given out by the 'government of anti-Christ', to renounce citizenship and to become vagrants, and to wander in expectation of the end of the world. At the insistence of the leaders of the sect people left

[20] Ibid., p. 173.

families, abandoned children, and renounced first and last names. Rank and file sectarians naively thought that thereby they would more truly be worthy of blessedness.[21]

There is an obvious affinity between this radical development among the True Orthodox Christians and the similar experience of the Old Believer sect of *Beguny* ('Runners'), which has been extant in Russia for two centuries. According to Pauline Taylor,

The published descriptions of the wanderers and their organization bear a striking resemblance to accounts of a sect of wanderers founded in the eighteenth century by Euphemius, a 'tramp' peasant and army deserter, who preached the rejection of all public duties, renunciation of family ties, and flight from the civil community. Nineteenth century followers of Euphemius are known to have spread his doctrine 'on a large scale in the wastelands of Siberia'.[22]

Indeed, there is considerable controversy among contemporary Soviet scholars as to whether the True Orthodox Christian Wanderers represent a sect growing out of Russian Orthodoxy, or whether it is more properly to be considered an intensification of the older movement, with its roots and sources among the Old Believers rather than the Orthodox. According to Milovidov, a champion of the latter opinion,

A special controversy on the Old Believer dogma on the reign of anti-Christ in 'the world' arose in the doctrine of the *Stranniki* (True Orthodox Christian Wanderers). According to the founder of the sect, Euphemius, anti-Christ was serially incarnate in the Russian tsars, beginning with Peter I. 'The apocalyptic beast,' writes Euphemius, 'is the tsarist power, its icon the civil power, its body the spiritual power.' Inasmuch as only God can vanquish anti-Christ and man cannot struggle with him openly, one must 'hide oneself' and 'run' so

---

[21] Okunev, op. cit., p. 31. In common with nearly all the reports concerning the True Orthodox Christian Wanderers (the chief exceptions being the treatment of the academicians V. F. Milovidov and, concerning the *Skrytniki*, Iu. V. Gagarin), this article is obviously sensationalized, designed for the broadest possible audience. The unalloyed hostility of such authors to the movement often threatens to vitiate their argument entirely, and always renders their treatment suspect, for exaggerations and mis-representations, intentional or otherwise, remain a real possibility. Hence particular care has been exercised in utilizing such materials, and it should be borne in mind that the treatment which follows may not be entirely inerrant owing to sources which, if others more reliable were available, would warrant use only sparingly, if at all.

[22] Taylor, op. cit., p. 282.

that in this way, all bonds may be broken with 'the world' and one may avoid all civil responsibilities, 'the visible marks of the rule of anti-Christ'.[23]

Milovidov takes specific issue with A. Trubnikova, who argues against this classification,[24] and his position is shared by Fedorenko, who treats the True Orthodox Christian Wanderers as a branch of the Old Believers,[25] as do some other Soviet scholars.[26]

However, the classification of the modern Wanderers as Old Believers would not seem to have been definitively established. Milovidov, for example, seems to base his interpretation on a rather tortuous argument concerning the social and economic class structure of the Old Believers during the 1920s, without asking himself the question whether the gap of forty years between that time and the present can be bridged with sufficient accuracy to ensure that his analysis based on the earlier developments within the Old Believer movement remains valid in the changed society of the present. Indeed, it would appear that his interpretation of the current movement is based chiefly on a single interview with a hermit of the True Orthodox Christian Wanderers who was interested in the history of the Old Believers, but at least in Milovidov's description of the interview it is not at all clear what the religious background of this hermit was—whether he was originally Orthodox or Old Believer.[27] Milovidov seems to be able to maintain his position despite acknowledged differences between the present movement and its older progenitor:

Even comparatively recently the Old Believers called tea 'a plant cursed by God', sugar 'an enticement of anti-Christ', potatoes 'a plant possessed with multifarious lecheries'. At the present time these products are everywhere used by the Old Believer population. Even in the Belotaezhnaia wilderness, located in the deep *taiga* forests of Tomsk *oblast*, the True Orthodox Christians have kitchen gardens sown with potatoes.[28]

---

[23] Milovidov, op. cit., pp. 214–15.
[24] Ibid., pp. 216–17.
[25] Fedorenko, op. cit., pp. 106–7, but contrast p. 108.
[26] *Nauka i Religiia*, No. 4 (December 1959), p. 69.
[27] Milovidov, op. cit., pp. 216–19.
[28] Ibid., p. 212. It should be noted that not all Old Believers subscribed to these peculiarities, some of which had sociological roots (e.g., due to Peter the Great's introduction of potatoes to Russia).

Finally, he even notes with unconscious irony, 'It is curious that even names of the believers are almost the same—True Orthodox Christians and True Orthodox Christian Wanderers.'[29]

As has been noted, some commentators within the U.S.S.R. disagree with this position. Trubnikova argues quite explicitly that this is a new movement which is similar to, but quite distinct from, its pre-revolutionary cognate. Unfortunately, her argument is based on a variant interpretation of the same social and class structure data which Milovidov uses to support the contrary conclusion, and suffers from the same inadequacies as the argument of her opposite number.[30]

In large measure this controversy seems somewhat academic, for in actual fact the Wanderers have a function in contemporary Soviet society which is exactly parallel with—if somewhat more extreme than—that of the True Orthodox Christians. Certainly, what little evidence is available concerning the membership would imply that the majority of the recruits are drawn not from Old Believer families but from the Orthodox tradition. In view of the fact that the members of the movement identify themselves by their very name with the True Orthodox Christians, it would seem appropriate (at least for the purposes of this study) to consider this a variant of the latter, and, indeed, a logical development of the approach of the True Orthodox Christians in a time of extreme tension.

Three gradations are observable within the membership of the movement. The first consists of the leaders of the movement, who are exceedingly experienced and adept at the difficult requirements of a totally clandestine form of life. Local leaders give guidance to the members not only in the mechanics and procedures necessary to ensure secrecy, but also (and probably more important) they are responsible for guiding the spiritual development of the members. Leaders above the local level fulfil similar functions for the regional and nationwide organization of the movement. The second classification is the Wanderers themselves, who have taken the vows of complete renunciation of society and have entered into the clandestine form of life. The third classification, without which the development of the movement would be severely hampered, are

[29] Ibid., p. 218.
[30] Alla Trubnikova, 'Tainik v taburetke' ('Hiding place in a taboret'), *Oktiabr'*, No. 9 (September 1964), p. 173.

the 'benefactors', or those adherents of the movement who have not, or have not yet, taken the vows of wandering. These people, who remain within society and work at various jobs, perform an exceedingly important function by supplying the clandestine organization with such funds as are necessary to its continued operation, with those materials from society (manufactured articles, literature) which are needed, and with safe, secure premises in which the Wanderers may secrete themselves.[31]

It is difficult to judge the geographic extent of the True Orthodox Christian Wanderers. Communities and cells are scattered over Siberia,[32] and as will become evident below, analogous groups are to be found in the far north, in the *taiga* regions, and in Soviet Central Asia. In addition, there are some indications that groups of True Orthodox Christian Wanderers exist in numerous of the larger cities of the U.S.S.R.[33]

The complete secrecy of this movement, together with the immense fluidity attendant upon a wandering life, in which it is incumbent upon the members to change their location frequently in order to avoid detection, are ideally suited to the development of a highly organized movement. The True Orthodox Christian Wanderers very quickly appear to have succeeded in founding a clandestine organization which embraces vast regions of the country, uniting the local cells of the movement in a highly centralized, tightly disciplined network strictly subordinated to the leadership.

Several cells made up a 'limit'. At the head of them stood senior 'limiters'. 'Limits' were found in Central Asia and Kazakhstan, in Saratov, Novosibirsk, Buisk, Cheliabinsk, and other cities. All the sect's activities were directed from the 'centre'. . . .

The head of the sect, the 'monk Varlaam,' carried the title of 'Pre-eminence' and regularly called 'Sobors' which passed on major problems in the life of the True Orthodox Christian Wanderers sect. Such meetings were held in 1960 in Novosibirsk and in 1963 in Alma-Ata. They dealt mainly with increasing the disruptive activities of the sect and particularly with attracting young people into its ranks. They

---

[31] Fedorenko, op. cit., p. 109; Okunev, op. cit., p. 31; for a detailed description of one benefactor, see Trubnikova, op. cit., pp. 169–72.

[32] Milovidov, op. cit., p. 216.

[33] Cf. Ovalov, op. cit., *Nauka i Religiia*, Nos. 1–6 (January–June 1966), *passim*.

worked on mothers with casuistry, flattery, and threats and often succeeded in leading young people astray.[34]

Naturally, the organized movement is highly skilled in clandestine practices, such as recognition signals and the like.[35]

The Soviet authorities have been greatly disturbed by the movement's evident ability to attract young people, who apparently form a significant portion of the membership. 'It is not by chance that the leaders of the sect directed their designs towards youth, from whom they attempted to fill the ranks of fanatic zealots.'[36] Numerous examples of young teenagers who have been recruited into the movement have been given in the Soviet press.[37] In one such case,

Religious fanaticism at last succeeded in convincing Mira of the existence of the heavenly kingdom and made her pray that the Lord quickly grant her death and heavenly blessedness.

If the school had been interested in how children are brought up at home, her teacher would have found out that the mother of Mira Strunnikova exercised a religious influence on the girl. Then they would have known where to find Mira [after she disappeared]. But the careless people believed in the absurd story of the sectarians that the girl had gone to relatives in another city and had died there.

Mira spent many years in a dungeon and lost her health there. When the girl, shaking with fright, came out of the dungeon [her mother] was asked:

'How could you treat your own daughter so pitilessly?'

'She is not a daughter to me,' she shouted, 'she is a *staritsa* [elder], the *staritsa* Nika. And I am not a mother to her but a fellow believer, a slave of God.'[38]

Apparently new initiates undergo a period of stern discipline directly after entering the movement. Generally attached, either singly or in groups, to a monk or nun, they spend a considerable period of time in hiding in a secret location (such as the basement of a benefactor's house or an isolated hut in the deep forest). 'Living

[34] *Kazakhstanskaia Pravda*, 8 December 1963; cf. V. Ilov, 'Konets peshchernykh apostolov' ('The end of the cave-dwelling apostles'), *Partiinaia Zhizn' Kazakhstana*, No. 4 (April 1964), p. 32; *Sel'skaia Zhizn'*, 10 September 1963.

[35] Trubnikova, op. cit., p. 168.

[36] Ilov, op. cit., p. 33.

[37] E.g., ibid., p. 32; Trubnikova, op. cit., *passim*.

[38] Okunev, op. cit., p. 31.

in a cell, a hiding place, the Wanderer leads a half-starved existence and works for the monk to exhaustion.'[39] During this period, the new member is subjected to exceedingly stern discipline, and must direct his energies exclusively towards prayer and the devotional life.

A fourteen-year-old girl, taken away from her parents by deceit, was baptized by three peasants, who subjected her to a disgraceful act: right on the street, in an old barrel, they plunged her nude into the water three times. Her tale of her life in the cells and hiding places cannot be heard without shuddering. She was fed food without fat once or twice a day; the fasts, which were prolonged for a great part of the year, and the uninterrupted prayer drove her to moral annihilation. The girl lived without air and light, surrounded by fanatics who stifled all humanity in her. They prohibited her from visiting with relatives, and even from thinking about them, from visiting the cinema, reading, listening to the radio. It was not permitted even to have recourse to a doctor. If an unknown person would appear, they hid her in a hiding place constructed in the basement.[40]

A similar case was discovered in 1963, in which a fifteen-year-old girl had spent her first two years in her initial training. Upon entry into the sect, she had been taken to a rude hut deep in the *taiga*.

Then came an endless succession of days filled with fastings and prayers. They lived on mushrooms, cabbage, and potatoes with meagre servings of sunflower oil. The food was brought by persons whom Margarita never saw.[41]

Eight to twelve hours a day, and more on religious festival days, were devoted to prayer and bowing before the icons.[42] All of the rites of the sect are conducted in deepest secrecy: 'The funeral for a Wanderer who has died is conducted in secret, usually at night in the house or in the woods, so no one will see.'[43]

The Wanderers seemed to be fairly well supplied with devotional and doctrinal literature, at least as compared with the other True Orthodox Christians. According to Fedorenko,

[39] Ibid.
[40] Ilov, op. cit., p. 33.
[41] *Kazakhstanskaia Pravda*, 8 December 1963.
[42] Trubnikova, op. cit., pp. 167–8.
[43] Okunev, op. cit., p. 31.

The doctrine, worship, and history of the sect are laid out in the hand-written book of a Wanderer, the *Flower Bed*. Mystical 'verses' are contained in it: 'On the Times,' 'The Birth of Anti-Christ,' 'The Sevens of Daniel,' 'Sacrifice,' 'Flight in the Presence of Anti-Christ,' 'Submission to the Government,' 'The Seal of Anti-Christ,' 'Marriage,' 'Do Not Communicate with Heretics,' 'The Three Beasts,' and others —they interpret them in an anti-Soviet spirit at the present time. In the analogous *Moral Flower Bed* similarly reactionary explanations are given to moral commandments, 'Concerning Obedience,' 'Humility,' 'Kindness,' 'Patience,' 'Virginity,' 'Lies,' 'Hospitality,' and the like. 'Never make friends with heretics, nor eat, nor drink with them, nor be their fellow traveller on the way, nor enter their homes nor their meetings because everything that there is of theirs is unclean. Do not become friends with heretics, that you be not joined to their society'— thus the authors of the *Moral Flower Bed* teach their followers, promising them recompense after the Second Coming of Christ as a reward for humility, kindness, obedience, hospitality, virginity, and separation from the world.[44]

It remains uncertain that the above compositions are of pre-revolutionary Old Believer origin or whether they have been recently composed by the Wanderers. In the former case, at least a portion of the apparent influence of the early Old Believer movement on the present day Wanderers would be accounted for.

Other pamphlets of the Wanderers include such titles as 'The Forty-Five Days', 'Anti-Christ Receives All Power From the Devil', 'The Defeat of Anti-Christ', and 'On the Education of Children'.[45]

Of particular interest is the large collection entitled *Universe*, which was discovered when members of the State security service raided a Wanderers Sobor in Alma-Ata in 1963. This work, of which more than one copy was recovered, was originally compiled in 1925,[46] and additions were inserted 'at various times, written on various typewriters' and included in a single binding.[47] *Inter alia*, it included such statements as the following: 'Not only Nero and Diocletian, persecutors of Christians, could be called betrayers, but

[44] Fedorenko, op. cit., p. 107. It is not clear whether or not the coincidence of title is indicative of a direct relationship between these works and the *Flower Bed* composed by Euphemius in the eighteenth century.

[45] Trubnikova, op. cit., p. 163.

[46] *Kazakhstanskaia Pravda*, 8 December 1963.

[47] Trubnikova, op. cit., p. 163.

many others have deserved the name—revolutionaries of all hues, communists.'[48] Curiously enough, a 'copy of an historical document', a letter of the wife of Pontius Pilate written in modern Russian, is also included in the collection.[49]

The major theme of the collection was an attempt to meet the propaganda of atheism on its own ground. According to *Universe*,

The spreading evil of unbelief attracts tens of thousands of people to itself in a raging torrent, without distinction of class, age, or sex. In order to help perishing mankind, we have found it necessary and essential to select materials from the literature we have in hand on various exceedingly militant contemporary questions in the struggle of religion with atheism.[50]

The book concentrates its attention on such themes as the creation of the world and of matter, and on the source of life on the earth.

The very deepest questions of the human soul—What is matter and whence? Where did the first movement in matter come from? What is the goal of the creation of the world? Where did life on earth come from and what is it? Where did human consciousness and intelligence come from? What is the goal of man's life on earth and in general that of all creatures?—remain inexplicable to the present time. We firmly believe that all these questions receive a correct answer only in religion. Only in faith in God can man correctly understand the goal of his commission. Only faith in God is able to solve all the enigmas, to enable him to rise above the level of the animal, to enable the achievement of wise, lofty, and noble goals.[51]

Apparently, *Universe* was continually receiving additional entries as the members of the Wanderers themselves continued their philosophical and theological research. A number of contemporary Soviet journals were discovered in the cell, supplied by the 'benefactor'.[52]

The Wanderers hermits, in dark hiding places, subterranean burrows, apparently in our time are seeking 'scientific' proofs of 'the divine

---

[48] *Kazakhstanskaia Pravda*, 9 February 1964; on 8 December 1963, the same newspaper had said that this sentence was a note hand-written by one of the leaders; whether it represents his addition to the *Universe* collection, or was copied therefrom by him, remains uncertain.

[49] Trubnikova, op. cit., p. 167.

[50] Quoted in Fedorenko, op. cit., p. 107.

[51] Quoted in ibid., pp. 107–8.

[52] Ilov, op. cit., p. 34.

inspiration of scriptures', 'the conditions for divine understanding', 'philosophical proofs of the being of God', and 'the authenticity of the Pentateuch'. With the help of idealist philosophers of all ages, they are trying to refute materialism, to demonstrate the limits of the world, the divine creation of the world and man, the eternity and invincibility of religion, considering it 'essential to give into the hands of believers the support of an intelligent foundation from scientific proofs', convincing their ignorant adherents that allegedly 'science does not alienate one from God, but draws one near to Him, inasmuch as the mysteries surrounding us at every step necessitate, on the part of science itself unconditional acceptance of the supernatural power which created all of its wise intelligence.'[53]

As yet no clear picture of the doctrinal positions taken by the True Orthodox Christian Wanderers has appeared. Considering the nature of the movement, it may well be that no coherent position is common to every member or group, although it would seem that with the movement's exceptional skill at establishing clandestine organizations a degree of doctrinal cohesion would eventually develop. At the present it would appear that their doctrinal stance remains vague and undefined, a somewhat eclectic combination of Orthodox, Old Believer, and sectarian traditions.[54] During their initial period in the movement, new members are thoroughly immersed in study of the Bible and are able to recite lengthy passages from memory (even though according to Soviet observers they seem astonishingly deficient in understanding that which they have memorized).[55] When he was arrested on 12 August 1963, one of the Wanderers leaders dated his signature to the protocol of his interrogation 30 July 7471 (the July date, of course, reflecting adherence to the Julian rather than the modern Gregorian calendar).[56] The computation of the year was subsequently found to be derived from a literal rendering of the Bible: adding the ages of the Old Testament patriarchs, etc., the Wanderers of this group computed 2242 years from Adam to the flood, and discovered that the Virgin Mary had been conceived in the year 5485.[57] Eschatology plays a considerable role in the doc-

[53] Fedorenko, op. cit., p. 108.
[54] See Teodorovich, 'The Catacomb Church in the U.S.S.R.,' op. cit., p. 13.
[55] Trubnikova, op. cit., p. 176.
[56] Ibid., p. 164.
[57] Ibid., p. 176.

trine of the Wanderers.[58] This is not an unexpected phenomenon in a movement whose alienation from society is total, but it may also reflect the general increase of interest in eschatological subjects during the period of extreme tension resulting from the rising anti-religious campaign.[59]

Perhaps the most notable phenomenon in considering the doctrinal position of the Wanderers is the great amount of energy which its adherents devote to the further development of the theological and philosophical bases of their position.[60] The results of this research, as apparent in the collection *Universe*, have been described above. In general, the attraction of literate, educated candidates into the movement seems of great importance to its leaders, and even young recruits who have the basic qualifications of literacy are quickly set to the task of research in Scripture and the other literature possessed by the Wanderers.[61]

The thought that all the spiritual richness of socialist culture was a myth was instilled into the minds of future preachers. Even space flights were interpreted as a manifestation of 'pride', which would inevitably be punished by 'divine wrath'. The sect called on its members not to obey Soviet authorities and to refuse to bear arms in defence of the Motherland.[62]

Soviet researchers discovered one of the eremetic Wanderers who devoted himself to problems of history, working with various historical compositions, including those of Old Believers and secular historical scholars.[63]

Nor are the Wanderers content with merely developing their doctrines. In order to disseminate them among the membership, networks of secret schools have been set up.[64] These schools consist not only of normal, more or less 'elementary', seminary-level schools, but also are supplemented by schools for advanced students, serving a university or academy function.[65] At one of the seminary-level schools,

[58] Milovidov, op. cit., pp. 214, 216.
[59] Malakhova, op. cit., p. 16.
[60] Skazhina, op. cit., p. 134.
[61] Ilov, op. cit., p. 34.
[62] *Kazakhstanskaia Pravda*, 8 December 1963.
[63] Milovidov, op. cit., pp. 218–19.
[64] Teodorovich, 'The Catacomb Church in the U.S.S.R.,' op. cit., p. 10; cf. Ovalov, op. cit., *Nauka i Religiia*, No. 5 (May 1966), pp. 79–83.
[65] Trubnikova, op. cit., p. 169; Ilov, op. cit., p. 33.

they rose before dawn, they prayed, and Gradislava, a woman of thirty with thin, pursed lips, began the 'lesson'. She read to them from manuscripts, explained the hidden meaning of the numbers 1,666 and 45, then taught them dogmas from the *Universe* book. This book spoke most of all about the anti-Christ, about the fact that his rule would come to an end, and by 'the power of the anti-Christ' was meant nothing else than Soviet rule.[66]

The work of the schools is supported by underground publishing houses using typewriters, hand-written copying, etc.[67]

Much of the data used by Soviet scholarship in evaluating the True Orthodox Christian Wanderers derives from a sensational trial which was held in Alma-Ata in 1963.[68] Members of the Committee of State Security raided a house, surrounded by a high wooden fence, with warnings of a vicious dog, and managed to apprehend district leaders of the True Orthodox Christian Wanderers, together with a number of relatively new members of the movement undergoing their initial disciplinary period. A widely publicized trial ensued, at which it was revealed that the organization had branches in many different regions of the U.S.S.R. The senior Wanderer present was G. Perevyshin.[69]

A decrepit, emaciated old man with a grey, sallow complexion, in a monastic hat. Under the wrinkled brow glare small, malicious eyes. This is Perevyshin, but for the fanatics he is the 'elder prior'. In his long and good-for-nothing life the 'prior' three times changed his name to cover his tracks, fleeing from responsibility for criminal deeds. He began with Grigorii, then became Vasilii, and then turned into the monk Varlaam. In 1930 he was sentenced to three years for anti-Soviet activity. In 1947 he again went to prison—for eight years. After he had served his sentence, he again acted as before: he energetically supplied 'marriages' [initiations into the True Orthodox Christian Wanderers] with prohibited literature and carried on active work to entice new members into the sect.[70]

His assistant was accused of desertion during the siege of Moscow where he had been sent for treatment of wounds, falsely spreading a rumour of his own death in order to avoid alimony payments to

[66] *Kazakhstanskaia Pravda*, 8 December 1963.

[67] Trubnikova, op. cit., p. 173.

[68] *Kazakhstanskaia Pravda*, 8 December 1963, 17 February 1963; Trubnikova, op. cit., Ilov, op. cit.; Okunev, op. cit.

[69] Ilov, op. cit., p. 32.

[70] Okunev, op. cit., p. 31.

his wife, and bigamous re-marriage and subsequent desertion.[71]
Together with them, the 'benefactor' who owned the house where
they were apprehended was also indicted.[72] As a result, Perevyshin
was sentenced to five years of imprisonment, his assistant to seven
years, and the 'benefactor' to three years, all at strict regime.[73]

Doubtless inspired in part by the publicity given to this single
court case, local atheist organizations began to devote considerable
attention to the threat imposed by this new movement. Although
the relative paucity of reports of success would seem to indicate that
it was exceedingly difficult to discover members of this movement,
whose existence was now widely recognized in the atheist propaganda, nevertheless there were some reports of success. In one case,
a local atheist devoted a long period of time to individual
work with one of the members of the movement and finally, by
developing his latent interest in machine technology, succeeded in
enlisting him in a tractor brigade.[74]

Also instructive was the fate of the girl M., a former activist of the sect
of True Orthodox Christians, who in correspondence to the beliefs of
her sect spent long years in 'wandering' about the villages and
nocturnal vigils before the icons. Not without the participation of the
atheists, who struggled persistently for the girl, M. began to work at
one of the swine enterprises of Penza. For the young sectarian, who had
considered even casual conversation with an atheist a great sin, a new
stage in life began. Now M. is a fine producer, a disciplined worker.
Already she does not avoid people and willingly enters into conversation, is a guest of atheists, attends the cinema, the theatre. Together
with her comrades from work she was on an excursion to Moscow. At
first glance, it seems that the victory has been a great one. But M. has
not yet departed from religion, she remains a believer. Yes, it is so. But
the conversion is already at hand. M. is herself already reaching out
to people, to the light, and this means that in her consciousness a
specific break has taken place. The comrades at work are doing everything to tear the girl away from religion at last.[75]

It would not seem, however, that these cases are typical, for the
reported successes in discovering and converting Wanderers back
to normal social intercourse have been exceedingly few. In one case,

---

[71] Ibid.; Ilov, op. cit., p. 33.
[72] Trubnikova, op. cit., pp. 169–72; *Kazakhstanskaia Pravda*, 8 December 1963.
[73] Ibid., 8 February 1964.
[74] Koltuniuk, op. cit., p. 91.
[75] Ibid., pp. 51–2.

17

a local Leningrad newspaper traced the movements of a member of the sect as far as possible and appealed for atheists to find the woman and rescue her six-year-old daughter.[76]

However anti-Soviet and anti-social the Soviet authorities may consider the leaders to be, Soviet researchers seem to remain in somewhat of a quandary with regard to identifying and understanding the motivations which impel new recruits, and especially youth, to join. Certainly political bias against the Soviet State has not been among the motives suggested by Soviet observers. In 1966, the chief anti-religious journal published a serialized novel dramatizing a young communist hero, Iury, and his romantic search for a girl-friend from school who had disappeared into the Wanderers movement. Although fictional, the story is well researched, generally accurate, and in most respects quite convincing. At the conclusion of the story, the narrator meets the girl, now happily married to Iury, and speculates:

One can still explain what impelled her to God—the search for consolation! Praskov'ia Semenovna [her mother] from childhood had accustomed her to church, to prayer. But—to the sectarians? And to such sectarians? Eccentricities of an unbalanced character? Flight from Iury? The threats of her mother to go to school [to complain about her behaviour]? The attraction of secrecy? A desire, even if unconscious, to submit herself to the will of another? It was not so simple to understand her![77]

In a non-fictional account based on interviews with the young people 'rescued' in the Alma-Ata case, a similar attempt is made to catalogue the motivations leading to entry into the Wanderers movement.

Various paths brought them to the sect. In one case, an unfortunate love and outraged virginal honour. In another, a drunken husband. In a third, the religious influence of a mother. In a fourth, conflict with teachers. And so forth and so on. However, the primary reason invariably was not so much unhappiness itself as that vacuum which was formed around each of them. For only as a consequence of the complete indifference of those around them could a trivial incident such as an incorrect grade at school grow into a desire to run away to anywhere so long as it is far away from school, where unjust teachers give unjust marks.[78]

[76] Radio Liberty dispatch, 27 August 1964, citing *Leningradskaia Pravda*.
[77] Ovalov, op. cit., *Nauka i Religiia*, No. 6 (June 1966), p. 80.
[78] Trubnikova, op. cit., p. 167.

It is exceedingly significant that Soviet observers have apparently found no trace of anti-Soviet political hostility in accounting for the motivations attracting new members to the movement. According to the Soviet sources, general social alienation of various sorts, none of them remotely connected with any sort of political hostility, attracts people to this mysterious and highly romantic form of life. Subsequent to their entry, the older leaders, who in the Alma-Ata case, at least, had good reason to fear and despise the political regime, transform this social alienation into a degree of political alienation. If this interpretation is correct, the Wanderers movement, at least in Soviet research, represents a new departure from the older movements, entry into which was universally attributed by Soviet scholarship to political hostility to the Soviet regime. It should be noted, however, that it seems just as likely that the difference is to be sought not so much in the peculiarities of the Wanderers movement, but in a more rational analysis by Soviet scholarship of this recent movement, as compared with the patterns of preconceived analysis applied by Soviet observers to the earlier movements.

In the far north, a movement analagous in many respects to the Wanderers uses the designation True Orthodox Christians in Hiding (*Skrytniki*). This movement is much more inclined towards the eremitic way of life than to the mobility of the Wanderers. The normative pattern would seem to be for an individual to flee into the deep forest, there build himself a hut, and lead a life of a hermit.

Similarities between the True Orthodox Christians in Hiding and the analogous sects among the Old Believers are much more pronounced than they are among the Wanderers. Indeed, it may be justifiable to classify this variant as more representative of the Old Believers movement than of modern Orthodoxy. At the very least, syncretism between the Old Believers and the modern Hidden ones is far advanced. In part this may be due to the ethnographic peculiarity of the region, which for two centuries was one of the strongholds of priestless sects of the Old Believers. The area has also served as a place of exile, and hence exiled representatives of modern underground Orthodox movements may have found the prevailing atmosphere congenial to their interests.

Numerous practices common to the Hidden ones give direct indication of the strong influence of the Old Believers. For example, the True Orthodox Christians in Hiding consider all unbelievers and all Christians who do not belong to their specific movement 'servants of anti-Christ' and make great efforts to avoid them at all times.[79]

They wash without soap, [they use] wooden utensils. You ask for a drink, and if they give it they do not do so in a ladle, lest it become 'defiled', but in something which they can throw away afterwards. Nor can you presume to smoke in the house. Formerly they did not give birth except in the cattle shed. They fast twice a week, and on Friday they do not eat at all. They preserve customs as laws. If, for example, an icon disappears from the hut, you will not have luck. Depart, build a new house.[80]

Apparently this movement can be traced back more or less intact to the middle twenties. In 1926 an organized network was extant which covered a large area of the northern part of the U.S.S.R. There were court trials of members of the movement in 1928, and again in the middle thirties.[81]

The contemporary movement is characterized by asceticism and a monastic form of life. A typical day would begin with rising at 3 a.m., and with one- and two-hour sessions of prayer interspersed with study. The Lord's Prayer would be recited before meals.[82]

Again it is difficult, on the basis of available information, to characterize the doctrinal position taken by the True Orthodox Christians in Hiding. Many of them seem to know very little about their faith, and often stray very far from the norm in their beliefs.[83]

The rituals of the True Orthodox Christians in Hiding, especially baptism, which is essential for moving from 'worldly Christians' to 'renouncers of the world', are distinguished by superstition. If in the twenties and thirties the rite of baptism was performed on people of any age, now this procedure is conducted only on elderly and sick believers. Special preparation precedes the rite: the candidate should observe a fast for seven weeks and pray zealously. Not infrequently the baptism is conducted in winter in holes in the ice, which often leads to colds and occasionally fatal results. During recent years, several elderly believers and two sick children have died

[79] Gagarin, op. cit., pp. 178–9.
[80] A. Romanov, 'Shuga' ('Sludge'), *Nauka i Religiia*, No. 7 (July 1968), p. 93.
[81] Gagarin, op. cit., pp. 169–70.
[82] Romanov, op. cit., p. 94.
[83] Gagarin, op. cit., p. 187.

as a result of this rite. Death of the [newly] baptized is considered as a sign of special 'divine grace'. Those whose spirits 'God does not take to himself' immediately after baptism should be worthy of this 'mercy' with fasts, prayers, an ascetic form of life, departure from native village and inhabiting a cell, inasmuch as relations with relatives would distract them from 'service of God'.[84]

Among their books are titles such as *John Chrysostom, The Holy Flower Bed*, and the *Psalter*.[85] The apocalyptic doctrine that anti-Christ rules in the world is highly developed among them and, indeed, in 1962 one group was predicting that the world would end in 1965.[86]

Other variants of the True Orthodox Christians movement display similar local peculiarities of nomenclature to those described above. Instead of Wanderers, some refer to themselves as 'Under-grounders', 'Butteryites',[87] 'Aliens',[88] and the like.[89] One exceptional group of True Orthodox Christians found in the Crimea, the Ukraine and in other regions, call themselves 'the Basic Link of Christ', and indulge in such novelties as electing Christs, apostles, prophets, and angels from their ranks, composing their own hymns to replace the *akafists*, and renouncing marriage.[90]

Thus the True Orthodox Christians movement has expanded considerably in the range of its approaches to the problem of preservation of the preferred religious life in increasingly difficult circumstances. The more extreme branches of the movement have drifted towards the doctrines, practices, and organizational patterns of the Old Believers on the one hand, and on the other towards some of the peculiarities characteristic of indigenous forms of Christianity and semi-Christianity, such as *Dukhobors* and *Khlysty* in the last case cited above. The True Orthodox Christians, however, continue to exist throughout the country. In many respects these recent variants appear to represent responses to the increasing pressure of the anti-religious campaign, which since its inception in the late fifties has exerted maximum effort to eradicate the

---

[84] Ibid., p. 184.
[85] Romanov, op. cit., p. 94.
[86] Gagarin, op. cit., pp. 183–4.
[87] Derived from *golbets*, the buttery or pantry under the floor.
[88] *Nenashi*, literally 'not ours'. This term would be used, for example, during the Living Church struggle to refer to people of the other persuasion.
[89] Fedorenko, op. cit., p. 109.
[90] Ibid., p. 216; Skazkina, op. cit., p. 135.

unregistered, illegal movements, of which the True Orthodox Christians are an important representative.

As has been noted, the innovation of complete silence seems to have been relatively ineffective in diverting the consequences of the rising anti-religious campaign. The same cannot be said, however, of the True Orthodox Christian Wanderers, for this form of clandestine religious life is ideally suited to avoiding detection and in some measure thrives on the regime's pressure. As less thoroughgoing options for underground Orthodox life became narrowed and closed by the increasing competence and vigilance of the police organs of the State, greater numbers of people find themselves reduced to the single alternative of giving up their illegal worship altogether, or joining this most extreme renunciation of normal society. In addition, the general romanticism of a vagabond life, coupled with the strong appeal of monasticism in Russian Orthodoxy (and the lives of the Wanderers would seem to be monastic in the extreme), enables this relatively recent innovation in underground Orthodoxy to attract new converts to this form of absolute and total commitment to religion.

There is no possibility of estimating the size of the Wanderers movement, just as the numerical strength of the True Orthodox Christians as a whole remains unknown. With regard to the recent innovations among the True Orthodox Christians, Soviet scholarship has presented only exceedingly scattered data. Indeed, it is not at all unlikely that in view of the considerable skill in the clandestine arts which those who have been apprehended have displayed, the Soviet regime itself is unable even to estimate the size or extent of these movements. Nevertheless, with regard to the Wanderers in particular, it would seem highly unlikely that the movement has attained any considerable magnitude or anything beyond an exceedingly modest size.

Even should its number of adherents be miniscule in comparison with the total number of Orthodox believers in the U.S.S.R.—or even with regard to the True Orthodox Christians as a whole—the Wanderers movement has a potential importance out of all proportion to its size. This extremely clandestine branch of the True Orthodox Christians has given to underground Orthodoxy that possibility of organizing on a regional and even nation-wide scale which the movement hitherto has lacked. With the appearance of this innovation, the True Orthodox Christians can avail themselves of a considerably greater range of flexibility, when necessary maintaining the diffusion which has contributed much to their power to survive the attacks of the State, but also giving them the opportunity of enjoying at least some form of organizational cohesion as conditions warrant.

In addition, the geographic mobility of the leaders and rank-and-file of the Wanderers promises considerable benefit to the True Orthodox Christians as a whole in providing spiritual and intellectual assistance to the discrete local groups. Of particular importance in this regard is the attention given by the Wanderers to the philosophical and theological development of their position. The possession of a core of specialists, however small in number, who devote their entire energies to such research aimed at equipping the believers for the challenges of the present time, together with the distributional capability inherent in the mobile, wandering form of life, promise immense benefit to the True Orthodox Christians movement as a whole in their struggle to preserve their religious beliefs and practices in a hostile society. If such services as these should continue to be rendered by the Wanderers and cognate branches of the movement for any great length of time, the True Orthodox Christians will have at their disposal a considerable fund of resources for continuing their survival, despite the attempts of the regime to eradicate all forms of underground religion during the past decade or more.

X

The Continuing Crisis

The anti-religious campaign which has been waged by the Soviet State for the past decade has created a general condition of extreme tension for all religious believers in the U.S.S.R. The True Ortho-dox Christians, as has been noted, have been under intense attack. By means of modifications equipping them for surviving such pressure, they have continued to exist and even in some respects to flourish. Other underground Orthodox groups have also felt the direct impact of this increase in State pressure, as will become evident below. But all religious people, whether in that minority which has consciously entered explicitly illegal organizations, or whether in the majority which still attempts to worship in the remaining legally permitted churches, have come under great pressure during the past decade. To some degree nearly all Christians have had to resort to practices which are technically illegal in order to continue even a truncated form of religious life. The result of the anti-religious campaign of the sixties has been to blur the distinction between the legalized Orthodox and the under-ground movements, to such a degree that the difference between the two groups becomes less categorically definable but more a difference of degree than of kind.

As has been noted, the early portents of the anti-religious campaign were already observable among illegal religious organizations as early as 1957. By the end of the decade it was obvious that this new campaign was to become general. The Moscow Patriarchate correctly read the omens and, in what seemed an almost desperate attempt to stem the tide, reacted strongly to the increasing State pressure by excommunicating three clerics who had defected to atheism. Then, on 25 February 1960, Patriarch Aleksii plainly warned of the coming storm:

In greeting you, our beloved archpastors, pastors and flock, with these festivities of the Moscow church, I express the hope that we all will be worthy of the prayers and protection of Saint Aleksii, by our life, our diligence, our faith, and our patience in bearing those unavoidable griefs which are rushing over us, over the Church of God, for the Lord Himself said, 'In the world you shall have tribulation'. We believe in the divine word of our Lord, 'But believe, for I have overcome the world'. That is, Christ has overcome all the insidious actions of the enemies of the Church, the enemies of God, and gives us the power to bear every grief which is unavoidable in this world.[1]

The attempt was unsuccessful. On 10 January, the anti-religious effort received the explicit support of the Central Committee.[2] In February, G. Karpov and Metropolitan Nikolai, who had symbolized the previous *détente* between State and Church respectively, were replaced.[3] Nikita Khrushchev personally endorsed the campaign in his key-note address to the Twenty-Second Party Congress in 1962,[4] and in 1964 L. Il'ichev, chairman of the Central Committee's Ideological Commission, called for even more increase in the anti-religious effort.[5] Obviously, the anti-religious campaign was being taken as seriously as any of the pre-war efforts, and it had the firm support of the highest levels of the regime.

The energies mobilized by the State for its campaign were formidable. The considerable efforts at expanding the theoretical bases of atheism, which had been in progress since Khrushchev's first official action regarding religion in 1954, were immensely augmented by the creation of universities and specialized schools of atheism throughout the country.[6]

Of primary concern to the regime was the infusion of atheism into the schools. Specialized courses were developed, and special textbooks and materials were produced to elaborate upon the

[1] *Z.M.P.*, No. 4 (April 1960).
[2] A. Hakimoglu, 'Forty Years of Antireligious Propaganda,' *East Turkic Review*, No. 2 (December 1960), p. 69.
[3] *Izvestiia*, 21 February 1960; *Z.M.P.*, No. 7 (July 1960), p. 6, and No. 10 (October 1960), p. 4.
[4] *Pravda*, 18 October 1962.
[5] L. Il'ichev, 'Formirovanie nauchnogo mirovozzreniia i ateisticheskoe vospitanie' ('The formation of a scientific world view and atheist education'), *Kommunist*, No. 1 (January 1964), pp. 23–46.
[6] 'V dobryi chas!' ('In good time!'), *Nauka i Religiia*, No. 9 (September 1964), p. 53; *Partiinaia Zhizn'*, No. 5 (March 1965), p. 80; D. Gegeshidze, 'Prisposabli-vaiutsia . . .' ('They are adapting themselves . . .'), *Agitator*, No. 21 (November 1964), pp. 46–7.

atheistic implications of all subjects at all levels. Where formerly the ideological commitment to introduce atheism in the schools had been largely observed in the breach, the subject now assumed considerable importance in the Soviet pedagogical sciences.[7]

Mass media were extensively employed in support of the propaganda campaign. Books on atheism appeared in thousands of titles and millions of copies, in every major language of the country and designed for every class of readership from the functional illiterate to the sophisticate. Articles on anti-religious themes became ubiquitous in newspapers and journals. Radio and television were enlisted in the campaign.[8] Films were produced to support the anti-religious effort.[9]

Numerous other forms of propaganda were used, such as public lectures, formal and informal conversations, and individual work with believers. The latter, whereby atheists would be individually assigned to specific, known believers, was thought highly effective and when properly applied, subjected the believer to a constant anti-religious pressure which was almost inescapable.[10]

Nor was the campaign confined to propaganda and persuasion. 'Administrative measures', ranging from minor harassment to forcible closure of the churches and arrest, imprisonment, and in a few cases death, of recalcitrant believers, were widespread.[11]

The fall of Khrushchev did not result in the cessation of the anti-religious effort. In the years subsequent to 1964, the campaign was ameliorated somewhat by avoidance of certain of the

[7] 'V institute nauchnogo ateizma' ('In the institute of scientific atheism'), *Politicheskoe Samoobrazovanie*, No. 4 (April 1965), p. 143; *Komsomol'skaia Pravda*, 14 June 1963; V. S. Ovchinnikov, 'Osnovy nauchnogo ateizma v technicheskom vuze' ('The foundations of scientific atheism in the technical schools'), *Voprosy Filosofii*, No. 7 (July 1961), pp. 141–4.

[8] Gegeshidze, op. cit., p. 47.

[9] *Komsomol'skaia Pravda*, 31 August 1962; *Literatura i Zhizn'*, 9 April 1961; 'Protiv ravnodushnykh' ('Against those who are indifferent'), *Nauka i Religiia*, No. 6 (June 1964), pp. 86–9.

[10] *Sovetskaia Moldaviia*, 8 July 1964; *Pravda*, 26 September 1962, 7 October 1963; *Krasnaia Zvezda*, 22 November 1961; *Kommunist Belorussii*, No. 9 (September 1964), p. 54. The chief difficulty of this approach, of course, was its staggering cost in man-hours when compared with other forms of persuasion.

[11] E.g., *Literaturnaia Gazeta*, 10 April 1962; *Sovetskaia Rossiia*, 21 June 1960; *Nauka i Religiia*, No. 6 (June 1964), p. 78; *Pravda*, 7 October 1963; S. Ivanov, 'Kak my organizuem nauchno-ateisticheskuiu propagandu' ('How we organize scientific atheistic propaganda'), *Kommunist Moldavii*, No. 7 (July 1961), pp. 52–7; cf. testimony of Paul B. Anderson in U.S. Congress, House, *Recent Developments in the Soviet Bloc* (Washington, D.C.: U.S. Government Printing Office, 1964), p. 99.

more brutish measures, such as forcible closure of the churches, and more selective use of others, such as arrest and imprisonment of believers. Perhaps most important is the fact that the campaign, which had been increasing in intensity from month to month until the fall of Khrushchev, has not shown any remarkable increase since. The effort exerted by the State has not been noticeably diminished, but neither has it intensified; it has remained on a plateau, at the approximate level it had reached late in 1964.[12]

Given these conditions, numerous pressures have developed in the religious life of the country. The anti-religious campaign has created a number of areas in which it is all but impossible for believers to satisfy their religious needs without compromising their position as conscientious, law-abiding citizens. Participation in illicit activities becomes more and more unavoidable. As a result of the regime's pressure, large numbers of religious people have been impelled further and further along the road which can eventually lead to outright underground activity, regardless of how fervently they may abhor this prospect and wish to retain their preferred status as loyal citizens of their country.

A large proportion of the believers, and particularly of the more devout, have regular or occasional recourse to religious worship or ceremonies which are technically illegal. Even where churches are open, the inadequate number induces many Orthodox to organize dinners and meetings at home which in fact are informal (and illegal) worship services.[13] In 1964, a letter to the editor of a national newspaper was published which asked why believers must pray in secret.[14] Even though it is strictly prohibited, many priests willingly conduct religious ceremonies in private homes when necessary (as in the case of bringing the Eucharist to the infirm).[15]

[12] The progress of the anti-religious campaign since the fall of Khrushchev may be followed by consulting the various translation services on religion in the U.S.S.R. and Eastern Europe, such as *Religion in Communist Dominated Areas* (hereafter *RCDA*), published by the National Council of Churches in New York, and, through 1969, *Research Materials*, published by the Centre de Recherches et d'Etude des Institutions Religieuses, Geneva, Switzerland.

[13] William C. Fletcher, 'Soviet Society and Religion: A Trip Report,' *Communist Affairs*, June–August 1963, p. 9.

[14] *Komsomol'skaia Pravda*, 5 January 1964.

[15] M. V. Demin, ' "Khristianskii kommunizm" kak otrazhenie krizisa sovremennoi religioznoi ideologii' (' "Christian communism" as a reflection of the crisis of contemporary religious ideology'), in I. D. Pantskhav, ed., *O nekotorykh osobennostiakh sovremennoi religioznoi ideologii* ('Certain peculiarities of contemporary religious ideology') (Moscow: Moscow University Press, 1964), p. 186.

Perhaps the most severe and widespread instance of the necessity to resort to illegal or quasi-legal ceremonies is the baptism of infants. With good reason, the regime has been much concerned over the continuing high incidence of this practice in the population, and relatively early in the campaign, a number of restrictions were applied to discourage it. Priests were prohibited from performing the rite without written permission from both parents, and in some cases from the local police or the father's place of employment.[16] By this measure, parents who wished their child to be baptized were faced with the alternative of publicly registering their desire, and hence suffering those consequences and sanctions which the regime liberally applies to believers in society, or having the rite conducted illegally. Furthermore, because both man and wife are employed in the great majority of families in the U.S.S.R., grandmothers are widely utilized as guardians for young children during the day; Russian grandmothers, always a mainstay of traditional Russian Orthodoxy, regularly persist in having their grandchild baptized according to the custom, regardless of the wishes of parents and regime alike.

Children and youth are by no means exempt from the pressure to maintain religious faith in secret. According to one Soviet author,

Children often try to hide their religiosity from others, and above all from the teachers. Externally they are no different from the others. They are often excellent pupils, well behaved in school, trying to give answers pleasing to their teacher. These are the little 'Tikhonites' or 'Jesus kids' of whom Makarenko once spoke, so it is not easy to know if they fulfil religious rites at home or go to church. . . .

Some children have neck crosses. It was remarkable, though, that we did not succeed in finding one child wearing his cross, among more than a thousand. Some have their crosses hanging over their beds at home or on a hook in the closet; some have it sewn into their pillows, some keep it in a little box; only a few wear the cross when they get home from school, or put it on when they go to bed.[17]

Such children are thus introduced at an early age to practice of secrecy and semi-clandestine skills in their religious life, and it

[16] Iu. Rozenbaum, 'Takoi zakon est'' ('There is such a law'), *Nauka i Religiia*, No. 4 (April 1964), pp. 83–5; P. Darmanskii, *Pobeg iz t'my* ('Flight from darkness') (Moscow: 'Sovetskaia Rossiia', 1961); *Nauka i Religiia*, No. 9 (September 1964), p. 89.

[17] *Nauka i Religiia*, No. 2 (February 1963), translated by Donald A. Lowrie, in *RCDA*, 20 May 1963, pp. 73–5.

would not be surprising if in later years they found such surreptitious religious practices congenial. Furthermore, the immense efforts to introduce atheism into the school system can be expected in some cases to have a contra-productive result, both in reinforcing the desire among religious children to avoid observation and, when conflict is created in a young, formative mind, by inducing parents to increase their efforts to give vigorous attention to religious education at home to counterbalance the indoctrination in atheism which prevails in the schools.

Further inducement was supplied by the stern measures introduced by the regime in the attempt to isolate children from the influence of the churches. As early as 1961 priests were prohibited from giving religious instruction to the children of their parishioners.[18] In 1962 it was explicitly stated that to teach the catechism was a violation of the law,[19] despite the fact that the laws of 1929, still in force, specifically permit religious instruction by clergymen on the invitation of parents.[20] Furthermore, by 1963 children between the ages of three and eighteen were prohibited from attending church services.

The law categorically forbids attracting minors into religious societies. This means that persons under eighteen years of age may not be members of religious organizations, and do not have the right to participate in church services or religious ceremonies of any kind.[21]

In some churches local authorities stationed guards at the entrances to the churches to enforce this ruling.[22] All of these measures could only induce devout parents to resort to extra-legal expedients.

The anti-religious campaign made it exceedingly costly for young people to allow their religious activities to become known. Expulsion from the communist youth organization was not unusual if a member was discovered to have taken part in a religious ceremony.[23] Because membership in the Komsomol is virtually

---

[18] Mitin, 'O nauchno-ateisticheskoi propaganda,' op. cit., p. 26.

[19] Donald A. Lowrie, 'Eastern Christians under Duress,' *Christian Century,* 21 November 1962, p. 1424, quoting *Nauka i Religiia,* No. 5 (May 1962).

[20] P. V. Gidulianov, *Otdelenie tserkvi ot gosudarstve* ('The separation of Church from State') (Moscow: State Publishing House for Juridical Literature, 1929), pp. 3–11.

[21] American Committee for Liberation, *The Beleaguered Fortress* (New York: The Committee, 1963), p. 16, quoting the booklet, *Freedom of Conscience in the U.S.S.R.*

[22] *Uchitel'skaia Gazeta,* 31 November 1963.

[23] N. Sviridov and G. Marchik, 'For the effectiveness of the ideological work,' *Molodoi Kommunist,* No. 8 (August 1962), translated in *RCDA,* 5 November 1962, p. 2.

mandatory at many universities, such action was often tantamount to virtual expulsion from the university. In one case a girl was expelled from an art institute when it was discovered that she was a member of a church choir.[24] Entrance into the Communist Party, a requisite for professional advancement in most fields, could be frustrated merely if the candidate's parents were known to be religious.[25] Indeed, in some areas, members of the Komsomol formed patrols to expose those who attended church.[26] Given such pressure, it would only be natural for religious youth to take whatever measures seemed necessary to avoid detection.

While the use of administrative measures, such as arrest and confinement, may have been intended as a deterrent, it is also possible that they had an opposite effect in some cases. Numerous religious cases were widely publicized in which it was evident that the culprits were convicted on the most arbitrary of charges.[27] When the regime felt it inadvisable to prefer charges, there were numerous cases of perfectly healthy monks arbitrarily confined to psychiatric asylums in lieu of arrest.[28] If religious citizens could be summarily disposed of in such manner, and particularly in view of the fact that great numbers of religious people, perforce, were already indulging in illegal religious activities at one time or another, the fear of arrest and imprisonment normally attaching to membership in the underground Orthodox organizations would lose much of its force.

The regime directly provided candidates for underground Orthodox life by such actions as the closure of monasteries. Of the 69 or 70 monasteries extant in 1959, only 32 were still functioning five years later.[29] *Kolkhozes* formed by monastics in order to continue cenobitic life were discovered and closed down early in the campaign.[30] Unless provision were made for the residents of these

[24] *Komsomol'skaia Pravda*, 31 March 1959.
[25] I. Volkov, 'Kto, esli ne ty?' ('Who, if not you?'), *Partiinaia Zhizn' Kazakhstana* No. 12 (December 1964), p. 46.
[26] *Leninskaia Smena*, 20 September 1959.
[27] For example, see the protest of a group of Baptists from Barnaul in Siberia translated in *RCDA*, 30 September 1964, pp. 123–5.
[28] See the petition to Khrushchev printed in *Letopis'*, 15 May 1963; Struve, op. cit. pp. 302–10.
[29] N. I. Iudin, *Pravda o petersburgskikh 'sviatyniakh'* ('The truth about the Petersburg "shrines" ') (Leningrad, 1962), translated in *RCDA*, 24 June 1963, p. 117; cf. S. D Bailey, op. cit., p. 305; Blake, op. cit., p. 114.
[30] *Izvestiia*, 24 January 1960.

now defunct communities, such forced closure could only swell the ranks of those who had no alternative other than underground religious life if they were to remain true to their vows.

The intensive effort to close churches during the first five years of the anti-religious campaign was of immense importance in providing candidates for clandestine religious life. Of the 15–16,000 Orthodox churches functioning at the start of the campaign,[31] half or more had been closed by the middle of the decade.[32] Even at its peak, the post-war Russian Church had possessed far too few churches to meet the needs of the Orthodox population, and with the precipitate decrease in the number of open churches during the anti-religious campaign the situation became quite impossible, and great masses of Orthodox citizens were left with no legal means whatsoever for the continuance of their faith. Some of the atheist practitioners were aware of the negative side of closing churches arbitrarily:

Recently one could notice that some administrative organs in the struggle with religion were somewhat carried away. The most striking examples of administrative measures against religious societies and clergy were some cases where houses of prayer have been illegally closed without any preliminary educational work with the believers; this evokes legitimate discontent in the population and imperils the work of the communist education of the working people.[33]

Russian Orthodox officials were deeply disturbed by the losses which the Church was suffering. According to one Orthodox clergyman,

If we have in mind the future of the Church of Christ, then no gates of hell can overcome it. But if we have in mind the perspective of some specific parish, then disquieting thoughts can arise: Christian congregations in our country rapidly decrease.[34]

[31] For detailed analysis of the number of churches during the post-war period, see William C. Fletcher, 'Statistics and Soviet Sociology of Religion,' in Hans Mol, ed., *Religion in the Western World* (Canberra: Australian National University, in preparation).

[32] *Commonweal*, 15 November 1963, p. 211; cf. the 'Open Letter' of the priests N. Eshliman and G. Iakunin, in *RCDA*, 15/30 June 1966, p. 93.

[33] *Komsomol'skaia Pravda*, 14 June 1963.

[34] A. Veschikov, 'Milestones of a great journey,' *Nauka i Religiia*, No. 11 (November 1962), translated in *RCDA*, 24 December 1962, p. 4.

This campaign to close churches was immensely successful in weakening the power of the institutional Church. At the same time, however, it created a vast and fertile field for practitioners of underground Orthodoxy.

Withdrawal of registered status frequently results in a mere increase in the number of unregistered but functioning religious societies and groups. Consequently the copying of figures from one column into another cannot be passed off as an indication of the success of atheistic efforts.[35]

Thus the results of the anti-religious campaign, if catastrophic to the Russian Orthodox Church, have not necessarily been completely deleterious to underground Orthodox organizations. Discontent with the present situation, always a prerequisite for any substantial underground movement, has increased enormously during the decade of tension. Vast numbers of religious people, clerics and laymen alike, have been religiously disfranchised, with no legally permissible outlet for their religious aspirations. Given such a situation, it would be strange indeed if there were not a considerable increase in underground religious activity within the country.

On the basis of evidence presently available, it would not appear that existing underground Orthodox organizations, other than the True Orthodox Christians, have greatly increased their activity during the past decade. Innokent'evtsy are still to be found,[36] but primarily as isolated individuals. Ioannity also remain active in several different areas of the country.[37] The Fedorovtsy were still extant at the beginning of the campaign,[38] but the evidence presently available is insufficient for determining their success (or lack of success) in weathering the anti-religious campaign. It may be that the large part of the membership of these earlier organiza-

---

[35] A. Valentinov, 'Sovetskoe zakonodatel'stvo o kul'takh' ('Soviet legislation on cults'), *Nauka i Religiia*, No. 10 (October 1961), p. 91.

[36] B. Zaikin, 'Pered samoi bol'shoi auditoriei' ('Before the largest audience'), *Agitator*, No. 20 (October 1966), pp. 44–5; Babii and Gazhos, op. cit., pp. 27–30; Skazkina, op. cit., p. 134.

[37] Ibid.; N. P. Krasnikov, 'Materialy issledovaniia religioznosti i praktika nauchno-ateisticheskogo vospitaniia' ('Materials on the research of religiousness and the practice of scientific atheistic education'), in Klibanov, *Konkretnye issledovaniia*, op. cit., p. 130.

[38] Aleksandrovich, op. cit., p. 65.

tions has been subsumed into the more vigorous True Orthodox Christians movement.

Perhaps even more important than such identifiable, organized underground Orthodox movements are the large numbers of individuals and groups who have abandoned the legal observance of religion and have independently begun underground Orthodox activity. Although there is no evidence to justify inclusion of such cases in the True Orthodox Christians movement, many of their expedients and practices are so similar as to suggest virtual, if not formal, identity with the movement.

In one case, clergy organized a 'profit-making enterprise' within a collective farm structure, and the local authorities were afraid to close it.[39] In 1960, an entire community of some sixty people cut themselves off from society entirely and made their living by truck gardening.[40] In another case, a woman suddenly began practising extreme asceticism.[41] One young girl was incarcerated in an informal chapel in the basement of her father's home,[42] and another youth was discovered living a life of seclusion underneath a house.[43] A hermit who had constructed a dug-out adorned with icons in the deep forest attracted numerous disciples.[44]

The great lack of religious literature and devotional materials has led to a vigorous clandestine production of such materials throughout the country. In July 1966 there was a scandal when it was discovered that crosses were being sold in the GUM (State Department Store) in Moscow.[45] This was merely an extreme example of the flourishing industry of the illicit production of crosses which has characterized the past decade.[46] In the open churches, informal (and hence technically illegal) production of literature continues.

All or at any rate very nearly all the words and music of the services are sung from hand-written exercise books. Printed scores are evidently

---

[39] Iu. Feofanov, 'Persistently, flexibly, intelligently!', *Sovety Deputatov Trudiashchikhsia*, No. 10 (October 1960), translated in *CDSP*, 18 January 1961, p. 36.

[40] *Nauka i Religiia*, No. 7 (July 1961), p. 25.

[41] Ibid., No. 3 (March 1963), p. 26.

[42] N. Lazarev, 'Teni proshlogo' ('Shadows of the past'), *Nauka i Religiia*, No. 8 (August 1963), pp. 88–9.

[43] M. Barykin, 'Pustotsvet na dvere zhizni' ('Delusion at the door of life'), *Nauka i Religiia*, No. 9 (September 1961), p. 48.

[44] *Sovetskaia Rossiia*, 27 September 1962.

[45] *Komsomol'skaia Pravda*, 10 July 1966.

[46] Cf. *Izvestiia*, 27 November 1963.

18

not to be had and those who sing must copy everything out for them-selves.[47]

There have been numerous reports of illegal production of litera-ture.[48] In 1960 a man was arrested for receiving a package con-taining 1,000 icons, 2,500 crosses, and much literature; even more religious literature was found at his home.[49] In 1963, a priest was arrested for colportage of illegal religious tracts.[50]

The critical incapacity of the relatively few remaining churches to meet the needs of the believing population has led to a number of innovations. Believers who for one reason or another find it inexpedient to attend church personally, are able to participate to some degree through the good offices of relatives or friends who do attend.[51] The earlier practices of participation in Church cere-monies by correspondence have been revived.[52] Many priests now consider it perfectly permissible to celebrate the marriage ceremony over the wedding ring of the woman in lieu of a church wedding and to perform a funeral ceremony over a bit of earth sent from, and subsequently returned to, the grave of a person who has been buried without an Orthodox funeral.[53] According to one Soviet study, in 1966, 63 of 100 church funerals in one locale were con-ducted 'by correspondence', while in another, 89 per cent were so conducted.[54]

Unknown numbers of individuals have been induced by the pressures of the times to enter a wandering life, similar to that of the True Orthodox Christian Wanderers. In one case, two sisters refused to work in a *kolkhoz* and wandered from village to village preaching their doctrine.[55] According to one Soviet author, such wanderers are exceedingly popular in the countryside: 'It is enough

[47] M. Shaw, 'Impressions of the Russian Orthodox Church,' *International Review of Missions*, No. 47 (October 1958), p. 442.

[48] *Uchitel'skaia Gazeta*, 16 February 1963; *Kazakhstanskaia Pravda*, 13 April 1963; *Izvestiia*, 27 November 1963; *Komsomol'skaia Pravda*, 10 July 1966.

[49] *Vechernaia Moskva*, 2 June 1960.

[50] *Pravda*, 18 August 1963.

[51] Iankova, 'O nekotorykh metodakh,' op. cit., p. 113.

[52] Listowel, op. cit., p. 107, citing Moscow Radio, 5 August 1954.

[53] Demin, op. cit., pp. 185–6.

[54] N. P. Andrianov, R. A. Lopatkin, and V. V. Pavliuk, *Osobennosti sovremennogo religioznogo soznaniia* ('Peculiarities of contemporary religious understanding') (Moscow: 'Mysl',' 1966), p. 213.

[55] O. Shestinskii, 'Pauki na mal'vakh' ('Spiders in the hollyhocks'), *Nauka i Religiia*, No. 3 (March 1960), p. 53.

to tell someone that a good woman has appeared in a certain place for people to start filing towards the gates of her house asking for prayers and bringing gifts.'[56] One young man, upon his conversion, wished to take monastic vows but could not because he was married; instead he began preaching. This angered the authorities and they forthwith banished him from the town, thereby forcing him into that mode of wandering life already popular in underground Orthodoxy.[57] The trials and tribulations of the Pochaev Monastery, which have received considerable publicity in the West,[58] made an oblique contribution to the continuing development of underground Orthodoxy in the U.S.S.R. Some of the monks living at Pochaev had been doing so illegally, without proper passports.[59] During the regime's abortive attack against the monastery, many of the monks were deprived of passports and ordered to leave; thus they were driven by the regime to embrace the wandering form of life.[60] Interestingly enough, the monastery was enjoying the services of informal (and strictly illegal) assistance in various places in the countryside, where funds and goods for the monks were collected.[61] Thus monks who had been expelled were already in the possession, in theory at least, of a network of sympathizers operational in illegal activity. Perhaps even more important, according to the Soviet press, beginning with 1958, members of the 'True Orthodox Church' (perhaps actually affiliated with the True Orthodox Christians, who had come under attack the preceding year) began to appear in the Pochaev monastery and from thence began to spread throughout the country.[62] This report, if true, raises the possibility that the monastery may have served some sort of function in the organized life of the Orthodox underground.

In another instance directly reminiscent of the True Orthodox Christians, action was taken to close down a newly found spring of

[56] A. Dubovka, 'Kto iz detei verit v boga?' ('Who among the children believe in God?'), *Nauka i Religiia*, No. 2 (February 1963), p. 75.

[57] *Sovetskaia Rossiia*, 27 September 1962.

[58] Cf. Struve, op. cit., pp. 303–10.

[59] A. Levitin, 'Monashestvo i sovremennost' ' ('Monasticism and contemporaneity'), in Archbishop Ioann (Shakovskoi), ed., *Zashchita very v SSSR* ('Defence of the faith in the U.S.S.R.') (Paris: Ikhthus, 1966), pp. 64–5, 82–5, *et passim*.

[60] D. Konstantinov, *Religious Persecution in U.S.S.R.* (London, Canada: SBONR, 1965), p. 7.

[61] *Nauka i Religiia*, No. 9 (September 1964), p. 89.

[62] *Trud*, 9 July 1960.

holy water, on the grounds that it was on State property and the crowds who were attracted 'disturb public order' by tramping down the meadow and forest.[63]

As has been indicated, illegal activities were by no means confined to those who had broken all their ties with the Church and with society. For unspecified reasons, but possibly because of the difficulty of obtaining apartments if one's vocation was discovered, clergymen of the Orthodox Church had long been accustomed to disguising their vocation when outside church premises.[64] Thus many of the legally operating priests had already had some small initiation into the arts of concealment. More unfortunate were those who through no fault of their own found it impossible to continue their vocation.

The church was closed and Mikhail Belov was left without work. How could he become reconciled with such a thing? Well, the dismissed priest began to think about getting busy. He understood quite well that he had to look for his living in some place where there is no respect for anti-religious propaganda. . . .

Belov established a clandestine chapel in the house of the [railway] track inspector [and was assisted by two women]. . . .

Upon Belov's instruction, these two God-loving women visited their neighbours and persuaded young mothers to have their children baptized and to hold prayer meetings.[65]

This was apparently a fairly common practice, for often, as has been noted, churches were closed by fiat despite the wishes of the clergy and the congregation. In one example, a year after a decision to close churches in one area, they apparently were functioning as normally as before.[66]

Such functioning churches, existing illegally and providing whatever services they can render depending on circumstances, are by far the most widespread phenomenon of present underground Orthodox life. Subject to immediate closure and severe penalties, these congregations continue as complete a religious life as is possible in difficult and trying circumstances. The exceedingly small number of churches, the severe limitations inherent in the

---

[63] Feofanov, op. cit., p. 36.

[64] Darmanskii, op. cit., pp. 104–6.

[65] *Gudok*, 23 February 1964.

[66] I. Brazhnik, 'Ateisticheskoe vospitanie—obshchepartiinoe delo' ('Atheist education—a matter for the entire Party'), *Partiinaia Zhizn'*, No. 24 (December 1963), p. 25.

capacity of individual churches to serve a vast surrounding populace, and the great distances between open churches in many
areas of the country force religious people to innovate and devise
new expedients, usually quite illegal, for continuing their religious
life.

People who know how to conduct church services are in great
demand, and believers constantly request such people, where they
are available, to perform the needed religious ceremonies. The
almost desperate lack of duly ordained priests precludes any great
insistence on corroboration of the individual's canonical right to
perform the ceremony in question; 'it's all the same now whether
a priest is licensed or not'.[67] Women often must fill the gap. One
such woman served as an example in the atheist press:

Long ago she traded her conscience for greed, abandoned honest work,
and profits from human plight.
'One requiem is not enough,' she blasphemes, 'The soul of the dead
will lament.'
Trusting people order memorial services from her again and again.
And she, having grabbed a bag of crosses and icons, goes out to the
villages to trade them.[68]

Believers who have no convenient access to an open church quite
commonly resort to various expedients. One such expedient which
has long been in vogue is to visit a church while on vacation. One
priest at Sochi, for example, explained that 'many people take
advantage of their stay in this seaside resort to "put themselves
right" with their religious duties since they are far away from the
criticism of friends and neighbours'.[69] Alternatively, some
Orthodox attend Old Believer churches when possible,[70] while
others 'sometimes look in on the Baptist prayer house and relate
sympathetically to the Baptists themselves'.[71] To a large degree, this
practice is indicative of the common phenomenon that in times of
trouble and pressure religious differences play a much lesser role
than at other times.[72]

Illegal churches seem to have sprung up throughout the country

[67] *Nauka i Religiia*, No. 2 (February 1963), p. 28.
[68] *Sel'skaia Zhizn'*, 13 February 1965.
[69] Constantin de Grunwald, *The Churches and the Soviet Union* (New York: Macmillan, 1962), p. 130.
[70] Milovidov, op. cit., p. 221.
[71] Fedorenko, op. cit., p. 235.
[72] Konstantinov, *Religioznoe dvizhenie soprotivleniia v SSSR*, op. cit., p. 12.

as a result of anti-religious pressure. As an example, in 1962 a Soviet scholar reported, 'The basic means of dissemination of religious ideas in Voronezh and the Voronezh *oblast* are the 55 Orthodox churches, 8 registered and a number of unregistered sectarian congregations and groups.'[73] The latter category included illegal Orthodox organizations, many of them operating in default of any available or nearby Orthodox church. House churches were not an uncommon phenomenon.[74] In 1965 an American student reportedly met a young girl in Moscow, attended such a house church, and learned of an entire organization of small circles within the city devoted to secret services, missionary activity, and the like. Interestingly enough, most of those at the service were youths.[75] Where churches are lacking, special services and religious events are organized for children.[76]

During the early part of the decade, when churches were being closed on a large scale, congregations whose churches had been closed would immediately commence underground Church activities.[77] One Soviet scholar reports a case which, if the causes for the closing of the church in question may be suspect, nevertheless is typical of this phenomenon:

The Orthodox church located in the centre of the *kolkhoz*, the village of Kutafino, functioned until 1960. As a result of a lingering dispute of the clergy with the church board [*dvadsatka*] over the division of monetary income, it ceased its functioning. In the pre-revolutionary past, judging by available church documents, the church was distinguished for skilfully prepared church propaganda. At the present time the active core of the Orthodox Church continues to exist in the *kolkhoz*, and organizes divine services of an amateur sort without the participation of a priest.[78]

Such illegal churches not only conduct regular services but also perform the rites of the sacraments as far as possible, and, indeed, seem to be able to attract many young people as well as the elderly.[79]

---

[73] Tepliakov, 'Sostoianie religioznosti naseleniia,' op. cit., p. 150.

[74] *Kazakhstanskaia Pravda*, 4 November 1965.

[75] Konstantinov, *Religioznoe dvizhenie soprotivleniia v SSSR*, op. cit., p. 46.

[76] Ibid., p. 30.

[77] *Current Developments in the Eastern European Churches*, May 1964, p. 16.

[78] N. P. Alekseev, 'Metodika i rezul'taty izucheniia religioznosti sel'skogo naseleniia' ('Methods and results of the study of religiosity of the village population'), in AN SSSR, *Voprosy nauchnogo ateizma*, op. cit., III, 138.

[79] Feofanov, op. cit., p. 37.

Authorities were much disturbed by the phenomenon of the underground churches continuing religious activity after all the open churches had been closed.[80] Indeed, in one case at least, countermeasures (other than force) were employed with some success. In the Crimea, a local atheist organized get-togethers to talk about atheism in order to counteract the influence of a lay church which was meeting informally in homes after the closure of the church. His lectures were reportedly so successful that eventually the lay services collapsed because of the small number of believers.[81]

Orthodox women have played a large role in such undertakings. Even in the open churches, women have been playing an increasingly prominent role, doubtless partly owing to the fact that many women are much less vulnerable to reprisal by the regime for such overt religious activity.

The Bible demands that women 'be silent' in the church, but women now quite often serve as deacons in the church and in sectarian congregations. Church regulations prohibit women (except the old nuns) to come to the altar, but now even young women serve at the altar.[82]

Not infrequently a *kolkhoz* which no longer has a church will have a number of old women who, according to atheist observers, perform healings and magic, crediting their success to prayer.[83] In one case, a woman set up an illegal chapel and performed baptisms, funerals, and the consecration of Easter cakes, and even provided candles for the worshippers.[84] A typical example was presented in some detail by a Soviet researcher:

In connection with the comparatively long distance of the village from the church, to which it is especially difficult to go during the winter, a few years ago in the village of Tsepelevo meetings of believers at home were organized for prayers and readings of church literature. They were held in the home of an old lady, N. K. (79 years old), who lived alone and who was the only one in the entire village who had two copies of the Bible, several copies of the Gospels, and other literature of religious content. The house of N. K. was chosen as a meeting place

[80] *Krasnaia Zvezda*, 14 February 1965.
[81] N. Rozenberg, 'Lektorii na domu' ('Lecture meetings in the home'), *Agitator*, No. 23 (December 1966), p. 45.
[82] *Komsomol'skaia Pravda*, 14 June 1963.
[83] Vasilov, 'Etnograficheskoe issledovanie,' op. cit., pp. 161–2.
[84] *Nauka i Religiia*, No. 3 (March 1963), p. 26.

for believers also because its owner, literate in comparison with other women of her age (N. K. completed the church parish school), easily read and interpreted religious texts, although she did not give the impression of being a typical fanatic believer. For her and for the other old ladies, these meetings for a long time were a place where they spent their leisure time and satisfied their religious demands. However, in recent times part of the participants in the meetings have switched to another form of spending their leisure time—playing lotto.[85]

In some cases there are stories that such women receive permission from priests to conduct such activities, and in particular the rite of baptism.[86] Naturally, services such as this are dependent on the availability of some person sufficiently familiar with church practices to conduct these services, and when they die or move away the services often lapse.[87]

It should not be imagined, however, that such *ad hoc* arrangements as these are everywhere sufficient to meet the needs of believers. Some areas which have been deprived of churches have been unable to provide for even their most fundamental needs, and the fires of religion burn low indeed.

Many of the old people consider that the Church 'is no longer fashionable.' . . . A similar evaluation by believers themselves of the role of the church in their daily life is very enlightening. Often to the question, 'Do you go to church?' one hears the answer, 'I don't know any prayers, I don't go to church. I believe, but I don't go to church: it's far away and I don't have the time. Here all the believers are like me.'[88]

Descriptions of the meagre attempts by laymen in areas which have had no churches for thirty years or more give vivid illustration of the general collapse which can envelop a religious population when no services, legal or illegal, are available.[89] One seventy-seven-year-old collective farmer described his attitude towards religion as follows:

The festivals I know; we do not work on them. At Easter the wife used to bless the *kulich* [cake]. Earlier I also used to understand the

[85] Nosova, op. cit., p. 154.
[86] Vasilov, 'Etnograficheskoe issledovanie,' op. cit., pp. 153–4.
[87] Ibid., p. 154.
[88] Nosova, op. cit., p. 154.
[89] Vasilov, 'Etnograficheskoe issledovanie,' op. cit., pp. 156–8.

church writing, but now I have forgotten everything. I knew the prayers, 'Worthy', 'Living Helpers', 'I Believe'—but now my memory is so bad, I have forgotten everything. Now I do not pray, but I have faith strongly. In the spirit I believe in God—this is the main thing. I make the sign of the cross. If there were a church, of course I would go, listen, watch—beautiful.[90]

Thus the decade-long anti-religious campaign, while vastly reducing the size and perhaps even the influence of the institutional Church, has left the large proportion of the population who are Orthodox in serious difficulty. Those who have no available opportunities for worship and who nevertheless remain deeply religious experience great frustration, and it would be unnatural if they would not willingly and enthusiastically embrace any form of religious worship which might be available, whether or not it is under the aegis of the duly constituted Church authorities, and even if, in some respects, it seems aberrational. Provided only that some answer to the unfulfilled religious needs is available, peculiarities which at first glance might seem a bit bizarre could easily be overlooked. Much more fortunate are those who have had recourse to some form of worship, whether spontaneous or organized, whether conducted by priest or layman, and quite obviously the benefits which they derive from such participation are sufficient to outweigh in their minds the fact that such services may be strictly illegal and run the risk of severe sanctions should hostile authorities descend upon them. Such people form an unknown portion of the religious population, who through no initial desire of their own have, perforce, become skilled in the clandestine arts of continuing religious worship despite the fact that the State in such unchurched areas has rendered any form of group worship illegal. The distinction between such clandestine groups as these, which conduct their secret religious activity independently, and those who affiliate themselves with the True Orthodox Christians or consider themselves a part of that underground Orthodox movement, is not a difference in kind, or even really in degree. In the extremely difficult conditions which prevail, the distinction amounts to little more than one of nomenclature.

Summarizing, the intense anti-religious campaign, which has lasted for more than a decade, has resulted in a total situation in which underground Orthodoxy assumes considerable importance

[90] Ibid., p. 159.

in the religious life of a large percentage of the people. Underground Orthodox movements, chief among them the True Orthodox Christians, have been able to survive the most concerted and vigorous efforts of the State to eradicate them and, indeed, in some respects have been able to thrive because of the general increase in tension in society. There is no way to determine the size of such movements as these. Even if they should be relatively small, however, the fact remains that the regime's religious policies over the past decade have reduced a significant portion of the Orthodox population to illegal and underground expedients in attempting to continue their religious life. In many areas of the country the religious situation is exceedingly unstable, if not volatile. The State must exert considerable vigilance in order to keep the precarious balance which forms the *status quo*. Large numbers of Orthodox believers have no legal recourse for satisfying their religious needs, and, given such a situation, the slightest change in State policy, whether towards leniency or towards even greater severity than at present, could expect untoward results in the Orthodox population. At present, a large and significant portion of the Orthodox population is reduced to illegal, underground expedients, partially or altogether, in order to preserve the most minimal satisfaction of their religious needs. The existence of a large body of Orthodox believers scattered throughout the country who have gained experience and have become habituated to the clandestine arts of worship presents fertile soil for the rise and expansion of underground Orthodox organizations. Even if the State has thus far succeeded, by and large, in keeping this underground Orthodox population unorganized and scattered, there is no guarantee that some catalytic event might not result in a rapid expansion of organized, underground Orthodoxy at any time.

Conclusions

The history of underground Orthodoxy in the U.S.S.R. has been directly related to the religious policy of the Soviet State, and in its pattern of historical development has reflected almost with exact precision the various changes in that policy. Indeed, in many respects it would be proper to consider the entire phenomenon a direct result of the State's religious policy. In many respects, the relations of Church and State may be read in the mirror image of the history of the underground movement.

Numerous schismatic sects of modern Orthodoxy, which had arisen in the decade immediately preceding the revolution, were already extant in 1917. Many of these movements survived for a considerable time in the new conditions and, indeed, some still exist. Most if not all of them shared the general historical pattern of underground Orthodoxy as a whole. Nevertheless, the influence of these movements has been relatively minor when compared with other movements of greater impact which have arisen in direct response to Soviet policy.

The Living Church Adventure was the harbinger of things to come. The massive popular dissatisfaction with this reforming movement, which bore so many marks of State connivance, caused an immediate reaction among the Orthodox people, a reaction which served to initiate them into the patterns and practices of independent, sometimes illegal, and occasionally clandestine religious life. Despite its huge initial success, however, the heyday of the Living Church was so brief that enduring, organized underground Orthodox movements did not take form in response to this challenge. Nevertheless, events were to show that numerous leaders and members of future underground Orthodox movements gained their initial baptism into this form of religious life during the Living Church Adventure.

It was the change in the Church's position from political neutrality to acceptance of the Soviet political regime which initiated
the rise of underground Orthodoxy as a whole. A number of
important and influential Church leaders refused to submit to
this change of course, and opposition movements formed around
them which, whatever their numerical strength at first, were
immensely serious challenges to the Russian Orthodox Church
from the point of view of the stature of their leadership. The
movements which arose around the dissident hierarchs were soon
to experience an immense growth, and would exercise a profound
influence on subsequent development of underground Orthodoxy
in the U.S.S.R.

In 1928, the regime embarked on an intense anti-religious
campaign concurrently with its industrialization and collectivization programmes. This campaign, which continued to be in force
with various degrees of severity for the next dozen years, impelled
large numbers of Orthodox believers towards illegal and clandestine religious activities, and if underground Orthodoxy assumed
proportions of a mass movement during the ensuing decade, the
excesses of the anti-religious campaign were primarily responsible.
Vast numbers of churches were closed with little reference, if any,
to the desires of the believers, and by the end of the decade only a
miniscule percentage of the Russian Orthodox churches were still
legally operational. As a result, the great majority of Russian
Orthodox believers were faced with the single alternative of
giving up any expression of their faith whatsoever, or engaging in
clandestine and illegal practices. In such conditions, numerous
underground Orthodox organizations sprang up throughout the
country and enjoyed great popularity, either temporarily or, in
some cases, throughout the entire period.

The regime's efforts to endow the country with an atheistic
society were abruptly terminated by the rise of World War II. In
the suddenly relaxed conditions, with the regime's entire energies
diverted away from religion, the religious life of the population
flourished. Multitudes of believers who had spent the preceding
years in the Orthodox underground returned to the surface. In
those parts of the country occupied by the Germans, new Orthodox
organizations sprang up independently of the Moscow Patriarchate
and without any noticeable loyalty to the previous Soviet regime.
With the Soviet reoccupation, these organizations were suppressed

and, in numerous instances, contributed candidates for the underground Orthodox movements which were rampant within the U.S.S.R. In addition, with the forcible incorporation of the Uniates in newly acquired territories into Russian Orthodoxy, the latter fell heir to new schismatic movements unrelated to the other underground organizations, and these Uniate underground movements, technically within the purview of Russian Orthodoxy, have continued to the present.

World War II ushered in a period of *détente* between Church and State which lasted for almost two decades. In return for the enthusiastic service of the legalized Church in political matters, a degree of religious permissiveness was allowed by the regime which, if still far from full religious freedom, contrasted markedly with the immediate pre-war situation. The anti-religious designs of the State were largely held in abeyance. In these more relaxed conditions, underground Orthodoxy flourished and gained immense strength throughout the country. Two parallel movements arose during this period.

The True Orthodox Church was a highly organized movement, opposing and in many respects challenging the legalized Russian Orthodox churches. The True Orthodox Church lacked bishops but possessed a priesthood, which enabled it to provide an almost complete liturgical worship life for its adherents, and, indeed, with the exception of such clandestine arts as were necessitated by its illegal position, its practices were hardly distinguishable from the legalized Church's worship patterns. It would not appear, however, that the True Orthodox Church was particularly well suited to surviving less relaxed conditions, for with the State's attack on illegal religion which commenced in 1948 the movement quickly declined, and well before the death of Stalin in 1953, was virtually defunct.

The True Orthodox Christians were a parallel movement, also arising during World War II. This movement, displaying remarkable powers of endurance, has survived the quarter century to the present day. A very diffuse and loosely organized movement, the True Orthodox Christians generally have been able to dispense with the institution of the priesthood and instead make full reliance on lay conduct of worship activities. If as a result this movement has been subject to aberrations which are sometimes far removed from traditional Orthodox practice, it nevertheless has been sufficiently resilient to withstand the most severe attacks of the State. It enjoyed immense influence during the immediate post-war years, and not even the vigorous attempt of the regime to eradicate such underground religious activity between 1948 and 1953 was sufficient to do more than cause a reduction in its membership. The movement flourished again in the interregnum after the death of Stalin, and even though it has suffered constant attack for the past dozen years it continues to operate on a wide scale in the U.S.S.R.

Throughout this history—and, presumably, at the present time as well—the Soviet penal system provided a background for participants in underground Orthodox activities. A large proportion of the members, and probably nearly all of the leaders, of underground Orthodox organizations were enrolled at one time or another in the prisons, the labour camps, and the exile system. Many of them did not return. Those who did, however, had been subjected to the experience of having to preserve their religious commitment in the most extreme of conditions, and as a result, practices and attitudes they had learned in the camps could be applied directly on their return to society. The impact of the penal system was especially pronounced during the middle fifties, when the great emancipation of prisoners resulted in the entry of large numbers of former convicts into the True Orthodox Christians and the other organizations of the Orthodox underground.

With the waning of the fifties, the regime began to mobilize its forces for a severe attack on religion, which soon assumed huge proportions and became a constant factor in the life of all religious people in the U.S.S.R. The True Orthodox Christians, as has been noted, were able to survive this attack. However, two new movements began within its ranks in response to the increasing pressure. The first of these, the movement of the Silent ones, in which the members would vow never to speak again, enjoyed only the briefest period of popularity before succumbing to the intelligently devised and exceedingly effective counter-measures instituted by the State. Nevertheless, even if it has been unable to preserve its organized existence, the movement characterized by the vow of silence has left its mark on the subsequent history of the True Orthodox Christians, and silence remains an option which is occasionally employed still.

The second development in the True Orthodox Christians movement in the new period of pressure was the practice of wandering. The True Orthodox Christians Wanderers gave up all attempts at maintaining any relationship whatsoever to society, and entered an absolutely clandestine life of hiding and of wandering about the countryside with no permanent residence. This movement, ideally suited as it was to conditions of extreme police and investigatory pressure, was able to organize quickly on a vast, virtually nation-wide scale. As such it has an influence on the religious life of Orthodoxy throughout the country and remains an attractive option for those Orthodox believers, clergy and laity alike, who have felt themselves particularly oppressed.

The rapid attrition in the size and strength of the legally existing Russian Orthodox Church, which has lost half of its parishes during the past decade and suffered exceedingly severe limitations on its activity, has resulted in a general condition within the believing population comparable to the immediate pre-war period. Vast numbers of believers are again faced with the alternative of giving up the practice of their faith, or of participating in illegal activities. Even the most conscientious of believing citizens can scarcely avoid engaging in some form of technically illegal religious activity at one time or another. In such conditions, underground Orthodox organizations which are capable of surviving despite the regime's immense effort to eradicate them have a field of opportunity which is very broad indeed. The restrictions of the present period against all religious believers have created a society in which underground Orthodox practices can, and very often do, flourish.

This historical pattern of underground Orthodox movements in the U.S.S.R., despite the poverty of concrete information which is available, is of considerable interest in a number of ways. Naturally, a study such as this can scarcely hope to do more than to suggest some of the implications and conclusions which may be derived from examining this phenomenon.

Perhaps most obvious is the potential of these movements for contributing to the sociological understanding of Soviet society. Other considerations apart, the underground Orthodox movements obviously form one of the existing sub-groupings within the complex totality of the society of the country. In some degree, the concrete forms taken by these organizations and the degree of popularity which they can achieve are determined by the total sociological structure of the country. The complex array of the social patterns and options of a given moment, together with the fund of social traditions within the local society and society at large, determine the forms which extreme sub-groupings such as these may take. Conversely, the forms taken by these organizations and groups can serve to define, in one respect at least, the maximum limit of variation which is possible to Soviet society.

From one point of view, at least, these movements may be considered a reaction to the evolution of society. Whatever other factors may enter into their motivation, in many respects these underground Orthodox movements represent a response, often negative, to changing society, to the process of modernization which has been convulsing twentieth-century Russia. As such, they may perhaps shed some light on the not uncommon phenomenon of a religious form being given to a general attempt to resist that loss of previously accepted values which is inevitable in the modernization process.

Finally, there is considerable importance from the sociological point of view in the social alienation which is observable in the underground Orthodox movements. This alienation from society has many parallels in other countries, and if alienation is becoming of increasing significance in modern societies, then this particular form of social alienation is of immense importance in illuminating at least one aspect of the general phenomenon.

The underground movements are of crucial importance to the understanding of the political realities of Soviet society. These movements have arisen and developed, with very few exceptions, exclusively in reaction to the political actions of the regime, and as such they provide an exceedingly important index to the country's political life, and especially to the religious policies of the ruling regime.

Regardless of the degree to which the various organizations of underground Orthodoxy have exhibited political hostility to the regime, their specific form of organization and the extent of their influence have in large measure been determined by the religious policy of the regime during the period in question. During times of extreme anti-religious pressure the underground movements have had immense opportunities for growth owing to the fact that the reduced availability of overt religious activity has provided them with masses of potential recruits in the population. At the same time, however, periods of intense anti-religious pressure have also restricted the opportunities of the underground organizations themselves to organize their religious life as they might wish. As a result, these periods have also been marked by a proliferation of abnormal and occasionally bizarre practices within underground Russian Orthodoxy.

Periods of relative relaxation in State policy towards religion have also resulted in changes within the underground Orthodox movements. These periods have been marked by great proliferation of the activities of the underground Orthodox organizations, for if the increased availability of legally permissible facilities for worship has reduced the number of potential candidates for the illegal movements, the corresponding relaxation of police and investigatory pressure has given to these organizations immensely amplified opportunities for activity. The underground Orthodox movements have been quick to take advantage of such relaxation as, for example, during the period from the advent of World War II until the rise of the *Zhdanovshchina* in 1947, and during the similar period of relaxation from 1953 to 1957. Underground Orthodox activity during these periods has displayed a tendency to move closer to normative Orthodox practice, and the more bizarre aberrations have been less in evidence. In this regard, it is ironic that despite their unwillingness to accept any compromise with the ruling regime, these underground organizations have in many respects been the beneficiaries of the dominant Church's willingness to make just such a compromise in the hope of gaining greater freedom of activity within society.

It is especially important to note that the political hostility of the underground Orthodox movement has in many respects been the direct result of State policies. The regime, in reacting and even over-reacting to the implied or actual political threat of such organizations, has made a signal contribution to the deepening—and in some cases the creation—of that political alienation which is the chief factor making such movements so abhorrent to the regime.

Great numbers of those who eventually enter into underground Orthodox organizations were themselves essentially apolitical in their persuasion and in their lives. When churches are arbitrarily closed, believers who might otherwise consider themselves eminently loyal citizens have no recourse other than activities which are defined by the State as disloyal, if they are to continue

19

their religious life at all. Furthermore, unjust penalties against those who merely wish to fulfil religious requirements can result in an adverse reaction in the victim, and a believing citizen who heretofore was politically neutral, or even positively loyal, might as a result of the injustice he has felt react negatively towards the regime and become politically hostile to it. Thus in many cases the anti-religious action of the State has bred political alienation in numerous citizens who might otherwise have remained quite untouched by any particular political disaffection.

Certain policies of the regime have unwittingly had the effect of inevitably ensuring that these underground religious organizations will be infected with a maximum degree of political hostility. The extreme restrictions against such activity have inadvertently resulted in a large measure of continuity in the leadership of the underground religious organizations, for in difficult circumstances only those leaders who have extensive experience may be expected to avoid detection by the State for very long. Thus the rise of new leaders is inhibited by the fact that the majority of them, because of their inexperience, can be apprehended early in their careers. Historically, the leadership of the underground Orthodox organizations has displayed a considerable degree of continuity, with many of the leaders direct descendants of the crisis of 1927, when the political attitude towards the State was the chief, if not the sole, issue.

Furthermore, the prison system has made an immense contribution towards ensuring that the leadership of the underground movements will remain exceedingly hostile to the regime. The concentration of investigatory and police energies upon detecting and apprehending leaders has ensured that nearly all of the dynamic elements in the Orthodox underground will at one time or another have passed through the prison system, where conditions are so severe as to make political alienation almost inevitable.

Finally, by its rigid prohibition of religious literature, the State has militated against the production of new literature. As has been noted, compositions of the twenties have remained of immense influence within the Orthodox underground to the present day. Were it not for the stringent restrictions against religious literature, it might well be that these earlier compositions, reflecting the pronounced political hostility of the early days of Bolshevik rule, might have been superseded by other productions reflecting a more congenial and less intensely political environment, such as that obtaining among the True Orthodox Christians in the immediate post-war period.

For the religious historian, there are numerous points of interest in surveying the patterns of development of underground Orthodoxy in the Soviet period. The difficulties experienced by religious organizations during the past fifty years in the U.S.S.R. have provided a sort of a laboratory experience for determining modes of development of religious movements. Conditions in which this evolution has taken place in the U.S.S.R. are, in many respects, without parallel in the modern history of the Church elsewhere in the world. Study of the evolutionary patterns of religious organizations in the peculiar climate of Soviet society promises to yield considerable insight into the dynamics of religious movements in general.

A process which in many respects is similar to the Protestant experience is observable in the developmental patterns of underground forms of Orthodox worship. It would be incautious, of course, to draw too close a parallel between the two experiences, for it should be borne in mind that these underground organizations, with a very few exceptions, are by no means intent on reforming or changing the Church. On the contrary, their chief goal has been to preserve their accustomed form of worship. Unlike the experience of Protestant movements in the West, the underground Orthodox in the U.S.S.R. have not been motivated by desires to change the doctrinal or worship structure of Orthodoxy. Their entrance into schismatic movements has been caused almost exclusively by political factors, and hence they represent somewhat of a unique experiment in modern Church development. Unwillingly, they have been driven to embracing innovations in Church life, innovations which in many respects are similar to those introduced by the Protestant movements.

One of the most obvious of these 'Protestantizing' innovations is to be found in the ecclesiology of the various underground Orthodox organizations. Quite against their desires, the exigencies of the times have driven these movements to a structure of the Church which is bereft of the traditional Orthodox reliance upon episcopal discipline. With the possible exception of the brief period following 1927, the underground Orthodox organizations have had to make do without an episcopate, and certainly without any claim to the Orthodox tradition of Apostolic succession through-out the episcopate. The difficulties of maintaining an actively functioning higher organization have forced many of the groups into a sort of presbyterian form of ecclesiastical structure, in which single parishes, or at best groups of parishes, must act independently in governing their own lives. Furthermore, the unavailability of priests has led many of the groups such as the True Orthodox Christians into that form of lay organization of the Church structure, its practices, and its decisions, which for other reasons many of the 'free churches' of Protestantism have long employed.

This departure from the traditional sacerdotal pattern of Orthodoxy is especially evident in the worship practices of the Orthodox underground. Regardless of their desires in the matter, the members have been reduced to a non-sacerdotal form of worship, in which laymen undertake what otherwise should be priestly functions simply because no priests are available. Thus movements such as the True Orthodox Christians have found it possible to practise lay administration of sacraments such as baptism and even the Eucharist.

Naturally, these innovations have, in many cases, led to changes in the theological doctrines, attitudes, and emphases among the underground Orthodox, which also find many parallels in Protestantism. In particular, the doctrine of the direct accessibility of the devout believer to Christ without the mediation of a priesthood, and the special presence of the Holy Spirit in a sanctified place even without canonical consecration, have become theologically prominent among the underground Orthodox. Furthermore, the emphasis on eschatology which is everywhere observable in these groups is also of significance. Naturally, eschatological themes are not foreign to traditional Orthodoxy (nor, indeed, to any historical Christian denomination). The special emphasis which this branch of theology receives, however, is not dissimilar to that same phenomenon in certain branches of Protestantism, particularly in the more pietistic sects.

In addition to such general points of similarity with Protestants, there are even specific practices of certain of the underground Orthodox groups which are curiously similar to practices which have appeared at one time or another among Protestants. For example, the worship services held at shrines and holy places, which last through the night, have many superficial similarities to the camp meeting tradition of U.S. Protestant history. Similarly, the emphasis on private or family devotional life also parallels practices which were widely utilized in some of the earlier Protestant denominations. Naturally, it would be unwise to press similarities too far, for even if the practices are outwardly cognate, the processes which led to these practices are so dissimilar as to suggest the possibility of coincidence rather than an intrinsic developmental process common to all non-sacerdotal Christian formations.

The similarity with Protestantism which might have the most impact for the future development of underground Orthodoxy would probably be found in its alienation from society. Perforce, the underground Orthodox movements are unable to continue the traditional Orthodox identification of Church with society. As a result, these groups seem much more prone to innovation and experiment than would religious denominations which are comfortably identified with the prevailing society. In some cases, at any rate, religious movements which have not identified themselves with current society have achieved remarkable transformations of that society over a considerable period of time; the hypothesis of Max Weber regarding the role of the Protestant ethic in the development of industrialized society is illustrative, as is the experience of the Old Believers in pre-revolutionary Russia. Especially after the Petrine reforms, the Old Believers refused to accept the prevailing social system, and hence were much better able to experiment and innovate in their attitudes and practices, especially within their own enclaves, than was the Russian Orthodox Church of the period. As a result, by the twentieth century the Old Believers were well on the way towards gaining great influence in the capitalistic sector of the industrializing society, and had it not been for the abrupt termination of this pattern of development in 1917, the resultant society might well have reflected in large measure the influence of the Old Believers and cognate groups alienated from the traditional, tsarist society.

The Old Believers show many points of similarity with the contemporary underground Orthodox movements. Even though the latter have been led to schismatic and illegal activities by factors considerably different from those which motivated the

Old Believers, their pattern of development over the past fifty years has in many instances paralleled the earlier experience. The various forms which modern underground Orthodoxy has taken, such as the True Orthodox Church and the True Orthodox Christians, have to some degree been parallel to the twin development of *Popovtsy* and *Bezpopovtsy* elements within the Old Believer tradition. The similarity between the True Orthodox Christians Wanderers and the Old Believer *Beguny* movement has already been noted. Even the economic success achieved by underground groups as opposed to their less fortunate brethren in the collective farm system in 1945–7 is similar to the economic success traditionally identified with the pre-revolutionary Old Believer movements. Furthermore, many of the modern underground Orthodox groups have displayed a degree of syncretism with non-Orthodox and indigenous religious movements (such as the *Khlysty*) which is reminiscent of the similar syncretism of the more extreme branches of the Old Believers movement.

Interesting as such comparisons with other Christian traditions may be, the chief benefit to be derived from study of these groups is to be found in considering them not so much in comparison with other groups but in their own right. The peculiarities of the Soviet tradition have created a kind of a laboratory experiment, in which other factors such as disagreement over doctrine and worship have been precluded. The single factor which has been dominant throughout the history of the modern underground Orthodox movements has not been religious at all, but rather has been of a secular nature: political pressure. Therefore the experience of these groups provides a uniquely controlled experiment in what happens to a highly liturgical, sacerdotal, episcopal tradition when it is no longer able to function according to its desires. Intensive study of the patterns, developments, and practices which have evolved in the course of this experience in Russian Orthodoxy as a whole promises to yield no little insight into the nature of the Orthodox tradition, its strength and weaknesses, and, in particular, the degree to which it is able to adjust to new and inclement changes in the environment. Indeed, close examination of these movements, which have had no special inclination or desire to become heretical or apostate, might be of immense value in seeking to define more accurately what is essential, as against what is merely desirable, for Orthodoxy, and thereby to give a clearer insight into the essence of Orthodox Christianity.

Of special importance are the conclusions which may be drawn from this historical experience with regard to the mechanics of survival in a society consciously designed to eliminate organized religion. Prior to World War II, the highly organized, episcopal Russian Orthodox Church all but succumbed to the pressure, and the vacuum left by its virtual disappearance from society was filled, if at all, by other, less complex religious structures of the Orthodox underground. The relaxed conditions during and after World War II gave rise to a relatively complex, sacerdotal movement, the True Orthodox Church. This form of underground Orthodox organization, however, was ill-equipped for survival, and collapsed almost immediately on the resumption of State pressure. Its place was taken by a much more diffuse, entirely non-sacerdotal form better able to survive, the True Orthodox Christians.

The implication would seem to be that a religious organization whose existence is conditional upon a functioning priesthood, and even more, an episcopacy, is not well adapted for survival of extreme conditions. Obviously, a hostile regime need only discover and remove that small portion of the membership which is the ordained clergy to effect the disruption of the organization. The more diffuse the organization, however, the less susceptible it is to such liquidation. If leaders of the True Orthodox Christians are arrested, replacements can arise immediately from among the rank-and-file. Furthermore, even should the large majority of a group's members be apprehended, the small number remaining at large, or even one individual, is fully equipped to re-organize a new group. Such flexible movements as the True Orthodox Christians thus have a Phoenix-like capacity for re-appearing time and again after apparently successful attempts by the State to eliminate them. In this regard, the conclusion would seem to be that the less an underground Orthodox movement adheres to Orthodox structural patterns, and the more it embraces Protestant innovations, the better will it be able to survive extreme conditions. A flexible organization can survive conditions which are fatal to a more rigid structure.

The rise of the True Orthodox Christians Wanderers would seem to imply that once a certain stage of repression has been reached, even an exceedingly diffuse movement is able to construct effective and widespread organizational patterns. If members of a movement are induced to sever all ties with society and practise absolute secrecy, apparently it once again becomes possible for them to enjoy an organized existence which, in its geographic structure at least, constitutes a partial return to the traditional Orthodox pattern, with regional leaders serving the same administrative functions as the episcopate. The difference, of course, is that structures such as those of the Wanderers are less susceptible to disruption, for its leaders, who have no requirement for a particular form of ordination, can be replaced with considerable facility.

The capability for survival, however, is not without its costs. Obviously, a movement which depends on secrecy is poorly equipped to influence society. The concordat of 1943 would seem to demonstrate that the traditional Russian Orthodox Church structure is best equipped for direct negotiation with a centralized secular authority, for its complex, hierarchical structure focuses its entire power in the single person of the Patriarch, enabling him to deal directly and from a position of strength with the individual or oligarchy in command of the State.

The most serious disability inherent in a flexible approach is that its ability to survive necessarily includes a diminished capacity for avoiding innovations in the religious life of the believers. Some sort of organizational authority is essential if heresies and breaches with accepted and proven traditions are to be avoided, and, at least to the Orthodox way of thinking, the traditional, authoritarian structure of the Russian Orthodox Church has proved best able to preserve the dogmatic and canonical heritage of Christianity intact. From the Old Believers to the present-day movements, all attempts to dispense with this structure have resulted in a proliferation of innovative practices which, in their extreme forms, seem foreign not only to Orthodoxy, but to historical Christianity itself. Not even the alternative authoritarian structure of the True Orthodox Christians Wanderers has been able to ensure complete freedom from non-Orthodox innovations. Underground Orthodox movements which have dispensed with the traditional organizational structure have proved their ability to survive; it is not yet certain, however, that over an extended period what survives will be *Orthodoxy*.

But what of the intrinsic importance of the underground movements themselves? Do they represent a development of exceedingly great importance for the people of the Soviet Union, or on the contrary, is this study primarily an examination of a movement which, however interesting it may be, is a minor and quite unimportant aberration on the far fringes of Soviet society, with little or no particular importance to that society?

Numerically speaking, the latter would seem to be the case with the underground Orthodox movement. Despite the nation-wide extent of these movements, in comparison with the 240,000,000 population of the U.S.S.R., the underground Orthodox movements would appear to embrace only the most miniscule of fractional percentages of the population. The impression gained from the study of available evidence would suggest that at present, at least, these underground groups by no means represent anything like a mass movement within the population, but instead consist of a scattered few adherents here and there throughout the Soviet Union. Naturally, such statements as this must be qualified, for the data are by no means complete and, particularly for the Sovietologist, the argument from silence is the most tenuous of all methodologies. Nevertheless, it would not appear that the underground Orthodox movements have approached even that degree of size which the Old Believers had achieved (10–20 per cent or more of the population at the turn of the century), and certainly do not represent anything like as many people as those who would identify themselves with the legalized Russian Orthodox Church, however truncated its present position may be. If one remains within the evidence at hand, at least, and denies oneself the luxury of speculation, it would appear that statistically speaking the underground Orthodox movements are quite insignificant.

It should be noted, however, that statistics are a poor criterion in evaluating anything so complex as a religious movement. Much more to the point is the question of what influence the movement has. Here again, it would seem that from the point of view of underground Orthodoxy's influence on society as a whole, the results are miniscule. It is highly improbable that more than a fraction of today's Soviet citizens have ever heard of these underground Orthodox organizations, and those who have doubtless have only the most hazy impression of their activity. These, after all, are clandestine organizations, which if they are to preserve their secrecy, simply are unable to reach out into society on any large scale. The underground Orthodox have provided the subject matter for exceedingly infrequent works of *belles lettres* in recent years. Nevertheless, in view of the general alienation of the intelligentsia from organized religion within the country, it would seem most unlikely that there is any considerable awareness of this rather esoteric, arcane phenomenon on the part of the educated, articulate sector of the population. To be sure, there was the curious episode late in 1967, when in Leningrad a secret discussion circle was discovered which had allegedly initiated a widespread conspiracy committed to the overthrow of the Government and the restoration of a State dominated by the Russian Orthodox Church.[1] But even this eccentric event showed little or no detectable relationship to the underground Orthodox movements. Certainly it would seem reasonable to predict that, barring catastrophe, the future evolution of Soviet society will be much less influenced by underground Orthodoxy than by the many other factors influencing the power structure of society.

At first glance, a similar conclusion would seem to be indicated with regard to the underground movement's influence on the Russian Orthodox Church itself. For the past two decades, at least, the Moscow Patriarchate had seemed quite content to order its affairs with no regard whatsoever for the dissidents in the Orthodox underground. The theological, ecclesiastical, and ecclesiological life of the Russian Orthodox Church has gone its own way, without a detectable backward glance at the underground movements, and if there is some contact between members of Russian Orthodoxy and the adherents of the clandestine churches on the local level (such as during the services at shrines and sacred places), this contact has not yet been reflected to any detectable degree in the evidence concerning the worship practices of the dominant Church. Hence it would appear that the underground movements have little effect on the life of the Russian Orthodox Church.

This judgement, however, must be tempered by certain indications of indirect influence of the underground movement on the life of the Russian Orthodox Church. These movements represent an intrinsic danger to the State, at least among those elements in the regime which seek to exercise the maximum possible control

[1] *New York Times*, 18 April 1968.

over the churches pending their eventual eradication. Control is possible in an open church, but a clandestine church cannot be controlled but only sought out by the most laborious of means, and prosecuted. It is not certain whether the implied danger of a massive increase in the underground movements has or has not induced the State to temper some of its more Draconian designs on the Russian Orthodox Church.

This hypothesis, however, remains a distinct possibility in view of the experience of another denomination in the U.S.S.R. In 1961, a formidable opposition movement arose within the Russian Baptist community, which claimed at its peak to represent twice as many congregations as did the legalized Russian Baptist organization.[2] So effective was the challenge by this dissident movement that the Russian Baptists were allowed by the State to hold nationwide congresses (the last previous congress had been held in 1945) in 1963 and 1966. At both of these congresses important concessions were made to the demands of the dissident movement. Obviously, the State considered it expedient to temper some of its actions designed to restrict the legalized Baptist Church in order to blunt the appeal of this underground movement. In view of this documentable example, it must remain a distinct possibility that the Russian Orthodox Church owes a certain measure of such freedom of action as it still retains precisely to the challenge the State sees in the underground movements.

A second indirect area of potential influence of the underground movements on Russian Orthodoxy as a whole, lies in the field of theology. As has been noted, the True Orthodox Christians Wanderers have been devoting considerable energy to attempting to work out theological positions in response to the needs of the present day. This is a most unusual phenomenon, all but unique in contemporary Russian Orthodoxy. Although the Moscow Patriarchate remains in possession of three theological seminaries and two academies, the theological research done at these schools, so far as is known, has assiduously avoided any attempt at the risky business of answering the challenges of present Soviet society. Instead, the theological schools have been devoting the bulk of their attention to such matters as patristics and dogmatics, or to ecumenical research. Neither of these fields seems to promise particular benefit in increasing Orthodoxy's ability to relate to

[2] Bourdeaux, op. cit.

modern society, for the former areas are in many respects anti-
quarian, while the latter deal with events more applicable outside
the U.S.S.R. than within contemporary Soviet society. Therefore,
the theological research and discoveries of the underground
Orthodox movement may be making a signal contribution to the
ability of Russian Orthodoxy, as a whole, to find its way in contemporary Soviet society.[3]

Naturally, there is no way to predict what the future of underground Russian Orthodoxy will be. The increasingly rapid process of change in modern society—and especially in the U.S.S.R.
—militates against any confident excursions into clairvoyance.
Nevertheless, certain probabilities may be suggested in view of the
history of the movements since 1917.

Should the future bring any considerable relaxation of the
regime's religious policy, then almost certainly the underground
Orthodox movements would make their contribution to a resurgence of religion in the country. This, after all, was the
experience during and immediately after World War II. In times
of difficulty, the underground movement serves as a sort of
reservoir of Orthodox belief within the country, providing the
most committed of the believers with a means of preserving their
faith even when all other outlets for Orthodox worship and
practice have been denied them. Certainly today, in view of the
truncated ability of the Russian Orthodox Church to serve its
members, the underground movement is fulfilling this function.
If an abrupt termination of pressure should occur, the underground movements would be able to supply important human
material for the reorganization of the seriously weakened structure
of Russian Orthodoxy. It should be noted, however, that the
present anti-religious effort of the regime has continued for a
dozen years, has handily survived the fall of Khrushchev, and
shows no signs whatsoever of diminishing.

Should conditions take a turn for the worse, then the under-

---

[3] It is difficult to estimate how large a role such literature plays in the religious life of
the Orthodox population as a whole, for this will depend, in part, on how vigorously
theological research is being conducted in *samizdat* (self-publishing, or informal [and
illegal] circulation of manuscripts) in the Church at large. Theological treatises are
known to have circulated in the fifties (*Nauka i Religiia*, No. 11 (November 1961), pp.
28–33, and cf. *RCDA*, 31 May 1964), and, in view of the vigorous production of clandestine religious literature reported in the Soviet press, similar works may be presumed
to continue to appear. However, none of these works, nor descriptions of them, have
reached the West.

ground Orthodox movements will become of even greater importance to the preservation of Russian Orthodoxy than they are now.
The contemporary organizations of underground Orthodoxy have
accumulated a fund of experience in the difficult and demanding
mechanics of surviving in clandestine circumstances, and any
further attrition suffered by the open churches would magnify the
importance of organizations which are capable of functioning
despite extreme pressure. The existing mass of believers who now
form potential or actual recruits for underground worship would
be multiplied, as fewer and fewer of the Orthodox population would
continue to have any other available outlet for religious practices.

The real importance of the underground movements, however,
is to be found in another area, and it is this consideration which,
in the last analysis, necessitates the study of the phenomenon. The
key factor for the future development of underground Russian
Orthodoxy, and the locus of any dramatic increase in its importance in the Russian Church, is to be found in the death of Aleksii,
Patriarch of Moscow and All Russia, on 17 April 1970. A successor
will have to be found. This event—the passing of the Patriarch
and the necessity to elect a new one—contains within it the seeds
of a profound transformation of the function and importance of
underground Orthodoxy in the U.S.S.R.

Late in 1965, a dissenting movement, apparently not connected
with the underground Orthodox, suddenly appeared within the
ranks of the Moscow Patriarchate.[4] Two priests in Moscow,
N. Eshliman and G. Iakunin, perhaps taking a page from the
Russian Baptists, reacted to the increased strictures on Church
life with two letters of protest. To the State they vigorously protested against the State's refusal to abide by its own laws in its
religious policy. To the Patriarch they suggested that the Russian
Orthodox Church had too supinely submitted to outrageous
demands of the State. This protest, which very quickly was
echoed in other dioceses, was led by the influential and highly
respected Archbishop Ermogen.

In 1967, Ermogen, who was involuntarily in retirement, wrote a
persuasive and intelligently conceived treatise which, *inter alia*,
examined the canonical requirements for a valid election of a
Patriarch.[5] He demonstrated that neither of the last two

---

[4] Michael Bourdeaux, *Patriarch and Prophets* (London: Macmillan, 1970).
[5] *Vestnik Russkogo Studencheskogo Khristianskogo Dvizheniia*, No. 4 (1967), pp. 75–7.

patriarchal elections (in 1943 and 1945) were satisfactory, because for one reason or another they were not a valid representation of the will of the Russian Church at large. His stern and uncompromising demonstration of the canonical invalidity of these past elections, and the obvious applicability of his treatise to the forthcoming selection of a new Patriarch, presented an ominous picture. Should the venality of Church officials or the connivance of the regime result in another inequitable and canonically irregular election, the present mood of Ermogen and bishops who may share his sentiments makes a schism of massive proportions seem almost inevitable.

In 1969, A. Levitin who, writing under his own name and the pseudonym of Krasnov, had been the leading publicist of this dissenting movement within the Russian Orthodox Church, was at last arrested.[6] In view of this action taken by the State, and in view of the total range of anti-religious efforts which continue strong in the country, it would seem most unlikely that any future election of a Patriarch would be able to revert to the salad days of 1917, with full and free representation of the Church electing the Patriarch of their choice. Should an improper election be held, dissatisfied elements in the episcopate would almost surely refuse to accept it, preferring instead, as in 1927, to sever relations with the Moscow Patriarchate.

It is this possibility which provides the focus for this study of contemporary underground Orthodoxy. If a schism of any magnitude should develop during coming months, then the underground segment of the Russian Orthodox population will be expanded immensely. The current underground organizations, whatever their present importance, will become crucial in the history of the Russian Orthodox Church, either through expanding their size and scope with the entrance of large numbers of erstwhile members of the legalized Church, or in providing the paradigm for any new schismatic movement which may develop. If this possible pattern of development should result from the death of the Patriarch, then underground Russian Orthodoxy, currently of considerable interest, will almost inevitably become of critical importance for an understanding of the Russian Orthodox Church in the U.S.S.R.

[6] *New York Times*, 15 September 1969.

List of Works Cited

Books

Academy of Sciences of the U.S.S.R. (AN SSSR), *Ezhegodnik muzeia istorii religii i ateizma* ('Annual of the Museum of the History of Religion and Atheism'). Moscow: AN SSSR, annually since 1957.

——, *Sovremennoe sektantstvo* ('Contemporary sectarianism'), Volume IX of the series AN SSSR, *Voprosy istorii religii i ateizma*. Moscow: AN SSSR, 1961.

——, *Uspekhi sovremennoi nauki i religiia* ('Contemporary science's successes and religion'). Moscow: AN SSSR, 1961.

——, *Voprosy istorii religii i ateizma* ('Problems of the history of religion and atheism'). Moscow: AN SSSR, annually, 1950–64.

——, *Voprosy nauchnogo ateizma* ('Problems of scientific atheism'). Moscow: 'Mysl' ', semi-annually since 1965.

Alexeev, Wassilij, *Russian Orthodox Bishops in the Soviet Union, 1941–1953* (mimeographed, in Russian). New York: Research Program on the U.S.S.R., 1954.

American Committee for Liberation, *The Beleaguered Fortress*. New York: The Committee, 1963.

Anderson, Paul B., *People, Church, and State in Modern Russia*. New York: Macmillan, 1944.

Andreev, Ivan Mikhailovich, *Kratkii obzor istorii russkoi tserkvi ot revoliutsii do nashikh dnei* ('A brief survey of the history of the Russian Church from the revolution to the present'). Jordanville, New York: Holy Trinity Monastery, 1952.

——, *O polozhenii pravoslavnoi tserkvi v sovetskom soiuze. Katakombnaia tserkov' v SSSR* ('The Position of the Orthodox Church in the Soviet Union. The catacomb Church in the U.S.S.R.'). Jordanville, New York: Holy Trinity Monastery, 1961.

Andrianov, N. P., R. A. Lopatkin, and V. V. Pavliuk, *Osobennosti sovremennogo religioznogo soznaniia* ('Peculiarities of contemporary religious understanding'). Moscow: 'Mysl' ', 1966.

Antonii, Bishop, *O polozhenii tserkvi v sovetskoi rossii i o dukhovnoi zhizni russkago naroda* ('The situation of the Church in Soviet Russia and the spiritual life of the Russian people'). Jordanville, New York: Holy Trinity Monastery, 1960.

Armstrong, John A., *Ukrainian Nationalism*. New York: Columbia University Press, 1955.

Attwater, Donald, *The Christian Churches of the East*. London: Chapman, 1961.

Beck, F., and W. Godin, *Russian Purge and the Extraction of Confession*. London: Hurst and Blackett, 1951.

Behr-Sigel, E., *Prière et Sainteté dans l'Eglise Russe*. Paris: Les Editions du Cerf, 1950.

Bissonette, Georges, *Moscow Was My Parish*. New York: McGraw-Hill, 1956.

Bociurkiw, Bohdan R., *Soviet Church Policy in the Ukraine, 1919–1939*. Unpublished Ph.D. dissertation, University of Chicago, 1961.

Bourdeaux, Michael, *Patriarch and Prophets*. London: Macmillan, 1970.

——, *Religious Ferment in Russia*. London: Macmillan, 1968.

Carroll, Wallace, *We're in This with Russia*. Boston: Houghton Mifflin, 1942.

Chamberlin, W. H., *Russia's Iron Age*. Boston: Little, Brown, 1934.

Cianfarra, Camille Maximilian, *The Vatican and the Kremlin*. New York: Dutton, 1950.

Ciliga, Anton, *The Russian Enigma*. London: Labour Book Service, 1940.

Ciszek, Walter J., S.J., *With God in Russia*. New York: McGraw-Hill, 1964.

Curtiss, John Shelton, *The Russian Church and the Soviet State, 1917–1950*. Boston: Little, Brown, 1953.

Dallin, David J., and Boris I. Nicolaevsky, *Forced Labor in Soviet Russia*. New Haven, Connecticut: Yale University Press, 1947.

Danzas, Iuliia Nikolaevna, *The Russian Church*. New York: Sheed and Ward, 1936.

Darmanskii, P., *Pobeg iz t'my* ('Flight from darkness'). Moscow: 'Sovetskaia Rossiia', 1961.

Davis, Nathaniel, *Religion and Communist Government in the Soviet Union and Eastern Europe* (unpublished Ph.D. dissertation), Fletcher School of Law and Diplomacy, 1960.

Delo Mitropolita Sergiia ('The Metropolitan Sergii affair'). Unpublished typescript, np, np, nd (1930?).

Evlogii, Mitropolit, *Put' moei zhizni* ('The path of my life'). Paris: Y.M.C.A. Press, 1947.

Fedorenko, F., *Sekty, ikh vera i dela* ('The sects, their faith and works'). Moscow: Publishing House for Political Literature, 1965.

Fireside, Harvey F., *The Russian Orthodox Church under German Occupation in World War II* (unpublished Ph.D. dissertation), New School for Social Research, 1968.

Fitzsimmons, Thomas, Peter Malov, and John C. Fiske, *U.S.S.R.: Its People, Its Society, Its Culture*. New Haven, Connecticut: Human Relations Area File Press, 1960.

Fletcher, William C., *Nikolai: Portrait of a Dilemma*. New York: Macmillan, 1968.

——, *A Study in Survival: The Church in Russia, 1927–1943*. New York: Macmillan, 1965.

'Father George', *God's Underground*. New York: Appleton-Century-Crofts, 1949.

Gidulianov, *Otdelenie tserkvi ot gosudarstva* ('The separation of Church from State'). Moscow: State Publishing House for Juridical Literature, 1929.

Gorchakov, Mikhail K., *Itogi politiki mitropolitov Sergiia i Evlogiia* ('The sum of the policy of Metropolitans Sergii and Evlogii'). Paris: 'Doroi zlo!', 1930.

Grabbe, Georgii, *Pravda o russkoi tserkvi na rodine i za rubezhom* ('The truth about the Russian Church in the motherland and abroad'). Jordanville, New York: Holy Trinity Monastery, 1961.

Grunwald, Constantin de, *The Churches and the Soviet Union*. New York: Macmillan, 1962.

Gubanov, N. I., et al., *Individual'naia rabota s veruiushchimi* ('Individual work with believers'). Moscow: 'Mysl' ', 1967.

Gurian, Waldemar, ed., *The Soviet Union, Background, Ideology, Reality*. Notre Dame, Indiana: University of Notre Dame Press, 1951.

Gussoni, Lino, and Aristide Brunello, *The Silent Church*. New York: Veritas, 1954.

Gustavson, Arfved, *The Catacomb Church*. Jordanville, New York: Holy Trinity Monastery, 1960.

Herling, Gustav, *A World Apart*. London: William Heinemann, 1951.

Iaroslavskii, Emel'ian, *O religii* ('On religion'). Moscow: State Publishing House for Political Literature, 1957.

Inkeles, Alex, and Raymond A. Bauer, *The Soviet Citizen*. Cambridge, Massachusetts: Harvard University Press, 1959.

Institute for the Study of the U.S.S.R., *Genocide in the U.S.S.R.* New York: Scarecrow Press, 1958.

Ioann (Shakovskoi), Bishop, *Russkaia tserkov' v SSSR* ('The Russian Church in the U.S.S.R.'). New York: Rausen Brothers, 1956.

——, *Zashchita very v SSSR* ('Defence of the faith in the U.S.S.R.'). Paris: Ikhthus, 1966.

Ioann (Snychev), Archimandrite, *Tserkovnye raskoly v russkoi tserkvi 20-kh i 30-kh godov XX stoletiia—grigorianskii, iaroslavskii, iosiflianskii, viktorianskii i drugie. Ikh osobennost' i istoriia* ('Church schisms in the Russian church of the 20s and 30s of the twentieth century—the

Grigorian, Iaroslav, Josephite, Viktorian, and others. Their peculiarity and history'). Unpublished Master's dissertation, Moscow Theological Academy, 1965.

Iswolsky, Hélène, *Soul of Russia*. London: Sheed and Ward, 1944.

Iudin, N. I., *Pravda o petersburgskikh 'sviatyniakh'* ('The truth about the Petersburg "shrines" '). Leningrad, 1962. Extracts translated in *RCDA*, 24 June, 1963, pp. 116–120.

Iwanow, Boris, ed., *Religion in the U.S.S.R.* Munich: Institute for the Study of the U.S.S.R., 1960.

Johnston, Joseph, *God's Secret Armies within the Soviet Union*. New York: Putnam, 1954.

Kandidov, Boris, *Tserkov' i shpionazh* ('The church and espionage'). Moscow: State Anti-religious Publishing House, 1938.

Keller, Adolph, *Religion and Revolution*. New York: Revell, 1934.

Kitchin, George, *Prisoner of the OGPU*. New York: Longmans, Green, 1935.

Klibanov, A. I., ed., *Konkretnye issledovaniia sovremennykh religioznykh verovanii (metodika, organizatsiia, rezul'taty)* ('Concrete research on contemporary religious faiths (methodology, organization, results)'). Moscow: 'Mysl' ', 1967.

Konstantinov, Dmitrii, *Gonimaia tserkov'* ('The persecuted Church'). New York: All-Slavic Press, 1967.

——, *Pravoslavnaia molodezh' v bor'be za tserkov' v SSSR* ('Orthodox youth in the struggle for the Church in the U.S.S.R.'). Munich: Institute for the Study of the U.S.S.R., 1956.

——, *Religious Persecution in USSR*. London, Canada: SBONR, 1965.

Krasnikov, N. P., ed., *Po etapam razvitiia ateizma v SSSR* ('Stages of the development of atheism in the U.S.S.R.'). Leningrad: 'Nauka', 1967.

——, *Voprosy preodoleniia religioznykh perezhitkov v SSSR* ('Problems of overcoming religious survivals in the U.S.S.R.'). Moscow: 'Nauka', 1966.

Kurdiumov, Mikhail Grigor'evich, *Komu nuzhna tserkovnaia smuta?* ('Who needs the Church confusion?'). Np, np, nd (1928?).

——, *Rim i Pravoslavnaia Tserkov'* ('Rome and the Orthodox Church'). Paris: Les Editeurs réunis, 1939.

——, *Tserkov' i novaia Rossiia* ('The church and modern Russia'). Paris: Y.M.C.A. Press, 1933.

Lipper, Elinor, *Eleven Years in Soviet Prison Camps*. London: Hollis and Carter, 1950.

Lowrie, Donald A., *The Light of Russia*. Prague: Y.M.C.A. Press, 1923.

Marshall, Richard H., Jr., ed., *Aspects of Religion in the Soviet Union, 1917–1967*. Chicago: University of Chicago Press, 1971.

Martsinkovskii, Vladimir Filimonovich, *With Christ in Soviet Russia*. Prague: Kniktiskarna V. Horak, 1933.

Mauriac, François, *Communism and Christians*. Westminster, Maryland: The Newman Press, 1949.

McCullagh, Francis, *The Bolshevik Persecution of Christianity*. New York: Dutton, 1924.

Mikhail, Sviashchennik (pseudonym of Mikhail Pol'skii), *Polozhenie tserkvi v Sovetskoi Rossii. Ocherk bezhavshego iz Rossii sviashchennika* ('The position of the Church in Soviet Russia. An essay by a priest who fled Russia'). Jerusalem: Goldberg's Press, 1931.

Mol, Hans, ed., *Religion in the Western World*. Canberra: Australian National University, in preparation.

Noble, John H., *I Found God in Soviet Russia*. New York: St. Martin's Press, 1959.

Nyaradi, Nicholas, *My Ringside Seat in Moscow*. New York: Thomas Y. Crowell, 1952.

Orthodox Eastern Church, Russian, *The Call of the Russian Church*. London: 'Soviet News', 1945.

——, *Patriarkh Sergii i ego dukhovnoe nasledstvo* ('Patriarch Sergii and his spiritual legacy'). Moscow: The Patriarchate, 1947.

——, *Pravda o religii v Rossii* ('The truth about religion in Russia'). Moscow: The Patriarchate, 1942.

——, *Russkaia pravoslavnaia tserkov' i velikaia otechestvennaia voina* ('The Russian Orthodox Church and the Great Patriotic War'). Moscow: Standard Press of the Unified State Publishing House, nd (1944?).

Pantskhav, I. D., ed., *O nekotorykh osobennostiakh sovremennoi religioznoi ideologii* ('Certain peculiarities of contemporary religious ideology'). Moscow: Moscow University Press, 1964.

Parvilahti, Unto, *Beria's Gardens: A Slave Laborer's Experiences in the Soviet Utopia*. New York: Dutton, 1960.

Pol'skii, Mikhail, *Kanonicheskoe polozhenie vysshei tserkovnoi vlasti v SSSR i zagranitsei* ('The canonical position of the supreme Church government in the U.S.S.R. and abroad'). Jordanville, New York: Holy Trinity Monastery, 1948.

——, *Novye mucheniki rossiiskie* ('Modern Russian martyrs'). Jordanville, New York: Holy Trinity Monastery, 1949 and 1957.

Raevskii, S., *Ukrainskaia avtokefal'naia tserkov'* ('The Ukrainian Autocephalous Church'). Jordanville, New York: Holy Trinity Monastery, 1948.

Rar, Gleb, (pseudonym of A. Vetrov), *Plenennaia tserkov'* ('The captive Church'). Frankfurt: Posev, 1954.

Roeder, Bernhard, *Katorga: An Aspect of Modern Slavery*. London: Heinemann, 1958.

Salisbury, Harrison E., *To Moscow—And Beyond*. New York: Harper, 1959.

Schakovskoy, Zinaida, *The Privilege Was Mine*. New York: Putnam's, 1959.

Sheinman, M. M., *Religion and the Church in U.S.S.R.* Moscow: Cooperative Publishing Society of Foreign Workers, 1933.

——, *Vatikan vo vtoroi mirovoi voine* ('The Vatican in the Second World War'). Moscow: AN SSSR, 1951.

Sherwood, M., *The Soviet War on Religion*. New York: Workers' Library Publishers, 1930.

Shiriaev, Boris, *Neugasimaia lampada* ('The inextinguishable icon-lamp'). New York: Chekhov Press, 1954.

Skazkina, S. D., ed., *Nastol'naia kniga ateista* ('Reference book for the atheist'). Moscow: Publishing House for Political Literature, 1968.

Smith, C. A., ed., *Escape from Paradise*. London: Hollis and Carter, 1954.

Spinka, Matthew, *Christianity Confronts Communism*. New York: Harper, 1936.

——, *The Church in Soviet Russia*. New York: Oxford University Press, 1956.

Stratonov, I., *Russkaia tserkovnaia smuta (1921–1931 gg)* ('The Russian Church confusion (1921–1931)'). Berlin: Parabola, 1932.

Struve, Nikita, *Christians in Contemporary Russia*. London: Harvill Press, 1963.

Szczesniak, Boleslaw, *The Russian Revolution and Religion*. Notre Dame, Indiana: University of Notre Dame Press, 1959.

Tchernavin, Tatiana, *Escape from the Soviets*. New York: Dutton, 1934.

Tchernavin, V., *I Speak for the Silent*. New York: Hale, Cushman, and Flint, 1935.

Terskoi, A., *U sektantov* ('Among the sectarians'). Moscow: Publishing House for Political Literature, 1965.

Timasheff, N. S., *Religion in Soviet Russia, 1917–1942*. New York: Sheed and Ward, 1942.

Titov, V. E., *Pravoslavie* ('Orthodoxy'). Moscow: Publishing House for Political Literature, 1967.

Tregubov, Iu. A., *Vosem' let vo vlasti lubianki* ('Eight years in the power of the Lubianka'). Frankfurt: Posev, 1957.

Troitskii, Sergei Viktorovich, *O nepravda Karlovatskogo raskola; razbor knigi Prot. M. Pol'skogo 'Kanonicheskoe polozhenie vysshei tserkovnoi vlasti v SSSR i zagranitsei'* ('On the falsity of the Karlovtsi schism; an analysis of the book by Protopriest M. Pol'skii, "The canonical position of the supreme Church government in the U.S.S.R. and abroad" '). Paris: Editions d l'Exarchat Patriarcal Russe in Europe Occidentale, 1960.

——, *Razmezhivanie ili raskol* ('Separation or schism'). Paris: Y.M.C.A. Press, 1932.

U.S. Congress, House, *The Crimes of Khrushchev*. Washington, D.C.: U.S. Government Printing Office, 1959.

——, *Recent Developments in the Soviet Bloc*. Washington, D.C.: U.S. Government Printing Office, 1964.

Valentinov, A. A., *The Assault of Heaven*. Berlin: Max Mattisson, 1924.

Wurmbrand, Richard, *Underground Saints*. Old Tappan, New Jersey: Fleming H. Revell, 1968.

Zernov, Nicholas, *The Russians and Their Church*. London: S.P.C.K., 1945.

Zybkovets, V. F., *Ot boga li nravstvennost'* ('Is morality from God'). Moscow: State Publishing House for Political Literature, 1961.

Articles

Aleksandrov, I., 'Dat' otpor agitatsii tserkovnikov' ('To repulse the agitation of the churchmen'), *Vlast' Sovetov*, No. 19 (October 1937), pp. 22–4.

Aleksandrovich, I. A., G. E. Kandaurov, and A. I. Nemirovskii, 'Sektantstvo v voronezhskoi oblasti i rabota po ego preodoleniiu' ('Sectarianism in Voronezh Oblast and work for overcoming it'), in AN SSSR, *Ezhegodnik muzeia istorii religii i ateizma*, op. cit., V, 58–75.

Alekseev, N. P., 'Metodika i rezul'taty izucheniia religioznosti sel'skogo naseleniia' ('Methods and results of the study of religiosity of the village population'), in AN SSSR, *Voprosy nauchnogo ateizma*, op. cit., III, 131–50.

Amosov, N., 'Oktiabr'skaia revoliutsiia i tserkov' ' ('The October Revolution and the Church'), *Antireligioznik*, No. 10 (October 1937), pp. 46–54.

'Antikhrist' (Anti-Christ), *Antireligioznik*, No. 5 (May 1941), p. 44.

Babii, A., and V. Gazhos, 'Tak lozhnaia mudrost' bledneet' ('Thus false wisdom fades'), *Nauka i Religiia*, No. 9 (September 1969), pp. 27–30.

Bailey, George, 'Religion in the Soviet Union', *The Reporter*, 16 July 1964.

Bailey, S. D., 'Religious Boom in Russia', *Christian Century*, 12 March 1958, pp. 304–6.

Barykin, M., 'Pustotsvet na dvere zhizni' ('Delusion at the door of life'), *Nauka i Religiia*, No. 9 (September 1961), pp. 45–55.

Blake, Patricia, 'Alliance with the Unholy', *Life*, 14 September 1959, pp. 114-26.

Brazhnik, I., 'Ateisticheskoe vospitanie—obshchepartiinoe delo' ('Atheist education—a matter for the entire Party'), *Partiinaia Zhizn'*, No. 24 (December 1963), pp. 21-6.

Chaikovskaia, O., 'Pochemu ushel topol' ' ('Why the poplar tree went away'), *Nauka i Religiia*, No. 6 (June 1966), pp. 4-10.

Demin, M. V., ' "Khristianskii kommunizm" kak otrazhenie krizisa sovremennoi religioznoi ideologii' (' "Christian communism" as a reflection of the crisis of contemporary religious ideology'), in Pantskhav, op. cit., pp. 178-215.

Dubovka, A., 'Kto iz detei verit v boga?' ('Who among the children believe in God?'), *Nauka i Religiia*, No. 2 (February 1963), p. 75.

Dunaevskii, L., 'II Vsesoiuznaia konferentsiia nauchno-issledovatelskikh uchrezhdenii po antireligioznoi rabote' ('The II National conference of scientific research institutions on anti-religious work'), *Vestnik Kommunisticheskoi Akademii*, No. 4 (1934), pp. 96-100.

Facey, Paul W., S.J., 'The Case of the Missing Underground', *America*, 16 July 1949.

Fedoseev, P., 'Marksizm-leninizm o bor'be s religiei' ('Marxism-Leninism on the struggle with religion'), *Pod Znamenem Marksizma*, No. 3 (March 1937), pp. 139-58.

Fedotov, Georgii Petrovich, 'K voprosu o polozhenii russkoi Tserkvi' ('On the question of the position of the Russian Church'), *Vestnik Russkago Studencheskago Khristianskago Dvizheniia*, No. 11 (November 1930), pp. 10-14.

Feofanov, Iu., 'Persistently, flexibly, intelligently!', *Sovety Deputatov Trudiashchikhsia*, No. 10 (October 1960), translated in *CDSP*, 18 January 1961, p. 36.

Filippova, R. F., 'K istorii otdeleniia shkoly ot tserkvi' ('The history of the separation of School from Church'), in Krasnikov, *Po etapam razvitiia*, op. cit., pp. 86-99.

Fletcher, William C., 'Soviet Society and Religion: A Trip Report', *Communist Affairs*, June-August 1963, pp. 8-11.

——, 'Statistics and Soviet Sociology of Religion', in Mol, op. cit.

Gagarin, Iu. V., 'Otkhod ot sektantstva v Komi ASSR' ('Departure from sectarianism in the Komi ASSR'), in Krasnikov, *Po etapam razvitiia*, op. cit., pp. 168-87.

Gegeshidze, D., 'Prisposablivaiutsia . . .' ('They are adapting themselves . . .'), *Agitator*, No. 21 (November 1964), pp. 45-7.

Glukhov, I., 'Patriarkh Sergii i ego deiatel'nost' ' ('Patriarch Sergii and his activity'), *ZMP*, No. 3 (March 1967), pp. 59-70.

Hackel, Sergei, 'New Perspectives and the Old Believers', *Eastern Churches Review*, I, 2 (Autumn 1966), pp. 104–17.

Hakimoglu, A., 'Forty Years of Anti-religious Propaganda', *East Turkic Review*, No. 2 (December 1960), pp. 67–9.

Hordienko, M., 'Is Orthodoxy Changing?', *Liudyna i Svit*, No. 3 (March 1969), pp. 18–23, translated in *Digest of the Soviet Ukrainian Press*, May 1969, pp. 16–17.

Huxley-Blythe, P. J., 'Modern Christian Martyrs', *American Mercury*, No. 88 (February 1959), pp. 23–6.

Iankova, Z. A., 'O nekotorykh metodakh konkretno-sotsial'nogo izucheniia religii' ('Certain methods of concrete social study of religion'), in Klibanov, *Konkretnye issledovaniia*, op. cit., pp. 111–18.

——, 'Sovremennoe pravoslavie i antiobshchestvennaia sushchnost' ego ideologii' ('Contemporary Orthodoxy and the anti-social essence of its ideology'), in AN SSSR, *Voprosy istorii religii i ateizma*, op. cit., XI, 67–94.

Iaroslavskii, Emel'ian, 'Zadachi antireligioznoi propagandy' ('The tasks of anti-religious propaganda'), *Antireligioznik*, No. 5 (May 1941), pp. 1–8.

——, 'Zadachi antireligioznoi propagandy v period sotsialisticheskogo nastupleniia' ('Tasks of anti-religious propaganda in the period of the advance of socialism'), *Pod Znamenem Marksizma*, No. 3 (March 1931), pp. 36–55.

Il'ichev, L., 'Formirovanie nauchnogo mirovozzreniia i ateisticheskoe vospitanie' ('The formation of a scientific world view and atheist education'), *Kommunist*, No. 1 (January 1964), pp. 23–46.

Ilov, V., 'Konets peshchernykh apostolov' ('The end of the cave-dwelling apostles'), *Partiinaia Zhizn' Kazakhstana*, No. 4 (April 1964), pp. 31–4.

Ivanov, S., 'Kak my organizuem nauchno-ateisticheskuiu propagandu' ('How we organize scientific atheistic propaganda'), *Kommunist Moldavii*, No. 7 (July 1961), pp. 52–7.

Klibanov, A. I., 'Nauchno-organizatsionnyi i metodicheskii opyt konkretnykh issledovanii religioznosti' ('Scientific organizational and methodological experience of concrete research on religiousness'), in Klibanov, *Konkretnye issledovaniia*, op. cit., pp. 5–34.

——, 'Sektantstvo v proshlom i v nastoiashchem' ('Sectarianism in the past and in the present'), in AN SSSR, *Sovremennoe Sektantstvo*, op. cit., pp. 9–34.

——, 'Sovremennoe sektantstvo v Lipetskoi oblasti' ('Contemporary sectarianism in Lipetsk Oblast'), in AN SSSR, *Voprosy istorii religii i ateizma*, op. cit., X, 157–85.

Klibanov, A. I., 'Sovremennoe sektantstvo v Tambovskoi oblasti' ('Contemporary sectarianism in Tambov Oblast'), in ibid., VIII, 59–101.

Kogan, P., 'Uchitelia-antireligiozniki v chuvashskom sele' ('Antireligious teachers in a Chuvash village'), *Antireligioznik*, No. 8 (August 1939), pp. 58–9.

Koltuniuk, S. V., 'Dokhodit' do kazhdogo—znachit uchityvat' osobennosti kazhdogo' ('To approach each means to study the peculiarities of each'), in Gubanov, op. cit., pp. 89–97.

Konstantinov, Dmitrii, 'The Results of Soviet Persecution of the Orthodox Church', *Bulletin of the Institute for the Study of the U.S.S.R.*, No. 5 (May 1965), pp. 38–47.

Koretskii, D., 'Iasna Hora' (Bright Mountain), *Liudyna i Svit*, No. 1 (January 1967), pp. 28–32.

Krasnikov, N. P., 'Materialy issledovaniia religioznosti i praktika nauchno-ateisticheskogo vospitaniia' ('Materials on the research of religiousness and the practice of scientific atheistic education'), in Klibanov, *Konkretnye issledovaniia*, op. cit., pp. 129–37.

Krupskaia, N., 'Antireligioznuiu propagandu—na bolee vysokuiu stupen' ' ('Anti-religious propaganda—on a higher level'), *Revoliutsiia i Natsional'nosti*, No. 3 (85) (March 1937), pp. 26–9.

Krypton, Constantine, 'Secret Religious Organizations in the U.S.S.R.,' *Russian Review*, No. 2 (April 1955), pp. 121–7.

Kurochkin, P., 'Evoliutsiia sovremennogo russkogo pravoslaviia' ('The evolution of contemporary Russian Orthodoxy'), *Nauka i Religiia*, No. 4 (April 1969), pp. 48–52.

Kuznetsov, M., 'Antireligioznoe vospitanie v shkolakh balashovskogo okruga' ('Anti-religious education in the schools of the Balashov region'), *Antireligioznik*, No. 5 (May 1930), pp. 82–7.

Ladorenko, V. E., 'K voprosu ob izmenenii politicheskoi orientatsii russkoi pravoslavnoi tserkve (1917–1945)' ('On the problem of the change of political orientation of the Russian Orthodox Church (1917–1945)'), in AN SSSR, *Voprosy istorii religii i ateizma*, op. cit., XII, 106–23.

Lagovskii, L., 'Itogi bezbozhnoi piatiletka' ('A summary of the godless five-year plan'), *Vestnik Russkago Studencheskago Khristianskago Dvizheniia*, No. 1 (January 1934), pp. 26–31.

Lazarev, N., 'Teni proshlogo' ('Shadows of the past'), *Nauka i Religiia*, No. 8 (August 1963), pp. 88–9.

Levitin, A., 'Monashestvo i sovremennost' ' ('Monasticism and contemporaneity'), in Ioann (Shakovskoi), *Zashchita very v SSSR*, op. cit., pp. 10–87.

Listowel, Judith, 'Is Soviet Youth Becoming Religious?', *Catholic World*, No. 180 (November 1954), pp. 102–9.

Lowrie, Donald A., 'Eastern Christians under Duress', *Christian Century*, 21 November 1962, pp. 1423–5.

Lowrie, Donald A., and William C. Fletcher, 'Khrushchev's Religious Policy, 1959–1964', in Marshall, op. cit., pp. 131–55.

Malakhova, I. A., 'Historians are studying present-day religious movements', *Istoriia SSSR*, No. 2 (March-April 1961), pp. 233–235, translated in *CDSP*, 24 May 1961, pp. 15–16.

Marc, Alexandre, 'The Outstretched (?) Hand . . . in the U.S.S.R.,' in Mauriac, op. cit.

'Materialy k kharakteristike sovremennogo sektantstva v tambovskoi oblasti' ('Materials characterizing contemporary sectarianism in Tambov Oblast'), in AN SSSR, *Sovremennoe sektantstvo*, op. cit., pp. 212–43.

Milovidov, V. F., 'Staroobriadchestvo i sotsial'nyi progress' ('The Old Believers and social progress'), in AN SSSR, *Voprosy nauchnogo ateizma*, op. cit., II, 198–224.

Mitin, M. B., 'O nauchno-ateisticheskoi propagande v svete postanovleniia TsK KPSS, "O zadachakh partiinoi propagandy v sovremennykh usloviiakh" ' ('Scientific atheistic propaganda in the light of the decision of the CC CPSU, "The tasks of Party propaganda in contemporary conditions" '), in AN SSSR, *Uspekhi sovremennoi nauki i religiia*, op. cit., pp. 11–35.

Mitin, M. 'O nashikh zadachakh na antireligioznom fronte' ('Our tasks on the anti-religious front'), *Pod Znamenem Marksizma*, No. 2–3 (March 1936), pp. 89–92.

Mitrokhin, L. N., 'Reaktsionnaia deiatel'nost' "istinno-pravoslavnoi tserkve" na Tambovshchine' ('The reactionary activity of the "True Orthodox Church" in the Tambov area'), in AN SSSR, *Sovremennoe sektantstvo*, op. cit., pp. 144–60.

Murav'ev, E. F., and Iu. V. Dmitrev, 'O konkretnosti v izuchenii i preodolenii religioznykh perezhitkov' ('Concreteness in studying and overcoming religious survivals'), *Voprosy Filosofii*, No. 3 (March 1961), pp. 63–73.

N. I., 'Zashchita magisterskoi dissertatsii v moskovskoi dukhovnoi akademii' ('Defence of a Master's dissertation in the Moscow Theological Academy'), *Z.M.P.*, No. 8 (August 1966), pp. 7–10.

Nikol'skaia, Z. A., 'K kharakteristike techeniia tak nazyvaemykh istinno-pravoslavnykh khristian' ('The characteristics of the movement of the so-called True Orthodox Christians'), in AN SSSR, *Sovremennoe sektantstvo*, op. cit., pp. 161–88.

Nosova, G. A., 'Opyt etnograficheskogo izucheniia bytovogo pravoslaviia' ('Experience of ethnographic study of the way of life of

Orthodoxy'), in AN SSSR, *Voprosy nauchnogo ateizma*, op. cit., III, 151–62.

Okunev, Il'ia, 'Konets sviatoi muzy' ('The end of the holy muse'), *Sovetskie Profsoiuzy*, No. 1 (January 1965), pp. 30–1.

Oleshchuk, F., 'O zadachakh antireligioznoi propagandy' ('Tasks of anti-religious propaganda'), *Pod Znamenem Marksizma*, No. 4 (April 1937), pp. 98–114.

——, 'Za konkretnost' nauchno-ateisticheskoi propagandy' ('For concreteness in scientific atheistic propaganda'), *Kommunist*, No. 5 (April 1958), p. 113.

Onishchenko, A. S., 'Tendentsii izmeneniia sovremennogo religioznogo soznaniia' ('Tendencies of change of contemporary religious understanding'), in AN SSSR, *Voprosy nauchnogo ateizma*, op. cit., pp. 91–109.

Osipov, A. A., ' "Sviatoe" pis'mo' ('A "Holy" letter'), *Nauka i Religiia*, No. 12 (December 1966), pp. 8–9.

Ovalov, Lev., 'Pomni obo mne' ('Remember me'), in six parts, *Nauka i Religiia*, No. 1–6 (January-June 1966).

Ovchinnikov, V. S., 'Osnovy nauchnogo ateizma v technicheskom vuze' ('The foundations of scientific atheism in the technical schools'), *Voprosy Filosofii*, No. 7 (July 1961), pp. 141–4.

Platonov, N. F., 'Pravoslavnaia tserkov' v 1917–1935 gg' ('The Orthodox Church, 1917–1935'), in AN SSSR, *Ezhegodnik muzeia istorii religii i ateizma*, op. cit., V, 206–71.

Podmazov, A., 'O sovremennom staroobriadchestve v Latvii' ('The contemporary Old Believers in Latvia'), *Kommunist Sovetskoi Latvii*, No. 1 (January 1967), pp. 69–74.

'Protiv ravnodushnykh' ('Against those who are indifferent'), *Nauka i Religiia*, No. 6 (June 1964), pp. 86–9.

Putintsev, O., 'O svobode sovesti v SSSR' ('Freedom of conscience in the U.S.S.R.'), *Pod Znamenem Marksizma*, No. 2 (February 1937), pp. 56–80.

Romanov, A., 'Shuga' ('Sludge'), *Nauka i Religiia*, No. 7 (July 1968), pp. 91–4.

Rozenbaum, Iu., 'Takoi zakon est' ' ('There is such a law'), *Nauka i Religiia*, No. 4 (April 1964), pp. 83–5.

Rozenberg, N., 'Lektorii na domu' ('Lecture meetings in the home'), *Agitator*, No. 23 (December 1966), p. 45.

Savushkina, N., 'Kitezh—byt' ili skazka' ('Kitezh—fact or tale'), *Nauka i Religiia*, No. 6 (June 1969), pp. 61–5.

Semashko, 'Odna iz zadach izbiratel'noi kampanii' ('One of the tasks of the election campaign'), *Vlast' Sovetov*, No. 10 (May 1938), pp. 19–21.

Semenov, M., 'Eto proizoshlo v Mud'iuge' ('This happened in Mud'iuga'), *Nauka i Religiia*, No. 2 (February 1966), p. 29.

Shabatin, I., 'Russkaia pravoslavnaia tserkov' v 1917–1967 gg' ('The Russian Orthodox Church, 1917–1967'), *Z.M.P.*, No. 10 (October 1967), pp. 32–46.

Shamaro, Aleksandr, 'Kerzhatskie tropy' ('Kerzhat footpaths'), *Nauka i Religiia*, No. 4 (December 1959), pp. 68–76.

Shaw, M., 'Impressions of the Russian Orthodox Church', *International Review of Missions*, No. 47 (October 1958), pp. 439–44.

Sheinman, M. M., 'Obnovlencheskoe techenie v russkoi pravoslavnoi tserkvi posle oktiabria' ('The renovation movement in the Russian Orthodox Church after October'), in AN SSSR, *Voprosy nauchnogo ateizma*, op. cit., II, 41–64.

Shestinskii, O., 'Pauki na mal'vakh' ('Spiders in the hollyhocks'), *Nauka i Religiia*, No. 3 (March 1960), pp. 53–6.

Shysh, A., 'The end and the means', *Liudyna i Svit*, No. 4 (April 1967), pp. 46–8, translated in *Digest of the Soviet Ukrainian Press*, No. 7 (July 1967), p. 23.

Smirnov, L., 'Iavlenie bogomateri—s pomoshch'iu nozhits i kleia' ('The appearance of the Mother of God—with the help of scissors and paste'), *Nauka i Religiia*, No. 1 (January 1966), p. 95.

Taylor, Pauline B., 'Sectarians in Soviet Courts', *Russian Review*, No. 3 (July 1965), pp. 278–88.

Teodorovich, Nadezhda A., 'The Belorussian Autocephalous Orthodox Church', in Iwanow, op. cit., pp. 70–5.

——, 'The Catacomb Church in the U.S.S.R.,' *Bulletin of the Institute for the Study of the U.S.S.R.*, No. 4 (April 1965), pp. 3–14.

——, 'The Political Role of the Moscow Patriarchate', ibid., No. 7 (July 1960), pp. 44–50.

——, 'The Russian Orthodox', in Institute for the Study of the U.S.S.R., op. cit., pp. 203–10.

Tepliakov, M. K., 'Pobeda ateizma v razlichnykh sotsial'nykh sloiakh sovetskogo obshchestva' ('The victory of atheism in various social strata of Soviet society'), in AN SSSR, *Voprosy nauchnogo ateizma*, op. cit., IV, 130–56.

——, 'Sostoianie religioznosti naseleniia i otkhod veruiushchikh ot religii v Voronezhskoi oblasti (1961–1964 gg)' ('The condition of religiousness of the population and the departure of believers from religion in Voronezh Oblast (1961–1964)'), in Krasnikov, *Voprosy preodoleniia religioznykh perezhitkov v SSSR*, op. cit., pp. 31–52.

Timasheff, N. S., 'Religion in Russia, 1941–1950', in Gurian, op. cit., pp. 153–94.

Trubnikova, Alla, 'Tainik v taburetke' ('Hiding place in a taboret'), *Oktiabr'*, No. 9 (September 1964), pp. 161–77.

'V dobryi chas!' ('In good time!'), *Nauka i Religiia*, No. 9 (September 1964), p. 53.

'V institute nauchnogo ateizma' ('In the institute of scientific atheism'), *Politicheskoe Samoobrazovanie*, No 4 (April 1965), p. 143.

Valentinov, A., 'Sovetskoe zakonodatel'stvo o kul'takh' ('Soviet legislation on cults'), *Nauka i Religiia*, No. 10 (October 1961), pp. 89–92.

Vasilov, V. N., 'Etnograficheskoe issledovanie religioznykh verovanii sel'skogo naseleniia' ('Ethnographic research on the religious faiths of the rural population'), in Klibanov, *Konkretnye issledovaniia*, op. cit., pp. 152–74.

——, 'O proiskhozhdenii kul'ta nevidimogo grada kitezha (monastyria) u ozera svetloiar' ('On the origins of the cult of the invisible city of Kitezh (monastery) at Lake Svetloiar'), in AN SSSR, *Voprosy istorii religii i ateizma*, op. cit., XII, 150–69.

Vasin, A., 'Nachalo polozheno' ('A beginning has been made'), *Nauka i Religiia*, No. 7 (July 1968), pp. 17–21.

Vdovichenko, P., 'Reaktsionnaia sushchnost' religioznogo sektantstva' ('The reactionary essence of religious sectarianism'), *Kommunist Belorussii*, No. 11 (November 1964), pp. 56–62.

Veschikov, A., 'Milestones of a great journey', *Nauka i Religiia*, No. 11 (November 1962), translated in *RCDA*, 24 December 1962, p. 4.

Volkov, I., 'Kto, esli ne ty?' ('Who, if not you?'), *Partiinaia Zhizn' Kazakhstana*, No. 12 (December 1964), pp. 45–7.

'Vreditel'skaia deiatel'nost' tserkovnikov i sektantov' ('Wrecking activity of churchmen and sectarians'), *Antireligioznik*, No. 5 (May 1930), pp. 97–9.

'II Vsesoiuznaia antireligioznaia konferentsiia' ('The II National anti-religious conference'), *Pod Znamenem Marksizma*, No. 5 (September-October 1934), pp. 173–87.

Ware, Kallistos Timothy, ' "Pray Without Ceasing": The Ideal of Continual Prayer in Eastern Monasticism', *Eastern Churches Review*, II, 3 (Spring 1969), pp. 253–61.

White, William C., 'The Triple-Barred Cross', *Scribner's Magazine*, No. 1 (July 1930), pp. 67–78.

Willetts, Harry, 'De-opiating the Masses', *Problems of Communism*, November-December 1964, pp. 32–41.

Zaikin, B., 'Pered samoi bol'shoi auditoriei' ('Before the largest audience'), *Agitator*, No. 20 (October 1966), pp. 44–5.

Zarin, P., 'Politicheskii maskarad tserkovnikov i sektantov' ('The political masquerade of churchmen and sectarians'), *Antireligioznik*, No. 10 (October 1931), pp. 9–16.

Zenkovsky, Vasily V., 'The Spirit of Russian Orthodoxy', *Russian Review*, No. 1 (January 1963), pp. 38–55.

Zybkovets, V., 'Put' sovetskogo ateizma' ('The path of Soviet atheism'), *Nauka i Religiia*, No. 9 (September 1967), p. 14.

Newspapers

Bakinski Rabochii (Baku worker), Baku.

Bezbozhnik (The godless), Moscow.

Gudok (Steam-whistle), Moscow.

Izvestiia (News), Moscow.

Kazakhstanskaia Pravda (Kazakhstan *Pravda*), Alma Ata.

Komsomol'skaia Pravda (Komsomol *Pravda*), Moscow.

Krasnaia Zvezda (Red Star), Moscow.

Leninskaia Smena (The Lenin generation), Alma Ata.

Literatura i Zhizn' (Literature and life), Moscow.

Literaturnaia Gazeta (Literary gazette), Moscow.

Molod' Ukrainy (Youth of the Ukraine), Kiev.

New York Times, New York.

Pravda (Truth), Moscow.

Sel'skaia Zhizn' (Rural life), Moscow.

Sotsialisticheskoe Zemledelie (Socialist agriculture), Moscow.

Sovetskaia Kul'tura (Soviet culture), Moscow.

Sovetskaia Moldaviia (Soviet Moldavia), Kishinev.

Sovetskaia Rossiia (Soviet Russia), Moscow.

Trud (Labour), Moscow.

Uchitel'skaia Gazeta (Teachers' gazette), Moscow.

Vechernaia Moskva (Evening Moscow), Moscow.

Za Kommunisticheskoe Prosveshchenie (For communist enlightenment), Moscow.

Periodicals

Agitator (The agitator), Moscow.

America, New York.

American Mercury, Washington, D.C.

Antireligioznik (The anti-religious), Moscow.

Bezbozhnik (The godless), Moscow.

Bulletin of the Institute for the Study of the U.S.S.R., Munich.

Catholic World, New York.

Christian Century, Chicago.

Colliers, New York.

Commonweal, New York.
Communist Affairs, Los Angeles.
Current Developments in the Eastern European Churches, Geneva.
Current Digest of the Soviet Press (*CDSP*), New York.
Digest of the Soviet Ukrainian Press, Munich.
East Turkic Review, Munich.
Eastern Churches Review, Oxford.
International Review of Missions, Geneva.
Istoriia SSSR (History of the U.S.S.R.), Moscow.
Kommunist (Communist), Moscow.
Kommunist Belorussii (Communist of Belorussia), Minsk.
Kommunist Moldavii (Communist of Moldavia), Kishinev.
Kommunist Sovetskoi Latvii (Communist of Soviet Latvia), Riga.
Liudyna i Svit (Man and the world), Moscow.
Molodoi Kommunist (Young communist), Moscow.
Ogonek (Light), Moscow.
One Church, New York.
Partiinaia Zhizn' (Party life), Moscow.
Partiinaia Zhizn' Kazakhstana (Party life of Kazakhstan), Alma Ata.
Pod Znamenem Marksizma (Under the banner of Marxism), Moscow.
Politicheskoe Samoobrazovanie (Political self-education), Moscow.
Problems of Communism, Washington, D.C.
Religion in Communist Dominated Areas (*RCDA*), New York.
Reporter, New York.
Research Materials, Geneva.
Revoliutsiia i Natsional'nosti (Revolution and the nationalities), Moscow.
Smena (Change), Moscow.
Sovetskie Profsoiuzy (Soviet trade unions), Moscow.
Sovety Deputatov Trudiashchikhsia (Councils of workers' deputies), Moscow.
Vestnik Kommunisticheskoi Akademii (Herald of the communist academy), Moscow.
Vestnik Russkogo Studencheskogo Khristianskogo Dvizheniia (Herald of the Russian Student Christian Movement), Paris.
Vlast' Sovetov (Rule of the Soviets), Moscow.
Voiovnychy Ateist (Militant atheist), Moscow.
Voprosy Filosofii (Problems of philosophy), Moscow.
Westminster Bookman, Philadelphia.
Zhurnal Moskovskoi Patriarkhii (*ZMP*) (Journal of the Moscow Patriarchate), Moscow.

Index

Note : Religious organizations and movements in the U.S.S.R. which are treated in the text as Underground Orthodox may be found under the heading, 'Underground Orthodox'. For religious denominations and sects, see the following entries: